Global Economic Prospects

A World Bank Group Flagship Report

JANUARY 2015

Global Economic Prospects

Having Fiscal Space and Using It

WORLD BANK GROUP

Table of Contents

Boxes

Figures

Tables

Acronyms

AME	advanced market countries
bbl	barrel
bcm	billion cubic meters
BIS	Bank for International Settlements
bp	basis point
BRICS	Brazil, Russia, India, China, and South Africa
CIS	Commonwealth of Independent States
CEE	Central and Eastern Europe
CPIA	Country Policy and Institutional Assessment (World Bank)
CY	calendar year
DSGE	dynamic stochastic general equilibrium
EAP	East Asia and Pacific
ECA	Europe and Central Asia
ECB	European Central Bank
EMBIG	Emerging Markets Bond Index Global
EMEs	emerging market economies
EU	European Union
FDI	foreign direct investment
FMEs	frontier market economies
FRED	Federal Reserve Bank St. Louis Economic Data
FTSE	Financial Times Stock Exchange
FY	fiscal year
GCC	Gulf Cooperation Council
GDP	gross domestic product
GEP	Global Economic Prospects
GMM	generalized method of moments
GNFS	goods and non-factor services
GNI	gross national income
G-7	Group of Seven countries: Canada, France, Germany, Italy, Japan, the United Kingdom, and the United States

G-20	Group of Twenty countries: Argentina, Australia, Brazil, Canada, China, the European Union, France, Germany, India, Indonesia, Italy, Japan, Mexico, Russia, Saudi Arabia, South Africa, South Korea, Turkey, the United Kingdom and the United States
GST	Non uniform goods and services tax
HIPC	Heavily Indebted Poor Countries Initiative
IDS	International Debt Statistics
IP	Industrial production
IPVAR	Interacted panel vector auto regression
ISIL	Islamic State of Iraq and Levant
ISIS	Islamic State of Iraq and Syria
JEDH	Joint External Debt Hub
LAC	Latin America and Caribbean
LIBOR	London Interbank Offered Rate
LIC	Low-income country
LMIC	Lower-middle-income countries
LNG	Liquefied natural gas
mb/d	Million barrels per day
MDRI	Multilateral Debt Relief Initiative
ODA	Official development assistance
ODs	Other developing countries
OECD	Organisation for Economic Co-operation and Development
OLS	ordinary least squares
OPEC	Organization of the Petroleum Exporting Countries
PIM	Public Investment Management
PMI	Purchasing Managers' Index
PPP	purchasing power parity
QEDS	Quarterly External Debt Statistics
RCA	Revealed comparative advantage
RCI	remittance and capital flow intensive
SAR	South Asia region

SARS	Severe acute respiratory syndrome
S&P	Standard & Poor's
SVAR	Structural vector auto regression
TTB	Temporary trade barriers
UMIC	Upper-middle-income countries
UNPD	United Nations Population Division
VAR	Vector auto regression
VAT	Value added tax
WDI	World Development Indicators
WEO	World Economic Outlook
WIOD	World Input Output Database
WTO	World Trade Organization

Acknowledgments

This World Bank Group Flagship report is a product of the Prospects Group in the Development Economics Vice Presidency. The project was managed by Ayhan Kose and Franziska Ohnsorge, under the general guidance of Kaushik Basu.

Several people contributed substantively to the report. The principal authors for Chapter 1 (Global Outlook) were Ayhan Kose, Franziska Ohnsorge, and Marc Stocker. Chapter 2 (Regional Outlook) was coordinated by Franziska Ohnsorge. The authors were Derek H. C. Chen (Latin America & the Caribbean), Damir Cosic (Middle East & North Africa), Gerard Kambou (Sub-Saharan Africa), Tehmina Shaukat Khan (South Asia), Mizuho Kida (Europe & Central Asia), and Ekaterine Vashakmadze (East Asia & Pacific). Chapter 3 was prepared by a team led by Ayhan Kose and Franziska Ohnsorge and including S. Amer Ahmed, Raju Huidrom, Sergio Kurlat, and Jamus J. Lim, with contributions from Israel Osorio-Rodarte and Nao Sugawara. The first essay of Chapter 4 was produced by a team led by John Baffes, Ayhan Kose, Franziska Ohnsorge, and Marc Stocker, and including Derek Chen, Damir Cosic, Xinghao Gong, Raju Huidrom, Ekaterine Vashakmadze, Jiayi Zhang, and Tianli Zhao. The second essay of Chapter 4 was prepared by Ileana Cristina-Constantinescu, Allen Dennis, Aaditya Mattoo, and Michele Ruta. The third essay of Chapter 4 was prepared by a team led by Ayhan Kose and Dilip Ratha, and including Supriyo De, Ergys Islamaj, and Seyed Reza Yousefi. The Special Focus was prepared by Tehmina Khan and Franziska Ohnsorge. The boxes were prepared by Vandana Chandra, Young Il Choi, Marcio Cruz, Poonam Gupta, Raju Huidrom, Tehmina Khan, Maryla Maliszewska, Franziska Ohnsorge, Dana Vorisek, and Tianli Zhao. Ajai Chopra, Kevin Clinton, Raphael Espinoza, Ugo Panizza, David Robinson, and Carlos Vegh provided consultancy support.

John Baffes and Damir Cosic provided inputs on commodity markets, and Eung Ju Kim and Marc Stocker on financial markets. Modeling and data work were led by Young Il Choi and Thi Thanh Thanh Bui assisted by Xinghao Gong, Vanessa Diaz Montelongo, Trang Thi Thuy Nguyen, Kiwako Sakamoto, and Jiayi Zhang.

The online publication was produced by a team overseen by Mikael Reventar and included Kristina Cathrine Mercado, Katherine Rollins, and Kiwako Sakamoto, with technical support from Marjorie Patricia Bennington, Ugendran Machakkalai, Praveen Penmetsa, and Prasanna Ramamoorthy.

Indira Chand and Merrell Tuck-Primdahl managed media relations and the dissemination. Kristina Cathrine Mercado managed the publication process.

Several reviewers offered extensive advice and comments. These included: Kishan Abeygunawardana, Pablo Acosta, Ahmad Ahsan, Asad Alam, Enrique Aldaz Carroll, Sara Alnashar, Enrique Blanco Amas, George Anayiotos, Kassia Antoine, Madelyn Antoncic, Matias Antonio, Matias Arnal, Luca Bandiera, Marina Bakanova, Andres Lajer Baron, Kevin Barnes, Kaushik Basu, Morgan Bazilian, Hans Anand Beck, Guillermo Beylis, Kirida Bhaopichitr, Deepak Bhattasali, Benu Bidani, Fernando Blanco, Zeljko Bogetic, Eric Le Borgne, Elizabeth, Ruppert Bulmer, Cesar Calderon, Jose R. Lopez Calix, Kevin Carey, Shubham Chaudhuri, Young Il Choi, Karl Kendrick Tiu Chua, Punam Chuhan-Pole, Natalia Cieslik, Mateo Clavijo, Maia Colodenco, Andre Coppola, Tito Cordella, Mariano Cortes, Marcio Cruz, Barbara Cunha, Somneuk Davading, Simon Davies, Hubertus De Leede, Donato De Rosa, Shantayanan Devarajan, Alain W. D'Hoore, Mame Fatou Irene Aminata Diagne, Tatiana Didier, Viet Dinh, Ndiame Diop, Calvin Zebaze Djiofack, Sascha Djumena, Ralph Van Doorn, Franz R. Dress-Gross, Bakyt Dubashov, Jozef Draaisma, Christian Eigen-Zucchi, Tilman D. Ehrbeck, Pablo Fajnzylber, Marianne Fay, Francisco H.G. Ferreira, Cornelius Fleischhaker, Samuel Freije-Rodriguez, German Galindo, Elisa Gamberoni, Fritzi Koehler-Geib, Michael Geiger, Ejaz Syed Ghani, Indermit S. Gill, Marcelo Giugale, Delfin Go, Chorching Goh, Sudarshan Gooptu, David Michael Gould, Poonam Gupta, Lea Hakim, Birgit Hansl, Wissam Harake, Jesko S. Hentschel, Marco Hernandez, Santiago Herrera, Sandra Hlivnjak, Bert Hofman, Vivian Y. N. Hon, Philippe H. Le Houerou, Bingjie Hu, Zahid Hussain, Elena Ianchovichina, Gabriela Inchauste, Yoichiro Ishihara, Roumeen Islam, Aleksandra Iwulska, Evans Jadotte, Markus Kitzmuller, Masami Kojima, Naoko Kojo, Daniel Enrique Kostzer, Auguste Tano Kouame, Ahmed Kouchouk, Aart C. Kraay, Aurelien Kruse, Chandana Kularatne, Praveen Kumar, Melanie Marie Laloum, Daniel Lederman, Tae Lee, Taehyun Lee, Soonwho Li, Joseph Louie C. Limkin, John Litwack, Julio Ricardo Loayza, Rohan Longmore, Sodeth Ly, Helen Marie Lynch, Samer Matta, Ernesto May, Paul Mariano, Miguel Eduardo Sanchez Martin, Denis Medvedev, Fabian Mendez Ramos, Elitza Mileva, Deepak Mishra, Jaba Misra, Sanket Mohapatra, Shabih Ali Mohib, Lars Moller, Maria Bru Munoz, Hannah Sibylle Nielsen, Irina A. Nikolic, Miguel Angel Saldarriaga Noel, Antonio Nucifora, Rei Odawara, Antonio Ollero, Camilo Gomez Osorio, Caglar Ozden, Robert Palacios, Lucy Pan, John Panzer, Marcelo Echague Pastore, Keomanivone Phimmahasay, Jaime de Piniés, Sonia Plaza, Alberto Portugal, Andrea Presbitero, Catriona Mary Purfield, Rong Qian, M. Zia Qureshi, Martin Rama, Luc Razafimandimby, Ana Revenga, Julio Revilla, Mick Riordan, Alberto Rodriguez, Petro L. Rodriguez, David Rosenblatt, German Galindo Rozo, Susana Sanchez, Frederico Gil Sander, Ilyas Sarsenov, Jose Gilberto Scandiucci, Philip Schellekens, Sergio Schmukler, Kirsten Schuettler, Phillip Schuler, Ethel Sennhauser, Luis Serven, Sudhir Shetty, Bojan Shimbov, Saurabh Shome, Sumeer Shukla, Peter Siegenthaler, Alex Sienaert, Raju Singh, Sandor Sipos, Karlis Smits, Nikola Spatafora, Vinaya SwaroopAshley Taylor, Gilles Thirion, Mark R. Thomas, Theo David Thomas, Antony Thompson, Hans Timmer, Augusto de la Torre, Volker Treichel, Sergei Ulatov, Robert Utz, Rogier J. E. Van Den Brink, Sona Varma, Julio Velasco, Mathew Verghis, Gallina Andronova Vincelette, Dana Vorisek, Ekaterina Vostroknutova, Ariel Yepez, Ayberk Yilmaz, Michele Savini Zangrandi, Albert Zeufack, Luan Zhao, May Thet Zin, Johannes Zutt. Regional projections and write-ups were produced in coordination with country teams, country directors, and the offices of the regional chief economists.

Foreword

The January 2015 edition of Global Economic Prospects marks a turning point in the World Bank Group's flagship publication on the world economy. While the report continues to present a detailed outlook for the global economy (Chapter 1) and for each of the world's developing regions (Chapter 2), its analytical content has been expanded significantly. Chapter 3 analyzes the evolution and effectiveness of fiscal policy in developing countries. Chapter 4 contains three essays examining key challenges and opportunities currently confronting developing countries: the causes and implications of the sharp drop in oil prices in the second half of 2014; factors underlying the slowdown in global trade in recent years; and consumption-smoothing properties of remittance flows.

The global economy is still struggling to gain momentum as many high-income countries continue to grapple with the legacies of the global financial crisis and emerging economies are less dynamic than in the past. After rising marginally in 2014, to 2.6 percent, world GDP will grow by an estimated 3.0 percent in 2015 and 3.3 percent in 2016, supported by gradual recovery in high-income countries, low oil prices, and receding domestic headwinds in developing countries. Developing economies are expected to see an increase in growth from 4.4 percent in 2014 to 4.8 percent and 5.3 percent in 2015 and 2016, respectively. Lower oil prices will lead to sizeable real income shifts to oil-importing countries from oil-exporting ones.

Risks to the global outlook remain tilted downwards. Weak global trade growth is anticipated to persist during the forecast period, potentially for longer than currently expected should the Euro Area or Japan experience a prolonged period of stagnation or deflation. Financial conditions could become volatile as high-income economies tighten monetary policy on diverging timelines. Rapid reassessment of risk could also be triggered by a spike in geopolitical tensions, bouts of volatility in commodity markets, or financial stress in major emerging market economies. Worryingly, the weak recovery in many high-income economies and slowdowns in several large emerging markets may be a symptom of deeper structural weaknesses.

Developing countries face significant policy challenges in an environment of weak global growth and considerable uncertainty. Fiscal buffers need to be rebuilt to ensure the effectiveness of fiscal policy in the future. Central banks need to balance policies to support growth against measures to stabilize inflation and currencies or to bolster financial stability. Progress on implementing structural reforms must be continued to boost long-term growth. The fragile global outlook makes the implementation of growth-enhancing policies and structural reforms even more urgent to improve the odds of achieving the World Bank Group's goal of ending extreme poverty by 2030.

The current juncture presents a window of opportunity for reform. The sharp decline in oil prices means that policymakers could implement subsidy and tax reforms to help rebuild fiscal space or finance better-targeted pro-poor policies while removing distortions that hinder activity. The challenge now is for policymakers to seize this opportunity.

Kaushik Basu

Chief Economist and
Senior Vice President
The World Bank

Executive Summary

Global growth in 2014 was lower than initially expected, continuing a pattern of disappointing outturns over the past several years. Growth picked up only marginally in 2014, to 2.6 percent, from 2.5 percent in 2013. Beneath these headline numbers, increasingly divergent trends are at work in major economies. While activity in the United States and the United Kingdom has gathered momentum as labor markets heal and monetary policy remains extremely accommodative, the recovery has been sputtering in the Euro Area and Japan as legacies of the financial crisis linger, intertwined with structural bottlenecks. China, meanwhile, is undergoing a carefully managed slowdown. Disappointing growth in other developing countries in 2014 reflected weak external demand, but also domestic policy tightening, political uncertainties and supply-side constraints.

Several major forces are driving the global outlook: soft commodity prices; persistently low interest rates but increasingly divergent monetary policies across major economies; and weak world trade. In particular, the sharp decline in oil prices since mid-2014 will support global activity and help offset some of the headwinds to growth in oil-importing developing economies. However, it will dampen growth prospects for oil-exporting countries, with significant regional repercussions.

Overall, global growth is expected to rise moderately, to 3.0 percent in 2015, and average about 3.3 percent through 2017. High-income countries are likely to see growth of 2.2 percent in 2015-17, up from 1.8 percent in 2014, on the back of gradually recovering labor markets, ebbing fiscal consolidation, and still-low financing costs. In developing countries, as the domestic headwinds that held back growth in 2014 ease and the recovery in high-income countries slowly strengthens, growth is projected to gradually accelerate, rising from 4.4 percent in 2014 to 4.8 percent in 2015 and 5.4 percent by 2017. Lower oil prices will contribute to diverging prospects for oil-exporting and -importing countries, particularly in 2015.

Risks to this slow-moving global recovery are significant and tilted to the downside. Financial market volatility, compounded by the risk of a sudden deterioration in liquidity conditions, could sharply raise developing countries' borrowing costs, an unwelcome development after several years of heavy capital market issuance in developing countries. Intensifying geopolitical tensions, bouts of volatility in commodity markets, or financial stress in a major emerging market could lead to a reassessment of risk assets. If the Euro Area or Japan slips into a prolonged period of stagnation or deflation, global trade could weaken even further. Although it is a low-probability event given China's substantial policy buffers, a sharper decline in growth could trigger a disorderly unwinding of financial vulnerabilities and would have considerable implications for the global economy.

The forces driving the global outlook and the associated risks pose significant policy challenges. In high-income countries, the still-fragile recovery calls for continued accommodative monetary policy and a flexible approach to fiscal policy, which supports growth but is also accompanied by concrete medium-term consolidation plans and structural reforms. In developing countries, global financial tightening could reduce capital flows and trigger further currency depreciations. Though depreciation may strengthen exports and help current account adjustments, they could weaken balance sheets and dampen the disinflationary effects of soft commodity prices. Some developing countries' central banks may thus have to weigh monetary policy measures to support growth against those needed to stabilize inflation and currencies or bolster financial system stability. Fiscal stimulus can also be considered in the event of a sharp cyclical downturn. In practice, however, the use of fiscal policy as a countercyclical policy tool may be constrained by a lack of fiscal space that limits the ability to use fiscal stimulus and its effectiveness. Both high-income and developing countries need to undertake comprehensive structural reforms, including improvements in institutions and public infrastructure, in order to promote growth and job creation. This will help lift growth towards rates needed to achieve poverty reduction targets by 2030.

This edition of the *Global Economic Prospects* also includes four essays that analyze key challenges and opportunities currently confronting developing countries: fiscal policy as a countercyclical policy tool; causes and implications of cheap oil; weak trade that fails to act as an engine of growth; and remittances as a means of steadying consumption during sudden stops.

Will fiscal policy be able to support activity effectively if needed? Over the past three decades, fiscal policy in developing countries has become increasingly countercyclical. The wide fiscal space accumulated prior to the global financial crisis not only made it possible for developing countries to implement fiscal stimulus during the crisis, but also made the stimulus more effective in supporting growth as fiscal multipliers tend to be higher in countries with greater fiscal space. However, in many developing countries, fiscal balances have yet to be restored to debt-stabilizing levels. This has likely dampened the effectiveness of fiscal policy, reducing fiscal multipliers by about one-third from pre-crisis levels. Over the medium-term, many countries need to rebuild fiscal buffers and to restore fiscal sustainability. The speed at which fiscal space should be restored depends on a host of country-specific factors. These include cyclical conditions as well as constraints on monetary policy, for example the post-crisis accumulation of private sector debt or still-elevated inflation in several developing countries. Well-designed and credible institutional arrangements—fiscal rules, stabilization funds, and medium-term expenditure frameworks—can help rebuild fiscal space and strengthen policy outcomes, enabling fiscal stimulus, and larger and more effective programs for poverty reduction.

What are the sources and implications of the recent decline in oil prices? Following four years of stability at around $105/bbl, oil prices have declined sharply since June 2014. A number of factors have driven the recent plunge in oil prices: several years of upward surprises in oil supply and downward surprises in demand, unwinding of some geopolitical risks that had threatened production, changing OPEC policy objectives, and appreciation of the U.S. dollar. Although it is difficult to precisely determine the relative importance of these factors, supply-related factors appear to have played a dominant role. If sustained, lower oil prices will contribute to global growth and lead to sizeable real income shifts to oil-importing countries from oil-exporting ones. For oil-importing countries, weak oil prices will support activity and reduce inflationary, external, and fiscal pressures. On the other hand, oil-exporting countries will be adversely impacted by deteriorating fiscal and external positions and weakening economic activity. Soft oil prices present a significant window of opportunity to reform energy taxes and fuel subsidies, which are substantial in several developing countries.

Why has global trade been weak in the post-crisis years? Global trade grew less than 4 percent a year during 2012-14, well below the pre-crisis average annual growth of about 7 percent. If global trade had continued to expand at its historical trend, it would have been some 20 percent above its actual level in 2014. The slowdown in global trade has been driven by both cyclical factors, notably persistently weak import demand in high-income countries, and structural factors, including the changing relationship between trade and income. Specifically, world trade has become less responsive to changes in global income because of slower expansions of global supply chains and a shift in demand toward less import-intensive items.

Can remittances help stabilize consumption? Remittance flows to developing economies are projected to continue to expand, while private capital flows might moderate as global interest rates begin rising or if growth in developing economies remains subdued. Remittances are generally a more stable source of external funding that is less correlated with the domestic business cycle than other types of private flows. Given these tendencies, remittances to heavily reliant developing countries can help ease liquidity constraints, improve access to financial services, and smooth household consumption, especially during periods of financial stress.

CHAPTER 1

GLOBAL OUTLOOK

Disappointments, Divergences, and Expectations

Summary and Key Messages

The world economy is still struggling to gain momentum as many high-income countries continue to grapple with the legacies of the global financial crisis. The recovery in high-income economies has been uneven, as some (the United States and the United Kingdom) have exceeded pre-crisis output peaks, but others (the Euro Area) are still below earlier peaks. Middle-income economies have also been less dynamic than in the past for cyclical reasons, but also due to a structural slowdown. Low-income countries continue to grow at a robust pace, despite a challenging global environment. The key features of the lackluster global recovery have been accommodative monetary policies, falling commodity prices, and weak trade. These are expected to persist, although financial conditions are projected to tighten gradually. Risks to this fragile recovery are significant and tilted to the downside. The key policy challenge for developing countries is to adjust monetary and fiscal policies to changing cyclical conditions while addressing headwinds to long-term growth by implementing structural reforms.

The recovery has been weaker than anticipated in June 2014, partly for one-off reasons, with a string of disappointing growth outturns in the Euro Area, Japan, parts of emerging Europe (especially Russia) and Latin America. The Euro Area and Japan accounted for more than half of the downward revisions to global growth in 2014 (and one-third of the downward revisions to global growth in 2015). Global growth picked up only marginally to 2.6 percent in 2014 from 2.5 percent in 2013 (Table 1.1). Some of the factors that set back activity, however, were slowly fading in the second half of the year, and growth is expected to settle at 3.0–3.3 percent for 2015-17 (Figure 1.1). Partly as a result of the modest growth outlook, commodity prices are expected to remain low and trade growth weak. In particular, following their sharp drop in the second half of 2014, soft oil prices are expected to persist, supporting global growth but dampening prospects for oil-exporting countries. With the recent decline of inflation expectations, monetary policy tightening is likely to be delayed in some high-income countries, and, even once it begins, policy rates are expected to remain low for an extended period. Growth in major economies has increasingly diverged, as the United States and the United Kingdom gained momentum, while the Euro Area and Japan lag behind. China is still growing at a robust pace but continues on a path of gradual deceleration.

Growth in middle- and low-income countries slipped to 4.4 percent in 2014. The slowdown in several large middle-income economies mainly reflects cyclical factors, domestic policy tightening, and political tensions. However, deeper, structural factors, including

FIGURE 1.1   Recent developments and global outlook

Global growth disappointed again in 2014 but is expected to pick up in 2015-17. Some high-income countries are projected to contribute more to global growth and gradually tighten monetary policy. Commodity prices are forecast to remain low.

A. Global GDP growth forecasts

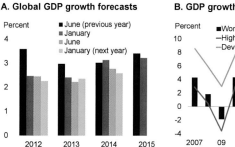

B. GDP growth, actual and projected

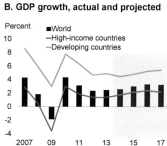

C. Global trade, industrial production and GDP

D. Contributions to global growth

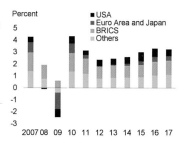

E. High-income countries: policy rate expectations[1]

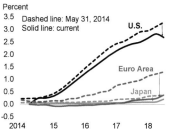

F. Commodity prices[2]

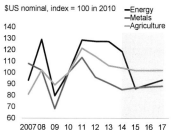

Sources: World Bank and Bloomberg.
1. Policy rate expectations are based on forward swap rates.
2. Energy consists of oil, natural gas and coal. Agriculture consists of grains, edible oils, oil seeds, and tropical commodities. Metals include the six base metals (aluminum, copper, lead, nickel, tin and zinc) and iron ore.

a trend slowdown in productivity, dampen growth prospects over the medium-term. Since the post-crisis rebound, output growth in the developing world has settled at a pace below that of the first decade of the 2000s. A sharp decline in oil and other commodity prices and softening growth, partly due to tighter monetary policies, is helping reduce inflation pressures in many developing countries (Figure 1.2). Low-income countries have been the exception: despite headwinds from the commodity price declines and in West Africa from the Ebola epidemic, growth strengthened on the back of rising public investment, robust capital inflows and solid harvests.

TABLE 1.1   The Global Outlook in Summary

(percentage change from previous year, except interest rates)

	2012	2013	2014e	2015f	2016f	2017f
REAL GDP[1]						
World	**2.4**	**2.5**	**2.6**	**3.0**	**3.3**	**3.2**
High income	**1.4**	**1.4**	**1.8**	**2.2**	**2.4**	**2.2**
United States	2.3	2.2	2.4	3.2	3.0	2.4
Euro Area	-0.7	-0.4	0.8	1.1	1.6	1.6
Japan	1.5	1.5	0.2	1.2	1.6	1.2
United Kingdom	0.7	1.7	2.6	2.9	2.6	2.2
Russia	3.4	1.3	0.7	-2.9	0.1	1.1
Developing countries	**4.8**	**4.9**	**4.4**	**4.8**	**5.3**	**5.4**
East Asia and Pacific	7.4	7.2	6.9	6.7	6.7	6.7
China	7.7	7.7	7.4	7.1	7.0	6.9
Indonesia	6.3	5.8	5.1	5.2	5.5	5.5
Thailand	6.5	2.9	0.5	3.5	4.0	4.5
Europe and Central Asia	1.9	3.7	2.4	3.0	3.6	4.0
Kazakhstan	5.0	6.0	4.1	1.8	3.2	4.7
Turkey	2.1	4.1	3.1	3.5	3.7	3.9
Romania	0.6	3.5	2.6	2.9	3.2	3.9
Latin America and the Caribbean	2.6	2.5	0.8	1.7	2.9	3.3
Brazil	1.0	2.5	0.1	1.0	2.5	2.7
Mexico	4.0	1.1	2.1	3.3	3.8	3.8
Argentina	0.9	2.9	-1.5	-0.3	1.6	3.1
Middle East and North Africa	1.4	0.5	1.2	2.5	3.0	3.5
Egypt[2]	2.2	2.1	2.2	3.5	3.8	4.0
Iran	-6.6	-1.9	1.5	0.9	1.0	2.2
Algeria	3.3	2.8	3.0	3.3	3.5	3.5
South Asia	5.0	4.9	5.5	6.1	6.6	6.8
India[2,3]	4.7	5.0	5.6	6.4	7.0	7.0
Pakistan[2,3]	3.5	4.4	5.4	4.6	4.8	4.9
Bangladesh[2]	6.5	6.0	6.1	6.2	6.5	7.0
Sub-Saharan Africa	4.0	4.2	4.5	4.6	4.9	5.1
South Africa	2.5	1.9	1.4	2.2	2.5	2.7
Nigeria	4.3	5.4	6.3	5.5	5.8	6.2
Angola	8.4	6.8	4.4	5.3	5.0	5.2
MEMORANDUM ITEMS						
World real GDP (2010 PPP weights)	3.1	3.2	3.3	3.6	4.0	4.0
OECD real GDP	1.2	1.3	1.7	2.3	2.4	2.1
Non-OECD real GDP	3.5	2.4	2.5	0.9	2.4	2.9
Developing country real GDP excluding BRICS	3.5	4.1	3.5	5.0	4.9	5.1
BRICS real GDP	5.4	5.4	5.0	5.1	5.5	5.6
World trade volume[4]	2.8	3.4	4.0	4.5	4.8	4.8
Non-oil commodity price index	-8.6	-7.2	-3.6	-1.1	0.2	0.3
Oil price[5]	1.0	-0.9	-7.7	-31.9	4.9	4.7
Manufactures unit export value[6]	-1.2	-1.4	-0.2	-0.2	1.9	1.7
6-month U.S. LIBOR interest rate (percent)[7]	0.7	0.4	0.3	...	...	...
6-month Euro LIBOR interest rate (percent)[7]	0.8	0.3	0.3	...	...	...
International capital flows to developing countries (% of GDP)						
Developing countries	**5.0**	**5.9**	**5.8**	**5.5**	**5.3**	**...**
East Asia and Pacific	4.6	6.4	6.3	5.9	5.5	...
Europe and Central Asia	8.0	7.4	5.4	6.0	6.2	...
Latin America and the Caribbean	5.4	5.9	6.2	5.9	5.7	...
Middle East and North Africa	1.8	2.3	1.8	1.8	1.9	...
South Asia	5.7	4.6	5.4	5.3	5.3	...
Sub-Saharan Africa	5.6	5.2	4.5	4.7	4.8	...

Source: World Bank.
Notes: PPP = purchasing power parity; e = estimate; f = forecast.
World Bank forecasts are frequently updated based on new information and changing (global) circumstances. Consequently, projections presented here may differ from those contained in other Bank documents, even if basic assessments of countries' prospects do not differ at any given moment in time.
1. Aggregate growth rates calculated using constant 2010 U.S. dollars GDP weights.
2. In keeping with national practice, data for Bangladesh, Egypt, India, and Pakistan are reported on a fiscal year basis in table 1.1. Aggregates that depend on these countries are calculated using data compiled on a calendar year basis.
3. Real GDP at factor cost, consistent with reporting practice in Pakistan and India.
4. World trade volume for goods and non-factor services.
5. Simple average of Dubai, Brent, and West Texas Intermediate.
6. Unit value index of manufactured exports from major economies, expressed in U.S. dollars.
7. The 2014e rates are the average of daily interest rates up to latest available data.

The baseline outlook embodies three global influences that are expected to affect developing economies significantly.

First, an eventual increase in the monetary policy rate in the United States is expected to result in gradually tightening global financial conditions from 2015 onward. Diverging cyclical positions and, as a result, prospects for asynchronous monetary policies in the major economies, have already been accompanied by U.S. dollar appreciation and pressure on some developing-country currencies.

Second, commodity prices are expected to remain soft on concerns about weak global growth and rising supply as well as a shift in market expectations about Organization of the Petroleum Exporting Countries (OPEC) policy objectives.

Third, developing countries' exports will be differentially impacted by the recovery in high-income economies. While faster growth in the United States is expected to propel some developing countries, others could be held back by the anemic recovery in the Euro Area and Japan.

Overall, global growth is expected to rise in 2015 to 3.0 percent, and to be sustained at 3.2-3.3 percent in 2016-17. This should be supported by continued recovery in the United States, a gradual acceleration of activity in the Euro Area, and receding headwinds to growth among slower growing developing regions. The sharp decline in oil prices since mid-2014 is projected to be sustained and to contribute to global growth, with significant income shifts from oil-exporting to oil-importing economies.

There are significant downside risks to the baseline outlook. Renewed bouts of financial market volatility could derail a still-fragile recovery. Tightening financial conditions, rising geopolitical tensions, financial market stress in a major emerging market, or repeated growth disappointments could cause investors to reappraise developing-country risks, push up risk premia, and expose some underlying vulnerabilities. In the Euro Area, stagnation, exacerbated by very low inflation or deflation, could prove to be protracted. Although a low-probability risk given significant policy buffers, the slowdown in China could turn into a disorderly unwinding of financial vulnerabilities with considerable implications for the global economy.

The forces driving the global outlook and the associated risks pose complex policy challenges. Among high-income countries, especially in the Euro Area and Japan, monetary accommodation needs to be maintained and fiscal policy needs to be flexible to support growth in the short-term complemented with concrete medium-term consolidation plans. These policies should be supported by long-term

FIGURE 1.2   Inflation

Slipping commodity prices and negative output gaps have helped dampen inflation in many high-income and developing countries.

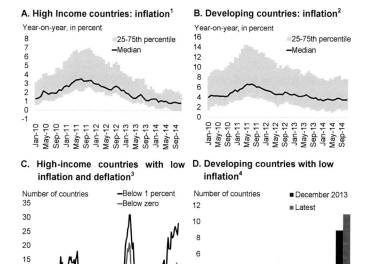

Sources: Haver Analytics, EIU, IFS.
1. The sample includes 55 high-income countries. Latest data is November 2014.
2. The sample includes 121 developing countries. Latest data is November 2014.
3. Number of high-income countries with year-on-year inflation below 1 percent and below zero. Excludes countries with a population of less than 1 million.
4. Number of developing countries with year-on-year inflation below 1 percent. Excludes countries with a population of less than 1 million and data unavailable after June 2014. Latest available data is November 2014 for most countries.

structural reforms to boost productivity and, especially in the Euro Area, strengthen banking systems and reduce financial fragmentation.

Developing countries face three major policy challenges. First, monetary and exchange rate policies might have to adapt to the more normal (i.e., less easy) financial conditions that will eventually accompany the recovery in high-income countries. Second, some developing countries that face benign cyclical environments should rebuild fiscal space, which would allow them to use countercyclical fiscal policy when needed. Third, developing countries need to implement structural reforms that promote job creation, growth, and trade. Such policies would mitigate the long-run adverse effects from less favorable demographics in many developing countries and weak global trade. Moreover, they will be instrumental in achieving higher growth rates that are necessary to achieve poverty targets.

Soft oil prices offer a window of opportunity to implement subsidy and energy tax reforms in oil-importing countries. This would make available additional

FIGURE 1.3   Major economies: Importance in the world economy

The United States, the Euro Area, China, Japan, and the United Kingdom account for a substantial share of global activity, trade and financial flows.

Distribution of global GDP, trade and financial assets, 2013

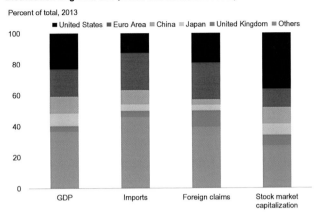

Percent of total, 2013

■ United States ■ Euro Area ■ China ■ Japan ■ United Kingdom ■ Others

Sources: World Bank, BIS, and World Federation of Exchanges (2013).
Note: Foreign claims refer to claims of BIS reporting banks on foreign banks and nonbanks. Stock market capitalization is the market value of all publicly traded shares.

fiscal resources which could be used to rebuild fiscal space or increase fiscal resources for better-targeted pro-poor spending or investment. At the same time, such reforms would reduce distortions that tilt economies towards energy-intensive activities.

Recent Developments and Outlook in Major Economies

The recovery in the United States and the United Kingdom appears robust, but is further delayed in the Euro Area and Japan. China looks set to continue on a path of gradual deceleration.

This section focuses on recent developments and the outlook for the five major economies most prominent in global activity, trade, and financial markets (Figure 1.3): the United States, the Euro Area, China, Japan, and the United Kingdom. In 2013, these economies together accounted for 63 and 54 percent of global gross domestic product (GDP) and imports, respectively, 60 percent of international banking system assets, and 72 percent of global stock market capitalization.

In the United States, apart from a temporary contraction at the beginning of 2014, growth has been above potential since mid-2013 and in the third quarter of 2014 reached its fastest pace since 2003. Growth is expected to reach 2.4 percent in 2014 and 3.2 percent in 2015 percent before gradually decelerating to 2.4 percent in

FIGURE 1.4   United States and United Kingdom

In the United States, the unemployment rate is falling, partly as a result of shrinking labor force participation rates, and growth is picking up. Nevertheless, the output gap remains negative though estimates of its exact size vary widely. In the United Kingdom, the growth rebound has been supported by a robust housing market and inflation undershot expectations.

A. Exports, domestic demand, and GDP growth[1]

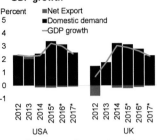

B. Output gap, 2014

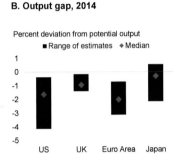

C. U.S.: Unemployment and participation rate

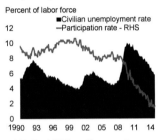

D. U.S.: Contribution to changes of labor force participation, 2008-2014Q1[2]

E. UK: Real GDP and house price growth

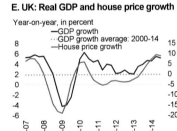

F. U.K.: inflation forecast[3]

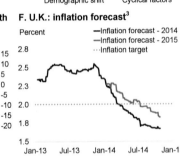

Sources: BLS, Consensus forecasts, Haver Analytics, World Bank, OECD, IMF, European Commission, UK HM Treasury, U.S. Congressional Budget Office, Bank of Japan., Aaronson and others (2014)
1. An asterisk indicates forecast.
2. Based on a least squares regression for 1976 – 2014.
3. Forecasts for 2014 and 2015 are consensus forecasts for average annual inflation made on a monthly basis.

2017. The recovery has been supported by highly accommodative monetary policy, which bolstered capital market valuations, and easing fiscal consolidation. Improving labor markets have been marked by robust job creation and gradually increasing, though still modest, wage growth. While unemployment has fallen sharply (Figure 1.4), labor force participation has declined to levels not seen since the early 1980s, when female labor force participation was much smaller. Demographic trends, such as changes in the age distribution of the population, and cohort effects, such as increased years of schooling, or earlier retirement, appear to explain a large part of the decline in the participation rate (Aaronson and others, 2014).

A number of factors support the recovery. Fiscal policy, which was strongly contractionary in 2012–13, is easing to an almost neutral stance in 2014–15. Housing market conditions have improved while declining oil prices are boosting real household incomes, maintaining private consumption as the main source of growth in 2015. Investment rates are expected to increase but remain below pre-crisis levels, while a strong dollar will dampen net exports and low oil prices affect negatively capital expenditure in the energy sector. Inflation is projected to remain below-target in 2015–16, partly as a result of sharply lower oil prices and a strengthening U.S. dollar. With slack in the economy diminishing, the first hike in the federal funds rate is expected around mid-2015, but the tightening is likely to be gradual due to subdued inflation expectations.

In the United Kingdom, the recovery has gained momentum, supported by robust housing markets and expanding credit. Growth reached 2.6 percent in 2014 and is expected to be above potential until 2016, despite slowing net exports partly as a result of weak euro area demand. Inflation was significantly below target in 2014 and should remain so until 2015, partly due to continued low oil prices. As the recovery broadens, also supported by low oil prices, the Bank of England is expected to begin modest tightening in the second half of 2015. However, subdued wage growth, low inflation, and spillovers from weak activity in the rest of Europe may delay the first rate hike.

As regards the Euro Area, activity has been weaker than anticipated, especially in France, Germany, and Italy (Figure 1.5). Concerns about long-term prospects and the legacies of the crisis (especially impaired balance sheets and high unemployment) weigh on a fragile recovery and diminish expected growth benefits from sustained low oil prices. In Greece, political uncertainty continues to fray investor sentiment. In contrast, in Ireland and Spain, a pickup appears underway, helped by gains in cost competitiveness and strengthening corporate balance sheets. The current account surplus in the Euro Area remains significant, reflecting ongoing import compression, competitiveness gains in the periphery and persistent surpluses in Germany. Bank recapitalization efforts and continued deleveraging could still constrain bank lending in some parts of the Euro Area, despite the successful completion of the European Central Bank's (ECB) Asset Quality Review and the move to place the largest banks under single supervision. Financial fragmentation, high unemployment, structural rigidities, and unresolved fiscal challenges are likely to dampen the

FIGURE 1.5   Euro Area and Japan

Growth slowed in much of the Euro Area during 2014 and inflation expectations have fallen. For 2015–17, the Euro Area periphery is expected to contribute more to growth. In Japan, a consumption tax hike caused sharp swings in retail sales and a partly temporary rise in inflation; export growth was slow despite a weak yen.

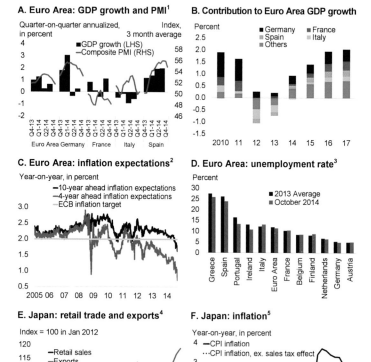

Sources: Bank of Japan, Bloomberg, Eurostat, Haver Analytics, ILO, and World Bank.
1. PMI denotes the Purchasing Managers' Index. A value above 50 indicates expansion, below 50 indicates contraction.
2. 10-year and 4-year ahead inflation expectations derived from 5 year forward contract on 5 year interest rate swap and 2 year forward contract on 2 year interest rate swaps, respectively.
3. Harmonized unemployment rate as per ILO definition.
4. Nominal retail sales and exports.
5. Inflation excluding sales tax effect estimated by the Bank of Japan Monthly Report (March to December 2014).

recovery. The sharp drop in oil prices in the second half of 2014 is expected to reduce headline inflation further in the short-term while core inflation remains low. Financial market indicators suggest that investors expect a prolonged period of below-target inflation. Euro Area growth is forecast at 1.1 percent in 2015, and 1.6 percent in 2016–17.

A persistent undershooting of the inflation target led the ECB to announce additional easing measures since June 2014. These included interest rate cuts, targeted liquidity

FIGURE 1.6   China

In China, a gradual slowdown is underway and also reflected in serial revisions to medium-term forecasts. House price inflation slowed as part of a broader slowdown, which was buffered by policy measures to stimulate infrastructure investment. Excess capacity is reflected in falling producer prices.

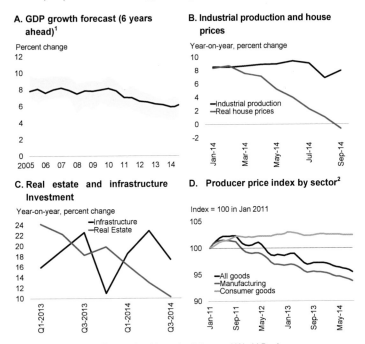

A. GDP growth forecast (6 years ahead)[1]

B. Industrial production and house prices

C. Real estate and infrastructure Investment

D. Producer price index by sector[2]

Sources: Consensus Economics, Haver Analytics, and World Bank.
1. Six-year-ahead GDP growth forecast, grey band indicates the range of forecasts, from minimum to maximum, compiled by Consensus Economics.
2. Latest data December 14, 2014.

provisions, and outright purchases of covered bonds and asset-backed securities. The central bank committed to expanding its balance sheet back to 2012 levels, which would amount to a 30 percent increase. These commitments contributed to some depreciation of the euro in trade-weighted terms, which should help support exports and help stabilize inflation. Aggregate fiscal policy continues to consolidate marginally, well short of the tightening in 2012–13.

In Japan, at 0.2 percent, growth in 2014 fell significantly short of expectations as the economy struggled to recover from a sales tax increase in April 2014, and, until mid-2014, exports remained subdued despite a weak yen. This export weakness reflected soft global demand, the relocation of production facilities overseas (Amiti, Itskhoki, and Konings, 2014), and rising cost of energy imports since the shutdown of nuclear reactors. Looking forward, however, soft oil prices should help contain the cost of energy imports and support the recovery. While unemployment is low, labor force participation remains below pre-crisis levels, and real wage growth is subdued. In June 2014, the government announced a range of

product and labor market reforms, broadly in line with Organisation for Economic Co-operation and Development (OECD) recommendations, and is expected to speed up their implementation in 2015. These should boost confidence in the short run and help foster growth in the medium term. The central bank announced additional monetary stimulus aiming at expanding its balance sheet to 70 percent of GDP to bolster growth and prevent a slowdown in inflation. Supported by these measures, growth is expected to reach 1.2 percent in 2015 and 1.6 percent in 2016, before decelerating to 1.2 in 2017 as a second sales tax hike is implemented in April that year.

China has adopted measures aimed at containing financial vulnerabilities and unwinding excess capacity (including in construction, shipping, and renewable energy sectors) and, at the same time, stemming a slowdown. Actions to rein in credit growth have slowed the real estate market (Figure 1.6) and investment while dampening growth, especially in early 2014. To reach its growth target, the government subsequently implemented a series of targeted stimulus measures. These included support for new public infrastructure and housing projects, tax relief to small and medium-sized enterprises, and targeted cuts in the banks' required reserves. In addition, benchmark deposit and lending rates were cut in November 2014 for the first time since 2012. As the authorities have balanced the competing goals of reducing vulnerabilities with supporting growth, the medium-term growth outlook has been revised downwards. For 2015, soft oil prices are expected to boost activity and reduce the need for additional policy stimulus. Growth is expected to slow below 7 percent by 2017 from 7.4 percent in 2014, broadly in line with the objectives of the current five-year plan. Reflecting excess capacity, weakening domestic demand, and reduced import costs, inflation is expected to remain below the central bank's indicative ceiling of 3 percent.

Global Trends and Spillovers

Developments in major economies are likely to shape the outlook for developing countries. First, the beginning of monetary policy rate hikes in the United States, combined with continued accommodative policies in the Euro Area and Japan, is expected to lead to modestly tighter global financing conditions in 2015–16. Second, commodity prices, which have fallen on expanding supply and concerns about global growth, are expected to remain soft. Third, the anemic recovery in the Euro Area and Japan—which together account for almost a third of global imports—will continue to weigh on global trade growth.

FIGURE 1.7   Global financial trends

Financial conditions generally remained easy as markets shrugged off negative news in 2014. However, financial market volatility has increased since October 2014 and the US dollar has strengthened.

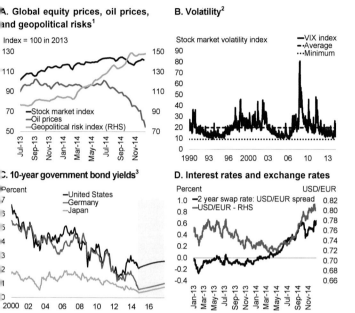

A. Global equity prices, oil prices, and geopolitical risks[1]

B. Volatility[2]

C. 10-year government bond yields[3]

D. Interest rates and exchange rates

Sources: Bloomberg, Chicago Board Options Exchange, Google Trends, Haver Analytics, World Bank.
1. Geopolitical Risk Index is the 6-month average weekly Google searches for Syria, Iraq, Gaza, ISIS, Ukraine, Russia, Geopolitical and Ebola; global stock market index is the Global FTSE stock market; oil prices are Brent crude prices in U.S. dollars.
2. VIX denotes the Volatility Index and measures market expectations of near-term volatility conveyed by S&P 500 stock index option prices.
3. Forecasted 10-years yields are based on the implied forward rates from Bloomberg, calculated by using the equation of a continuously compounded forward rate.

FIGURE 1.8   Financing conditions for developing countries

Renewed volatility since October 2014 brought a modest correction in developing country equity markets and slowing net inflows into mutual funds. Developing-country bond yields increased but international debt issuance was robust throughout 2014.

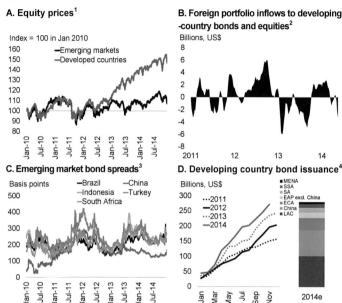

A. Equity prices[1]

B. Foreign portfolio inflows to developing-country bonds and equities[2]

C. Emerging market bond spreads[3]

D. Developing country bond issuance[4]

Sources: Bloomberg, Dealogic, Emerging Portfolio Fund Research, JPMorgan Chase, World Bank.
1. MSCI Equity Index in local currency.
2. 6-week moving average of net inflows.
3. JPMorgan EMBIG spread.
4. Face values for bond issues.

Easy but Gradually Tightening Financial Conditions

Since the 2008-09 global crisis, major central banks have maintained exceptionally accommodative policies to support activity. As markets focused on central banks' support for the recovery, they tended to interpret negative news as a reason for continued monetary policy accommodation. This has resulted in low bond yields, and has lifted global credit markets (Figure 1.7). As a result, corrections in equity and high-yield bond markets were quickly recouped.[1] Financial

market volatility spiked briefly in October and December 2014 on geopolitical risks, concerns about global growth, and oil market volatility. Global equity markets dropped initially and long-term interest rates remained low in the United States and fell further in core Euro Area countries on safe-haven flows. Bond spreads of developing countries widened, but by less than during the volatility episode of May/June 2013.

Benign financing conditions through much of 2014 have allowed developing countries to tap international bond markets at a record pace (Figure 1.8). In Latin America, energy companies have been substantial issuers. In Sub-Saharan Africa, several sovereign issuers went to international capital markets, partly in anticipation of rising borrowing costs. New issues by Chinese corporates reached record volumes, as tight funding conditions in the domestic market encouraged many to turn abroad.

The expected divergence of monetary policies in the United States and the United Kingdom, versus the Euro Area and

---

[1] Tensions between Russia and other high-income countries intensified over the conflict between Russia and Ukraine, leading to a series of sanctions and growing disruptions to regional trade and capital flows. In the Middle East, the capture of large swaths of territory in Iraq and Syrian Arab Republic by the Islamic State of Iraq and Levant has raised security risks in an already fragile region. The rapid spread of the Ebola epidemic across West Africa has caused a human tragedy for local populations, and growing economic losses.

FIGURE 1.9 Exchange rate movements in developing countries

Many developing country currencies have depreciated against the U.S. dollar.

A. Nominal effective appreciation, May–December 2014[1]

A. Non-financial Corporate Debt[2]

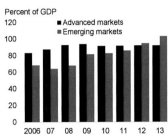

Sources: BIS, Haver Analytics, and World Bank.
1. A negative sign indicates depreciation.
2. Weighted average. Advanced Markets include the Euro Area, United States, United Kingdom and Japan. Emerging Markets include China, Czech Republic, Hungary, Indonesia, India, South Korea, Mexico, Poland, Thailand, Turkey and South Africa.

Japan, became increasingly evident over the course of 2014. The U.S. dollar appreciated against other reserve currencies, and exchange rate volatility increased. In a sign that markets expect the differential growth and policy outlook to persist, long-term interest rates in the Euro Area and Japan are projected to remain about 160 and 200 basis point (bp), respectively, below equivalent U.S. interest rates in 2015–17.

Eastern European currencies, closely tied to the euro, and affected by geopolitical turmoil in the region, have depreciated substantially against the U.S. dollar, but less in nominal effective terms (Figure 1.9). A number of commodity exporters have also seen renewed exchange rate pressures, reflecting the combined impact of a broad-based dollar strengthening, softening commodity prices, and domestic uncertainties.

After several years of rapid credit growth and record debt issuance on international bond markets, corporations in many developing countries have accumulated significant liabilities and exposure to both global interest rate and exchange rate fluctuations. Although global financing conditions should generally remain favorable over the coming years, a broad-based appreciation of the U.S. dollar adds to currency risks and balance sheet pressures, potentially inducing a faster tightening of borrowing costs and rising bond spreads.

Soft Commodity Prices

Expanding supply and concerns about global growth prospects have reduced commodity prices—and especially sharply oil prices. Commodity prices are likely to remain soft into 2015-17 (Figure 1.10).

- *Oil:* Faster-than-expected unwinding of supply disruptions and unconventional oil production, weaker-than-expected global growth, receding geopolitical risks, shifting OPEC policy objectives, and U.S. dollar appreciation contributed to an unusually sharp drop in oil prices in the second half of 2014 (Chapter 4). Cumulatively, the fall in oil prices from early-2011 peaks has been larger than that for other commodities. With underlying weak demand growth, implementation of new policy objectives of OPEC, and falling cost of shale oil production in the United States, oil prices are expected to remain low through 2016.

- *Metals:* China is a major importer of industrial commodities: it consumes almost one-quarter of global energy output and one-half of global metal supply. Just as China's burgeoning investments in commodity-intensive manufacturing, construction, and real estate raised global demand for commodities, its slowing has depressed demand, especially for copper, iron ore, steel, and nickel. Prices of these metals have recently been 33 percent off their record highs of 2011. They are expected to stay low over the period 2015-16 as expanding supply is only gradually absorbed by rising demand.

- *Agriculture:* Crops in 2014-15 have turned out better than originally anticipated. Stock-to-utilization ratios (a measure of the size of harvests) are expected to increase for key grains and oilseeds, including wheat and maize (U.S. Department of Agriculture, 2014).[2] Fears that 2015 will be a strong El Niño year have dissipated.[3] The expected mild El Niño would have, at most, local implications, for example in Central America, whereas global prices are likely to remain unaffected. With supply set to remain robust (absent unexpected weather shocks) and low oil prices compressing the cost of energy-intensive agricultural production, prices should remain soft through 2015-16.

- *Side effects of U.S. dollar appreciation:* In addition to these broad trends in supply and demand, the U.S. dollar appreciation in 2014 has, as in earlier episodes, been associated with falling U.S. dollar denominated commodity prices over the short-term.

---

[2]Some price increases, e.g., Arabica coffee, cocoa, and rice, reflect specific supply conditions.

[3]El Nino is an irregular and prolonged warming of the surface temperature of the Pacific Ocean that can change rainfall patterns and fishing stocks.

Historical estimates suggest that a 30 percent decline oil prices (as projected for 2015) could be associated with an increase in global GDP by about 0.5 percent. These types of sizeable growth effects are possible if the decline in oil prices is mostly driven by supply related factors. Recent developments, including upward surprises in oil supply, unwinding of some geopolitical risks, and changes in OPEC's policy objectives, all indicate that supply related factors have been playing a significant role in explaining the plunge in oil prices.

However, the growth impact can be expected to be smaller in 2015-2016 for several reasons. First, low oil prices coincide with low growth prospects and other country-specific headwinds, including weak confidence that may encourage households and corporates to save real income windfalls. Second, monetary policy rates of some major central banks are currently at the zero lower bound; hence, central banks' ability to stimulate activity with the goal of supporting inflation expectations is limited. While low oil prices will support global growth, they will cause significant real income shifts from oil-exporting countries to oil-importing ones. Unless offset by depreciations or food and fuel subsidies, falling commodity prices will temporarily reduce inflation in developing countries. To the extent that subsidies are not fixed in nominal terms, fiscal pressures will also ease.

Current low oil prices are mostly below oil exporters' fiscal break-even prices, although still above extraction cost in all but the highest-cost producers of shale oil in the United States, oil from tar sands in Canada and deepwater oil in Brazil and Mexico. Weakening fiscal balances are expected to be accompanied by declining current account surpluses. For now, many oil-exporting economies have substantial reserves to buffer extended periods of low prices. However, sustained low prices could severely undermine fiscal resources and external balances in several already-fragile oil-exporting economies in the Middle East, Europe and Central Asia, and Latin America. Slowing growth across large oil-exporting economies, including in Russia, will have important regional repercussions.

In contrast, for oil-importing economies across the world, low oil prices are expected to yield real income gains (World Bank, 2013a). Low oil prices will reduce current account deficits and, in countries with substantial fuel and food subsidies, fiscal deficits—at a time when many governments need to rebuild fiscal room and central banks are weighing their response to the possible increase in global financial conditions. In particular, if softer commodity prices lessen inflation pressures, central banks would have greater room to implement

FIGURE 1.10 Commodity markets

Commodity prices have declined—due to US. dollar appreciation, rising supplies, and slowing global demand including from China, a major buyer of commodities—and are expected to remain soft. As a result, deteriorating terms of trade of some large developing countries, which account for much of the supply in commodity markets, are expected to weaken their trade balances.

A. Changes in trade balance due to terms of trade effects, 2013-2014[1]

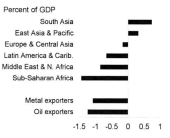

B. Commodity prices and the U.S. dollar[2]

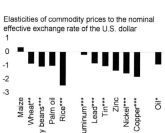

C. Shares of China and India in global commodity imports[3]

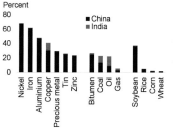

D. Shares of selected emerging economies in global commodity exports[3]

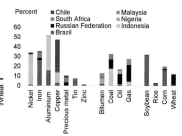

Sources: Baffes and Savescu (2014), Baffes and Dennis (2013), Zhang et al., (2008), UN Comtrade, USDA, and World Bank.
1. Effect of 20 percent decline in oil, 5 percent decline in agricultural prices and 10 percent decline in metal prices on the difference between exports and imports in percent of GDP, assuming no supply response. Excludes re-exports.
2. Elasticities show the percentage change in oil associated with a 1 percent U.S. dollar appreciation. Based on coefficient estimates from an OLS regression of the logarithm of U.S. dollar-denominated commodity prices on the logarithm of nominal effective exchange rate of the U.S. dollar and a number of control variables. Data from 1960-2012. Asterisks denote significance * significance at 10, ** significant at 5%, and *** significance at 1%.
3. Average over 2008-2013. Including exports of ores (e.g. bauxite) and oil products.

more accommodative monetary policy stances. Lower commodity prices would also provide an opportunity for governments to rebuild fiscal space and remove distortions associated with food and fuel subsidies, while limiting the impact on households.

Beyond oil, developing countries have large market shares for various other commodities. Conversely, many are heavily dependent on the exports of a few raw materials. The broad-based commodity price declines of 2013–14 have considerably worsened their terms of trade, and dampened growth. Countries in Latin America and the Caribbean and Sub-Saharan Africa, which export agricultural produce and metals, saw export revenues

FIGURE 1.11   Global trade

Global trade has grown along a weak post-crisis trend. With the recovery in the United States gaining momentum and growth in the Euro Area gradually picking up, high-income countries are expected to contribute more to global trade.

A. Trade volumes[1]

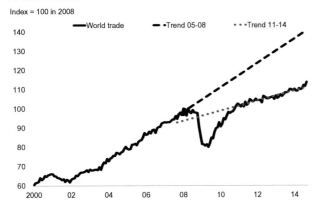

B. Contributions to global import growth

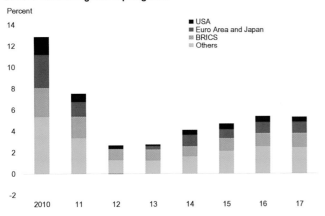

Sources: CPB Netherlands Bureau for Economic Policy Analysis -World Trade Monitor and World Bank.
1. Blue dotted line: trend during 2005Q1–2008Q1; red dotted line: trend since 2011Q1.

access to trade credit may have contributed to the latter development (Chapter 4).

Until 2013, the halting recovery in Europe, which accounts for a quarter of global merchandise trade, dampened trade growth. Since then, the modest expansion in global import demand has been driven by growing demand from the United States and the Euro Area, notwithstanding its fragile recovery. In contrast, developing country import growth has decelerated to its slowest pace since the 2008 global financial crisis, reflecting weaker domestic demand in some large middle-income economies, and exchange rate depreciations since the financial market turmoil of May 2013.

Despite some projected pick-up, global trade growth is not expected to revert to the steeply rising path of the pre-crisis years. Strengthening demand from high-income countries is expected to lift exports of developing countries to different degrees, depending on their major trading partners, and the composition of their export baskets. For 2015–17, the acceleration in the United States will support manufacturing exports from Central America and Asia. Stabilizing, or slowly expanding, activity in other high-income countries, particularly the Euro Area and Japan, would also add some momentum.

Recent Developments and Outlook in Developing Countries

Recent Developments

Compared to the rapid expansion in the pre-crisis years, growth in the developing world has been moderate since 2010. Growth slowed in 2014 but is expected to accelerate in 2015. In large middle-income countries, cyclical factors, a round of policy tightening, and political tensions, have interacted with a trend slowdown in productivity growth.

Growth in many emerging market economies disappointed in 2014, and forecasts were repeatedly downgraded (Figure 1.12). Several factors contributed to slower-than-expected growth:

decline sharply. In contrast, falling commodity prices have helped narrow trade deficits in the commodity importers of east and south Asia. Elsewhere, the net effect on trade balances depended on the relative strength of agricultural, metal, and oil price declines and the composition of import and export baskets. For example, trade balances of countries in the Middle East and North Africa (heavy importers of grains and oilseeds) improved.

Weak Global Trade

Since the global financial crisis, world trade growth has slowed significantly from the trend of the 1990s and early 2000s, as a result of both weak global growth and what appears to be lower responsiveness of world trade to activity (Figure 1.11). Changes in global value chains, a shifting composition of import demand, and impaired

- *Export weakness.* Deteriorating terms of trade and falling commodity prices dampened growth in commodity exporters (although the growth impact was mitigated by strong harvests in Argentina and Zambia, and strong services growth in Nigeria). Elsewhere, the narrowing of current account deficits in several large developing countries in the first half of 2014 was reversed in the second.

- *Setbacks to confidence.* In Argentina, Brazil, Ghana, South Africa, Thailand, and República Bolivariana de Venezuela, policy or electoral uncertainty, or social or labor tensions, combined with slow progress in structural reforms dented confidence and contributed to a slowdown. In India and Mexico, weak sentiment early on in the year on election uncertainties and reform fatigue initially held back investment but was reversed later.

- *Domestic policy tightening.* Brazil, Mexico, the Philippines, and Turkey enacted fiscal or monetary policy tightening measures to contain credit growth or inflation and improve fiscal positions. In some economies in Sub-Saharan Africa that have high inflation and large fiscal and current account deficits (e.g., Ghana and Zambia), fiscal and monetary policy tightening and weakening confidence weighed on activity.

Fiscal deficits generally widened modestly in developing countries and remained high in frontier markets.[4] Sovereign bond issuance in frontier markets has doubled between 2011 and 2013 and increased further in 2014. This has financed significant fiscal deficits, in some cases in excess of 8 percent of GDP (Ghana, Lebanon, and Mongolia). As a result, government debt in frontier markets has steadily increased to almost 60 percent of GDP in 2014 from about 30 percent of GDP in 2008.

Inflation has started slowing in many developing countries as commodity prices declined and, in some, macroeconomic policies tightened, which also helped slow private sector credit growth and domestic demand pressures more generally. This was the case in Brazil, Malaysia, Thailand, and Turkey (Figure 1.13) although inflation remains above target in Brazil and Turkey. In Hungary, Romania, and Serbia, inflation has fallen below the lower bounds of central bank target ranges against the backdrop of anemic growth. In contrast, in some countries where inflation was already elevated, exchange rate and domestic demand pressures, VAT hikes, severe weather, or sanctions have pushed inflation rates higher (República Bolivariana de Venezuela, Egypt, or Ghana).

---

[4]Frontier markets, such as those used in indices developed by S&P and FTSE, are typically smaller, less developed, and in investors' views riskier developing economies with recent access to international capital markets. They include, among others, Bangladesh, Côte d'Ivoire, Ghana, Jamaica, Kenya, Lebanon, Mongolia, Senegal, Vietnam, and Zambia.

FIGURE 1.12   Growth in developing countries

Growth disappointed in several large developing countries, partly for one-off reasons that reduced growth below potential and widened output gaps. In all developing country regions, except Sub-Saharan Africa and the Middle East and North Africa, growth has declined and in most regions is below long-term growth rates, partly reflecting slowing productivity growth.

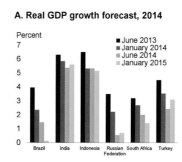

A. Real GDP growth forecast, 2014

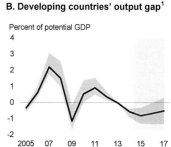

B. Developing countries' output gap[1]

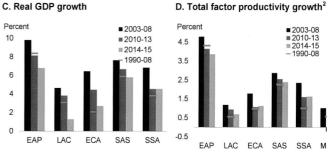

C. Real GDP growth   D. Total factor productivity growth[2]

Sources: World Bank and World Bank calculations.
1. Output gap estimates using production function approach, Hodrick-Prescott filter, and band-pass filter. The shade indicates the range of output gap estimates.
2. Total factor productivity growth estimates are based on a production function approach.

Despite slowing growth and in contrast to high-income countries, employment growth has typically been sufficient to absorb a growing working age population and rising labor force participation. Exceptions are the Middle East, North Africa, South Asia, and Eastern and Central Europe where unemployment increased or remained high. Wage growth has moderated, especially in countries that tightened monetary policy (e.g., Indonesia) or suffered sharp contractions (e.g., Ukraine).

Long-term growth has been on a secular decline in larger developing countries, especially in East Asia and Eastern Europe. Population growth is slowing and the share of the working-age cohort is decelerating (Figure 1.14). Although potential growth is difficult to measure, different methodologies suggest a slowdown started with the global financial crisis. This largely reflected weak global demand and sluggish productivity growth—partly as a result of limited reallocation of labor out of low-productivity into high-productivity sectors in some countries (World Bank, 2014a). Investment and, in some countries, the labor force, have also grown slowly. In the larger developing

FIGURE 1.13   Inflation, credit, and labor markets in developing countries

Tightening macroeconomic policies helped slow inflation and credit growth. Inflation fell in most developing countries—in some Eastern European countries below target ranges—but rose in a few countries with already high inflation. Employment mostly grew to absorb rising working age populations and labor forces while wage growth was broadly steady. Fiscal balances widened and debt rose, especially in some frontier markets.

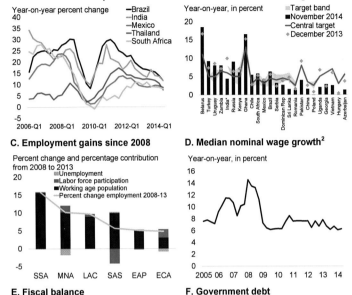

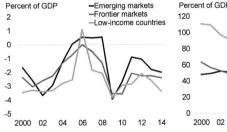

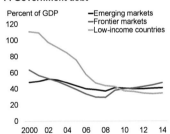

Sources: BIS, Centralbanking.com, Haver Analytics, IMF World Economic Outlook, National Central Banks, World Bank, and World Bank estimates.
1. Latest available data for November 2014; for Ghana September 2014. Targets include both formal inflation targets and implicit or indicative, nonbinding guidance compiled by centralbanking.com. An asterisks (*) denotes a proposed inflation target.
2. Sample includes Albania, Azerbaijan, Brazil, Belarus, Bosnia and Herzegovina, Bulgaria, Colombia, Ecuador, Georgia, Hungary, Indonesia, Kazakhstan, Macedonia, Malaysia, Mexico, Moldova, Paraguay, Peru, Romania, South Africa, Thailand, Turkey, and Ukraine.

FIGURE 1.14   Long-term growth pressures

Potential growth has been slowing, partly as a result of limited reallocation of resources from low-productivity to high-productivity sectors. In the medium-term, it may decline further as a shrinking share of the working-age population reduces the "demographic dividend."

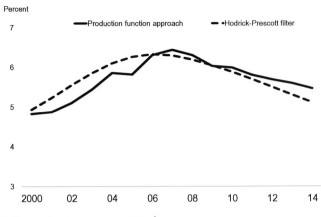

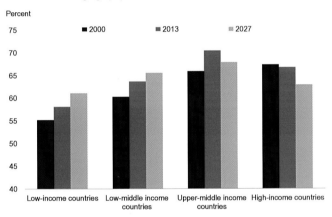

Sources: UN Population Statistics and World Bank.
1. Hodrick-Prescott filter applied to quarterly seasonally adjusted real GDP levels.
2. Projections for working age and total population based on "medium fertility" scenario (UN Population projection, 2014).

countries, a shrinking demographic dividend as the population ages and the share of the working age group declines, will further depress potential growth.

In low-income countries, growth remained robust at about 6 percent in 2014 on the back of rising public investment, robust capital inflows, good harvests (Ethiopia, Rwanda), and improving security in a few conflict countries (Myanmar, Central African Republic, Mali, see Special Focus at the end of this chapter). Many low-income countries are heavily reliant on remittances that can help smooth consumption

fluctuations (Chapter 4). In South Asia and Sub-Saharan Africa, robust remittances supported consumption growth whereas a sharp drop in the value of remittances from Russia dented domestic demand in Europe and Central Asia. The moderation in global food and energy prices in 2014 contributed to a decline in inflation which was particularly substantial in Sub-Saharan Africa.

Outlook

The baseline forecast assumes that the domestic headwinds that held back growth in 2014 will gradually subside. Developing countries will also benefit from the slowly strengthening recovery in high-income countries, and easing commodity prices should help commodity importers. Growth is expected to rise to 4.8 percent in 2015 and reach 5.4 percent by 2017.

External drivers of growth. Developments in the major economies will shape developing countries' prospects to varying degrees.

- Growth in developing countries with high trade exposure to the United States (especially in parts of Latin America and East Asia) are expected to gain momentum, while those reliant on demand from the Euro Area will face headwinds (Eastern Europe, Northern and Sub-Saharan Africa).

- With oil, metal and coal prices expected to remain well below 2013 levels, producers in Latin America (Chile, Colombia), Sub-Saharan Africa (Zambia, South Africa), and Central and East Asia (Mongolia, Indonesia) may eventually struggle to maintain high post-crisis growth rates.

- Sustained low oil prices will weaken activity in exporting countries, with spillovers to trading partners and recipient countries of remittances or official support (Chapter 4). A sharp recession in Russia will dampen growth in Central Asia, while weakening external accounts in the República Bolivariana de Venezuela or GCC countries may put at risk external financing support they provide to neighboring countries.

- The ability to adjust to global shocks depends importantly on the credibility of a country's policy framework and its implementation. Countries with relatively more credible policy frameworks and reform-oriented governments (India, Kenya, Mexico, Senegal) will adjust more easily to tightening or volatile global financial conditions than countries with limited policy buffers, weakening growth prospects, high exposure to short-term portfolio flows, and a large stock of debt held by foreign investors.

Domestic drivers of growth. In several countries, easing political uncertainty and social tensions (Brazil, Indonesia, South Africa, Thailand) or the implementation of structural reforms (India, Kenya, Malaysia, Mexico, Nigeria, Senegal) should raise confidence, and encourage stronger investment and consumption. In some countries (Ghana, Mongolia, and Turkey), additional policy tightening would be needed to decisively reduce external and internal imbalances. Investment in the maintenance of the capital stock or in new capacity is expected to ease capacity constraints in several countries in Sub-Saharan Africa (including Nigeria and South Africa).

Finally, some fragile states should see increased growth in 2015–17 as the spread of Ebola slows, security improves, and peacebuilding efforts progress (as they did in 2014 in the Central African Republic and Mali).

Poverty implications. Growth is central to poverty reduction. Sustained per capita growth rates on the order of 4 percent would allow the share of the global population living on less than $1.25 a day to fall toward 3 percent by 2030 from 14 percent in 2011 (Box 1.1). However, under the baseline scenario, achieving this growth rate will be a major challenge that emphasizes the need for growth-enhancing macroeconomic policies and structural reforms.

Regional Prospects

The broad global and domestic trends above are also reflected in regional prospects (Chapter 2).

- *East Asia and Pacific, excluding China:* As a result of political tensions; tightening monetary, fiscal, and macro-prudential policies in 2013 and early 2014; and soft commodity prices, activity, credit growth and inflation slowed (in most countries). This has allowed several central banks to keep policy rates on hold for the time being but monetary policy room remains constrained by high domestic debt. Recent volatility in global financial markets put some pressure on asset prices and currencies in commodity-exporting economies. Although the region has so far been resilient to the growth slowdown in China from post-crisis peaks (with the exception of some commodity exporters, such as Indonesia), a sustained slowdown in China may feed through via integrated supply chains. Nevertheless, growth is expected to gain momentum as the investment cycle turns (Indonesia), political unrest subsides (Thailand), and countries integrated into global value chains (Cambodia, Malaysia, Thailand, and Vietnam) benefit from the pickup in the United States and other major markets for manufactures. Adjustment to softer commodity prices will continue to weigh on growth of the commodity exporters of the region but should help commodity-importing countries.

- *Europe and Central Asia:* Weak activity in the Euro Area; a severe slowdown in Russia combined with a sharp depreciation of the ruble against the U.S. dollar between January and mid-December 2014; and a sharp contraction in Ukraine present difficult headwinds to the region. Some Central Asian countries already experienced double-digit declines in exports to Russia and sharp drops in the value of

BOX 1.1   What does weak growth mean for poverty in the future?[1]

The Millennium Development Goal to halve extreme poverty was reached in 2010. Since then, the World Bank Group set a new goal, to reduce extreme poverty to below 3 percent by 2030. Under current growth projections, reaching this goal will be challenging. This increases the urgency of implementing growth-enhancing policies and structural reforms.

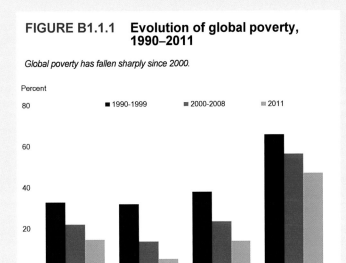

FIGURE B1.1.1   Evolution of global poverty, 1990–2011

Global poverty has fallen sharply since 2000.

Percent

■ 1990-1999   ■ 2000-2008   ■ 2011

Source: PovcalNet (2014).
Note: Simple average over the respective years. Poverty defined as share of population living on less than US $1.25 per day (in constant 2005 prices).

Global poverty has declined steeply over the past half century. The Millennium Development Goal of halving extreme poverty by 2015 was achieved ahead of schedule, as the share of the world's population living on less than $1.25 per day in constant 2005 prices declined from 36 percent in 1990 to 14.5 percent in 2011 (Figure B1.1.1). The reduction in poverty between 2000 and 2011 was aided by relatively high growth rates in developing economies, especially prior to the global financial crisis. Fast-growing Asian emerging markets—namely, China and, to a lesser extent, India—accounted for most of the decline in poverty.

Despite the rapid decline in poverty overall, it remains widespread. Almost half of the population of low-income countries still lives in extreme poverty. At the global level, more than one billion people, mostly in Sub-Saharan Africa and South Asia, are in extreme poverty. In April 2013, the World Bank set an ambitious new poverty target of reducing the share of people living in extreme poverty to 3 percent of the global population by 2030.[2]

Weaker growth in developing countries during the past three years raises questions about whether the significant decline in

poverty achieved in recent decades can be repeated in the future. In 2012–14, growth in developing countries slowed to 4.5–4.9 percent, well below the average rate during the early 2000s, and is expected to rise only slowly, to about 5.4 percent by 2017. Moreover, the post-crisis slowdown in developing countries has been taking place in an environment of weak global growth.

In light of the fragile medium-term growth outlook, this box briefly examines the implications of various growth projections for the global poverty rate in 2030.

Why is growth so important for poverty reduction?

Growth is central to poverty reduction. Between 1970 and 2010, growth in average per capita income accounted for three-quarters of the income growth of the poor.[3] In particular, a significant part of poverty reduction was attributed to growth in labor income (Inchauste et al., 2014; Inchauste and Saavedra-Chanduvi, 2013). Increases in labor income are associated with a reduction in poverty through at least two channels. First, growth in the agricultural sector, the primary source of income for the poor, raises incomes more than growth in less labor-intensive sectors, in particular the natural resource sector. Second, the movement of labor from the low-productivity agriculture sector to the higher-productivity manufacturing and service sectors raises labor incomes, including of those of the poor (Kuznets 1955; Chenery, 1979; Ngai and Pissarides, 2008).

---

[1] The main author of this box is Vandana Chandra.

[2] The poverty goal is one of the World Bank's twin goals. The other goal is to promote shared prosperity by improving the living standards of the bottom 40 percent of the population in every country. The poverty target is 3 percent (as opposed to zero) in order to accommodate persistence due to exogenous shocks, such as conflict and drought, as well as the churning that occurs when vulnerable families fall back into extreme poverty. Basu (2013) presents a detailed discussion of the normative properties of these goals, their strengths and weaknesses, and their implications for policies.

[3] This finding is based on regressions of growth rates of the income of the poor on average income growth. The underlying data for the exercise is compiled from household surveys of 151 developed and developing countries. Despite the increase in inequality in some countries, growth was sufficiently strong to reduce poverty sharply. For example, in East Asia, poverty declined steeply as the incomes of the poor grew at 3.2 percent per year, close to growth of 3.4 percent in average incomes. In the early 1980s, East Asia was the poorest region in the world by headcount poverty rate and Sub-Saharan Africa the third poorest. By the early 1990s, Sub-Saharan Africa had swapped positions with East Asia (Dollar, Kleineberg and Kraay, 2013; Chen and Ravallion, 2007, 2013; Ravallion, 2007, 2012).

BOX 1.1   *(continued)*

What do different growth projections imply for poverty?

A simple simulation exercise is conducted to study the implications of different growth projections for the percentage of the world's population who will live below the international poverty line of $1.25 a day in 2030.[4] The exercise begins by aligning each country's household survey-based mean per capita income or consumption expenditure for 2011 (reference year) and then applies per capita GDP growth rates to simulate country-specific poverty in 2030. The country-specific poverty rates are aggregated to derive regional estimates and the latter are aggregated to obtain global poverty estimates.[5] The five growth scenarios are as follows:

- Baseline scenario: Annual per capita growth rates for each country during 2015–17 are as projected in this report. For 2018–30, growth is assumed to remain at the 2015–17 average.

- Pessimistic scenario: Per capita growth rates during 2015-30 are 1.5 percentage points below those in the baseline scenario. This scenario illustrates the effect of a sustained slowdown in the global economy.

- Historical growth scenario: Throughout 2015–30, per capita growth rates are the long-run average of actual growth rates during 1991–2010.

- Pre-crisis growth scenario: Throughout 2015–30, per capita growth rates are the average of growth rates during 2003–08. This scenario illustrates the effect of a repeat of the exceptionally strong performance during the pre-crisis years.

- Optimistic scenario: Throughout 2015–30, per capita growth rates are assumed to be 4 percent per year, which would be unprecedented (Commission on Growth and Development, 2008).

FIGURE B1.1.2 Global poverty in 2030

Meeting the poverty target will be a challenge.

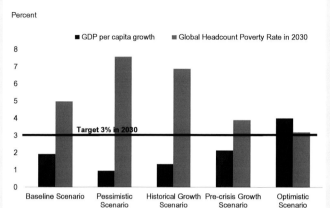

Sources: World Bank (2014ij) and Chapter 2.
Note: GDP per capita growth is the aggregate for the developing world. Global poverty estimates in the optimistic and historical scenarios are based on the growth assumptions in World Bank (2014j). The pre-crisis scenario is based on historical average growth between 2003 and 2008. Poverty estimates for the baseline and pessimistic scenarios are based on the per capita growth of household final consumption expenditure for 2011-2014 in World Bank (2014k) and per capita GDP growth projections in this report for 2015-2017. Population growth assumptions in all scenarios are based on the UN population growth projections.

Although forecasts of growth and corresponding projections of poverty rates are highly uncertain, the results of the scenarios elaborated here show the difficulty of achieving the 2030 poverty target of 3 percent. The target is met only in the optimistic scenario (Figure B1.1.2).[6] Under the baseline scenario, the global poverty rate will stand at 5.0 percent in 2030, while in the pessimistic scenario of persistent slow growth in developing economies it would fall to only 7.6 percent.[7] A significantly higher per capita growth rate in China and South Asia enables poverty to decline rapidly in the optimistic scenario. Given that South Asia has almost as many poor as Sub-Saharan Africa, higher growth in the former would make a large contribution to poverty reduction in the world.[8]

---

[4]These exercises closely follow those in World Bank (2014j, 2014k).

[5]The main assumptions underlying the scenarios are: (i) the distribution of consumption or income in each country remains unchanged throughout the projection period for all scenarios; (ii) the population growth rates are country-specific and based on the UN population growth projections, except in the optimistic scenario, in which population growth in each country is assumed to be equal to the world average population growth rate in order to keep between-country inequality unchanged; and (iii) growth rates are country specific and are based on either national-accounts-based per capita income/consumption expenditure growth projections or the historical mean of per capita household income/consumption expenditure, except for the optimistic scenario, as noted above. Some of the findings are quite sensitive to changes in these assumptions.

[6]For simplicity, all the scenarios here assume stable growth rates over the 2015–2030 period. In reality, variability in growth rates is more likely. If the assumption of each country's population growing at the world average is replaced by country-specific population growth, the poverty rate in the optimistic scenario declines to only 4.1 percent. The results reported here convey the same headline messages as World Bank (2014a). Minor differences between the results here and those in World Bank (2014a) stem from small variations in the household survey datasets. The findings here are also broadly consistent with Chandy, Ledlie and Penciakova (2013), Edward and Sumner (2013), and Bluhm, de Crombrugghe, and Szirmai (2014).

[7]The scenarios here assume that the distribution of income in each country does not change. However, if the incomes of the bottom 40 percent grow faster than the mean, it would be easier to achieve the World Bank's poverty goal by 2030 (Lakner, Negri, and Prydz, 2014).

BOX 1.1   *(continued)*

Challenges beyond growth

High growth rates will be necessary for reducing poverty in the future, but poverty reduction will likely face two additional challenges. First, poverty reduction will need to be broader based than it has been in the past. Rapid growth in a single country, China, helped halve the number of extreme poor over 2000–2011. Going forward, slowing growth and a shrinking number of poor in China will reduce its contribution to global poverty reduction. Instead, the main drivers of poverty reduction should be Sub-Saharan Africa and South Asia, where most of the world's poor are now concentrated. Second, although Sub-Saharan Africa is expected to be among the fastest-growing developing regions, its growth is likely to be driven by the capital-intensive natural resource sector, limiting the scope for positive trickle-down effects to the labor incomes of the poor.

Poverty reduction: Role of policies

The growth scenarios presented here and the highlighted additional challenges indicate the importance of policies for improving the odds of achieving the 2030 poverty target. The fragile medium-term global outlook makes the implementation of growth-enhancing policies and structural reforms even more urgent. Adverse growth shocks—whether caused by domestic or external factors, drought, or conflict—can stall or reverse poverty reduction.

The experiences of countries with sustained progress in poverty reduction point to two equally important policy components. First, these countries implemented policies that promote the productive use of the poor's most abundant asset—labor. This calls for the wider adoption of policies aimed at harnessing market incentives, social and political institutions, infrastructure, and technology to better utilize the poor's labor. Second, countries that have been successful at reducing poverty designed policies to provide basic social services to the poor, including primary health care, family planning, nutrition, and primary education (World Bank, 1990). In addition to these two components, which support each other, a comprehensive strategy to alleviate poverty also requires well-designed social safety nets, which can help sustain poverty reduction and foster inclusive human development especially during economic downturns (World Bank, 2014k).

---

[8]The regional poverty projections indicate that the poverty outcomes associated with slow global growth will be worse for Sub-Saharan Africa. For example, in the optimistic scenario, the poverty rate for Sub-Saharan Africa is close to 18 percent by 2030, whereas it is about 34 percent in the pessimistic scenario.

---

remittances. Additional monetary policy accommodation and a gradual, though weak, recovery in the Euro Area would support strengthening growth in Central and Eastern Europe. In contrast, despite a gradual tilt toward increased ties to China, contraction in Russia, low commodity prices and an unfinished domestic reform agenda will hold back activity in CIS countries. In Turkey, despite robust exports and government spending, growth slowed somewhat in 2014 as election-related uncertainties and geopolitical tensions dampened confidence and policy tightening slowed credit growth. In 2015–16, growth is expected to gradually accelerate on the back of strengthening consumption growth, and lower oil prices will reduce current account deficits.

- *Latin America and the Caribbean:* Growth decelerated sharply in 2014, as a consequence of domestic difficulties and declining commodity prices. A number of the larger economies are currently grappling with low growth, high or rising inflation, and weak investor confidence. Over the next two years, negative terms of trade effects should taper off in commodity-exporting countries and domestic constraints should ease to some extent. But growth is expected to remain modest by pre-crisis standards. Productivity-enhancing reforms, and the extensive trade exposure to the United States, should support growth in Mexico. Prospects of a rapid rebound in Brazil, however, are constrained by an unfinished reform agenda and weak confidence. Since Brazil is a significant importer from the rest of the region, this may weigh on growth in neighboring countries. Macroeconomic imbalances and soft prices of key commodities dampen growth prospects in Argentina (compounded by the unresolved dispute with some bondholders) and República Bolivariana de Venezuela. Should República Bolivariana de Venezuela's preferential energy export arrangements with countries in the Caribbean, Central America and South America be altered, external financing needs could rise sharply in recipient countries and funding for some related social programs could be affected.

- *Middle East and North Africa:* The recovery is strengthening, in particular in oil-importing countries, but it remains fragile and uneven. Substantial official assistance from Gulf Co-operation Council countries has helped firm consumption, investor confidence, and raise investment in Egypt and Jordan. Some oil-exporting countries, however, will face weak growth, and deteriorating fiscal and external balances as a result of low oil prices or continue to struggle with security concerns (Iraq, Libya, and the Republic of Yemen) that have prevented them from restoring full production. Although activity in the region should pickup and softening commodity prices should help dampen inflation, unemployment remains high—partly as a result of recessions after the Arab Spring uprisings—and government service delivery as well as the business environment has been chronically weak. Energy subsidies, which are often a poorly targeted way of assisting those in need, burden budgets. Domestic security concerns as well as spillovers from conflicts in Iraq and Syria (including refugee flows and militant incursions) add to the challenges.

- *South Asia:* Growth in South Asia strengthened in 2014. In India, export growth has been robust, and investor confidence has been bolstered by the election of a reform-minded government. The current account deficit and elevated inflation—both persistent vulnerabilities—have declined considerably. Over the medium-term, growth is expected to rise steadily to 7 percent as reforms begin to yield productivity gains. This is expected to benefit other countries in the region which receive remittances from India. In Pakistan, political tensions in the second half of 2014 and a difficult security situation are projected to continue to weigh on activity. In contrast, in Bangladesh, continued reform efforts and robust remittances have helped and should continue to promote domestic demand and activity more generally.

- *Sub-Saharan Africa:* The region expanded moderately in 2014 but the pace of expansion was slower in many of the larger economies (Angola, Ghana, Kenya, and South Africa) as a result of subdued global demand, soft commodity prices, weak foreign direct investment flows, low business confidence, and capacity shortages, especially infrastructure constraints. The Ebola epidemic has severely disrupted activity in Guinea, Liberia, and Sierra Leone. Economic losses in these countries, however, should begin diminish as effective containment strategies are put in place. Regional spillovers from Ebola should then remain modest. The sharp oil price decline will benefit oil-importing countries but adversely affect several countries in Subsaharan Africa that are oil exporters. Large fiscal and current account deficits persist in Ghana, Kenya, and South Africa. South Africa is exposed to potential capital outflows, due to its reliance on portfolio investment. Public investment in infrastructure and mining, improved agricultural production, and buoyant service sectors are expected to continue to support growth in the region.

Risks

The baseline global economic scenario assumes a strengthening recovery in major economies, a modest rebalancing of demand in China, a smooth transition of developing countries to tighter global financing conditions, and soft commodity prices. However, these assumptions are subject to downside risks. In financial markets, changes in perceptions about growth and policy prospects could result in abruptly tighter credit conditions, and another bout of financial volatility. Financial markets could also reassess country risk in oil-exporting countries against the backdrop of soft oil prices, raising their borrowing cost. Such setbacks could in turn expose underlying vulnerabilities and result in contagion to many emerging and frontier economies. Stagnation in the Euro Area could be exacerbated by deflation, and become protracted. The slowdown in China, so far carefully managed, could become more disorderly. An intensification of the Ebola epidemic would pose a grave threat to human life and economic well-being in West Africa.

Financial Market Stress

Financial risks have continued to build, especially in the non-bank financial sector and securities markets. A renewed bout of increased risk aversion could sharpen sensitivity to underlying country vulnerabilities and policy credibility and adversely affect growth prospects. This could trigger a reappraisal of sovereign and corporate risks and precipitate sharp swings in capital flows.

Separately, an extended period of low oil prices could gradually erode fiscal and external buffers of oil producers (Chapter 4). As buffers weaken, episodes of sharp currency depreciations and associated financial stress could intensify. Corporates, banks or sovereigns in several major oil producers, including Russia and Nigeria, have also borrowed substantially in financial markets. Financial stress in one or more of them could trigger a reassessment of emerging market assets more broadly.

While financial markets have thus far largely shrugged off risks in a low volatility environment, sentiment could easily turn, and markets could react more strongly to negative news. A sudden deterioration in liquidity conditions as foreign investors attempt to exit emerging markets could lead to sharp asset price and exchange rate movements. Countries that have substantial macroeconomic imbalances are most vulnerable to potential financial market stress.

FIGURE 1.15 Vulnerability to financial market stress

The average maturity of developing country bond issuance has increased and current account deficits have narrowed. However, many countries remain vulnerable to financial market turmoil because foreign investors have a strong presence in local bond markets. Central bank balance sheets in the Euro Area and Japan will expand in 2015

A. Average maturities of corporate international bond issuance

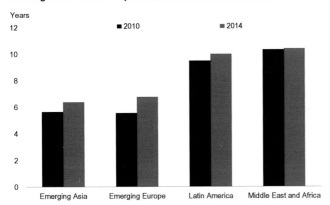

B. Nonresident local sovereign bond holdings[1]

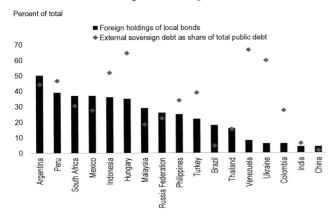

C. Central Bank balance sheets

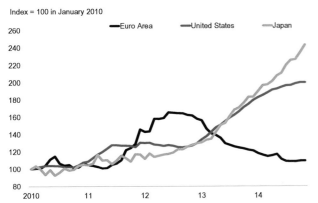

Sources: Dealogic, JP Morgan Chase, Barclays, Haver Analytics, and World Bank.
1. Based on latest 2014 data (foreign holdings of local bonds for China, the Philippines, and República Bolivariana de Venezuela are World Bank estimates). Foreign and foreign currency shares include non-resident holdings of all outstanding sovereign bonds.

As the monetary policy tightening in high-income countries proceeds on an asynchronous timeline, exchange rates of reserve currencies may swing abruptly as expectations adjust. This may reveal underlying vulnerabilities in countries with significant currency mismatches, for example, countries with export earnings predominantly denominated in euros but corporate borrowing or external liabilities predominantly denominated in U.S. dollars. Corporate and financial sector exposure to rapid currency depreciations could be amplified by rollover difficulties for existing debt or bond market funding. In such a context, investors may reassess country risk, and borrowing costs may rise abruptly.

Previous episodes of financial market turmoil are an indication of the speed with which market sentiment can turn and of the potential impact on developing countries. Capital flight in May–June 2013 followed a public debate on the timing of tapering of the U.S. Federal Reserve's program of extraordinary asset purchases. Financial market volatility again rose in January–February 2014, partly over rising concerns about growth in China, and again since October on weakening global economic prospects. In these episodes, portfolio adjustments were generally greater in larger, more liquid and more financially integrated emerging markets, and in countries where macroeconomic imbalances were more significant and policy credibility less established.

Countries with a large presence of foreign investors in local bond markets, a large share of foreign-currency denominated bonds and short-maturity bonds, and a heavy reliance on short-term portfolio flows to finance current account deficits tend to be more vulnerable to sharp financial market corrections (Figure 1.15). These factors are partly mitigated by smaller exposures of retail investors, which had driven capital outflows in May–June 2013, and a narrowing of current account deficits, partly due to domestic policy tightening and softer commodity prices, in some countries with international financial market access (e.g., Ghana, India, and Turkey).

Stagnation in the Euro Area and Japan

Below-target and declining inflation in the Euro Area could be a symptom of secular stagnation associated with a shortfall of aggregate demand as well as declining growth potential (Figure 1.16). If inflation expectations become de-anchored, falling well below the ECB target of close to 2 percent, weak consumption, anemic investment, and low inflation could feed on each other in a deflationary spiral. The danger of deflation would be compounded by the difficulties already afflicting countries in the Euro Area: a shrinking working age population, slowing productivity growth (reflecting a lack of capital-embodied new technologies), and a loss of skills among the large number of long-term unemployed. In addition, some Euro Area countries have still-unresolved banking sector weaknesses.

Secular stagnation would be accompanied by continued high saving rates and demand for safe assets, while investment rates would remain depressed (Summers, 2013). Even with the ECB holding short-term interest rates near the zero floor, the real cost of borrowing in the private sector could be substantially higher, as a result of increased risk premia in an unstable economic environment, and falling prices. Low growth would depress tax revenues, and raise budget deficits, throughout the area, which would worsen concerns about solvency in the periphery. In the absence of significant Euro Area-wide capital backstops, negative feedback loops between bank and sovereign debt would amplify the threat to macro-financial stability.

Given the Euro Area's economic size and international integration, stagnation would have global repercussions. The Euro Area accounts for one-sixth of global GDP and a quarter of global trade and cross-border banking system assets. While neighboring high-income countries, including Switzerland and the United Kingdom, may be hardest hit by stagnation in the Euro Area, it would also directly dampen activity in Eastern Europe, North Africa and South Asia, which depend heavily on European export markets (IMF, 2014a). European banks could find their capital cushions eroding as borrowers struggle in a low-growth environment. Subsidiaries of European banks, especially those in Eastern Europe, could find their parent banks reluctant to fund new lending.

Separately, there is a risk that Japan relapses into deflation and stagnation. The Bank of Japan's aggressive monetary easing program and fiscal stimulus may fail to permanently lift inflation expectations and sustainably revive growth. Stagnation in Japan would particularly dampen growth prospects in trading partners in East Asia.

Disorderly Slowdown in China

Although a low-probability scenario, China's carefully managed slowdown could turn into a disorderly unwinding of financial sector vulnerabilities. Should growth slow abruptly, or credit conditions tighten sharply, a self-reinforcing cycle of weakening growth and deteriorating credit quality could ensue. It could also include a sharp correction in the real estate market, which currently accounts for a sizable proportion of local government revenues.

FIGURE 1.16   Stagnation in the Euro Area

Stagnation and/or deflation risks have increased in the Euro Area in 2014. Deflation would raise real borrowing costs despite policy rates near the zero lower bound, and weak investment would lower potential growth. Among developing countries, stagnation would most immediately reduce growth in trading partners in Eastern Europe and North Africa.

A. Euro Area: inflation forecast, 2015

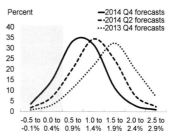

B. Euro Area: growth forecast, 2015

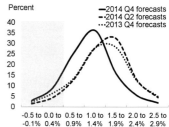

C. Euro Area: interest rates[1]

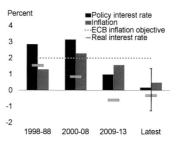

D. Inflation forecasts, 2015[2]

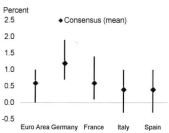

E. Euro Area: potential GDP growth

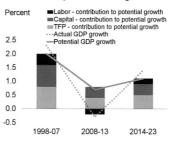

F. Share of exports to the Euro Area[3]

Sources: Bloomberg, Consensus, European Commission (2013), IMF World Economic Outlook, and World Bank calculations.
1. Vertical line shows latest range of real monetary policy rates across Euro Area countries.
2. Vertical line indicates the range of Consensus forecasts as of December 2014.
3. A darker shade indicates a greater share of exports to the Euro Area. The share of exports to the Euro Area ranges from 0.3–84.2 percent in the country sample.

China's corporate sector and local government debt has grown rapidly and is high, with an increasing share intermediated by the non-bank financial system.[5] Total (household, corporate, and government) debt stands at 250 percent of GDP. Borrowing has financed investment,

---

[5]Nontraditional credit has accounted for more than half of (broadly defined) net lending flows since 2009 and about 70 percent during mid-2012-13, compared with only 20 percent before the global financial crisis. By mid-2014, in terms of stocks, these instruments accounted for one-third of broadly defined credit.

FIGURE 1.17   (Dis)orderly slowdown in China?

Growth has increasingly decoupled from the rapid debt buildup that has fuelled investment. Investment growth has been strong by comparison with investment booms in East Asia in the 1990s. It has contributed most to real GDP growth while TFP growth was weak in the 2000s. A disorderly slowdown in China would sharply reduce commodity prices and growth in key trading partners.

A. China: stock of debt [1]

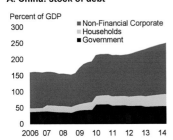

B. China: debt and growth[1]

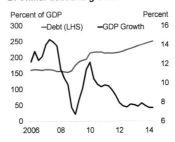

C. China, Korea, and Japan: Gross fixed investment

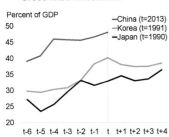

D. China: contribution to GDP growth

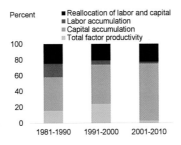

E. Impact of 1 percentage point decline in growth of China's industrial production[2]

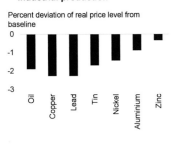

F. Impact of 1 percentage point decline in growth in China[3]

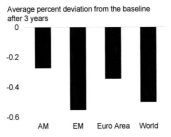

Sources: Cesa-Bianchi and others (2012), BIS, Standard Chartered, World Bank and DRC (2013), Haver Analytics, IMF World Economic Outlook, IMF Spillover Report (2013), Gauvin and Rebillard (2014), Gruss (2014), Roache (2012), and World Bank.
1. Government debt includes general government debt and debt of local government financing vehicles. 2014 refers to the latest available data.
2. Based in vector autoregression estimation for 2000 - 2011.

which has been the main driver of growth since the global financial crisis. By 2014, investment had risen to 45 percent of GDP, well in excess of the levels seen in the Republic of Korea and Japan in the 1990s (Figure 1.17). As capital accumulation increasingly contributed to growth in China, total factor productivity growth fell below its 1990s average. The widening gap between real GDP growth and debt accumulation suggests that diminishing returns to credit-fuelled investment may be setting in.

However, China currently has sufficient policy buffers to intervene at times of stress.

- *Fiscal buffers.* At less than 60 percent of GDP, public debt levels provide fiscal space to employ stimulus in the event of a slowdown. It also provides some room to bail out banks if nonperforming loans were to rise sharply.

- *Institutional buffers.* Sovereign debt is currently predominantly domestically held, by a small group of institutions. Regulations restrict savings instruments outside the banking system and the financial system is still predominantly state-owned. Capital controls on portfolio investment and bank lending can prevent sharp capital outflows.

- *Foreign exchange buffers.* While institutional buffers can retain savings within the country in the event of a loss of confidence in the financial system, they would not a priori preclude a loss of confidence among depositors in the currency. A bank run could be associated with attempts to convert local currency deposits into foreign currency, at least up to the regulatory ceiling. However, spikes in demand for foreign currency could be met by ample central bank reserves, which amount to $4 trillion (22 percent of broad money).

Estimates suggest that a 5 percent decline in China's real fixed asset investment growth would adversely affect demand for metals, and hence weaken activity in trading partners in Latin America and Africa by some 0.3–0.6 percent. World output could fall by 0.3–0.5 percent relative to the baseline (IMF, 2012; World Bank, 2013d; Gauvin and Rebillard, 2014).

Weak Potential Growth in Developing Economies

Growth in developing economies has repeatedly disappointed since 2011. Despite a string of downward revisions in forecasts, growth eventually fell short of even these revised forecasts. In an increasing number of countries, growth has fallen below historical averages (Figure 1.18). Whereas in 2011–13, forecast revisions for developing countries followed those for high-income countries, reflecting spillovers from weak growth in major economies, in 2014 developing country forecasts themselves had to be revised downwards repeatedly. This may be a symptom of weaker-than-anticipated underlying, potential growth in large emerging markets.

Weaker potential growth may reflect both a less favorable external environment and structural factors. External conditions could turn less favorable as trade growth is expected to remain weak and financing costs are set to rise. Structural factors include complacency on reforms during the pre-crisis boom period that continues weighing on productivity growth (Cubeddu et al., 2014; IMF, 2014b). In addition, the crisis has widened income inequality between the bottom and the top 10 percent of the income distribution. The negative impact of rising inequality on growth has been attributed to underinvestment, especially in human capital, by the poor; political economy considerations; and smaller domestic markets to encourage the development of new technologies (Cingano, 2014).

Geopolitical Tensions

Geopolitical tensions, currently concentrated in Eastern Europe, the Middle East, and, to a lesser extent, South East Asia, could rise in the short- and medium-term (Figure 1.19). The direct impact on the affected regions has already been significant. Global repercussions of uncertainty associated with these tensions on financial markets and investment—although limited in earlier episodes —could exceed that of the actual disruptions to supply chains, trade, and travel. If investor confidence were sufficiently shaken, geopolitical tensions could trigger a general repricing of risky assets, including those of emerging and frontier markets.

Significant geopolitical risks exist in several areas of the world:

- An escalation of tensions between the *European Union (EU) and Russia* could disrupt gas supplies to Europe for a sustained period. Given the reliance of many European countries on Russian gas, this could stifle the fragile recovery in the continent. Disruptions could also deepen the recession in Russia, which would dampen growth in trading partners and remittance recipients across the region.

- A further escalation of violence in *Syria and Iraq* would aggravate the existing spillovers. These conflicts have already forced heavy migration internally and to neighboring countries. Over 3 million Syrian refugees are hosted in other countries in the Middle East, amounting to 25 percent of the population in Lebanon, and 10 percent in Jordan. The presence of these refugees could intensify economic, social, and fiscal pressures (although, in the longer term, it might increase labor supply and aggregate demand in host countries).

- Setbacks in *political transitions* in Egypt, Iraq, Libya, Tunisia, and the Republic of Yemen or rising political tensions between Israel and West Bank and Gaza may further undermine confidence and adversely affect

FIGURE 1.18 Countries with slowing growth

In middle-income countries, growth has increasingly fallen below historical averages.

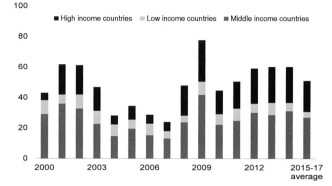

Source: World Bank estimates.
Note: For each year, share of countries (in percent) in which growth is slower than average growth over the period 1990-2007.

FIGURE 1.19 Geopolitical tensions

If the tensions between the Russian Federation and Ukraine were to disrupt gas supplies, several core Euro Area countries could face rapidly rising energy cost. Should political tensions prevent the increase in Iraq's capacity from materializing, oil prices may rise over the medium term. Conversely, a sustained decline in oil prices would widen fiscal imbalances in higher-cost oil producers.

A. Dependence of European countries on Russian gas, 2013[1] **B. Impact of 1 percentage point decline in growth in Russia**

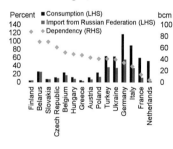

C. Oil Producers: fiscal break-even price[2] **D. Expected capacity increase in oil production, 2014-2019**

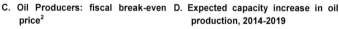

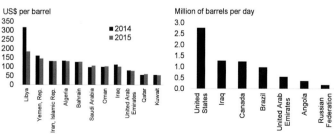

Sources: BP, Bloomberg, Solomon (2014). Husabo (2014), Alturki et al., (2009); Obiora (2009). Haver Analytics, International Energy Agency, World Bank.
1. Dependency is defined as imports from Russia relative to gas consumption. bcm denotes billion cubic meters.
2. Fiscal break-even prices are the oil prices at which general government balances are zero.

FIGURE 1.20   Ebola epidemic

Ebola is the deadliest epidemic recorded since the 1970s.

A. Ebola and other epidemics: cases and deaths, 1970–2014[1]

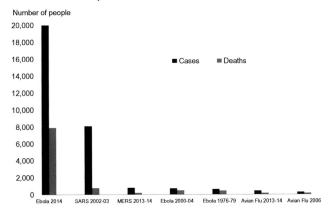

B. Ebola and SARS: cases and deaths[2]

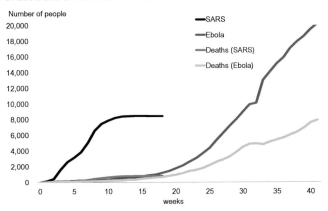

Source: World Health Organization.
1. SARS refers to the outbreak in East Asia in 2003. Ebola refers to the outbreak in West Africa in 2014. Chart does not include the Spanish Flu of 1918–19 in which one -quarter of the world population was infected and which took a human toll of 40-50 million people (IMF, 2003).
2. SARS refers to the outbreak in East Asia in 2003. Ebola refers to the outbreak in West Africa in 2014.

tourism, trade, investment, and foreign direct investment (FDI) flows.

Although oil prices have fallen sharply since mid-2014, renewed tensions in the Middle East could potentially lead to more volatility in response to intensifying or receding geopolitical risk. As regards oil production, Iraq is currently poised for a substantial increase in output, but the deteriorating security situation could spread to core production facilities. Intensifying turmoil in Libya could derail the current recovery in oil exports. Failure to reach an international agreement with Iran could result in tighter sanctions that dent oil exports.

In countries like Afghanistan, Central African Republic, Democratic Republic of Congo, Nigeria, and Republic

of South Sudan, intensifying conflict and violence could take a heavy human toll and potentially draw in neighboring countries.

Ebola Epidemic

In West Africa, the Ebola epidemic—the deadliest since the 1970s—has sharply reduced growth in Liberia, Sierra Leone, and Guinea. By end-December 2014, the number of both cases and deaths exceeded those of the severe acute respiratory syndrome (SARS) epidemic in 2003 (Figure 1.20). The virus continued to spread through 2014, with new cases surging again in Liberia in December.

If uncontained, the epidemic could spread to neighboring countries with potentially global repercussions (World Bank, 2014b). Economic activity would suffer sharply in the affected areas, as a result of both the direct effects of sickness and death, and the indirect effects of disruptions to planting and harvesting in agriculture, to transport including shipping and flights, to domestic and cross-border trade, and to government services as state resources are diverted toward stemming the epidemic. Fear of Ebola would undermine consumer and investor confidence. Estimates of the possible cumulative loss in GDP for West Africa over two years range from $3.8 billion, on the low side, to as much as $32.6 billion (which represents a range of 0.5 percent to more than 4 percent of regional GDP), depending on containment measures and the extent to which fear of infection depresses investment and travel (World Bank, 2014c).

Containment hinges on well-equipped health care systems and a resolute policy response, both to reduce mortality rates from around 40 percent and to halt contagion. Nigeria and Senegal provide examples of successful containment. As a result of the epidemic, Liberia's fiscal deficit is estimated to have doubled to 14 percent of GDP in 2014 as tax revenues fell sharply and the health care system struggled to respond to the epidemic. Unless the epidemic is contained, fiscal costs will continue to climb, straining the sustainability of already fragile government finances.

Policy Challenges

Among high-income countries, short-term measures to support domestic demand need to be reinforced with long-term structural reforms. Developing country policy makers face three challenges: adapting monetary and exchange rate policies to an expected tightening of global financial conditions; rebuilding fiscal space at an appropriate pace to preserve the ability to conduct countercyclical fiscal policy; and implementing structural reforms that promote growth, create jobs, and mitigate the effects of less favorable demographics and weak global trade.

Major Economies

As the U.S. Federal Reserve Bank nears its first interest rate hike, clear guidance will help prevent disorderly market adjustments. The gradual tightening of monetary policy should be complemented with targeted macro-prudential measures to contain pockets of excessive risk-taking in domestic credit markets (e.g., high-yield bond markets). A comprehensive long-term plan to ensure fiscal sustainability would include efforts to reform taxation and improve the quality of public spending, and to restore and expand public infrastructure (Congressional Budget Office, 2014). Reforms to improve education and vocational training should increase productivity and facilitate entry (or re-entry) into the labor market and thereby help raise participation in the labor market from its current low level.

With cost pressures and inflation contained, and downside risks to growth in the rest of Europe, monetary policy rates in the United Kingdom are expected to rise only gradually from 2015 onwards, despite prospects of diminishing slack. Macro-prudential policy could help contain risks associated with a housing market boom, such as increasing vulnerabilities of households to income and interest rate shocks. As the fiscal consolidation program implemented over the past several years winds down, the recovery will strengthen. However, revenue and expenditure reforms are needed to meet medium-term fiscal objectives. Continuing to reduce bottlenecks in infrastructure and investing in human capital will be key to supporting the needed improvements in productivity.

In view of the weak recovery and undesirably low inflation in the Euro Area, the ECB needs to maintain an extended period of policy accommodation. Further action could include extending outright purchase programs to sovereign bonds. Fiscal policy should respond flexibly to support growth along with concrete medium-term consolidation plans. The EU budget, as well as European Investment Bank instruments, should be used more effectively to stimulate both public and private investments. These measures should be reinforced by growth- and job-enhancing structural reforms and measures to strengthen the financial system—including ensuring that the Single Supervisory Mechanism gains traction in mitigating the current fragmentation and complementing a banking union with appropriate financial backstops.

Determined monetary policy easing in Japan remains appropriate as the economy struggles to gain momentum and the government implements gradual fiscal consolidation over the medium term. Although a potential drag on growth, fiscal consolidation measures will eventually be a necessary step towards restoring fiscal sustainability and to signal the government's commitment to stabilizing high and growing public debt. The large—albeit declining—exposure of the Japanese banking sector to sovereign debt remains a concern. Strengthening capital standards for regional banks and funding sources of major banks could mitigate some of these concerns (IMF, 2014c). The government has set a goal of around 2 percent for annual growth over FY2013-22, while announcing a series of reforms to the tax system. Agricultural, energy, and labor market policies are being modernized in line with OECD recommendations (OECD, 2014). The focus should now shift to full and swift implementation of these reforms.

China faces the challenge of containing financial vulnerabilities in the short term, while putting long-term growth on a secure footing. To contain financial vulnerabilities, the authorities have tightened regulation and supervision, especially of shadow banking, and raised interest rates in the interbank market, where much of shadow banking activity is funded. Nontraditional lending has slowed considerably as a result, and lending appears to be shifting back to conventional bank loans and corporate bonds.

Financial sector reform initiatives are being complemented by a comprehensive blueprint for reforms announced in November 2013 (World Bank, 2014d). It aims to give markets a more decisive role in the economy, to encourage the reallocation of resources to high-productivity sectors, and to strengthen institutions and governance. Instead of outright privatization of state-owned enterprises, the reform aims to remove some of their privileges and encourage competition. Land reform has the potential to increase productivity of the agricultural sector, which is predominantly household-owned and -operated. A reform of public finances would reduce reliance of local governments on land sales as a source of revenue. At the same time, the local government tax revenue base could be better aligned with expenditure responsibilities. Financial sector reforms, including the introduction of a deposit insurance scheme, will help address risks arising from the rapid growth of credit and improve the allocation of capital towards the most productive uses. The government has already taken several steps. These include identifying six pilot state-owned enterprises for reform; improving the documentation of farmers' land rights; and authorizing bond issuance for 10 provincial and local governments.

FIGURE 1.21 Monetary policy in developing countries

Monetary policy rates have been on hold since mid-2014 and expectations for policy rates in 2015 have been revised downwards in many developing countries.

A. Policy interest rates

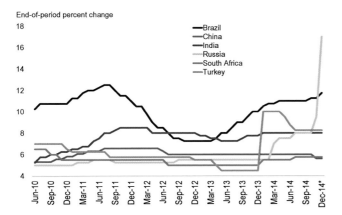

B. Policy rate expectations for 2015Q2

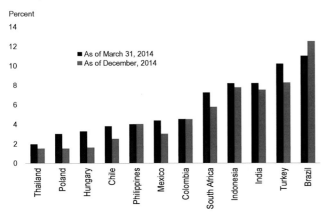

Sources: Bloomberg and Haver.
Note: Official/policy interest rates: Brazil: Selec-Target Rate, China: Prime Lending Rate, India: Repo Rate, Russia: Minimum 1 Week Lombard & REPO Auctions Loan Rate, South Africa: Repurchase Rate, and Turkey: 1-Week Repo Rate. *Latest rate as of December 31, 2014.

The reform agenda has the potential to raise output by 2–3 percent in the long term. In the short term, however, it may dampen growth as factor reallocation across sectors proceeds gradually and companies adjust to new factor prices.[6]

---

[6]Assuming full and immediate implementation of the reform agenda, model projections indicate that in the near-term growth would slow by just under 1 percentage point below a no-reform baseline as public investment would fall (IMF, 2013). But, over the longer term, productivity gains would boost growth by 2.5–2.7 percentage points above the baseline. Household incomes and consumption would rise, despite the lower investment.

Developing Countries

Monetary and Financial Policies

During the 2000s, monetary policy in developing countries appears to have become increasingly countercyclical. This was supported by rising foreign currency positions and strengthening monetary policy frameworks as many developing countries moved toward inflation targeting frameworks (Box 1.2).

Early in 2014, many developing country central banks in Asia (India, Malaysia, Mongolia, and the Philippines), Latin America (Brazil, Colombia, and Costa Rica), Europe (Turkey and Ukraine) and Africa (Ghana and South Africa) raised interest rates or implemented macroprudential tightening to curtail inflation, mitigate currency pressures or contain strong credit growth (Figure 1.21). However, since mid-2014, monetary policy rates have been on hold in several of these countries as inflationary pressures eased whereas, in others, central banks continued to hike rates in the fourth quarter of 2014 (Angola, Brazil, Ghana, Indonesia, Malawi, Nigeria, Zambia). In Eastern Europe, central banks have cut rates to support weak economies, and markets expect further policy rate cuts for most developing countries in 2015.

Looking ahead, commodity price declines are expected to reduce inflation pressures in countries that do not offset commodity price fluctuations with food and fuel subsidies. At the same time, tightening global financial conditions may dampen capital flows that trigger depreciations and weaken domestic demand growth in developing countries. Depending on the exchange rate and commodity price pass-through into inflation, inflation pressures may ease or intensify.

- In some countries, where growth has been cyclically strong and accompanied by rapid credit growth and above-target inflation, easing inflation and capital flows would provide a welcome cooling (e.g., in Indonesia, Mongolia, and Turkey).

- Elsewhere, where growth has been weak and inflation elevated (e.g., Brazil and South Africa), monetary policy would gain room for greater accommodation if inflation pressures and inflation expectations eased. If, however, the pass-through of depreciation intensified inflation expectations instead, central banks will have to weigh two objectives. On the one hand, policy rate hikes could stem inflation but would trigger a stronger cyclical slowdown in growth. On the other hand, policy rate cuts could increase the risk of capital outflows and depreciation, weakening

BOX 1.2   Countercyclical monetary policy in emerging markets: Review and evidence[1]

Procyclical capital flows have induced monetary policy responses in many developing countries. In the 2000s, however, monetary policy in developing countries has become less procyclical, partly as a result of stronger monetary frameworks and net foreign asset positions.

FIGURE B1.2.1   Capital flows and exchange rate cyclicality and net foreign assets

Procyclical capital flows have been associated with procyclical monetary policy, partly as a result of negative net foreign asset positions until the mid-2000s.

A. Capital flow and currency cyclicality

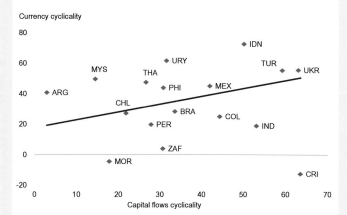

B. Net foreign assets

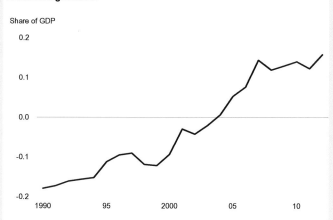

Source: Cordella and Gupta (2014).
Note: Currency, monetary policy, and capital flows cyclicality are defined as the correlation coefficient between the cyclical component (deviation from Hodrick-Prescott-filtered trend) of nominal effective exchange rates, short term interest rates, and net private capital flows, respectively, and the cyclical component (deviation from Hodrick-Prescott-filtered trend) of real GDP during 1975-2013. Exchange rates are defined such that an increase is an appreciation; hence, a positive currency cyclicality indicates that an increase in cyclical GDP was associated with appreciation. In the left panel, emerging markets in the EU are excluded. For the right panel, the median for the net foreign currency position is calculated for 33 emerging markets included in Cordella and Gupta (2014), wherein more details are provided.

Monetary policy, especially in emerging markets, became increasingly countercyclical during the 2000s. This countercyclicality to developing countries' own business cycle may, however, be put to the test in the coming years: In many emerging markets, weaker growth prospects than pre-crisis are expected to coincide with rising global interest rates. Emerging markets would, thus, need to use a mix of policies to cushion the impact of higher global interest rates on capital inflows while simultaneously addressing the challenge of a weak growth outlook.

This box addresses the following three questions:

- What is the relationship between the cyclicality of capital flows, exchange rates, and monetary policies?
- How has the cyclical stance of monetary policy in emerging markets evolved?
- What are the implications of changes in the cyclical stance for monetary policy in the coming years?

Relationship between the cyclicality of capital flows, exchange rates, and monetary policies

Procyclicality of monetary policy can be traced back to the procyclicality of capital flows (Cordella and Gupta, 2014, and Kaminsky, Reinhart, and Végh, 2004). Capital flows to emerging markets have historically been procyclical, rising during times of high growth and falling when activity contracted. Over the past three decades, for example, the correlation between the cyclical component of net private capital inflows and the cyclical component of real GDP in developing countries has risen by up to 60 percent in some emerging markets (Costa Rica and Ukraine) and almost 40 percent on average. These procyclical swings in capital flows have generated procyclical exchange rate pressures.

A priori, the relationship between growth and exchange rates is ambiguous. The original Mundell-Fleming framework suggests a negative correlation: exchange rates should depreciate when growth is high because a positive income shock worsens the current account and adjustment occurs through (real) depreciation. In contrast, monetary models suggest a positive correlation: stronger

---

[1]The main author of this box is Poonam Gupta.

BOX 1.2   *(continued)*

growth increases the demand for money and causes appreciation.[2] In practice, as capital flows into economies with strong growth, exchange rates appreciate. Sustained exchange rate appreciation, in turn, encourages further capital inflows. In contrast, when activity weakens, capital flows slow or reverse and exchange rates depreciate, which in turn may sharpen capital outflow pressures. This was reflected in a positive correlation between the cyclical component of GDP and the cyclical component of exchange rates over the past three decades (Figure B1.2.1). Countries with more procyclical capital flows were also those with a positive and larger cyclical comovement of exchange rates and GDP.

The response of monetary policy to these cyclical exchange rate pressures depends on a wide range of factors, including the exchange rate regime, balance sheet vulnerabilities, and the openness of capital accounts (Calvo and Reinhart, 2002). For example, in countries with a high stock of foreign-currency denominated liabilities, policy makers may resist currency depreciation to limit balance sheet losses by tightening monetary policy. This, in turn, weakens the prospects of recovery. Végh and Vuletin (2012) attribute such reluctance of policy makers to allow depreciation to a "fear of free falling" that is less pronounced in countries with stronger institutions.

Evolution of the cyclical stance of monetary policy

Since about 2000, emerging economies have begun to transition from procyclical to countercyclical monetary policy.[3] This change in the 2000s was partly, but not solely, due to a countercyclical policy response by central banks in developing countries, and in Latin America specifically (Didier, Hevia, and Schmukler, 2012; and de la Torre, Didier, Hevia, and Schmukler, 2012), during the global financial crisis in 2008/09. However, even excluding data for 2009–13, the correlation between the cyclical component of monetary policy and real GDP increased.

Many factors have contributed to the movement towards greater countercyclicality. These included the move towards inflation targeting in many emerging markets and declining financial vulnerabilities but also, more generally, improving institutions (Végh and Vuletin, 2012) and financial market development

(McGettigan et al., 2013).

- *Inflation targeting.* Countries that have implemented inflation targeting regimes tended to have significantly more countercyclical monetary policy. Since 2000, 13 emerging and frontier market central banks have adopted inflation targeting frameworks, bringing the number of inflation targeting emerging markets to 18 (Bank of England, 2012).

- *Shrinking financial vulnerabilities.* The net foreign currency position of emerging markets has steadily improved over the 2000s. This has been attributed to rising current account balances and foreign reserves; a shift in capital flows to equity from debt; and the financial deepening of local currency debt markets (Lane and Shambaugh, 2010). As a result, central banks may have been able to implement less procyclical monetary policy.

- *Macroprudential measures:* Macroprudential measures can constrain lending or capital flows that are deemed to undermine financial stability. In this, they can supplement monetary policy in reducing the procyclicality of credit driven by capital flows. Since the mid-1990s, the use of macroprudential measures has increased (Dell'Arriccia et al., 2012).

The most notable example of graduation from procyclical monetary policy is Chile (Frankel, Végh, and Vuletin, 2013). Following a steep recession and a banking crisis in the 1980s, Chile introduced partial inflation targeting in the 1990s which also included a loose real exchange rate band and maintained capital controls. In 1999, once inflation had been reduced through a broad-based macroeconomic stabilization program, the inflation target was narrowed to 3 percent and the exchange rate and capital account liberalized. From then on, monetary policy became significantly more countercyclical (McGettigan et al., 2013).

Notwithstanding the broader trend towards countercyclicality since 2000, there were sporadic episodes of policy tightening in response to capital flow pressures. These included the financial market turmoil of May–June 2013, which triggered capital outflows and asset price corrections in several emerging markets. For example, Brazil, India, and Indonesia tightened monetary policy to stem market volatility in 2013. Policy tightening was accompanied by other measures such as removing remaining capital controls and targeted liquidity injections (Sahay et al., 2014).

Looking forward: Implications for monetary policy

Since 2000, monetary policy in emerging markets has become increasingly countercyclical. This trend has been supported by

---

[2]This has been established for both flexible price models (Frenkel, 1976) and sticky price models (Dornbush, 1976)

[3]Vegh and Vuletin (2012) and Cordella and Gupta (2014) find greater countercyclicality since 2000. McGettigan et al (2013) find an earlier break point in this transition around 1996-97.

BOX 1.2   *(continued)*

strengthening institutions, especially monetary policy frameworks, more active use of macroprudential policies, and shrinking vulnerabilities, including net foreign currency positions.

Looking ahead, monetary policy frameworks in developing countries may be tested when global financial conditions tighten amidst modest growth prospects. Past episodes of monetary policy tightening in the United States were associated with declines or reversals in capital flows to emerging markets. At the time, many emerging markets maintained fixed exchange rate regimes so in most countries real depreciations occurred gradually (IMF, 2013). Some countries with large underlying vulnerabilities, however, were forced to abandon their currency pegs under capital outflow pressures, triggering the "tequila crisis."

Going forward, the adjustment in developing countries to financial tightening is expected to proceed more smoothly, as a result of stronger institutions, larger buffers, as well as mitigating global developments. In particular, declining commodity prices are expected to reduce inflation pressures in many developing countries (unless offset by depreciating currencies or large subsidies for food and fuel consumption). This may provide monetary policy additional room to support growth. In addition, monetary policy frameworks have strengthened as an increasing number of developing countries have put in place inflation targeting regimes. This allows exchange rates to bear a greater burden of adjustment; some of this adjustment has already occurred with the depreciations following the turmoil of May/June 2013. In addition, monetary policy buffers such as reserves and net foreign currency positions have grown significantly over the 2000s, thus easing constraints on monetary policy.

balance sheets with foreign-currency exposures. This may especially be the case in some oil-exporting countries which have come under strong depreciation pressures as oil prices declined.

Strengthened monetary policy frameworks, improved foreign currency positions, as well as other policy buffers such as capital flow management measures, should facilitate the use of exchange rates as shock absorbers and enable a countercyclical monetary policy response.

Fiscal Policies

Especially if monetary policy is constrained by inflation or financial stability concerns, a cyclical growth slowdown could require the use of countercyclical fiscal policy to support activity. A structural growth slowdown, however, weakens fiscal space and constrains a country's ability to engage in countercyclical fiscal policy (Chapter 3).

During the early 2000s, fiscal policy in developing countries, especially in large developing countries and frontier markets with international market access, became increasingly countercyclical (Figure 1.22). On the eve of the crisis, developing countries had built fiscal space by lowering debt-to-GDP ratios to below 2001 levels, and by closing deficits. During the crisis, many of them used this space to support growth with countercyclical stimulus measures or to allow automatic stabilizers to operate. Nevertheless, in most developing countries, debt levels at

end-2013 remain below those in the early 2000s—with the notable exception of some large frontier markets.

Fiscal deficits, however, have yet to return to pre-crisis levels and, if allowed to persist, could accumulate into unsustainable stocks of debt. In about three-quarters of developing countries with international capital market access, primary balances are below levels that would stabilize debt at benchmark levels (Chapter 3). In addition, current conditions flatter the sustainability of primary balances: real interest rates are at historic lows and some recent entrants into international capital markets have growth rates substantially above their historical averages.

Developing countries facing benign cyclical environments need to build fiscal buffers and to restore fiscal sustainability. This would allow them to have access to the countercyclical fiscal policy that has served them well since 2000. The desirable speed of rebuilding buffers depends on a host of country-specific factors, including cyclical positions and the degree to which countercyclical monetary policy may be encumbered by high or rising private sector indebtedness. The manner in which buffers are rebuilt should take into account long-term structural reform needs. Many developing countries provide generous energy subsidies that distort activity and are poorly targeted. Especially in countries with limited economic slack, the fall in oil prices that is expected to persist provides an opportunity to rebuild fiscal space while removing the economic distortions associated with subsidies.

FIGURE 1.22   Fiscal policy in developing countries

Fiscal deficits widened during the crisis and have yet to return to pre-crisis levels. As a result, primary balances in many countries would be too large to stabilize the debt stock if interest rates and growth rates were at historical averages.

A. Overall fiscal balance[1]

Percent of GDP

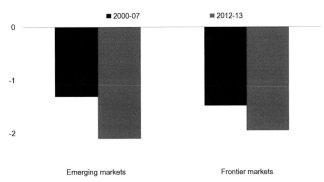

B. Sustainability gap[2]

Percent of GDP

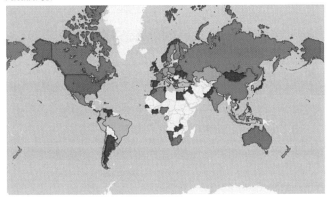

Sources: IMF and World Bank.
1. Overall fiscal balance is the general government balance.
2. Sustainability gap is defined as the difference between the primary balance and the debt-stabilizing primary balance assuming historical average interest rates and growth rates. A negative sustainability gap indicates that the primary balance is debt-increasing; a positive gap indicates that the primary balance is debt-reducing. A redder color indicates a more negative gap; a greener color a more positive gap.

Structural Reforms

In view of weakening medium-term prospects, growth-sustaining reforms are needed. Reform needs range widely, with subsidy reform, improvements in public infrastructure, and strengthened institutions ranking among the most common.

Among developing countries of all regions, food and fuel subsidies are common with a fiscal cost of up to 25 percent of GDP (the Islamic Republic of Iran). At the same time, they tend to be poorly targeted and distortionary (IMF 2014d, World Bank, 2014e, AfDB, 2014). In 2013 and 2014, several countries undertook subsidy reform. Egypt

raised fuel prices by 78 percent in 2014 and is doubling electricity prices over the next five years; Indonesia raised gasoline and diesel prices by an average of 33 percent in 2013 and by another 34 percent in 2014; India eliminated diesel subsidies in October 2014 after incremental hikes over the preceding two years; the Islamic Republic of Iran raised petrol prices by 75 percent in April; and Malaysia raised fuel prices by 10–20 percent in 2013 and further in 2014. Unless fiscal space is severely constrained, funds saved in subsidy reform should be reallocated to expanded and better targeted social safety nets or to efficiently chosen priority investment. These more efficient and better targeted expenditures should be maintained and a reversal of subsidy reforms resisted even once oil prices begin to rise again.

Enterprise surveys persistently highlight reform needs in two areas: fostering an environment that enables sound institutions and improving public infrastructure. These surveys consistently suggest that a major obstacle to growth in the developing world is corruption (Figure 1.23). To varying degrees in South Asia, Sub-Saharan Africa, the Middle East and North Africa, and Latin America and the Caribbean, corruption is facilitated by burdensome practices for licenses and permits, inefficient tax administration, heavy-handed customs and trade regulations, and weak judicial systems that fail to robustly protect investor and property rights.

Enterprise and expert surveys also point to infrastructure constraints, especially with respect to access to reliable electricity supplies (Sub-Saharan Africa, Central Asia, the Middle East, and South Asia). Infrastructure bottlenecks impede trade within and between regions. They are endemic in Sub-Saharan Africa, South Asia, Central Asia, and in parts of East Asia (World Bank, 2014f). Increased or improved infrastructure investment could reduce bottlenecks and support long-run growth (World Bank, 2003; IMF, 2014b). The benefits, however, are conditional on the efficiency of public investment, which requires good regulatory and institutional frameworks for project appraisal and selection and transparent procurement practices. In countries with high existing levels of debt (including some countries in East Asia) or substantial deficits (parts of South Asia and Middle East and North Africa), the scope for additional debt-financed public investment may be limited. Even when room for public investment is scarce, frameworks for private infrastructure investment can be strengthened and capital market development facilitated to support long-term investment.

Easing labor regulations and trade restrictions could help reduce corruption and incentives to resort to informal economic activities. It could also facilitate a more dynamic reallocation of labor into the most productive sectors which, in many countries, has been limited in the 2000s. Burdensome labor regulations encourage informal employment and constrain firm size (World Bank, 2013b). These include high minimum wages and restrictions on overtime (Brazil) or the length of fixed-term contracts (Brazil, South Africa) and substantial hurdles to redundancy (e.g., India World Bank, 2014f). Reforms should combine policies to improve the flexibility of employment contracts with adequate social protection for the most vulnerable. In developing countries with high youth unemployment (e.g., in the Middle East and North Africa), rapid urbanization (e.g., South Asia and Sub-Saharan Africa), or aging populations (Eastern Europe), there may be a need for active labor market policies and selective interventions.

New protectionist trade measures should be avoided and measures enacted since 2008 should be unwound (Chapter 4). Trade-restrictions have risen since 2008. For example, the number of product lines subject to import restrictions by G-20 members has increased by half since 2007 (to 3 percent of all import product lines, World Bank, 2014g). Reforms should include reducing barriers to merchandise trade, services liberalization, and addressing "at-the-borders" constraints, such as congestion at customs. Logistical obstacles to trade have risen since 2007 and, in all developing country regions, are significantly greater than in high-income countries. In several low-income and lower-middle-income countries, restrictions on services trade remain particularly onerous.

Among reform needs in these broad areas, priorities vary within and across regions. The relative urgency of these reforms also differs depending on country circumstances. Two regional examples help illustrate different reform priorities.

- *East Asia and Pacific* (World Bank, 2014d). (i) Institutions need to be strengthened by improving government effectiveness (including efficiency in policy formulation and implementation) and regulatory quality (including faciliating business startups and access to credit). (ii) Trade costs need to be reduced by eliminating inefficient border procedures and significant behind-the-border obstacles. Services trade should be liberalized by reforming domestic regulations. (iii) Infrastructure and logistics gaps need to be addressed by better prioritizing public investment projects, thus taking account of constraints on the public sector's absorptive and implementation capacity. (iv) In labor markets, skills gaps between job requirements and worker education need to be narrowed by shifting the focus from access to quality of education and lifelong skills development. Migrant workers should be used more effectively to promote prosperity. In labor-receiving countries, this

FIGURE 1.23 Constraints to doing business

Structural reforms need to address infrastructure bottlenecks, especially in energy, and strengthen institutions, partly to resist corruption. Trade impediments need to be eased, including by reducing logistical obstacles and reversing recent trade restrictions.

A. Major constraints to firm activity[1]

B. Ease of doing business indicators

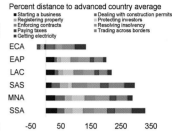

C. Logistics performance index[2]

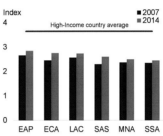

D. Import protection and temporary trade barriers, trade-weighted[3]

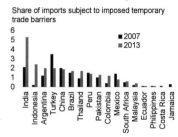

Sources: World Bank Doing Business, World Bank Enterprise Surveys, World Bank Logistics Performance Index, and Temporary Trade Barriers Database, World Bank (2012).
1. Balance of responses to the question "What is the biggest obstacle to your business?".
2. A higher index indicates fewer challenges in trade logistics (based on a qualitative assessment in a survey of global freight forwarders and express carriers).
3. Share of imports subject to temporary trade barriers (TTB) in effect under all TTB policies.

requires greater focus on addressing market failures that prevent their own workers from upgrading their skills, so as to complement rather than compete with migrants. In labor-sending countries, it requires improved financial services available to migrant families. (v) Spending on regressive subsidies should be reallocated to better-targeted safety nets and other antipoverty programs.

- *Middle East and North Africa* (World Bank, 2013c, 2014h). The region's key reform priority is strengthening the labor market and fostering a vibrant private sector. (i) Labor market reform requires reducing the gap between private and public sector employment and strengthening the quality of education more broadly. (ii) Access to economic opportunities need to be improved and the playing field needs to be leveled between firms by eliminating privileges for connected firms and barriers to competition. (iii) Institutional quality, governance, and transparency need to be strengthened to ensure better public sector service delivery. (iv) Energy subsidies need to be reformed to open fiscal space for growth-enhancing public investments.

Several countries have committed to structural reforms, in various cases as part of the G-20 process (World Bank, 2014i). The actual programs have been of varying degrees of ambition and alignment with priorities.[7]

---

[7]Mexico has announced an ambitious and well-targeted set of reforms. These invite private investment and FDI, e.g. in the telecommunications and oil sectors; strengthen competition, by establishing new regulatory bodies; overhaul labor regulation; and encourage trade through long-haul trucking agreements and trade partnership negotiations. India's newly elected government has announced and begun to implement reforms, with a focus on streamlining administrative processes and easing business registration and licensing requirements. In addition, it has begun to address long-standing weaknesses in the energy sector, by introducing market-based diesel pricing, partially deregulating gas prices, and taking steps towards increased private sector participation in the coal sector. Turkey's 10th Five-Year Development Plan, adopted in 2013, prioritizes infrastructure investment and labor market reform to raise labor force participation and reduce informality. The plan also includes promotion of integration into global value chains through greater trade facilitation, services trade liberalization, and expanded free trade areas.

References

Aaronson, S., T. Cajner, B. Fallick, F. Galbis-Reig, C. L. Smith, and W. Wascher. 2014. "Labor Force Participation: Recent Developments and Future Prospects." Federal Reserve Bank of Cleveland Working Paper.

African Development Bank. 2014. Innovation and Productivity Empirical Analysis for North African Countries. Tunis: African Development Bank.

Alturki, F., J. Espinosa-Bowen, and N. Ilahi. 2009. "How Russia Affects the Neighborhood: Trade, Financial, and Remittance Channels." Working Paper WP/09/277, International Monetary Fund, Washington, DC.

Amiti, M., O. Itskhoki, and J. Konings. 2014. "Why Hasn't the Yen Depreciation Spurred Japanese Exports?" Liberty Street Economics (blog), New York Federal Reserve.

Baffes, J., and A. Dennis. 2013. "Long-Term Drivers of Food Prices." Policy Research Working Paper 6455, World Bank, Washington, DC.

Baffes, J., and C. Savescu. 2014. "Causes of the Post-2000 Metals Supercycle." Mimeo, Development Prospects Group, World Bank, Washington DC.

———. 2014. "Monetary Conditions and Metal Prices." Applied Economics Letters 21 (7): 447–52.

Bank of England. 2012. "State of the Art of Inflation Targeting". Centre for Central Banking Studies Handbook 29. Bank of England.

Bank of Japan. 2014. "Monthly Report of Recent Economic and Financial Developments, October 2014." Bank of Japan, Tokyo.

Basu, K. 2013. "Shared Prosperity and the Mitigation of Poverty: In Practice and in Precept." Policy Research Working Paper 6700, World Bank, Washington, DC.

Berument, H. M., Nildag Basak Ceylan, and N. Dogan. 2010. "The Impact of Oil Price Shocks on the Economic Growth of Selected MENA Countries." Energy Journal 31 (1): 149–76.

Blanchard, O. J., and Jordi G. 2009. "The Macroeconomic Effects of Oil Shocks: Why Are the 2000s So Different from the 1970s?" In International Dimensions of Monetary Policy, ed. Jordi Gali and Mark Gertler, 373–428. Chicago: University of Chicago Press.

Blanchard, O. J., and M. Riggi. 2013. "Why Are the 2000s So Different from the 1970s? A Structural Interpretation of Changes in the Macroeconomic Effects of Oil Prices." Journal of the European Economic Association 11 (5): 1032–52.

Bluhm, R., D. de Crombrugghe, and A. Szirmai. 2014. "Poor Trends: The Pace of Poverty Reduction after the Millennium Development Agenda." Working Paper 2014-006, UNU Merit, Maastricht, The Netherlands.

Calvo, G. A., and C. M. Reinhart. 2002. "Fear of Floating." Quarterly Journal of Economics 107 (2): 379–408.

Canuto, O. 2014. "The Commodity Supercycle: Is This Time Different?" Economic Premise 150, World Bank, Washington, DC.

CBO (Congressional Budget Office). 2014. "An Update to the Budget and Economic Outlook: Fiscal Years 2014 to 2024." Report, CBO, Washington, DC.

Cesa-Bianchi, A., M. Hasehm Pesaran, A. Rebucci, and T.T. Xu. 2012. "China's Emergence in the World Economy and Business Cycles in Latin America." Journal of Lacea Economica, 12 (2): 1-75.

Chandy, L., N. Ledlie, and V. Penciakova. 2013. "The Final Countdown: Prospects for Ending Extreme Poverty by 2030." Global Views Policy Paper 2013-04, Brookings Institution, Washington, DC.

Chen, S., and M. Ravallion. 2007. "China's (Uneven) Progress Against Poverty." Journal of Development Economics 82 (2007): 1–42.

————. 2013. "More Relatively-Poor People in a Less Absolutely-Poor World." Policy Research Working Paper 6114, World Bank, Washington, DC.

Chenery, H. 1979. Structural Change and Development Policy. New York: Oxford University Press.

Cologni, A., and M. Manera. 2008. "Oil Prices, Inflation, and Interest Rates in a Structural Cointegrated VAR Model for the G-7 Countries." Energy Economics 30 (3): 856–88.

Commission on Growth and Development. 2008. The Growth Report—Strategies for Sustained Growth and Inclusive Development. Washington, DC: World Bank.

Cordella, T., and P. Gupta. 2014. "What Makes a Currency Procyclical? An Empirical Investigation." Policy Research Working Paper 7113, World Bank, Washington, DC.

CPB Netherlands Bureau for Economic Policy Analysis. 2014. "CPB World Trade Monitor July 2014." CPB Netherlands Bureau for Economic Policy Analysis, The Hague.

Cubeddu, L., A. Culiuc, G. Fayad, Y. Gao, K. Kochhar, A. Kyobe, C. Oner, R. Perrelli, S. Sanya, E. Tsounta, and Z. Zhang. 2014. "Emerging Markets in Transition: Growth Prospects and Challenges." Staff Discussion Note, International Monetary Fund, Washington, DC.

Cuddington, J., and D. Jerrett. 2008. "Supercycles in Real Metals Prices?" IMF Staff Papers 55 (4): 541–65.

de la Torre, A., T. Didier, C. Hevia, and S. Schmukler. 2012. "Latin America Copes with Volatility: The Dark Side of Globalization." Spring Meetings Report, World Bank, Washington, DC.

Dell'Arriccia, G., D. Igan, L. Laeven, H. Tong, B. Bakker, and J. Vandenbusche. 2012. "Policies for Macrofinancial Stability: How to Deal with Credit Booms." Staff Discussion Note 12/06, International Monetary Fund, Washington, DC.

Deutsche Bank Research. 2014. "EM Oil Producers: Breakeven Pain Thresholds." Deutsche Bank, Frankfurt.

Didier, T., Constantino H., and S. Schmukler. 2012. "How Resilient and Countercyclical Were Emerging Economies to the Global Financial Crisis?" Journal of International Money and Finance 31 (8): 2052–77.

Dollar, D., T. Kleineberg, and A. Kraay. 2013. "Growth Still Is Good for the Poor." Policy Research Working Paper 6568, World Bank, Washington DC.

Dornbusch, R. 1978. "Monetary Policy under Exchange-Rate Flexibility." In Managed Exchange-Rate Flexibility: The Recent Experience, ed. Federal Reserve Bank of Boston, 90–122. Boston: Federal Reserve Bank of Boston.

Edward, P., and A. Sumner. 2013. "The Future of Global Poverty in a Multi-Speed World: New Estimates of Scale and Location, 2010–2030." Working Paper 327, Center for Global Development, Washington, DC.

Erten, B., and J.A. Ocampo. 2013. "Super Cycles of Commodity Prices since the Mid-Nineteenth Century." World Development 44: 14–30.

European Commission. 2013. "Quarterly Report on the Euro Area." European Commission 12 (4).

Feldkircher, M., and I. Korhonen. 2012. "The Rise of China and Its Implications for Emerging Markets: Evidence from a GVAR Model." Institute for Economies in Transition Discussion Papers 2012-20, Bank of Finland, Helsinki.

Frankel, J. A., C. A. Végh, and G. Vuletin. 2013. "On Graduation from Fiscal Procyclicality." Journal of Development Economics 100 (1): 32–47.

FRED. 2014. "Trade-Weighted Exchange Rate Indices." Federal Reserve Economic Data. Federal Reserve Bank, St. Louis, MO.

Frenkel, J. A. 1976. "A Monetary Approach to the Exchange Rate: Doctrinal Aspects and Empirical Evidence." Scandinavian Journal of Economics 78 (2): 200–24.

Gauvin, L., and C. Rebillard. 2014. "Towards Recoupling? Assessing the Impact of a Chinese Hard Landing on Commodity Exporters: Results from Conditional Forecast in a GVAR Model." Mimeo. Lyon Meeting.

Gruss, B. 2014. "After the Boom—Commodity Prices and Economic Growth in Latin America and the Caribbean." Working Paper 14/154, International Monetary Fund, Washington, DC.

HM Treasury. 2014. "Forecasts for the UK Economy: A Comparison of Independent Forecasts, October." HM Treasury, London.

Husabo, E. 2014. "Spillovers to Europe from the Crisis in Russia and Ukraine." Economic Commentaries 6, Norges Bank, Oslo.

IEA (International Energy Agency). 2014a. "Oil Market Report, June 13." Paris.

———. 2014b. "Oil Market Report, November 14." Paris.

IMF (International Monetary Fund). 2003. "Public Debt in Emerging Markets." World Economic Outlook, IMF, Washington, DC.

———. 2012. "China's Trade Balance Adjustment: Spillover Effects: 2012 Spillover Report." Background Paper, IMF, Washington, DC.

———. 2013. "World Economic Outlook, October 2013." IMF, Washington, DC.

———. 2014a. "IMF Multilateral Policy Issues Report," IMF, Washington, DC.

———. 2014b. "Legacies, Clouds, Uncertainties," World Economic Outlook, October, IMF, Washington, DC.

———. 2014c. "Japan: 2014 Article IV Consultation—Staff Report." Country Report 14/236, IMF, Washington, DC.

———. 2014d. Subsidy Reforms in the Middle East and North Africa: Recent Progress and Challenges Ahead. Washington, DC: IMF.

Inchauste, G. J.P. Azevedo, B. Essama-Nssah, S. Olivieri, T. Van Nguyen, J. Saavedra-Chanduvi, and H. Winkler. 2014. "Understanding Changes in Poverty." World Bank, Washington, DC.

Inchauste, G., and J. Saavedra-Chanduvi. 2013. "Opportunity Knocks: Deepening Our Understanding of Poverty Reduction," In Understanding Changes in Poverty, ed. Gabriela Inchauste, João Pedro Azevedo, B. Essama-Nssah, Sergio Olivieri, Trang Van Nguyen, Jaime Saavedra-Chanduvi, and Hernan Winkler, 1–12. Washington, DC: World Bank.

Jiménez-Rodríguez, R., and M. Sánchez. 2004. "Oil Price Shocks and Real GDP Growth: Empirical Evidence for Some OECD Countries." Working Paper Series 362, European Central Bank, Frankfurt.

Jongwanich, J., and D. Park. 2009. "Inflation in Developing Asia." Journal of Asian Economics 20 (5): 507–18.

Kaminsky, G., C. Reinhart, and C. Végh. 2004. "When It Rains, It Pours: Procyclical Capital Flows and Macroeconomic Policies." NBER Macroeconomics Annual 19: 11–82.

Kiersz, A. 2014. "Here's What a Sustained $20 Drop in Oil Prices Does to the World's Major Economies." Business Insider, November 12. http://www.businessinsider.com/societe-generale-oil-price-drop-effects-2014-11.

Kilian, L. 2009. "Not All Oil Price Shocks Are Alike: Disentangling Demand and Supply Shocks in the Crude Oil Market." American Economic Review 99 (3): 1053–69.

Kilian, L., A. Rebucci, and N. Spatafora. 2009. "Oil Shocks and External Balances." Journal of International Economics 77 (2): 181–94.

Kuznets, S. 1955. "Economic Growth and Income Inequality." American Economic Review 45 (1): 1–28.

Lakner, C., M. Negre, and E. Beer Prydz. 2014. "Twinning the Goals—How Can Promoting Shared Prosperity Help to Reduce Global Poverty?" Policy Research Working Paper 7106, World Bank, Washington, DC.

Lane, P. R., and J. C. Shambaugh. 2010. "Financial Exchange Rates and International Currency Exposures." American Economic Review 100 (1): 518–40.

McGettigan, D., Kenji M., J. N. N. Ntsama, F. Painchaud, H. Qu, and C. Steinberg. 2013. "Monetary Policy in Emerging Markets: Taming the Cycle." Working Paper 13/96, International Monetary Fund, Washington, DC.

Morck, R., B. Yeung, and W. Yu. 2000. "The Information Content of Stock Markets: Why Do Emerging Markets Have Synchronous Stock Price Movements?" Journal of Financial Economics 58: 160–215.

Ngai, L. R., and C. Pissarides. 2008. "Employment Outcomes in the Welfare State." CEP Discussion Papers 0856, Centre for Economic Performance, London School of Economics.

Obiora, K. 2009. "Decoupling from the East toward the West? Analyses of spillovers to the Baltic countries." Working Paper 09/125, International Monetary Fund, Washington, DC.

OECD (Organisation for Economic Co-operation and Development). 2014. Global Economic Outlook, OECD, Paris.

Rasmussen, T., and A. Roitman. 2011. "Oil Shocks in a Global Perspective: Are They Really That Bad?" Working Paper 11/194, International Monetary Fund, Washington, DC.

Ravallion, M. 2007. "Economic Growth and Poverty Reduction: Do Poor Countries Need to Worry about Inequality?" 2020 Vision Briefs BB08 Special Edition, International Food Policy Research Institute, Washington, DC.

———. 2012. "Why Don't We See Poverty Convergence?" American Economic Review 102 (1): 504–23.

Roache, S. K. 2012. "China's Impact on World Commodity Markets." Working Paper 12/115, International Monetary Fund, Washington, DC.

Sahay, R., V. Arora, T. Arvanitis, H. Faruqee, P. N'Diaye, T. Mancini-Griffoli. 2014. "Emerging Market Volatility: Lessons from the Taper Tantrum," Staff Discussion Note 14/09, International Monetary Fund, Washington, DC.

Segal, P. 2011. "Oil Price Shocks and the Macroeconomy." Oxford Review of Economic Policy 27 (1): 169–85.

Summers, L., "Speech at the 14th Annual Research Conference in Honor of Stanley Fisher." International Monetary Fund, Washington, DC, November 8.

U.S. Department of Agriculture. 2014. "World Agricultural Supply and Demand Estimates Report, October." U.S. Department of Agriculture, Washington, DC.

Végh, C., and G. Vuletin. 2012. "Overcoming the Fear of Free Falling: Monetary Policy Graduation in Emerging Markets." Working Paper 17753, National Bureau of Economic Research, Cambridge, MA.

World Bank. 1990. World Development Report 1990: Poverty. New York: Oxford University Press, World Bank.

———. 2003. Global Economic Prospects, June. World Bank, Washington, DC.

———. 2013a. Global Economic Prospects, June. World Bank, Washington, DC.

———. 2013b. Doing Business 2014: Understanding Regulations for Small and Medium-Size Enterprises. Washington, DC: World Bank.

———. 2013c. Middle East and North Africa—Economic Developments and Prospects: Investing in Turbulent Times. Washington, DC: World Bank.

———. 2013d. Global Economic Prospects, January. World Bank, Washington, DC.

———. 2014a. Africa's Pulse 10 (October), World Bank, Washington, DC.

———. 2014b. Update on the Economic Impact of the 2014 Ebola Epidemic on Liberia, Sierra Leone, and Guinea. World Bank, Washington, DC.

———. 2014c. The Economic Impact of the 2014 Ebola Epidemic: Short and Medium-Term Estimates for West Africa. Washington, DC: World Bank.

———. 2014d. "Enhancing Competitiveness in an Uncertain World." East Asia Update, October, World Bank, Washington, DC.

———. 2014e. "Corrosive Subsidies," MENA Economic Monitor, October, World Bank, Washington, DC.

———. 2014f. Doing Business 2015, World Bank.

———. 2014g. "Temporary Trade Barriers Database: Update through 2013." World Bank, Washington, DC.

———. 2014h. MENA Quarterly Economic Brief. July 2014, Issue 3, World Bank, Washington, DC.

———. 2014i. Growth Strategies: G20 Emerging Market Economies—World Bank Assessments. Washington, DC: World Bank.

———. 2014j. Ending Poverty and Sharing Prosperity. Global Monitoring Report 2014/2015. Washington, DC: World Bank.

———. 2014k. A Measured Approach to Ending Poverty and Boosting Shared Prosperity: Concepts, Data, and the Twin Goals. Washington, DC: World Bank.

World Bank and Development Research Center of the State Council, the People's Republic of China. 2014, Urban China: Toward Efficient, Inclusive, and Sustainable Urbanization, World Bank.

Zhang, Y.J., Y. Fan, H.T. Tsai, and Y.M. Wei. 2008. "Spillover Effect of US Dollar Exchange Rate on Oil Prices." Journal of Policy Modeling 30 (6): 973–91.

SPECIAL FOCUS

Low-Income Countries:
Graduation, Recent
Developments,
and Prospects

Special Focus:
Low-Income Countries: Graduation, Recent Developments, and Prospects[1]

The number of low-income countries has almost halved since 2001. As of 2013, 34 countries were classified as "low income" according to the World Bank definition, down from 65 in 2001, following the graduation of 31 mostly metal-exporting and transition economies to "middle-income" status.[2] Today, low-income countries are predominantly agriculture based, small, and fragile, and they tend to have weak institutions. Yet in contrast to middle-income countries, economic activity in low-income countries strengthened in 2014 on the back of rising public investment, significant expansion of service sectors, solid harvests, and substantial capital inflows. Growth in low-income countries is expected to remain strong in 2015–17.

This Special Focus section puts in perspective the graduation of some low-income countries to middle-income status and examines the main features of and growth outlook for today's low-income countries. Specifically, it briefly addresses three questions:

- What were the main characteristics of low-income countries that "graduated" to middle-income status between 2001 and 2013?
- What are the main characteristics of today's low-income countries?
- What are the prospects and outlook for countries currently classified as low-income?

Graduation into the Middle-Income Category

In more than half of the 31 low-income countries that attained middle-income status between 2001 and 2013

(Figure SF.1), graduation followed new discoveries or intensified exploitation of metal and oil reserves. Another five graduating countries, mostly in Europe and Central Asia, had seen per capita incomes fall precipitously in the 1990s during deep "transition" recessions, but subsequently rebounded. In several other countries, graduation followed the implementation of structural reforms.

- *Metal and oil exporters.* A sustained increase in commodity prices significantly improved the terms of trade for metal- and energy-exporting low-income countries in Sub-Saharan Africa and East Asia. At the same time, rising commodity demand spurred greater exploration for energy and metal resources. New discoveries of commodities (such as in Ghana, Indonesia, the Lao People's Democratic Republic, Mauritania, São Tomé and Príncipe, Timor-Leste) and large investments in the resource sector (as in Azerbaijan, Cameroon, Lao PDR, Mongolia) then supported graduation to middle-income status.[3] In graduating countries with new resource discoveries or exploitation, governance was on average substantially weaker than in those without natural resources and remained broadly on par with low-income countries that did not graduate.

- *Transition economies.* Disruptive transitions to market economies and regional political conflicts in the first half of the 1990s led to precipitous growth collapses in several countries, with output falling by 50 percent or more in Armenia, Azerbaijan, Georgia, Kyrgyz Republic, and Moldova by the mid-to late-1990s (Iradian, 2007). As a consequence, per capita incomes in many of these (at the time) middle-income economies dropped below low-income thresholds. Subsequently, however, growth rebounded, supported by strong remittances from migrants that found income-earning opportunities in the Russian Federation and Europe (Armenia, Kyrgyz Republic, and Moldova), and foreign direct investment (FDI)-led reconstruction of the energy sector (Azerbaijan). With the exception of the Kyrgyz Republic, per capita income had returned to middle-income levels in all of these countries by 2005.

---

[1]The main authors of this Special Focus are Tehmina S. Khan and Franziska Ohnsorge.

[2]As of July 1, 2014, low-income economies are defined as those with a gross national income (GNI) per capita, calculated using the World Bank Atlas method, of $1,045 or less in 2013; between $1,045 and $12,745 for middle income; and $12,746 or more for high income. Lower-middle-income and upper-middle-income economies are separated at a GNI per capita of $4,125. The comparable per capita thresholds in 2000 were $755 for low-income economies, $756–9,265 for middle-income economies (with a cutoff of $2,995 separating the lower-middle-income and upper-middle-income classifications); and greater than $9,265 for high-income economies. These classifications are revised in July of every year, and are a key input into the World Bank's operational classification of countries, which determines lending eligibility for the International Bank for Reconstruction and Development and the International Development Association lending (Heckelman, Knack, and Rogers, 2011). During the 2000s, only two countries reverted briefly (for one year) from middle-income to low-income status: Mauritania in 2011 and the Solomon Islands in 2009.

---

[3]In Ghana, the increase in per capita income became apparent with the rebasing of GDP in 2010 (Moss and Majerowicz, 2012).

FIGURE SF.1 Trends in graduation from low-income to middle-income status

The number of low-income countries has halved since 2001. Many countries that graduated from low-income to middle-income discovered metals or energy resources or were transition economies emerging from deep recessions. Growth is higher and the decline in volatility sharper in countries that have graduated. Countries that received debt relief experienced smaller poverty declines than those that graduated without debt relief, despite rising expenditures for poverty alleviation.

A. Low-income countries, 2001 and 2013[1]

B. Governance indicators, 2000 and 2013[1]

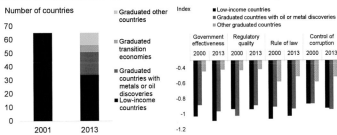

C. GDP growth and volatility[2]

D. Expenditure on poverty reduction by graduating countries that received debt relief[3]

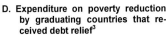

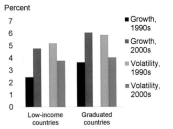

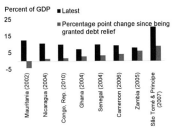

E. Decline in poverty headcount ratios after graduation[4]

Percentage of population living on less than $1.25 per day

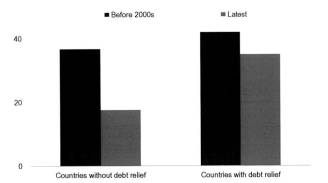

Source: World Bank, IMF (2013), and World Development Indicators.
1.   Graduated countries with new discoveries or exploitation of metals, oil, or gas resources are Angola, Azerbaijan, Cameroon, Republic of Congo, Equatorial Guinea, Ghana, Indonesia, Lao PDR, Lesotho, Mauritania, Mongolia, Nigeria, Sudan, Timor-Leste, Republic of Yemen, Uzbekistan, and Zambia. Graduated transition economies without metals or oil resources are Armenia, Georgia, Kyrgyz Republic, Moldova, and Ukraine. Other graduated countries are Bhutan, Côte d'Ivoire, India, Nicaragua, Pakistan, Senegal, Vietnam, and Solomon Islands. The countries that have remained low income include Afghanistan, Bangladesh, Benin, Burkina Faso, Burundi, Cambodia, Central African Republic, Chad, Comoros, Democratic Republic of Congo, Eritrea, Ethiopia, The Gambia, Guinea, Guinea-Bissau, Haiti, Kenya, Liberia, Madagascar, Malawi, Mali, Mozambique, Myanmar, Nepal, Niger, Rwanda, Sierra Leone, Somalia, Tajikistan, Tanzania, Togo, Uganda, Zimbabwe, and Democratic People's Republic of Korea.
2.   Growth is calculated as average for the respective period. Volatility refers to the standard deviation of GDP growth from 2000 till 2010.
3.   Data in parentheses are the years in which full debt relief was made available.
4.   Countries that received debt relief include: Cameroon, Republic of Congo, Côte d'Ivoire, Ghana, Mauritania, Nicaragua, São Tomé and Príncipe, Senegal, and Zambia. Those that did not include: Angola, Armenia, Azerbaijan, Bhutan, Georgia, Equatorial Guinea, Indonesia, India, Kyrgyz Republic, Lao PDR, Lesotho, Moldova, Mongolia, Nigeria, Pakistan, Sudan, Solomon Islands, Timor-Leste, Ukraine, Uzbekistan, Vietnam, and Yemen.

• *Structural and political reformers.* Accelerating growth in some countries reflected dividends from earlier structural reforms (India, Indonesia), and political and economic reforms (Vietnam). Several economies have also benefited from greater political stability or an easing of conflict that allowed faster growth during the 2000s (Pakistan, Solomon Islands).

In countries that graduated, growth accelerated markedly to rates above those in countries that remained in the low-income category. A moderation in the volatility of output growth also coincided with a decline in the frequency of growth collapses that undermined poverty reduction in earlier decades (Arbache et al., 2008). One-third of graduating countries received debt relief between 2000 and 2014 under the Heavily Indebted Poor Countries (HIPC) Initiative, Multilateral Debt Relief Initiative (MDRI), or bilateral initiatives.[4] For Cameroon, Republic of Congo, Ghana, Kyrgyz Republic, São Tomé and Príncipe, Senegal, and Zambia, the fall in debt servicing burdens associated with debt relief initiatives enabled an increase of, on average, 3.9 percent of gross domestic product (GDP) in expenditures allocated for poverty reduction, although poverty has been relatively slower to decline compared to other graduating countries.

Main Characteristics of Today's Low-Income Countries

Today's low-income countries are typically agricultural economies and often heavily reliant on worker remittances from abroad (Figure SF.2). Three-quarters of low-income countries are in Sub-Saharan Africa, where challenging climatic conditions (especially in the Sahel region) at times strain activity in predominantly subsistence economies (Sheffield and Wood, 2011; Devarajan et al., 2013).

• *Agriculture.* On average, agriculture accounts for about 25 percent of GDP in low-income countries. In many cases, exports are dominated by agricultural commodities, especially coffee and tea (Burundi, Ethiopia, Kenya, Rwanda, Uganda) and cocoa (Guinea, The Gambia, Liberia, Togo).[5] With most parts of Africa having been exposed to drought over the past three decades, and given the dominance of rain-fed agriculture in economic activity and food

---

[4]Barring countries that graduated to middle-income status before they received full debt relief under HIPC (Republic of Congo and Côte d'Ivoire), graduation followed debt relief after 1 to 6 years (3.6 years, on average).
[5]Minerals, notably tantalum, are increasingly a major source of export revenue in Rwanda.

consumption in many household budgets, weather related shocks can have a disproportionate impact on growth and poverty (Devarajan et al., 2013).[6]

- *Remittances.* Many low-income countries are heavily dependent on remittances to support consumption and investment (Chapter 4). On average, remittances accounted for almost 6 percent of GDP in low-income countries in 2013, significantly more than FDI.

- *Fragility.* More than half of today's low-income countries are fragile states with weak governments and poor institutions.[7] Most, particularly fragile countries, are also heavily reliant upon foreign aid to finance critical government spending (IMF, 2014). Government revenues in fragile states tend to be lower than in other low-income countries, making it difficult to provide basic public services. Public investment management tends to be weak, hindering efficient investment in new public infrastructure as well as impinging on needed maintenance.

Notwithstanding soft commodity prices in the near term, several low-income countries could be set to grow into middle-income countries, on the back of substantial resource discoveries. East Africa, in particular, has emerged as a "new frontier" for oil and gas in the past half-decade. Mozambique's deep-water gas fields are estimated to hold around 20 billion barrels of oil equivalent, more than in Angola or Nigeria, and there have been significant discoveries of gas reserves in Tanzania as well (although more modest than in Mozambique). Newly discovered oil reserves in Uganda (estimated at around 2.5 billion barrels, the fourth-largest in Sub-Saharan Africa; Alkadiri, Raad, and Natznet Tesfay, 2014) and Kenya have the potential of coming onstream by the end of the decade (IEA, 2014). Some low-income countries have also been steadily pursuing both structural and public financial management reforms (Bangladesh, Myanmar, and Rwanda), facilitated by the end of civil conflict (Myanmar).

Recent Developments and Outlook for Low-Income Countries

Growth remained robust in low-income countries at about 6 percent in 2014, on the back of rising public investment, strong capital inflows, good harvests (Ethiopia, Rwanda), and improving security conditions in a number of conflict countries (Myanmar, Central African Republic, Mali). The moderation in global food and energy prices in 2014 contributed to a deceleration in inflation in low-income countries, particularly those in Sub-Saharan Africa (except in Malawi, where fuel prices have been deregulated and the currency devalued by 30 percent).

FIGURE SF.2   Features of low-income countries

About three-quarters of today's low-income countries are in Sub-Saharan Africa. Low-income countries tend to be predominantly agricultural economies and often heavily reliant on remittances. More than half of them are fragile states with weak government institutions. Nearly half of low-income countries that have seen debt burdens fall under the HIPC and MDRI Initiatives are fragile.

A. Low and middle income countries: remittances, 2013

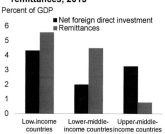

B. Share of commodity exports

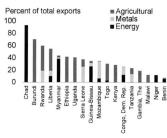

C. Share of agriculture in output, 2012

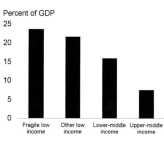

D. Indicators of government institutions[1]

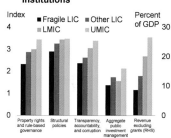

E. Countries currently classified as low-income that have received debt relief and/or are fragile[2]

F. Low-income countries granted full debt relief under HIPC and MDRI[2]

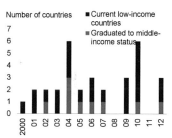

Source: IMF (World Economic Outlook), UN Comtrade, and World Bank (CPIA Indicators, and Public Investment Management, PIM).
1.   Data for PIM are as of 2010, for revenues in percent of GDP as of 2014, and for other indicators as of 2012.The PIM Index is a composite index of the efficiency of the PIM process ranging from 1 to 4 (higher = better); the index covers strategic guidance and project appraisal, selection, management and implementation, and evaluation and audit. Values for the aggregate PIM index denote the residuals from a regression on purchasing-power-parity-adjusted GDP per capita. LIC, LMIC, and UMIC stands for low-income countries, lower-middle-income countries, and upper-middle-income countries, respectively.
2.   Fragile countries are defined according to the Harmonized List of Fragile Situations, and comprise countries whose World Bank Country Policy and Institutional Assessment (CPIA) score are 3.2 is less, or where UN or other peace-keeping forces have been present for the past three years.

---

[6]For low-income economies in Sub-Saharan Africa, it is estimated that 1 percentage point of agricultural growth is three times as effective in reducing poverty as 1 percentage point of growth in the non-agricultural sector (Christiaensen, Demery, and Jesper, 2011).

[7]Fragile states are defined according to the Harmonized List of Fragile Situations, and comprise countries whose World Bank Country Policy and Institutional Assessment (CPIA) score are 3.2 or less, or where the United Nations and/or other peace-keeping forces have been present for the past three years. Of the 34 countries currently classified as low income, 16 are also categorized as fragile.

FIGURE SF.3   Recent low-income countries developments and outlook

Most low-income countries, heavily reliant on commodity exports, suffered terms of trade deteriorations from commodity price declines during 2014. Nevertheless, driven by (often remittance-fueled) domestic demand, growth was robust and, in some, increased. Twin fiscal and current account deficits remain large in several countries, however. Weak state capacity has allowed the rapid spread of the Ebola epidemic in affected countries.

A. GDP growth[1]

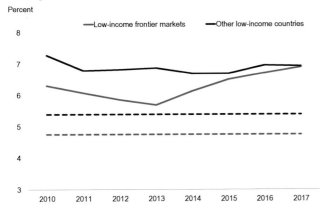

B. Fiscal and current account balance of select LICs, 2014[2]

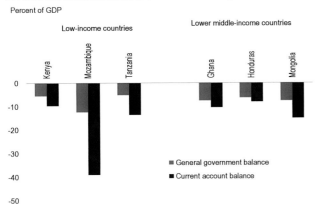

C. Impact of Ebola outbreak on GDP growth in affected countries[3]

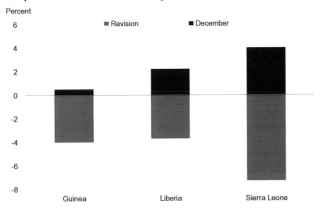

Source: Dealogic, JP Morgan Chase, and World Bank.
1. Dashed lines indicate 1990-2009 average.
2. Selected nonfragile low- and lower-middle-income frontier markets for which both current acount and fiscal deficits exceed 5 percent of GDP.
3. Revision is calculated as forecast revision to 2014 real GDP growth from June 2014 to January 2015 Global Economic Prospects.

While a few countries that export tropical agricultural goods benefited from rising prices in 2014 (such as Burundi and Ethiopia), the terms of trade of most others deteriorated. Among noncommodity producers, Bangladesh saw export growth slow, as demand in key export markets softened. In addition, textile manufacturing production in Bangladesh was affected by disruptions due to social unrest and by stricter enforcement of regulations on working conditions following the collapse of a commercial building that took a heavy human toll.

Domestic demand grew briskly in many low-income countries, for a variety of reasons. Investment in public infrastructure (Benin, the Gambia, Mozambique, and Togo) and in coal, gas, or oil extraction (Mozambique and Niger) grew rapidly. Rising real incomes, due to robust growth, in Kenya and Tanzania encouraged consumption. Strengthening growth in some key remittance-sending economies (India, the Gulf Cooperation Council countries, and the United States), meanwhile, bolstered domestic demand growth in several remittance-receiving countries (including Bangladesh and Nepal). Remittances to low-income countries in Central Asia, however, fell sharply as growth stalled in Russia.

As a result of growing demand for imports, current account deficits have recently widened in about one-third of low-income countries and remain high in several others (Figure SF.3). Fiscal deficits have also widened in some low-income countries on the back of slowing growth in commodity export revenues, increasing expenditure on public infrastructure projects (Mali, Niger, and Uganda), rising wage bills (Kenya and Mozambique), or expanding security- or health-related programs (Afghanistan, Guinea, Liberia, and Sierra Leone). However, several countries have taken advantage of benign international financing conditions to issue sovereign bonds in international markets—for some (Kenya), the first issuance in many years. While foreign capital flows are supporting public investment and growth, they are also financing substantial fiscal deficits and leading to an increase in the share of non concessional loans in public debt (though from a low base).

In several fragile states where government institutions are weak (Guinea, Liberia, and Sierra Leone), lack of adequate public health care services has facilitated the rapid spread of the Ebola virus. In addition to the heavy human toll, the spread of the disease has interrupted trade, agriculture, mining and investment, shaving 3–7 percentage points off growth in affected countries. For now, the spread of the disease outside these three countries appears to have been mostly contained.

For low-income countries as a whole, growth is expected to remain around 6 percent in 2015–17. Soft commodity prices, especially for oil exporters, as well as weak growth in the Euro Area, an important trading partner for West Africa, are expected to hold back growth in many low-income countries. However, strong government consumption and investment growth is expected to mitigate these headwinds. Some fragile states should see increased growth in 2015–17 as the Ebola epidemic abates, security improves, and peacebuilding efforts progress.

References

Alkadiri, R., and N. Tesfay. 2014. "Africa's New Energy Frontier: The Promise and the Peril." Q2–2014. IHS Quarterly, Englewood, CO. http://www.ihs.com/tl/quarterly/features/promise-and-the-peril.aspx Arbache, Jorge, Delfin S. Go, and John Page. 2008. "Is Africa's Economy at a Turning Point?" In *Africa at a Turning Point: Growth, Aid, and External Shocks*, ed. Delfin Go and John Page, 13–85. Washington, DC: World Bank.

Christiaensen, L., L. Demery, and J. Kuhl. 2011. "The (Evolving) Role of Agriculture in Poverty Reduction: An Empirical Perspective." *Journal of Development Economics* 96 (2): 239–54.

Devarajan, S., D. S. Go, M. Maliszewska, I. Osorio-Rodarte, and H. Timmer. 2013 "Stress-Testing Africa's Recent Growth and Poverty Performance." Policy Research Working Paper 6517, World Bank, Washington, DC.

Heckelman, J., S. Knack, and F. Halsey Rogers. 2011. "Crossing the Threshold: An Analysis of IBRD Graduation Policy." Working Paper 5531, World Bank, Washington, DC.

IEA (International Energy Agency). 2014. *Africa Energy Outlook: A Focus on Energy Prospects in Sub-Saharan Africa.* Paris: IEA.

IMF (International Monetary Fund). 2013. "Heavily Indebted Poor Countries (HIPC) Initiative and Multilateral Debt Relief Initiative (MDRI): Statistical Update, December." IMF, Washington, DC.

———. 2014. "Macroeconomic Developments in Low-Income Developing Countries." Policy Paper, IMF, Washington, DC.

Iradian, G.. 2007. "Rapid Growth in Transition Economies: Growth-Accounting Approach." Working Paper 07/164, International Monetary Fund, Washington, DC.

Moss, T., and S. Majerowicz. 2012. "No Longer Poor: Ghana's New Income Status and Implications of Graduation from IDA." Working Paper 300, Center for Global Development, London.

Sheffield, J., and E. F. Wood. 2011: Drought: Past Problems and Future Scenarios. London: Earthscan.

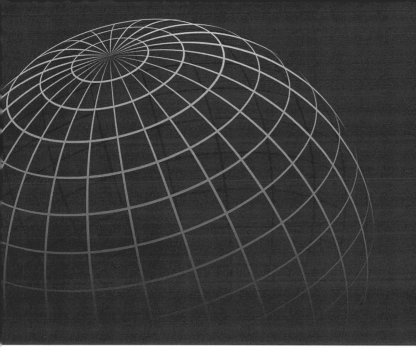

REGIONAL OUTLOOKS

CHAPTER 2
EAST ASIA & PACIFIC

The East Asia and Pacific (EAP) region continued its gradual adjustment to slower but more balanced growth. Regional growth slipped to 6.9 percent in 2014 as a result of policy tightening and political tensions that offset a rise in exports in line with the ongoing recovery in some high-income economies. The medium-term outlook is for a further easing of growth to 6.7 percent in 2015 and a stable outlook thereafter reflecting a gradual slowdown in China that starts to be offset by a pickup in the rest of the region in 2016-17. In China, structural reforms, a gradual withdrawal of fiscal stimulus, and continued prudential measures to slow credit expansion will result in slowing growth to 6.9 percent by 2017 from 7.4 percent in 2014. In the rest of the region, growth will strengthen to 5.5 percent by 2017 supported by firming exports, improved political stability, and strengthening investment. Adjustment to softer commodity prices will continue to weigh on growth of the commodity exporters of the region. A stalled global recovery, a sharp slowdown in China, financial market volatility, and eventual tightening of global financing conditions represent key risks to the regional outlook.

Recent Developments

At 6.9 percent in 2014, growth was only 0.3 percentage point slower than in 2013, and the region remained the fastest-growing developing region in the world (Figure 2.1, Table 2.1). In most economies, the slowdown largely reflected domestic developments. In China, the impact of policy measures to contain financial vulnerabilities was mitigated by offsetting policy measures to avoid a sharper slowdown. As a result, growth has slowed marginally. In the rest of the region, growth slowed to 4.6 percent largely reflecting domestic policy tightening, and political turmoil in Thailand that was only resolved in late 2014. External conditions have been broadly supportive, reflecting weak but sustained recovery in demand, especially from the United States, for the region's exports and favorable global financing conditions.

In China, policy measures guided a gradual slowdown to 7.4 percent in 2014 from 7.7 percent in 2013 (Table 2.2). Since 2013, various policy measures have been enacted to contain the buildup of financial sector vulnerabilities by slowing credit growth, especially in innovative lending products. These have included tightened regulations and supervision for nontraditional lending products, the introduction of quotas for local government borrowing, and liquidity tightening in the interbank market where much of shadow banking is financed.

Credit growth decelerated somewhat, especially in innovative lending products such as trust loans. These measures were complemented by efforts to curb activity in sectors with overcapacity or that are environmentally polluting (such as aluminum, cement, coal, sheet glass, steel, and shipbuilding), including revised performance criteria for local government officials. Partly as a result of these measures, production in these sectors declined sharply.

FIGURE 2.1 GDP growth

In most countries, growth slipped in 2014, but a modest recovery is expected.

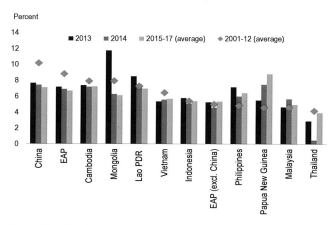

Source: World Bank.
Note: EAP and EAP (excluding China) are GDP-weighted averages.

49

FIGURE 2.2 China: House price growth

House price growth has slowed sharply.

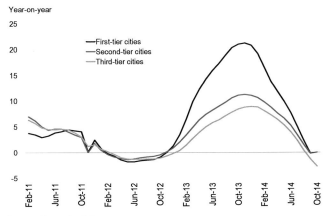

Source: Haver Analytics.
Note: Year-on-year house price growth.

FIGURE 2.3 Credit growth

Bank credit growth continued to slow except in China and the Philippines.

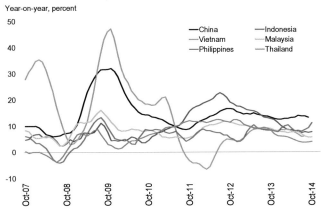

Sources: IMF and IFS.
Note: Data is for year-on-year real credit growth, deflated by the GDP deflator.

FIGURE 2.4 Monetary policy rates

Policy rates have been on hold in most EAP countries since mid-2014.

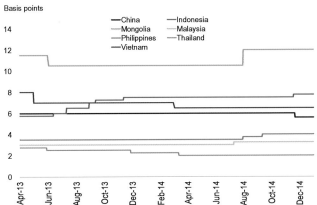

Sources: Haver Analytics and World Bank.
Note: Official policy/interest rates: China: Prime Lending Rate, Indonesia: Bank Indonesia Rate, Malaysia: Overnight Policy Rate, Philippines: Reverse repo rate: overnight borrowing, Vietnam: refinance rate, Thailand: Policy Target Rate, Mongolia: Policy Rate.

This targeted policy tightening was accompanied by a parallel set of growth-stimulating measures designed to cushion the slowdown, especially in the real estate market where house price growth has dropped steeply (Figure 2.2). As a result, housing starts and the inventory-to-sales ratio stabilized in the last quarter of 2014, but activity remains weak and excess inventory high (World Bank, 2014a). Monetary policy was eased with a cut in the rediscount rate, liquidity support for individual banks, cuts in mortgage rates, steps to increase financing for real estate developers, and a lending and deposit rate cut in mid-November.

Elsewhere in the region, domestic policy tightening has continued to weigh on credit and investment growth (Figure 2.3). Partly to anchor inflation expectations following fuel subsidy cuts, central banks in Indonesia and Malaysia raised policy rates in 2014 to ease price pressures and contain credit growth (Figure 2.4). Mongolia and the Philippines also raised policy rates to contain price pressures reflecting capacity constraints. China, Thailand, and Vietnam were the exceptions, with rate cuts aimed at supporting activity amidst a sharp decline in inflation that suggests risks of deflationary pressures. Fiscal balances generally weakened as growth slowed, except in Malaysia where the structural deficit remained at over 3 percent of GDP (Figure 2.5) prompting the authorities to implement several rounds of fuel subsidy cuts. While investment growth slowed from post-crisis highs, robust demand for labor, strong inflows of remittances and buoyant capital markets supported resilient consumption. In Thailand, where political turmoil in the second quarter caused a temporary but sharp slowdown, consumption and activity more broadly rebounded strongly as political tensions subsided.

Current account balances improved, by virtue of rising exports, soft domestic demand, and robust remittances (Figure 2.6). Cambodia, Malaysia, Vietnam, and the Philippines were able to capitalize on firming global demand for the region's exports through a diversified manufacturing base, integration into regional supply chains, competitive unit labor costs and relative political stability. In commodity-exporting countries, however, the decline in commodity prices reduced exports (except in Mongolia, where a newly operational copper mine raised export volumes). Remittances continued to benefit the Philippines and Pacific Island economies (e.g., Samoa and Tonga), but at a slower pace than in 2013, reflecting moderate growth in Australia and uncertainties related to the oil price decline for Gulf Cooperation Council countries.

Capital flows rebounded strongly from first quarter weakness, especially into equities and bond issuances but came under renewed pressure in December following a sharp decline in oil prices and increased global uncertainty (Figure 2.7). Equity issuance in the region doubled, largely because of the $25 billion initial public offering of China's Alibaba Group in September. Through much of the year, strong equity flows into Malaysia and Thailand, and, to a lesser extent, into Indonesia and the Philippines buoyed local stock markets but eased in late 2014. In contrast, in China, stock markets rallied in the last two months of 2014, encouraged by a sharp trading volume increase of retail investors and foreigners' access to A shares through the recently launched Shanghai–Hong Kong Stock Connect scheme and the expectations of the renewed policy easing.

Bond issuance was particularly strong in Indonesia, the Philippines, and China, where tight domestic funding conditions encouraged many corporations to borrow in international bond markets. In the last quarter of 2014, however, issuance declined reflecting increased global uncertainty and volatility. China accounted for more than one-quarter of all developing-country bonds sold in the first nine months of 2014. In contrast, overall bank lending fell to its lowest level since 2010, largely reflecting a sharp slowdown in lending to China as the property sector cooled. Foreign direct investment (FDI) flows into Indonesia and Vietnam rose strongly, reflecting subsiding political uncertainty in Indonesia and easing tensions between China and Vietnam.

Regional currencies, which were firm for most of 2014, came under pressure in December. This reflected increased financial and external vulnerabilities, especially in oil– and gas-producing economies and economies with a significant share of foreign holdings of domestic assets. Given Japan's importance as a regional trading partner, the impact of the sharp depreciation of the Japanese yen on the competitiveness of developing countries in the region was only partly offset by the ongoing U.S. dollar appreciation. The Chinese renminbi continued its steady appreciation, reflecting gradual liberalization and renminbi internationalization..

Outlook

Regional growth is expected to ease slightly to 6.7 percent in 2015 from 6.9 percent in 2014 and remain stable over the projected period. A gradual pick-up of growth in the region excluding China is expected to gradually offset moderating growth in China. In China, structural reforms, a gradual withdrawal of stimulus, and continued measures to tighten credit will slow investment and gradually dampen growth to 6.9 percent by 2017. The unwinding of excess inventory in the housing sector

FIGURE 2.5   Structural fiscal balance

Fiscal policy was mostly neutral, except for tightening in Malaysia on subsidy reform and loosening in Thailand and the Philippines.

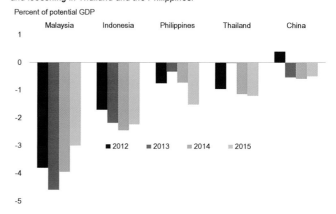

Source: IMF World Economic Outlook.
Note: The structural balance adjusts the overall balance for the business cycle and one-off factors.

FIGURE 2.6   Contributions to growth

Exports increasingly contributed to growth, in contrast with domestic demand.

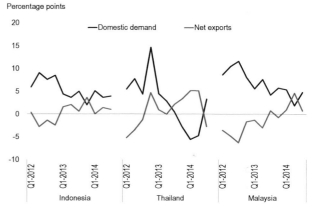

Source: World Bank.
Note: Contribution to year-on-year real GDP growth.

FIGURE 2.7   Gross capital inflows

Gross capital inflows have rebounded strongly from the disruptions in January/ February 2014.

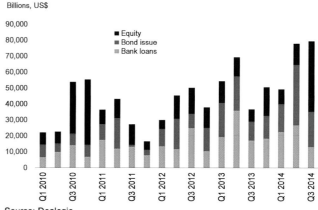

Source: Dealogic.
Note: Gross issuance of equity initial public offerings; corporate and sovereign bonds, and syndicated loans. Exclude secondary market trading.

will continue to depress housing prices and the removal of excess capacity in other industries will be a drag on activity (Wang, 2011). In the short term, central government infrastructure and social housing projects, monetary support measures, and rising net exports will moderate the slowdown in the real estate sector and in industries with excess capacity.

In the baseline scenario, activity in East Asia other than China is expected to accelerate modestly, as exports firm, and political tensions in Thailand recede. Rising demand from high-income countries is expected to benefit the region given its integration into global value chains. In addition, portfolio and FDI flows will be attracted by improving terms of trade (except for commodity-exporting Indonesia, Mongolia, and to some extent Malaysia), by favorable growth prospects—the region being the fastest-growing developing country region—and by the resolution of domestic political uncertainty. This will encourage the return of temporarily relocated export production from neighboring countries to Thailand. It will also benefit neighboring Cambodia by reviving tourism. Investment is expected to strengthen in Vietnam and Myanmar as macroeconomic stabilization programs boost confidence. The recent sharp drop in oil prices, if sustained, is expected to improve terms of trade and current account balances for commodity importers but weigh on growth in oil exporters.

Myanmar should receive an additional boost from continued policy and institutional reforms, and a revival of trade. Post-typhoon reconstruction will raise activity in the Philippines. In Indonesia, the impact of the increase in subsidized fuel prices and policy rate hikes in November 2014 on private consumption will be partly offset by higher targeted social transfers. Growth is expected to pick up gradually as investment recovers. However, over the medium-term, growth will depend crucially on the implementation of long-standing structural reforms and key infrastructure investments.

In a few countries, growth will be held back by domestic policy tightening and weak commodity prices. Continued fuel subsidy reform and the introduction of a goods and services tax are expected to slow growth in Malaysia to 4.7 percent in 2015 from an estimated 5.7 percent in 2014. In the Lao People's Democratic Republic and Mongolia, fiscal and monetary tightening in 2015 to contain fiscal and current account deficits, and to reduce credit growth and inflation are expected to dampen growth.

Growth in Pacific Island countries will be buoyed by improved trade, tourism, and remittances, as well as by a series of country-specific factors. In Papua New Guinea, growth is forecast at 16 percent in 2015, as rising liquefied natural gas (LNG) exports more than offset declines in LNG-related construction. In the Solomon Islands, reconstruction following the April 2014 flooding is expected to boost growth in 2015–16. In Timor-Leste, however, where activity has been driven by government spending, a flat 2015 draft budget compared with the 2014 budget is expected to keep non-oil growth constant at around 7 percent. In Fiji, the necessary fiscal consolidation to contain a further buildup of debt and contingent liabilities will contribute to a growth slowdown.

Risks

Risks to this baseline outlook, as elsewhere around the globe, are tilted to the downside. Key risks stem from weaker-than-anticipated global growth and, although a low -probability scenario, a sharper-than-expected slowdown in China. In addition, the regional outlook is sensitive to the risk of a sharp tightening of global financial conditions.

The countries in the region are highly open economies, deeply integrated into global supply chains or commodity markets, and hence particularly sensitive to global growth (Box 2.1). Overall, global growth is expected to rise in 2015 to 3.0 percent, and to be sustained at around 3.3 percent in 2016-2017 led by continued recovery in the United States and a gradual acceleration of activity in the Euro Area. However, should the global recovery stall, e.g. because of the Euro Area or Japan slipping into stagnation or because of a faltering recovery in the United States, many countries in the region are likely to slow, with the impact transmitted through trade and investment channels. On the other hand, a faster-than-anticipated recovery in global growth and trade, and a steeper-than-expected and sustained decline in commodity prices should lead to higher growth than is envisaged under the baseline scenario, except in commodity-exporting countries.

Although unlikely, a failure to address vulnerabilities in the financial sector in China could increasingly weigh on activity, by allowing inefficient firms to continue operating and by weakening financial institutions (Jian, Lingxiu, and Yiping, 2013). This would reduce productivity growth and increase capital misallocation. In addition, the housing sector could weaken more than expected, thus undermining consumer confidence and investment activity (Chapter 1). A slowdown in China would dampen activity in the entire region, because of the size of the Chinese market and the close trade and investment links. Since it would likely be associated with commodity price declines, commodity exporters (Indonesia and Mongolia) would suffer a double blow (Gauvin and Rébillard, 2014).

Financial market volatility, or abruptly tightening financial conditions, could lead to sharp reductions or reversals in capital inflows, exposing some countries to considerable pressures. Under the baseline scenario, financial conditions are expected to tighten modestly in 2015 and capital flows are expected to moderate smoothly. However, there is a risk that adjustments would happen abruptly. Portfolio flows are particularly prone to disruption. A flight out of risk assets would likely extend to emerging market debt. Tightening external financing conditions would feed into rising domestic interest rates. This would raise debt service burdens, and put pressure on the balance sheets of banks, businesses, and households. A rise in non-performing loans could impair banking system capital, and raise questions about financial stability. Countries with historically high private sector debt service ratios, resulting from rapid debt accumulation since the global financial crisis, are particularly at risk.[1] Other sources of vulnerability are reliance on short-term borrowing to finance current account deficits or rollovers (Indonesia, Malaysia, Mongolia, and Thailand)[2], a heavy foreign currency debt load (Indonesia and the Philippines), and a large stock of domestic debt held abroad (Indonesia, Malaysia, and the Philippines).

Rising interest rates could trigger real estate market downturns, which could in turn prompt a sharp deleveraging of exposed financial institutions and a drop in investment. After a rapid rise in recent years, real housing prices began falling in Malaysia in the fourth quarter of 2013 and in China and Thailand in the first quarter of 2014. Housing prices in the larger EAP economies remain broadly within levels consistent with fundamentals, but an abrupt adjustment in real estate prices could trigger a chain reaction of banking system stress because of its high exposure to the housing sector and high leverage rates (World Bank, 2014b).

Policy Challenges

In China, the key policy challenge is to put growth on a sustainable path while reducing financial risks. Two

FIGURE 2.8   Sectoral distribution of credit

Credit has grown rapidly and exceeds GDP in some countries.

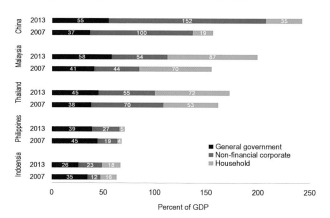

Sources: World Bank, Haver Analytics, and BIS.
Note: Data are for credit from the financial system to the government and the private sector.

reform areas stand out as candidates for early action: fiscal reforms to place local government finances on a more solid footing; and financial sector reforms to strengthen market discipline, contain further buildup of vulnerabilities and engineer their gradual unwinding. Such measures need to be complemented with state-owned enterprise and land reform to boost productivity and to offset the impact of a shrinking labor force and decreasing returns to capital accumulation (World Bank and Development Research Center of the State Council, the People's Republic of China, 2014). The authorities have initiated several pilot programs to implement the comprehensive reform agenda announced in November 2013 (World Bank, 2014a).

Elsewhere in the region, countries face the challenge of containing a further buildup of debt while adjusting monetary and exchange rate policies in response to tightening global financing conditions and soft commodity prices. Although they would also reduce inflation pressures across the region, monetary policy remains constrained by high levels of domestic debt in several countries. The need for slowing the growth of debt is particularly acute in Malaysia and Thailand (Figure 2.8). In some smaller economies, including Lao PDR, Papua New Guinea, and Vietnam, containing the further buildup of external debt is a key policy challenge.

Governments across the region should preserve the recently achieved countercyclicality of fiscal policy and rebuild buffers where cyclical conditions are conducive (Chapter 3). Building policy buffers is especially important in Cambodia, Lao PDR, Mongolia, and Vietnam, where fiscal deficits are in excess of 5 percent

---

[1]Household debt expanded rapidly to 72 percent of GDP in Thailand, and has reached 87.1 percent of GDP in Malaysia in Q3 2014.

[2]In Indonesia, short-term external financing needs are estimated at 10 percent of GDP and 77 percent of foreign exchange reserves in 2014. External financing relies heavily on volatile portfolio inflows, which reached record levels in 2014. In Mongolia, short-term external financing needs amounted to almost 30 percent of GDP and 130 percent of reserves in 2014.

of gross domestic product (GDP). In Indonesia, the Philippines, and Thailand, measures to bolster revenues and to reduce further poorly targeted subsidies (as seen in the recent fuel price increases in Indonesia) would create space for productivity-enhancing infrastructure investments and a well-targeted poverty-reduction program. In Vietnam, although macroeconomic stability is solidifying, banking sector balance sheets need to be strengthened to improve access to credit; and regulatory reform is needed to level the playing field for private business—especially domestic—in relation to state-owned enterprises.

These measures should be supported by structural reforms to mitigate the effects of weak global trade growth and declining productivity growth. Indonesia, where growth has slowed as a result of the sharp fall in commodity prices since 2012, has a pressing need to address long-standing structural reforms, which can help to deliver the necessary improved performance in the manufacturing sector to support export performance and diversification, and quality job creation. Many countries in the region will benefit from addressing infrastructure and logistics obstacles and from the removal of restrictions on service trade. Finally, the region will benefit from implementing a comprehensive strategy to address skills gaps and other human capital constraints, ranging from early childhood development to higher education and lifelong learning.

TABLE 2.1   East Asia and Pacific forecast summary

(Annual percent change unless indicated otherwise)

	00-10[a]	2011	2012	2013	2014e	2015f	2016f	2017f
GDP at market prices[b]	9.0	8.3	7.4	7.2	6.9	6.7	6.7	6.7
(Average including countries with full national accounts and balance of payments data only)[c]								
GDP at market prices[c]	9.0	8.3	7.4	7.2	6.9	6.7	6.7	6.7
GDP per capita (units in US$)	8.2	7.6	6.7	6.5	6.2	6.1	6.2	6.1
PPP GDP	8.8	8.1	7.3	7.1	6.7	6.6	6.7	6.6
Private consumption	6.7	9.0	7.7	6.8	7.4	7.4	7.5	7.6
Public consumption	8.4	8.7	8.1	7.7	7.4	7.4	7.4	7.4
Fixed investment	11.9	8.6	9.4	8.6	6.7	6.9	6.8	6.7
Exports, GNFS[d]	11.3	8.7	4.7	7.4	6.8	7.6	7.3	7.0
Imports, GNFS[d]	11.0	9.8	6.1	8.6	7.1	8.2	8.1	8.3
Net exports, contribution to growth	0.4	0.0	-0.3	-0.1	0.1	0.0	-0.1	-0.2
Current account balance (percent of GDP)	4.6	2.0	2.1	1.6	1.8	2.0	1.9	1.7
Consumer prices (annual average)	2.6	5.6	2.8	3.0	2.5	…	…	…
Fiscal balance (percent of GDP)	-1.6	0.2	-0.3	-2.3	-2.1	-2.1	-2.1	-2.0
Memo items: GDP								
East Asia excluding China	5.0	4.8	6.3	5.3	4.6	5.2	5.4	5.5
China	10.5	9.3	7.7	7.7	7.4	7.1	7.0	6.9
Indonesia	5.2	6.5	6.3	5.8	5.1	5.2	5.5	5.5
Thailand	4.3	0.1	6.5	2.9	0.5	3.5	4.0	4.5

Source: World Bank.

World Bank forecasts are frequently updated based on new information and changing (global) circumstances. Consequently, projections presented here may differ from those contained in other Bank documents, even if basic assessments of countries' prospects do not differ at any given moment in time.

a. Growth rates over intervals are compound weighted averages; average growth contributions, ratios and deflators are calculated as simple averages of the annual weighted averages for the region.

b. GDP at market prices and expenditure components are measured in constant 2010 U.S. dollars.

c. Sub-region aggregate excludes Fiji, Myanmar and Timor-Leste, for which data limitations prevent the forecasting of GDP components or Balance of Payments details.

d. Exports and imports of goods and non-factor services (GNFS).

TABLE 2.2   East Asia and Pacific country forecast

(Real GDP grow th at market prices in percent and current account balance in percent of GDP, unless indicated otherw ise)

	00-10ᵃ	2011	2012	2013	2014e	2015f	2016f	2017f
Cambodia								
GDP	8.0	7.1	7.3	7.4	7.2	7.5	7.2	7.0
Current account balance	-4.7	-6.8	-9.6	-10.7	-11.3	-11.2	-9.6	-8.7
China								
GDP	10.5	9.3	7.7	7.7	7.4	7.1	7.0	6.9
Current account balance	5.0	1.9	2.6	2.0	2.0	2.3	2.2	2.0
Fiji								
GDP	1.6	2.7	1.7	3.5	3.7	2.5	2.5	2.6
Current account balance	-6.6	-5.0	-1.8	-15.5	-8.7	-9.3	-9.7	-9.3
Indonesia								
GDP	5.2	6.5	6.3	5.8	5.1	5.2	5.5	5.5
Current account balance	2.3	0.2	-2.8	-3.3	-3.2	-2.8	-2.8	-2.6
Lao PDR								
GDP	7.1	8.0	8.0	8.5	7.5	6.4	7.0	6.9
Current account balance	-10.6	-10.3	-12.7	-11.5	-11.2	-14.9	-15.4	-13.8
Malaysia								
GDP	4.6	5.2	5.6	4.7	5.7	4.7	5.1	5.2
Current account balance	11.7	11.6	5.8	4.0	4.2	3.1	3.4	3.4
Mongolia								
GDP	6.5	17.5	12.4	11.7	6.3	6.0	6.1	6.3
Current account balance	-4.6	-26.5	-27.4	-25.1	-11.3	-9.0	-10.1	-13.6
Myanmar								
GDP	10.3	5.9	7.3	8.3	8.5	8.5	8.2	8.0
Current account balance	...	-1.9	-4.3	-5.4	-5.3	-5.1	-5.0	-4.9
Philippines								
GDP	4.8	3.6	6.8	7.2	6.0	6.5	6.5	6.3
Current account balance	1.4	2.5	2.8	3.8	3.0	2.7	2.4	1.7
Papua New Guineaᵇ								
GDP	3.5	10.7	8.1	5.5	7.5	16.0	5.1	5.4
Current account balance	4.5	-23.6	-53.6	-30.8	-8.5	12.5	10.8	9.5
Solomon Islands								
GDP	2.9	10.7	4.9	3.0	0.1	3.5	3.5	3.5
Current account balance	-16.6	-6.9	0.2	-8.4	-14.7	-15.5	-14.6	-12.0
Thailand								
GDP	4.3	0.1	6.5	2.9	0.5	3.5	4.0	4.5
Current account balance	3.3	2.6	-0.4	-0.5	3.4	2.3	1.6	1.9
Timor-Lesteᶜ								
GDP	4.3	14.7	7.8	5.6	7.1	7.0	7.0	7.0
Current account balance	19.1	40.4	43.5	34.3	32.1	27.0	27.7	27.0
Vietnam								
GDP	6.6	6.2	5.2	5.4	5.6	5.6	5.8	6.0
Current account balance	-3.3	0.2	6.0	5.6	4.1	3.4	2.6	1.2

Source: World Bank.
World Bank forecasts are frequently updated based on new information and changing (global) circumstances.
Consequently, projections presented here may differ from those contained in other Bank documents, even if basic
assessments of countries' prospects do not significantly differ at any given moment in time.
Samoa; Tuvalu; Kiribati; Democratic People's Republic of Korea; Marshall Islands; Micronesia, Federated States; N. Mariana
Islands; Palau; and Tonga are not forecast ow ing to data limitations.
a. GDP grow th rates over intervals are compound average; current account balance shares are simple averages over the
period.
b. The start of production at Papua New Guinea Liquefied Natural Gas (PNG-LNG) is expected to boost GDP grow th to 16
percent and shift the current account to a surplus in 2015.
c. Non-oil GDP. Timor-Leste's total GDP, including the oil economy, is roughly four times the non-oil economy, and highly
volatile, sensitive to changes in global oil prices and local production levels.

BOX 2.1   China's integration in global supply chains: Review and implications[1]

Since 2001, China has rapidly integrated into global supply chains. Rising foreign content has been associated with robust growth in the domestic content of exports, especially in knowledge-intensive sectors. This has shifted China's comparative advantage towards these sectors.

FIGURE B2.1.1 Growth of foreign and domestic value added of exports and total exports

Strong growth in foreign and domestic value added of exports followed China's WTO accession.

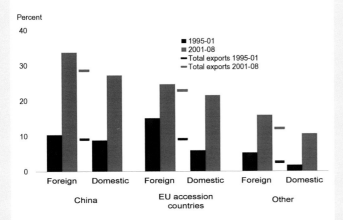

Sources: WIOD and World Bank.
Note: Average annual growth for manufacturing goods exports. EU accession countries are Bulgaria, Czech Republic, Estonia, Hungary, Latvia, Lithuania, Poland, Romania, Slovenia, and Slovak Republic.

FIGURE B2.1.2   Source of foreign content of China's exports

The share of foreign content of China's exports from outside East Asia has grown significantly.

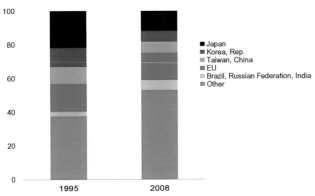

Sources: WIOD and World Bank.
Note: In both bars, EU includes the 15 member countries of the European Union before 2004, excluding the accession countries from 2004 onwards.

Between 2001 and 2008, manufacturing exports from China surged by 29 percent per year, on average. This rate was significantly faster than that of other Asian countries and other regions, including Eastern Europe, which over the same period rapidly integrated into Western European production processes. The brisk growth of China's manufacturing exports reflected a surge in both foreign content (i.e., the intermediate inputs and raw materials that are shipped from abroad and processed in China into exports) and domestic content (i.e., the domestic factor inputs that complement foreign intermediate inputs and raw materials to produce China's exports), which grew on average by 34 and 27 percent per year, respectively (Figure B2.1.1). The increase in foreign content is partly attributable to China's World Trade Organization (WTO) accession in 2001.

This box examines the episode during which China integrated into global supply chains with a focus on two questions:

- How has China's participation in global supply chains evolved?
- What are the implications of China's vertical integration on trade balances and comparative advantage?

The analysis employs sector-by-sector and country-by-country input-output and import-export matrices from the World Input-Output Database (WIOD) to calculate the shares of foreign content and domestic content in exports for each of 35 sectors in 41 countries from 1995, the first year for which WIOD data is available, until the start of the global financial crisis in 2008.[2] This time period was chosen because it represents a unique episode in China's process of integration into global supply chains.

Evolution of China's integration in global supply chains

China initially participated mainly in the East Asian supply chain. In 1995, nearly half of the foreign content in China's exports was sourced from three economies: Japan; the Republic of Korea; and Taiwan, China. After its WTO accession, China

---

[1]The main authors of this box are Tianli Zhao and Dana Vorisek.
[2]The World Input-Output Database (WIOD) by Timmer and others (2012) includes data on 35 sectors for 41 countries (Australia; Austria; Belgium; Brazil; Bulgaria; Canada; China; Cyprus; Czech Republic; Denmark; Estonia; Finland; France; Germany; Great Britain; Greece; Hungary; Ireland; Italy; India; Indonesia; Japan; South Korea; Lithuania; Luxembourg; Latvia; Malta; Mexico; Netherlands; Poland; Portugal; Romania; Russian Federation; Spain; Slovak Republic; Slovenia; Sweden; Taiwan, China; Turkey; United States; and rest of the world) for the period 1995 to 2009. The analysis in this box is based on the framework employed by Koopman, Wang, and Wei (2014).

BOX 2.1 *(continued)*

FIGURE B2.1.3 Foreign content in exports

China's position relative to other countries in the global value added chain has shifted.

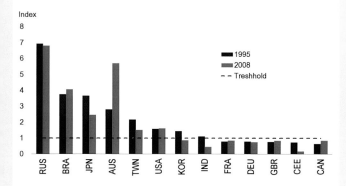

Sources: WIOD and World Bank.
Note: The index is constructed as a ratio of each country's value added in China's exports to China's value added in the other country's exports. An index value greater than 1 indicates China is downstream relative to the country, while an index value less than 1 indicates China is upstream relative to the country.

FIGURE B2.1.4 Decomposition of foreign content in China's iPhone exports, 2009

Only 4 percent of the value added of China's iPhone exports was domestic as of 2009.

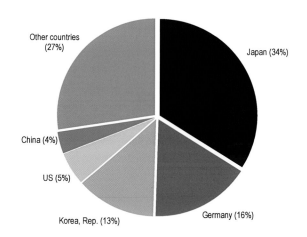

Source: Xing and Detert, 2010.

began to expand beyond the regional supply chain into the global network and, as a result, the share of foreign content from Japan; Korea; and Taiwan, China in China's exports declined to less than a quarter in 2008 (Figure B2.1.2).

As it became vertically integrated with a more diverse set of countries, China moved "downstream" to several resource exporters (such as Australia and the Russian Federation) and high-tech intermediate component exporters (such as the United States)—that is, these economies' content in China's exports increased more than Chinese content in their exports (Koopman, and others, 2010). Meanwhile, China gradually moved "upstream" to Central and Eastern European countries that, over the same period, rapidly integrated into Western European production processes (Figure B2.1.3).

Implications for trade balances and comparative advantage

Integration into global supply chains increased bilateral trade imbalances between China and other countries. The production chain for iPhones constitutes a good example: prior to the financial crisis, iPhones were entirely assembled in China, using inputs from nine companies in other countries, before being exported to the United States. Of the total value of China's iPhone exports, 96 percent was from Japan, Germany, South Korea, and the United States and other countries, while only 4 percent was domestic Chinese content (Figure B2.1.4). Although predominantly produced with foreign content, the full value of Chinese exports of iPhones to the United States was recorded in China's trade surplus in *gross terms* to the United States (Xing and Detert, 2010). In contrast, only 4 percent of Chinese content in iPhones would be recorded in China's trade surplus with the United States in *value-added terms*.

Because China's exports embed content from other countries in the global supply chain, its bilateral trade balances in value-added terms can differ significantly from bilateral trade balances in gross terms (Figure B2.1.5).[3] China's bilateral trade deficit with Japan, for example, is about three times larger in gross terms than in value-added terms. This reflects significant exports of intermediate goods from Japan to China, which are used not for domestic Chinese consumption, but rather in the production of China's exports to the world. China's bilateral trade surplus with the United States is about one-quarter larger in gross terms than in value-added terms because intermediate inputs produced by other countries (e.g., in

---

[3]The bilateral trade balance between China and the United States, in value-added terms is China's value added that is eventually absorbed by the United States net of the value added of the United States eventually absorbed by China—as opposed to the bilateral trade balance in gross terms, which is simply the difference between total exports and imports between China and the United States (Koopman, Wang, and Wei, 2014).

BOX 2.1   *(continued)*

the iPhone) are used extensively in Chinese goods made for export to the United States (Cheung, Chinn, and Qian, 2014).

As it integrated into global supply chains, China also rapidly expanded its domestic content of exports.[4] This was most pronounced in knowledge-intensive sectors.[5] With foreign content growth of 30 percent per year during 1995–2008, vertical integration in the knowledge-intensive manufacturing sectors was almost twice as fast as that in most other sectors. Although the share of domestic content in knowledge-intensive exports remained lower than in other sectors, rapid vertical integration in this sector was accompanied by brisk growth in domestic content, also well in excess of that in most other sectors (Figure B2.1.6).

As expected, this rapid vertical integration contributed to a gradual shift in comparative advantage (Bahar and others, 2014). China's revealed comparative advantage (RCA) captures this process, where RCA is defined as the share of an industry's exports in China's total exports compared with the share in world exports—all based on domestic content of exports.[6] In 1995, China had a comparative disadvantage in knowledge-intensive sectors. By 2008, however, following a period of rapid vertical integration in these sectors, this comparative disadvantage had turned into a comparative advantage (Figure B2.1.7). As a result, the value-added trade deficits that China ran in these sectors in 1995 had turned into, in some cases, large value-added trade surpluses in 2008 (Figure B2.1.8).

Conclusion

Since joining the WTO in 2001, China has rapidly integrated into global supply chains, especially in knowledge-intensive industries. While the analysis here is limited by data availability, it shows that the process of integration was accompanied by a rapid expansion of domestic production for exports and led to an increase in the degree of comparative advantage in knowledge-intensive industries. The results also suggest that trade balances in value added terms can provide additional information about bilateral trade positions, especially for countries that are integrated in global supply chains.

---

[4]The positive correlation between the growth of foreign content in exports and growth of domestic content in exports is also found in the European supply network (Rahman and Zhao, 2013).

[5]The classification of knowledge-intensive sectors follows the Organisation for Economic Co-operation and Development (OECD) Technology Intensity Definition. Specifically, the industries belonging to "high-technology" or "medium-high-technology" in the OECD definition are classified as knowledge-intensive sectors here.

[6]Recent research shows that a RCA based on the value-added decomposition of exports eliminates double counting and is more accurate than a RCA based on gross trade (Koopman, Wang, and Wei, 2014; Rahman and Zhao, 2013).

FIGURE B2.1.5   China's bilateral trade balance in value-added and gross terms, 2008

Because of vertical integration, China's bilateral trade balance with Japan is more negative in gross terms than in value-added terms (and vice versa with the United States).

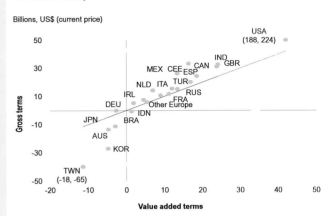

Sources: WIOD and World Bank.
Note: China's bilateral trade deficit with Taiwan, China and bilateral trade surplus with the United States is off the scale in the figure; the relevant amounts are shown in parenthesis.

FIGURE B2.1.6   Average annual growth in domestic and foreign content in Chinese merchandise exports by sector, 1995–2008

Growth in foreign value added of China's exports was accompanied by growth in domestic value added.

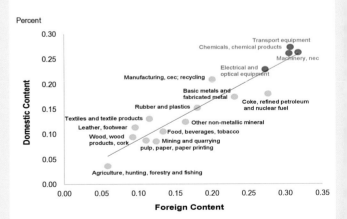

Sources: WIOD and World Bank.
Note: Knowledge-Intensive manufacturing sectors are shown in red.

BOX 2.1 *(continued)*

FIGURE B2.1.7 **China's revealed comparative advantage in three sectors**

China's comparative advantage in knowledge-intensive industries has grown as the economy became increasingly vertically integrated.

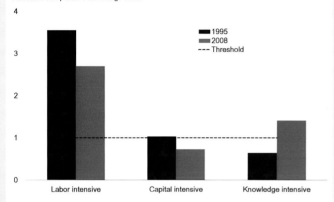

Revealed comparative advantage index

Sources: WIOD and World Bank.
Note: An RCA above the threshold of 1 indicates comparative advantage. Revealed comparative advantage is defined as an industry's share of China's exports (in terms of domestic value added of exports) relative to the same industry's share in world exports (also in terms of domestic value added of exports).

FIGURE B2.1.8 **China's value-added trade balances**

China's value-added trade balance in knowledge-intensive sectors turned from deficit to surplus between 1995 and 2008.

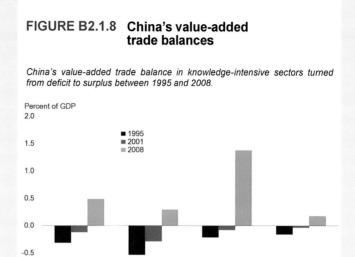

Percent of GDP

Sources: WIOD and World Bank.

EUROPE & CENTRAL ASIA

Growth in Europe and Central Asia is estimated to have slowed to a lower-than-expected 2.4 percent in 2014 as a stuttering recovery in the Euro Area and stagnation in the Russian Federation posed headwinds. In contrast, growth in Turkey exceeded expectations despite slowing to about 3.1 percent. Growth in the region is expected to rebound to 3.0 percent in 2015 and 3.8 percent in 2016–17 but with considerable divergence. Recession in Russia holds back growth in Commonwealth of Independent States whereas a gradual recovery in the Euro Area should lift growth in Central and Eastern Europe and Turkey. The tensions between Russia and Ukraine and the associated economic sanctions, the possibility of prolonged stagnation in the Euro Area, and sustained commodity price declines remain key downside risks for the region. Long-term growth is held back by structural impediments, including weak business environments and institutions and fragile banking systems.

Recent Developments

A stuttering recovery in the Euro Area and slowing growth in the Russian Federation have posed headwinds to developing Europe and Central Asia (ECA).[1] Growth in the region is estimated to have slowed to a lower-than-expected 2.4 percent in 2014, from 3.7 percent in 2013. This reflected a sharp contraction in Ukraine, spillovers from weakness in Russia and the Euro Area, and slowing capital inflows (Table 2.3).

Activity in Russia slowed further to 0.7 percent in 2014 (Figure 2.9, Table 2.4). Tensions with Ukraine, sanctions, and falling crude oil prices interacted with a structural slowdown, although a depreciating ruble and increased public spending supported exports and industrial production in the final quarter of 2014 after a sharp contraction in mid-2014. Capital flight and the loss of access to international capital markets by Russian banks and

corporates under sanctions led to over 75 percent depreciation of the ruble against the U.S. dollar between January and mid-December 2014 despite repeated interest rate hikes and interventions in the currency markets by the central bank. Borrowing and rollover costs have risen sharply and business confidence and investment have sagged. Rising inflation was exacerbated by the retaliatory sanctions that Russia imposed on the imports of a range of food items. In turn, rising prices have had adverse effects on household real income and consumer spending in Russia.

FIGURE 2.9   Russian Federation and CIS: GDP

Spillovers from stagnation in the Russian Federation have dampened growth in the CIS.

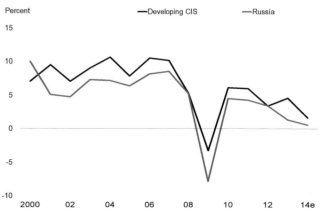

Sources: Haver Analytics and World Bank.
Note: GDP-weighted average real GDP growth for CIS.

---

[1]Countries in developing ECA region include only the low- and middle-income countries of the geographic region. Developing countries in Central and Eastern Europe (CEE) are Albania, Bosnia and Herzegovina, Bulgaria, Georgia, Hungary, Kosovo, the Former Yugoslav Republic of Macedonia, Montenegro, Romania, and Serbia. Recently high-income CEE countries include Croatia, the Czech Republic, Estonia, Latvia, Lithuania, Poland, the Slovak Republic, and Slovenia. Developing countries in the Commonwealth of Independent States (CIS) are Armenia, Azerbaijan, Belarus, Kazakhstan, Kyrgyz Republic, Moldova, Tajikistan, Turkmenistan, Ukraine, and Uzbekistan.

FIGURE 2.10   CEE: Industrial production and export volume growth

Exports and industrial production in CEE countries slowed partly as a result of weak Euro Area growth.

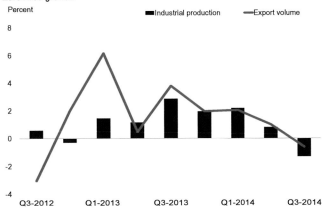

Sources: Haver Analytics and World Bank.
Note: The figure reflects quarter-on-quarter growth in GDP-weighted export volumes and industrial production.

FIGURE 2.11   Inflation and inflation targets

Inflation is above target in several CIS countries and Turkey and below target in the CEE countries.

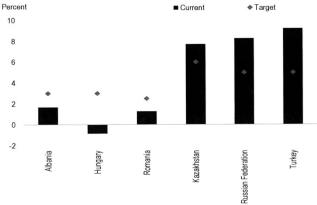

Sources: World Bank and centralbanking.com.
Note: "Current" denotes year-on-year inflation in November 2014. Formal and informal non binding inflation targets compiled by centralbanking.com.

FIGURE 2.12   Policy interest rates

Policy rates have dropped to historic lows in a number of countries.

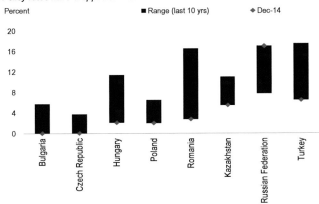

Source: World Bank.
Note: Monetary policy rates at end-November 2014.

Conflict has taken a severe toll on Ukraine's economy, with output estimated to have contracted an estimated 8.2 percent in 2014. An 85 percent depreciation of the currency against the U.S. dollar in 2014 and a sharp import compression led to a significant current account adjustment. The fiscal deficit remains high amid weakness in revenue collection and increased security-related spending. High debt refinancing needs weigh on the balance of payments. Although an EU-brokered ceasefire agreement was reached in October, disputes with Russia over natural gas supplies, prices, and debts, as well as over pipeline transit, have heightened uncertainties.

In countries in the Commonwealth of Independent States (CIS), growth slowed sharply to 1.5 percent, mainly attributable to the sharp output contraction in Ukraine. Russia's slowdown has had negative spillovers on trade and remittances, notwithstanding recent declines in exposure to Russia. In the first half of 2014, export volumes to Russia fell more than 10 percent year on year in Kazakhstan, and by almost 20 percent in Uzbekistan. Others have been hit hard by a significant decline in the dollar value of remittances, partly due to a sharp depreciation of Russian ruble. Tajikistan and the Kyrgyz Republic, where remittances from Russia represent 46 and 29 percent of GDP, respectively, are most exposed. Some governments, in an effort to offset the impact of currency depreciations on purchasing power and safeguard political stability, raised public sector wages and social benefits (Belarus, Kazakhstan, the Kyrgyz Republic, and Uzbekistan). This has pushed inflation higher or kept it in double-digits.

Growth in Central and Eastern Europe (CEE) was broadly steady at an estimated 2.6 percent, reflecting close trade ties to struggling core Euro Area countries (Figure 2.10). In addition, the escalating economic sanctions between Russia and other high-income countries reduced confidence and slowed FDI inflows. Investment was further damped by sluggish bank lending, and by rising real interest rates as inflation approached zero or even turned negative.

Many CEE countries are in or near deflation (Figure 2.11), because of negative output gaps, significant cuts in regulated energy prices (in Bulgaria, Croatia, Czech Republic, Hungary, and FYR Macedonia), and declining food and fuel prices. Falling food prices reflected bumper harvests (especially in Bulgaria and Romania), as well as weaker demand because of the Russian ban on food imports. Several central banks cut interest rates to historic lows to support weak economies in the second half of 2014 (Figure 2.12). However, the high share of foreign currency-denominated lending and nonresident debt holdings has constrained central banks' ability to support growth, because of the risk that interest rate cuts might lead to large depreciations, and thereby impair balance sheets.

Growth in Turkey was an estimated 3.1 percent in 2014, exceeding earlier expectations. Strong government spending and export growth mitigated investment and consumption weakness associated with high inflation, domestic policy uncertainties, and rising geopolitical risk. The combination of robust export growth and slowing domestic demand, as well as a temporary decline in gold imports, helped narrow the current account deficit to 5.6 percent of GDP in 2014, down from 7.9 percent in 2013. Inflation rose to almost double the central bank's target rate of 5 percent. This increase was partly the result of one-off factors, such as high food prices following a drought in mid-2014. However, demand pressures were also at work, as evidenced by tight capacity, and by sustained growth in employment. In response, the central bank raised interest rates in early 2014. This move was also motivated by concerns about the exchange rate, and Turkey's heavy reliance on short-term foreign borrowing (Figure 2.13). However, the rate increase was partially reversed in the second half of 2014, as domestic demand softened.

Capital inflows into the ECA region as a whole have been weak, reflecting the region's economic struggles. A few countries did nevertheless successfully place modest-sized bond issues in international markets (Azerbaijan, Bulgaria, Kazakhstan, Romania, and Turkey). Gross capital flows to Turkey remained strong, partly because global investors diverted funds from Russia.

Outlook

After a sharp deceleration in 2014, growth in the region is projected to recover moderately, with growth in developing countries in the region averaging 3.5 percent in 2015–17, but with considerable divergence across countries. In the baseline scenario, the expected contraction in Russia in 2015 and gradually tightening global financial conditions are expected to be offset to some extent by a modest recovery in Euro Area demand, diminishing political tensions, and the benefits of lower international energy prices on net importers.

The outlook for Russia hinges on geopolitical tensions and related sanctions and on oil prices. The baseline scenario assumes that geopolitical tensions remain contained, but that current sanctions on banks, energy, and defense sectors stay in place for an extended period. Increased funding difficulties and uncertainty will depress private investment,

FIGURE 2.13 External vulnerability, Q2 2014

Financing needs remain high and reserve coverage moderate in some countries.

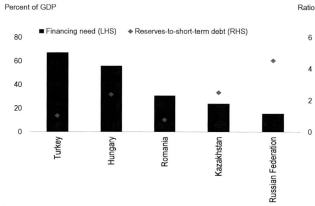

Source: World Bank.
Note: Financing need calculated as current account balance plus short-term debt in Q232014. Reserves-to-short-term debt based on Q3 2014 data. Short-term debt data for Q3 2014 proxied by data for Q2 2014 and debt repayments, assuming no rollover.

while continued currency depreciation, high inflation and weak real wage growth will dampen consumption, the main engine of growth for the past decade. Banks and corporates that have lost access to international capital markets will continue to struggle to roll over debt and may need to resort to central bank funding, resources from the National Welfare Fund, and domestic market funding (at sharply higher interest rates than earlier in 2014). Absent major structural reforms, import substitution stimulated by the weaker ruble and import restrictions is expected to be limited. Low oil prices will put significant pressure on the budget, limiting fiscal space for further public investment and other stimulus. Growth is expected to be negative in 2015 and barely positive in 2016.

Ukraine's economy faces a highly uncertain outlook. In the baseline scenario, which assumes no further escalation of tensions, activity is expected to bottom out in 2015 and to recover in 2016–17.

Among energy—exporting CIS countries, a slowdown in emerging market trading partners (especially China and Russia) and continued weakness in crude oil and other key commodity prices are expected to reduce growth in 2015, before the onset of a recovery in 2016–17. In particular, growth is expected to decelerate in Azerbaijan and Kazakhstan as oil prices remain soft and domestic oil production stagnates because of persistent production difficulties at key oil fields. Non-oil sector growth is also expected to weaken as tight macroprudential regulations slow bank lending (in particular to households), and as Chinese and Russian import demand softens. In Uzbekistan, buoyant natural gas exports will be offset by

FIGURE 2.14 Changes in trade balance due to terms of trade effects, 2014–2017

Trade balances of some CIS oil producers could deteriorate sharply if the recent softening in commodity prices is sustained.

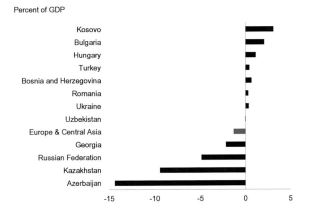

Source: World Bank.
Note: Effect of 30 percent decline in oil, 5 percent decline in agricultural prices, and 10 percent decline in metal prices on the difference between exports and imports in percent of GDP, assuming no supply response.

falling prices in other key commodities (gold and cotton), weaker remittances from migrant workers in Russia, and softening Russian demand for manufactured goods. Turkmenistan is especially exposed to China, which accounts for two-thirds of the country's exports.

Among non-energy-exporting CIS countries, Belarus is expected to benefit from increased agricultural exports to Russia in the wake of the ban on Western food imports. Nevertheless, recession in Russia and large depreciation of the Russian ruble will reduce manufacturing exports and investment. The state's substantial footprint on the economy will continue to deter foreign investment, while still-high inflation will dampen consumption growth.

Armenia, the Kyrgyz Republic, Moldova, and Tajikistan are vulnerable to dislocations in the Russian labor market because of the importance of remittances from Russia. Declining prices of agricultural commodities, metals, and raw materials are expected to weaken the terms of trade and reduce trade balances.

In oil-importing CEE countries, a gradual strengthening in the Euro Area, additional monetary accommodation and a decline in international energy prices should support industrial activity and export growth. In Hungary and Romania, domestic demand is expected to increasingly drive growth, supported by improving labor market conditions and consumer confidence, and by public investment in infrastructure largely financed by the EU. In South and Eastern European countries,

including Bulgaria, Bosnia and Herzegovina, FYR Macedonia, and Serbia, external demand will remain the key driver of growth as consumer and business confidence remain weak over lingering political uncertainty, chronically high unemployment, and still-fragile banking systems saddled with high nonperforming loans. Russia's ban on food imports from the EU could affect some of the Baltic countries, Hungary, and Poland to varying degrees.

In Turkey, growth is expected to gradually pick up in 2015–17 on the back of stronger private consumption. Nevertheless, growth will remain below its historical average. With softening commodity prices and stronger export demand from the Euro Area, the current account deficit is expected to continue narrowing but remain elevated in the forecast period. Short-term portfolio flows continued to finance much of this deficit through 2014 (Figure 2.13).

Risks

The balance of risks to the region's outlook remains tilted to the downside. Further escalation in political tensions with Russia, persistent stagnation in the Euro Area, or a sudden tightening of global financial conditions are key downside risks to the region's outlook.

Tensions between Russia and Western countries escalated throughout 2014, resulting in a series of sanctions and countersanctions that disrupted trade and financial flows, and curtailed access to international financial markets for Russia's oil, finance, and defense industries. Although the natural gas sector has thus far been largely excluded from the sanctions, and gas stocks remain ample following a mild winter, several countries in the region are vulnerable to disruptions in supply. The recent cancellation of the South Stream gas pipeline project, which was to supply Russian gas to southern Europe, has raised the stakes. Should sanctions materially disrupt the gas sector, protracted weakness in both EU and Russia could ensue, with negative spillovers to the entire region. In such a high-risk scenario, activity in Russia could contract by more than 2.9 percent in 2015, with domestic demand falling by more, and for longer, than projected. The relaxation of the fiscal rule by the government, and greater public investment, would only partly offset the contraction in private demand.[2] In addition, there is a risk that exchange rate pressures in Russia increase and some borrowers, including some large corporates or banks, begin to struggle to roll over debt.

Sharp or sustained declines in commodity prices or remittance inflows from Russia—the major source of remittances to the region—represent major risks for CIS countries. A significant slowdown in remittances from Russia would weaken these countries' current account balances, household consumption, and poverty dynamics. Most countries are heavily reliant on a few commodity exports, which make them vulnerable to commodity price swings. Furthermore, some CIS countries trade extensively with each other, increasing the risk of self-reinforcing declines. A further decline in crude oil prices could reduce the trade balance in Russia, Azerbaijan, and Kazakhstan by 5–14 percentage points of GDP (Figure 2.14). In contrast, such a decline would benefit net oil importers in the region, improving their trade balance by 1.2 percentage point of GDP on average, and more than 2 percentage points in Bulgaria and Kosovo.

Failure of the expected modest upturn in the Euro Area to materialize represents a significant risk to the outlook of CEE countries that could derail their already-weak recovery. Because of their integration in Euro Area production chains, persistent stagnation in the core Euro Area would reduce exports and investments in the manufacturing sector, and weigh on consumer demand through confidence and employment.

Financial market volatility is another potential source of uncertainty for countries with large financing needs. Several countries have reduced their vulnerability to external shocks, through tightened policies or exchange rate depreciations, which have helped narrow current account deficits. But others, still rely on short-term foreign capital (Turkey), or their balance sheets reflect currency and maturity mismatches (Hungary,).

Policy Challenges

Notwithstanding recent improvements, countries in the region face further challenges in implementing fiscal and monetary policies to counteract the projected gradual tightening of global financial conditions and weak growth in major trading partners, such as Russia and the Euro Area. A legacy of fiscal deficits and high public debt has reduced fiscal space in several countries, especially in

South Eastern Europe (Albania, Serbia, and FYR Macedonia). Efforts so far to reduce public expenditure have focused on cutting capital investment rather than tackling structural rigidities such as large public wage bills and poorly targeted social benefits (World Bank, 2014c). Room for monetary policy easing also remains limited, especially in CEE countries where policy rates are already very low or where foreign-currency denominated debt is high. In countries facing high inflation or the risk of capital outflows further tightening may be in order to anchor inflation expectations and sustain capital inflows (Kazakhstan and Turkey).

Long-term growth is held back by structural weaknesses, including weak business environments and institutions and fragile banking sectors across the region. Perceived corruption, weak competition, and excessive government intervention remain significant obstacles for diversification and private sector growth in resource-rich Central Asia (World Bank, 2014d). Lack of reliable access to electricity supplies, along with other infrastructure bottlenecks, are also perceived as significant constraints. In some countries, dependence on a few commodities for export revenues is a further structural weakness.

In several countries, banking systems remain saddled with an overhang of nonperforming loans. Fourteen of the twenty developing countries with the highest share of nonperforming loans are in Europe and Central Asia, led by Kazakhstan, Serbia, Albania, Bulgaria, Romania, and Ukraine. Even though these loans appear to be well provisioned and backed by adequate bank capital, they weigh on new lending for efficient investment and job-creating growth, and pose a contingent liability for the public sector.[3] Recognizing this, authorities have recently introduced measures to jump-start the resolution process. For example, in Kazakhstan, the authorities are increasing the capitalization of the Problem Loan Fund, expanding the eligible loans for purchase by the entity, and changing the tax rules and insolvency regime to incentivize debt write-offs. In Ukraine, the authorities, with the financial and technical assistance from the International Monetary Fund and the World Bank, are introducing changes to the legal and regulatory framework to facilitate the workout of nonperforming loans.

[2]Russia's fiscal rule, approved in 2012 and aimed at medium-term fiscal adjustment, caps federal government expenditures at the projected sum of non-oil revenues, oil and gas revenues calculated at benchmark prices, and net financing of 1 percent of GDP. The benchmark price is a backward-looking 10-year average (in 2013, however, 5-year average) of the Urals oil price (IMF, 2013a).

[3]See, for example, Caballero, Hoshi, and Kashyap (2008) and Barnett et al., (2014).

TABLE 2.3   Europe and Central Asia forecast summary

(Annual percent change unless indicated otherwise)

	00-10[a]	2011	2012	2013	2014e	2015f	2016f	2017f
GDP at market prices[b]	4.6	6.2	1.9	3.7	2.4	3.0	3.6	4.0
(Average including countries with full national accounts and balance of payments data only)[c]								
GDP at market prices[c]	4.6	6.3	1.9	3.6	2.4	3.0	3.6	3.9
GDP per capita (units in US$)	4.1	5.5	1.2	2.9	1.8	2.3	2.9	3.4
PPP GDP	4.8	6.0	2.0	3.6	2.2	2.9	3.6	4.0
Private consumption	5.2	7.2	2.2	5.0	2.4	3.0	3.7	3.8
Public consumption	3.0	2.8	4.4	3.7	4.5	4.9	4.0	4.0
Fixed investment	6.1	11.0	-0.1	4.1	1.6	3.0	2.3	3.8
Exports, GNFS[d]	5.9	9.0	4.9	1.0	3.7	4.6	4.8	4.9
Imports, GNFS[d]	6.5	11.7	2.5	4.2	1.2	5.5	6.2	7.2
Net exports, contribution to growth	-0.3	-1.2	0.8	-1.3	0.9	-0.5	-0.7	-1.2
Current account balance (percent of GDP)	-3.6	-4.3	-3.5	-4.0	-2.3	-2.2	-2.8	-2.9
Consumer prices (annual average)	13.9	8.2	8.7	6.2	7.1	...	...	...
Fiscal balance (percent of GDP)	-4.4	0.7	-0.6	-1.3	-1.5	-1.6	-1.5	-1.4
Memo items: GDP								
Broader geographic region (incl. recently high income countries)[e]	4.5	4.9	2.3	2.2	1.8	0.8	2.2	2.8
Central and Eastern Europe[f]	3.3	2.0	-0.2	2.2	2.6	2.4	2.8	3.3
Commonwealth of Independent States[g]	7.2	6.0	3.4	4.0	1.5	2.8	4.1	4.7
Kazakhstan	8.3	7.5	5.0	6.0	4.1	1.8	3.2	4.7
Turkey	3.9	8.8	2.1	4.1	3.1	3.5	3.7	3.9
Romania	4.1	2.3	0.6	3.5	2.6	2.9	3.2	3.9
Russian Federation	4.8	4.3	3.4	1.3	0.7	-2.9	0.1	1.1

Source: World Bank.
World Bank forecasts are frequently updated based on new information and changing (global) circumstances. Consequently, projections presented here may differ from those contained in other Bank documents, even if basic assessments of countries' prospects do not differ at any given moment in time.
a. Growth rates over intervals are compound weighted averages; average growth contributions, ratios and deflators are calculated as simple averages of the annual weighted averages for the region.
b. GDP at market prices and expenditure components are measured in constant 2010 U.S. dollars.
c. Sub-region aggregate excludes Bosnia and Herzegovina, Kosovo, Montenegro, Serbia, Tajikistan and Turkmenistan. Data limitations prevent the forecasting of GDP components or Balance of Payments details for these countries.
d. Exports and imports of goods and non-factor services (GNFS).
e. Recently high-income countries include Croatia, Czech Republic, Estonia, Latvia, Lithuania, Poland, Russian Federation, and Slovak Republic.
f. Central and Eastern Europe: Albania; Bosnia and Herzegovina; Bulgaria; Georgia; Kosovo; Lithuania; Macedonia, FYR; Montenegro; Romania; Serbia.
g. Commonwealth of Independent States: Armenia, Azerbaijan, Belarus, Kazakhstan, Kyrgyz Republic, Moldova, Tajikistan, Turkmenistan, Ukraine, Uzbekistan.

TABLE 2.4   Europe Central Asia country forecast

(Real GDP grow th at market prices in percent and current account balance in percent of GDP, unless indicated otherw ise)

	00-10[a]	2011	2012	2013	2014e	2015f	2016f	2017f
Albania								
GDP	5.5	2.5	1.6	1.4	2.1	3.0	4.0	4.5
Current account balance	-7.7	-13.4	-10.2	-10.6	-11.9	-11.8	-11.7	-11.5
Armenia								
GDP	7.9	4.7	7.2	3.5	2.6	3.3	3.7	4.1
Current account balance	-9.3	-10.9	-11.2	-8.0	-9.2	-7.2	-7.1	-6.7
Azerbaijan								
GDP	14.9	0.1	2.2	5.8	4.5	4.4	4.1	3.8
Current account balance	5.1	26.0	21.7	16.5	12.6	9.8	8.1	5.3
Belarus								
GDP	7.4	5.5	1.7	0.9	1.5	1.8	2.0	2.0
Current account balance	-5.5	-8.6	-2.7	-10.2	-8.1	-6.3	-8.5	-8.8
Bosnia and Herzegovina								
GDP	4.1	1.0	-1.2	2.5	0.4	1.5	2.5	3.0
Current account balance	-12.3	-9.5	-9.3	-5.4	-9.7	-8.6	-6.9	-6.2
Bulgaria								
GDP	4.1	1.8	0.6	1.1	1.4	1.1	2.0	2.7
Current account balance	-10.3	0.1	-0.8	2.1	1.2	-0.5	1.9	0.7
Georgia								
GDP	6.2	7.2	6.2	3.3	5.0	5.0	5.0	5.5
Current account balance	-11.4	-12.7	-11.7	-5.7	-8.5	-7.8	-7.1	-6.7
Hungary								
GDP	1.9	1.6	-1.7	1.5	3.2	2.0	2.5	2.7
Current account balance	-6.2	0.4	0.9	4.2	4.3	4.3	4.3	4.4
Kazakhstan								
GDP	8.3	7.5	5.0	6.0	4.1	1.8	3.2	4.7
Current account balance	-1.7	5.4	0.5	0.5	2.0	-1.1	-1.1	0.0
Kosovo								
GDP	6.2	4.5	2.8	3.4	2.5	3.0	3.5	3.5
Current account balance	-7.9	-20.3	-7.5	-6.4	-7.7	-6.8	-6.5	-6.1
Kyrgyz Republic								
GDP	4.1	6.0	-0.1	10.9	3.0	2.0	4.0	5.0
Current account balance	-3.1	-6.5	-15.1	-13.9	-12.4	-15.0	-13.8	-13.1
Macedonia, FYR								
GDP	3.0	2.3	-0.5	2.7	3.3	3.5	3.8	4.0
Current account balance	-5.6	-2.5	-2.9	-1.8	-2.2	-3.0	-4.9	-5.5
Moldova								
GDP	5.1	6.8	-0.7	8.9	2.0	3.0	3.5	5.0
Current account balance	-7.7	-11.2	-6.8	5.0	-4.5	-4.8	-6.6	-7.0
Montenegro								
GDP	3.6	3.2	-2.5	3.3	1.5	3.4	2.9	3.0
Current account balance	-20.6	-17.7	-18.7	-14.6	-15.7	-16.3	-16.8	-17.5
Romania								
GDP	4.1	2.3	0.6	3.5	2.6	2.9	3.2	3.9
Current account balance	-7.1	-4.5	-4.5	-1.4	-2.0	-2.5	-2.5	-2.9
Serbia								
GDP	3.7	1.6	-1.5	2.5	-2.0	-0.5	1.5	2.0
Current account balance	-9.5	-9.1	-12.3	-6.5	-6.1	-4.7	-4.3	-4.1

TABLE 2.4   *(continued)*

(Real GDP growth at market prices in percent and current account balance in percent of GDP, unless indicated otherwise)

	00-10[a]	2011	2012	2013	2014e	2015f	2016f	2017f
Tajikistan								
GDP	8.3	7.4	7.5	7.4	6.4	4.2	5.3	6.2
Current account balance	-4.4	-4.7	-1.3	-0.7	-6.1	-5.7	-5.2	-4.7
Turkey								
GDP	3.9	8.8	2.1	4.1	3.1	3.5	3.7	3.9
Current account balance	-3.5	-9.7	-6.2	-7.9	-5.6	-4.5	-4.9	-5.0
Turkmenistan								
GDP	13.6	14.7	11.1	10.2	10.1	10.0	10.4	10.6
Current account balance	5.8	2.0	0.0	0.2	0.6	-1.5	-1.5	-1.7
Ukraine								
GDP	4.3	5.2	0.3	0.0	-8.2	-2.3	3.5	3.8
Current account balance	1.8	-6.3	-8.1	-9.2	-2.7	-2.7	-2.9	-2.7
Uzbekistan								
GDP	6.9	8.3	8.2	8.0	7.9	7.4	8.2	8.1
Current account balance	5.1	5.8	1.2	1.8	1.7	1.5	1.7	1.3

	00-10[a]	2011	2012	2013	2014e	2015f	2016f	2017f
Recently transitioned to high income countries [b]								
Croatia								
GDP	2.4	-0.2	-2.2	-0.9	-0.5	0.5	1.2	1.5
Current account balance	-5.2	-0.9	-0.1	0.9	1.3	1.3	1.2	0.5
Czech Republic								
GDP	3.4	1.9	-1.0	-0.7	2.5	2.7	2.7	2.7
Current account balance	-3.8	-2.9	-1.3	-2.2	-1.3	-0.9	-0.4	-0.6
Estonia								
GDP	3.3	8.3	4.7	1.6	1.9	2.0	2.8	3.6
Current account balance	-8.4	0.0	-2.1	-1.4	-2.8	-3.1	-3.7	-2.5
Latvia								
GDP	4.1	5.3	5.2	4.2	2.5	2.6	3.4	4.1
Current account balance	-9.1	-2.9	-3.3	-2.3	-2.1	-2.2	-2.8	-2.6
Lithuania								
GDP	4.4	6.0	3.7	3.3	2.9	3.2	3.5	3.7
Current account balance	-6.5	-3.7	-0.2	1.6	0.8	-0.4	-1.4	-0.4
Poland								
GDP	3.9	4.5	2.0	1.7	3.2	3.2	3.3	3.5
Current account balance	-4.4	-5.0	-3.7	-1.4	-1.2	-1.6	-1.8	-2.5
Russian Federation								
GDP	4.8	4.3	3.4	1.3	0.7	-2.9	0.1	1.1
Current account balance	8.8	5.1	3.6	1.6	3.1	7.3	4.4	2.1
Slovak Republic								
GDP	4.8	3.0	1.8	1.4	2.4	2.7	3.4	3.4
Current account balance	-4.9	-3.8	2.2	0.8	0.5	0.2	0.3	0.6

Source: World Bank.

World Bank forecasts are frequently updated based on new information and changing (global) circumstances. Consequently, projections presented here may differ from those contained in other Bank documents, even if basic assessments of countries' prospects do not significantly differ at any given moment in time.

Bosnia and Herzegovina and Turkmenistan are not forecast owing to data limitations.

a. GDP growth rates over intervals are compound average; current account balance shares are simple averages over the period.

b. The recently high-income countries are based on World Bank's reclassification from 2004 to 2014.

CHAPTER 2
LATIN AMERICA
& THE CARIBBEAN

Growth in Latin America and the Caribbean slowed markedly to 0.8 percent in 2014 but with diverging developments across the region. South America slowed sharply as domestic factors, exacerbated by China's cooling economy and declining global commodity prices, took their toll on some of the largest economies in the region. In contrast, growth in North and Central America was robust, lifted by strengthening activity in the United States. Strengthening exports on the back of the continued recovery among high-income countries and robust capital flows should lift regional GDP growth to an average of around 2.6 percent in 2015–17. A sharper-than-expected slowdown in China and a steeper decline in commodity prices represent major downward risks to the outlook.

Recent Developments

Aggregate regional growth declined considerably to 0.8 percent in 2014 because of declining commodity prices, a slowdown in major trading partners, and domestic tensions in some of the larger economies (Figure 2.15, Table 2.5). Regional growth was less than a third of that in 2013, and was the slowest in over 13 years, with the exception of 2009. Nevertheless, there were diverging trends across sub-regions and countries. With continued robust expansions in Bolivia, Colombia, Ecuador, and Paraguay and sharp slowdowns in Argentina, Brazil, and República Bolivariana de Venezuela, South America decelerated sharply from 2.9 in 2013 to 0.2 percent in 2014. In contrast, because of its close proximity to a strengthening United States, growth in developing North and Central America picked up to 2.4 percent in 2014, led by Mexico. Underpinned by robust mining exports and services, rapid growth in the Dominican Republic contributed to stronger growth in the Caribbean of 4.6 percent in 2014.

In the region's largest economy, Brazil, protracted declines in commodity prices, weak growth in major trading partners, severe droughts in agricultural areas, election uncertainty, and contracting investment have contributed to a steep decline in growth. The central bank has raised interest rates to fight inflation and credit conditions have tightened. Growth in Brazil is therefore expected to remain weak at least in the short run, with a

contraction in the first half of 2014. Argentina's credit rating downgrade to selective default will hinder access to international capital markets, adding downside risks to its outlook, which was partly mitigated by a bumper soy harvest. Recent sharp declines in oil prices have raised investors' doubts about República Bolivariana de Venezuela's ability to service its debts, pushing yields on its U.S. dollar denominated sovereign bonds to 26 percent, the highest sovereign yield in the world.

With continued strengthening of the United States and the Euro Area recovering slowly, export growth picked

FIGURE 2.15 GDP growth, 2013 and 2014

Growth slowed down in 2014 with divergence among sub-regions

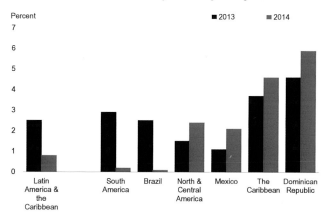

Source: World Bank.
Note: GDP-weighted real GDP growth.

FIGURE 2.16 Exchange rates, 2013–14

The depreciations of mid-2013 have persisted and intensified in some countries in late 2014.

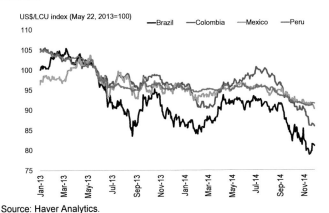

Source: Haver Analytics.

FIGURE 2.17 Impact of declining commodity prices on trade balances, 2013–14

Projected declines in commodity prices are expected to worsen trade balances less than in 2013.

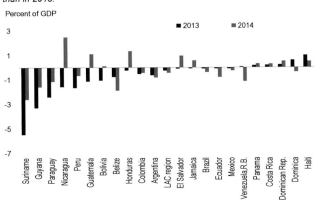

Source: World Bank.
Note: Based on the assumption of a 7 percent annual average decline in oil prices, a 2 percent annual average decline in agricultural commodity prices and a 6 percent annual average decline in metals and minerals prices between 2013 and 2014.

FIGURE 2.18 Gross capital flows, 2013–14

Capital flows initially rebounded from January/February weakness but then softened again on policy uncertainty.

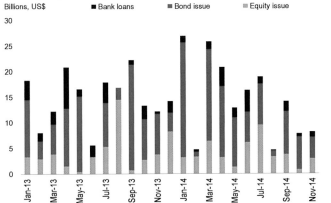

Sources: Dealogic and World Bank.
Note: Gross capital flows includes gross equity and bond issuance and syndicated lending. Secondary trading in securities not included.

up in 2014 despite softening global commodity demand. Aside from trading partner growth, a variety of country-specific factors buoyed exports. These included a bumper soy harvest (Argentina), strong gas production and exports to Argentina and Brazil (Bolivia), and large gold shipments (Dominican Republic). In contrast and as an exception in the region, Brazilian exports contracted modestly because of weak demand in major trading partners Argentina and China.

Substantial currency depreciations since May 2013 have persisted and, in some cases, intensified in late 2014, bolstering competitiveness (Figure 2.16). By end-November 2014, the Colombian peso, Costa Rican colon, Mexican peso, and Peruvian nuevo sol had depreciated, on average, by 10.7 percent in nominal terms and around 5.8 percent in real effective terms since April 2013, just prior to the mid-2013 financial market volatility. The depreciations of the Brazilian real (20.1 percent nominal, 12.2 percent real) and Jamaican dollar (13.1 percent nominal) were especially deep, largely because of investor concerns about macroeconomic imbalances. Following the 18 percent devaluation in late January 2014, the Argentine peso gradually depreciated further throughout the year. Through a new dollar auction system created in early 2014, the Venezuelan government has effectively devalued the bolivar.[1]

Falling commodity prices led to diverging terms of trade effects, especially between oil exporters and oil importers (Figure 2.17). While declining oil, metal, agriculture, and precious metal prices worsened the terms-of-trade for regional commodity exports in 2014 and dented regional exports—although less than in 2013—they improved the terms-of-trade of commodity importers. Nicaragua, in particular, benefited from the rebound in beef and coffee prices, which surged 23–40 percent in 2014, after falling 2013. In contrast, metals price declines hit Suriname, a major exporter of gold and aluminum (around 90 percent of its exports), particularly hard. On balance, the region's current account deficit was broadly stable at about 2.6 percent of GDP in 2014.

---

[1]Public-sector and high priority imports are eligible for the official rate (BsF6.3:US$1), while the private sector may purchase U.S. dollars through one of the two auction system in place: Sicad was created in early 2013 and auctions dollar at the around BsF12:US$1; Sicad 2 was created in early 2014 and auctions dollar at around BsF50:US$1. Additionally, due to difficulties in accessing dollar through these official mechanism, private sector has had buy dollar or on the black market, where the exchange rate is currently around BsF175:US$1. In real effective terms, however, the bolivar has appreciated more than 100 percent because of high inflation rates.

FIGURE 2.19   Monetary policy rates

Except in Brazil and Colombia, monetary policy rates were on hold or lowered since mid-2014.

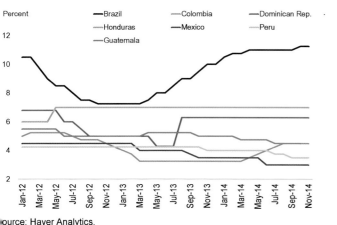

Source: Haver Analytics.

Note: Official (nominal) policy interest rates: Brazil (Selic), Colombia (BDLR Intervention Rate), Dominican Republic (Overnight Rate), Honduras (Monetary Policy Rate), Mexico (Tasa Objetivo), Peru (Tasa de Interés de Referencia), Guatemala (Leading Interest Rate).

FIGURE 2.20   Change in fiscal balances, 2013–14

Structural fiscal deficits widened in an effort to support growth.

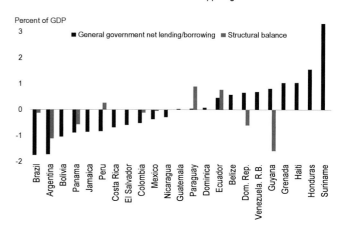

Sources: IMF World Economic Outlook and Brazilian Central Bank.

Note: The structural fiscal balance adjusts the overall fiscal balance for the business cycle and one-off revenues and expenditures.

Gross capital flows to the region slowed significantly in 2014 (Figure 2.18), partly reflecting weak activity. This was largely accounted for by a sharp drop in equity flows to Brazil and Mexico, where weakening growth prospects discouraged investors. In contrast, bond issuance reached the highest volumes on record in late 2014, as prospects of U.S. monetary tightening spurred a surge of refinancing and pre-financing by Latin American borrowers, especially in Brazil and Mexico, which combined accounted for 76 percent of region's total bond issues in 2014.

Amid generally modest inflation, monetary policy continues to be accommodative with recent cuts in Guatemala, Mexico, and Peru to support growth. Policy rates in most countries remained below 3 percent in real terms in 2014 (Figure 2.19), with real rates in a few countries even turning negative. In contrast, the Central Bank of Brazil, citing inflation concerns, resumed tightening after a six-month pause, raising the benchmark Selic rate to 11.75 percent, a cumulative increase of 450 basis points in the tightening cycle that began April 2013. The central bank of Colombia also increased the benchmark interest rate, in several smaller steps, in 2014, from 3.25 percent to 4.5 percent. To support growth in the medium term, monetary policy in the region is expected to remain broadly accommodative provided that inflation pressures remain contained.

Fiscal balances deteriorated and fiscal policy loosened in much of the region in 2014 (Figure 2.20). Amid lower commodity prices, slower growth, and weakening

government revenues, fiscal deficits, on average, widened somewhat from 4.0 percent in 2013 to around 5.2 percent of GDP in 2014. Structural balances deteriorated as governments loosened fiscal policies to support growth. For example, Brazil's fiscal deficit surged in 2014 as the government implemented stimulus measures, including tax breaks and an expansion of public lending to stem the growth slowdown.

Outlook

Aggregate regional growth is expected to accelerate on strengthening exports and investment. The recovery in advanced countries is expected to support external demand growth despite the carefully managed slowdown in China and soft commodity prices. Although financing conditions gradually tighten in the baseline forecast, domestic demand growth should pick up after bottoming out in 2014. On balance, regional growth is expected to further strengthen to 2.6 percent on average over 2015–17. While continuing to be positive, the current outlook is significantly less favorable than the pre-crisis period of 2004–2008, when growth averaged more than 5 percent per annum, driven by the double tailwinds of booming commodity markets and surging external demand.

The Caribbean is projected to lead regional growth, averaging 4.1 percent over 2015–17 (Figure 2.21), benefiting from stronger external demand and rising tourism receipts. Countries in developing North and

FIGURE 2.21 GDP growth, 2014–17

Growth is expected to gradually accelerate in all subregions except the Caribbean.

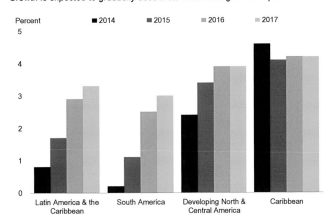

Source: World Bank.
Note: GDP-weighted averages.

Central America are expected to expand at an average of 3.7 percent as potential growth rises on reform dividends. As a result of persistent policy uncertainty and soft commodity prices, South American economies will likely accelerate at a somewhat lower pace, averaging 2.2 percent over the forecast horizon. Across the region, the tilting of growth away from domestic demand towards exports is expected to narrow current account deficits.

The recovery taking hold in advanced economies will strengthen export demand, offsetting the impact of China's adjustment to a more sustainable long-term rate of growth. While there are substantial compositional differences between the export baskets to China and to advanced countries, the increased demand from the latter (mainly manufactures) is projected to more than offset the decline in Chinese demand (mainly primary commodities). In addition, rising tourism receipts will support activity. Competitiveness gains from depreciated local currencies will help some countries gain global market share. Following their fall in 2014, commodity prices are expected to remain soft. Balance of payments pressures for non—energy commodity exporters will be further mitigated by rising remittances from high-income economies. Despite tightening global financial conditions expected for 2015, net capital flows to the region are expected to rise gradually, supporting investment growth.

Domestic constraints among the regions' largest economies are also expected to gradually loosen in the medium term. Despite the removal of electoral uncertainty, uncertainty about monetary and fiscal policies and the structural reform agenda remains elevated in Brazil. However, the baseline forecast for

Brazil assumes that with the new economic team in place, growth-supporting policies will strengthen. In that light, the tepid recovery in the second half of 2014 is expected to continue into 2015, with investment slowly strengthening, as a result of improved investor confidence and the boost to exports created by the depreciated real. In the medium term, however, structural impediments to growth, such as poor infrastructure and cumbersome tax and labor regulations, will continue to subdue growth. While projected to still undergo adjustment and remain weak in 2015, Argentina and República Bolivariana de Venezuela are expected to slowly rein in government expenditures, re-anchor inflation expectations, and thereby reduce inflation. Consumer and investor confidence will gradually return, leading to strengthening domestic demand in the second half of the forecasting horizon.

However, a number of other countries are projected to see favorable developments in the medium term, partially offsetting the slow recovery of the largest countries and lifting regional growth. While the partial withdrawal of Intel will have significant near-term effects on growth, prospects remain positive for Costa Rica in the medium term on robust investment growth, spurred by the Dominican Republic-Central America-United States Free Trade Agreement and supported by increasing economic openness and a business-friendly tax regime. Colombia, the fourth largest recipient of FDI in the region, will continue to be attractive to investors with its sound macroeconomic fundamentals, and continued focus on further improving the business environment, leading to robust fixed investment growth in the medium term. Similarly, despite the continued delay in elections, Haiti is projected to see a modest pickup in growth with strong expansion in construction, industrial output and commerce, and, in particular, apparel exports with the opening of the new Caracol Industrial Park in the northeast.

With the soft oil prices posing substantial downside risks for oil exporters, Ecuador is expected to see even stronger growth from 2016 as new production from the Ishpingo, Tambococha, and Tiputini (ITT) fields comes onstream. Driven by large-scale investment projects, Panama has the most rapid rate of expansion in 2014 in the region. The stimulus provided by public construction is projected to subside in the medium term, especially after the conclusion of the canal expansion in 2016, but should be partially replaced by increased tourism and services exports generated by the expanded canal. Despite the plunge in copper prices, Peru's outlook remains positive on sound macroeconomic policies and substantial commodity wealth. Peruvian GDP growth is expected to rebound sharply in the medium term, supported by government stimulus, implementation of large new infrastructure projects, and two mining mega-projects coming online in the next two years.

Risks

The balance of risks in the Latin America and Caribbean (LAC) region, as in others, leans heavily towards the downside. The downside risks are both external and internal to the region and include the following:

- *Financial volatility.* Tightening global liquidity conditions following the expected first monetary policy hikes in the United States could trigger sharp swings in capital flows and large asset price and exchange rate movements, as investors reappraise long-term returns and attempt to exit less profitable investments. Given a continued strong U.S. dollar, capital flows to the region could stall or reverse, choking off financing for consumer durables and investment, and weighing on growth. Risks will be most pronounced among developing economies where short-term or foreign debt or both represents a large proportion of overall debt, or where credit has been expanding rapidly in recent years.

- *Disorderly slowdown in the region's largest economies.* Three of the region's largest economies, Argentina, República Bolivariana de Venezuela, and to a much less severe extent, Brazil, are currently grappling with elevated inflation in a low-growth environment, and risks to their outlooks are tilted to the downside. Given the systemic nature of these economies in the region, weaker-than-expected growth in one or more of these three economies could have a contagion effect across the region. For example, a disruption to low-priced oil supplies from República Bolivariana de Venezuela, under the Petrocaribe program, could sharply dent activity in some Caribbean and South American countries.

- *Sharper-than-expected decline in commodity prices.* The baseline assumes that commodity prices remain soft, following their slides in late 2014. A sharper-than-expected slowdown in China could lead to more severe declines in commodity prices, which could further erode exports and government revenues of regional commodity exporters and widen current account deficits in the region (Box 2.2). Investment, especially in mining industries, would fall. Countries with higher shares of commodity exports would be more sensitive

FIGURE 2.22 Share of commodities in total exports, 2010–12 average

Countries with large shares of commodity exports will be more sensitive to commodity price declines.

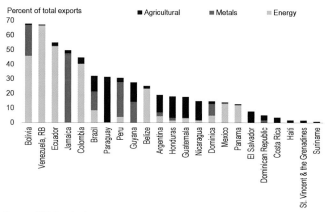

Source: UN Comtrade.
Note: Using a consistent cross-country methodology; may differ from country sources (e.g. for Peru) that use a different classification or more updated data.

to commodity price declines (Figure 2.22). However, lower oil prices in the medium term will represent an upside risk for oil-importing economies in the region.

- *Escalation in violence.* The region remains one of the most violent in the world. Compared to the global average murder rate of 6.2 per 100,000 population, the murder rate in South America, Central America, and the Caribbean are around 24, 26, and 19 respectively (United Nations Office on Drugs and Crime, 2014). If crime and violence escalate, the region's business environment will turn less conducive and become a drag on investment and economic growth in the medium and extended term.

Policy Challenges

Tax revenues in the region remain overreliant on indirect taxes, which are regressive, and on commodity exports, which are volatile and leave public finances heavily exposed to external shocks. Across the region, reforms are needed to simplify and rebalance the complex tax systems, so as to reduce incentives to shift to informal economic activities and to achieve a more resilient revenue base.

Underdeveloped infrastructure is another major constraint on the region's ability to achieve higher sustained growth. Public investment in infrastructure has never recovered from the substantial cuts made under the stabilization programs of the 1990s. Regional infrastructure investment averaged 2.7 percent of GDP per annum in the last decade. However, an investment of 6.2 percent of GDP is estimated to be required to satisfy the region's infrastructure demand in the period 2012–20 (ECLAC, 2014). To ease fiscal constraints, recent efforts to increase infrastructure investment include greater private sector involvement, for example, through public-private partnerships.

A key concern for the region is that slower long-term growth—around 2–3 percent per annum—might become the "new normal." The past 15 years may, ex post, turn out to have been a double tailwind era—booming commodity market and rapidly growing export demand. With this era fading, economies near or at full employment, and domestic credit growth slowing, the region must sustain long-term growth through enhanced productivity growth. The quality of the workforce, especially in the informal sector, needs to be upgraded; research, development, and innovation fostered; and more competitive environment, especially in the service sector, nurtured.

Several governments have proceeded to implemented reforms, although often slowly and in an uncoordinated manner, partly as a result of fragile governments. Mexico, the Dominican Republic, and Chile have had particular reform momentum.

- In Mexico, a number of reforms were signed into law in 2013 and 2014, including education, energy, and telecommunications reforms. Full implementation should remove some of Mexico's binding constraints to growth.

- The Dominican Republic is pursuing education, labor, energy, and fiscal pacts, with the first already agreed, and other reforms currently under discussion.

- Chile enacted a tax reform in September 2014 that is expected to yield additional revenue. The government is now focused on education reform and the pension system.

TABLE 2.5   Latin America and the Caribbean forecast summary

(Annual percent change unless indicated otherwise)

	00-10ᵃ	2011	2012	2013	2014e	2015f	2016f	2017f
GDP at market pricesᵇ	3.3	4.2	2.6	2.5	0.8	1.7	2.9	3.3
(Average including countries with full national accounts and balance of payments data only)ᶜ								
GDP at market pricesᶜ	3.3	4.2	2.6	2.5	0.8	1.7	2.9	3.3
GDP per capita	1.9	3.0	1.4	1.4	-0.3	0.7	1.9	2.2
PPP GDP	3.2	4.4	2.7	2.7	1.1	2.0	3.1	3.4
Private consumption	3.6	5.1	4.1	3.2	0.9	1.5	2.3	2.7
Public consumption	3.3	3.0	4.1	2.6	2.4	1.6	2.3	2.4
Fixed investment	4.8	8.0	2.0	2.2	-2.3	1.7	4.2	5.0
Exports, GNFSᵈ	2.8	6.8	3.1	0.9	2.0	3.3	4.2	4.7
Imports, GNFSᵈ	5.7	11.0	4.8	2.6	0.5	2.2	3.2	3.9
Net exports, contribution to growth	-0.4	-0.8	-0.4	-0.4	0.3	0.2	0.2	0.1
Current account balance (percent of GDP)	-0.5	-1.5	-1.8	-2.5	-2.6	-2.8	-2.5	-2.2
Consumer prices (annual average)	7.0	7.5	6.7	9.8	13.9	...	...	...
Fiscal balance (percent of GDP)	-2.6	-3.1	-3.6	-4.0	-5.2	-4.2	-4.1	-4.1
Memo items: GDP								
Broader geographic region (incl. recently high income countries)ᵉ	3.3	4.2	2.7	2.6	0.9	1.8	2.9	3.3
South Americaᶠ	3.7	4.2	2.1	2.9	0.2	1.1	2.5	3.0
Developing Central and North Americaᵍ	2.0	4.2	4.1	1.5	2.4	3.4	3.9	3.9
Caribbeanʰ	3.4	2.8	2.0	3.7	4.6	4.1	4.2	4.2
Brazil	3.6	2.7	1.0	2.5	0.1	1.0	2.5	2.7
Mexico	1.8	4.0	4.0	1.1	2.1	3.3	3.8	3.8
Argentina ⁱ	3.8	8.6	0.9	2.9	-1.5	-0.3	1.6	3.1

Source: World Bank.

World Bank forecasts are frequently updated based on new information and changing (global) circumstances. Consequently, projections presented here may differ from those contained in other Bank documents, even if basic assessments of countries' prospects do not differ at any given moment in time.

a. Growth rates over intervals are compound weighted averages; average growth contributions, ratios and deflators are calculated as simple averages of the annual weighted averages for the region.

b. GDP at market prices and expenditure components are measured in constant 2010 U.S. dollars.

c. Sub-region aggregate excludes Cuba, Grenada, and Suriname, for which data limitations prevent the forecasting of GDP components or balance of payments details.

d. Exports and imports of goods and non-factor services (GNFS).

e. Recently high-income countries include Chile, Trinidad and Tobago, and Uruguay.

f. South America: Argentina, Bolivia, Brazil, Colombia, Ecuador, Guyana, Paraguay, Peru, Venezuela

g. Developing Central & North America: Costa Rica, Guatemala, Honduras, Mexico, Nicaragua, Panama, El Salvador.

h. Caribbean: Belize, Dominica, Dominican Republic, Haiti, Jamaica, St. Lucia, St. Vincent and the Grenadines.

i. Preliminary for long-term average. Data was recently rebased; missing data up to 2003 was spliced with the earlier data.

TABLE 2.6   Latin America and the Caribbean country forecast

(Real GDP growth at market prices in percent and current account balance in percent of GDP, unless indicated otherwise)

	00-10[a]	2011	2012	2013	2014e	2015f	2016f	2017f
Argentina [b]								
GDP	3.8	8.6	0.9	2.9	-1.5	-0.3	1.6	3.1
Current account balance	1.8	-0.7	-0.2	-0.8	-1.4	-1.2	-0.7	-0.1
Belize								
GDP	4.0	2.1	4.0	0.7	2.6	2.6	2.7	2.8
Current account balance	-11.8	-1.1	-1.2	-4.5	-5.3	-6.2	-6.4	-6.5
Bolivia								
GDP	3.8	5.2	5.2	6.8	5.3	4.5	4.3	4.0
Current account balance	4.0	2.2	7.9	4.3	2.3	-0.2	-1.3	-2.0
Brazil								
GDP	3.6	2.7	1.0	2.5	0.1	1.0	2.5	2.7
Current account balance	-0.9	-2.1	-2.4	-3.6	-3.8	-3.6	-3.4	-3.2
Colombia								
GDP	4.1	6.6	4.0	4.7	4.7	4.4	4.3	4.3
Current account balance	-1.5	-2.9	-3.1	-3.2	-4.0	-4.3	-4.0	-3.7
Costa Rica								
GDP	4.4	4.5	5.1	3.5	3.7	4.1	4.2	4.5
Current account balance	-4.8	-5.4	-5.3	-4.9	-4.7	-4.1	-4.0	-3.8
Dominica								
GDP	2.6	0.2	-1.1	0.8	1.5	1.3	1.5	1.6
Current account balance	-18.6	-14.5	-18.9	-16.6	-17.0	-16.1	-15.2	-14.0
Dominican Republic								
GDP	4.9	2.9	2.6	4.6	5.9	4.9	4.7	4.7
Current account balance	-3.5	-7.9	-6.8	-4.1	-3.4	-3.1	-2.9	-2.8
Ecuador								
GDP	4.1	7.8	5.1	4.5	4.0	3.8	4.3	5.0
Current account balance	0.1	-0.4	-0.4	-1.3	-0.2	-2.9	-1.8	-0.6
El Salvador								
GDP	1.9	2.2	1.9	1.7	1.9	2.4	2.7	2.9
Current account balance	-4.1	-4.8	-5.4	-6.5	-5.9	-5.8	-5.7	-5.6
Guatemala								
GDP	3.3	4.2	3.0	3.7	3.5	3.6	3.6	3.5
Current account balance	-4.3	-3.4	-2.6	-2.7	-2.0	-1.9	-1.8	-1.7
Guyana								
GDP	2.4	5.4	4.8	5.2	3.6	3.7	3.8	4.0
Current account balance	-10.1	-13.1	-11.6	-12.9	-15.4	-15.3	-15.0	-14.6
Haiti								
GDP	0.1	5.5	2.9	4.3	3.6	3.8	4.1	4.1
Current account balance	1.3	-4.3	-5.7	-6.7	-6.2	-6.1	-5.9	-5.8
Honduras								
GDP	4.1	3.8	4.1	2.6	3.0	3.0	3.3	3.5
Current account balance	-6.6	-8.0	-8.5	-9.5	-7.1	-6.8	-6.6	-6.6
Jamaica [c]								
GDP	0.7	1.7	-0.6	0.6	0.9	1.1	2.2	2.5
Current account balance	-9.8	-13.4	-13.0	-11.1	-8.4	-7.1	-5.9	-5.0
Mexico								
GDP	1.8	4.0	4.0	1.1	2.1	3.3	3.8	3.8
Current account balance	-1.4	-1.1	-1.3	-2.1	-2.1	-2.4	-2.2	-2.2

TABLE 2.6   *(continued)*

(Real GDP grow th at market prices in percent and current account balance in percent of GDP, unless indicated otherw ise)

	00-10[a]	2011	2012	2013	2014e	2015f	2016f	2017f
Nicaragua [b]								
GDP	2.8	5.7	5.0	4.6	4.2	4.4	4.5	4.3
Current account balance	-12.4	-12.8	-12.7	-11.4	-10.8	-9.2	-9.5	-10.1
Panam a								
GDP	6.3	10.9	10.8	8.4	6.5	6.1	5.8	5.6
Current account balance	-5.2	-15.9	-10.6	-11.9	-12.3	-12.0	-11.1	-10.0
Paraguay								
GDP	3.4	4.3	-1.2	14.2	4.0	4.3	4.3	4.6
Current account balance	1.5	-1.1	-0.9	2.1	1.1	-1.1	-0.6	-0.7
Peru [b]								
GDP	5.6	6.5	6.0	5.8	2.4	4.8	5.5	5.9
Current account balance	-0.9	-1.9	-3.3	-4.5	-4.8	-4.2	-3.9	-3.6
St. Lucia								
GDP	1.8	1.2	-1.6	-0.4	-1.0	-0.6	0.8	1.4
Current account balance	-18.1	-18.9	-14.2	-7.4	-7.7	-8.6	-9.4	-10.0
St. Vincent and the Grenadines								
GDP	2.9	-0.5	1.2	1.7	1.5	2.6	2.9	3.4
Current account balance	-19.9	-29.4	-31.1	-32.9	-33.5	-33.0	-32.4	-31.6
Venezuela, RB								
GDP	3.1	4.2	5.6	1.3	-3.0	-2.0	0.5	1.5
Current account balance	9.0	7.7	2.9	2.5	2.0	-0.3	-0.5	-0.6

Source: World B ank.
World Bank forecasts are frequently updated based on new information and changing (global) circumstances. Consequently, projections
presented here may differ from those contained in other B ank documents, even if basic assessments of countries' prospects do not significantly
differ at any given moment in time.
Cuba, Grenada, St. Kitts and Nevis, and Suriname are not forecast owing to data limitations.
a. GDP growth rates over intervals are compound average; current account balance shares are simple averages over the period.
b. Preliminary for long-term average. Data was recently rebased; missing earlier data was spliced with the previous series.
c. Fiscal year basis.

	00-10[a]	2011	2012	2013	2014e	2015f	2016f	2017f
Recently transitioned to high income countries [b]								
Chile								
GDP	4.1	5.8	5.5	4.2	1.7	2.9	3.8	4.2
Current account balance	0.8	-1.4	-3.5	-3.4	-1.7	-1.1	-1.3	-1.3
Trinidad and Tobago								
GDP	5.7	-2.6	1.2	1.6	2.1	2.3	2.5	2.6
Current account balance	16.2	12.4	5.0	11.8	10.5	10.3	10.2	10.1
Uruguay								
GDP	2.9	7.3	3.7	4.4	2.9	3.3	3.5	3.1
Current account balance	-1.3	-2.9	-5.4	-5.4	-5.5	-4.9	-4.5	-4.0

Source: World B ank.
World B ank forecasts are frequently updated based on new information and changing (global) circumstances. Consequently, projections
presented here may differ from those contained in other B ank documents, even if basic assessments of countries' prospects do not significantly
differ at any given moment in time.
a. GDP growth rates over intervals are compound average; current account balance shares are simple averages over the period.
b. The recently high-income countries are based on World B ank's country reclassification from 2004 to 2014.

BOX 2.2   What does a slowdown in China mean for Latin America and the Caribbean?[1]

Growth in Latin America and the Caribbean (LAC) has become increasingly dependent on activity in China, partly as a result of heavy reliance on commodity exports. A 1 percentage point deceleration of growth in China has been associated with a 0.6 percentage point slowing of growth in the LAC region.

FIGURE B2.2.1   Correlations between China and Latin America and the Caribbean

Growth in LAC region has increasingly become tied to growth in China.

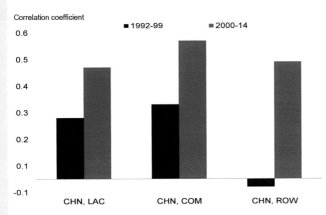

Source: World Bank calculations.
Note: "CHN, LAC" refers to the correlation between China's GDP growth and Latin America and the Caribbean's GDP growth; correlation coefficients are statistically significant at 5 percent for both periods. "CHN, COM" refers to the correlation between China's GDP growth and metal commodity prices; correlation coefficients are statistically significant at 5 percent only for the second period (2000-2014). "CHN, ROW" refers to the correlation between China's GDP growth and the rest of the world's GDP growth; correlation coefficients are statistically significant at 5 percent only for the second period (2000-14). Estimations are based on quarterly data covering 1992Q2 -2014Q2.

FIGURE B2.2.2   Share of exports from Latin America and the Caribbean to China and the United States

China has become an increasingly important export destination for LAC countries while the share of exports to the United States has declined.

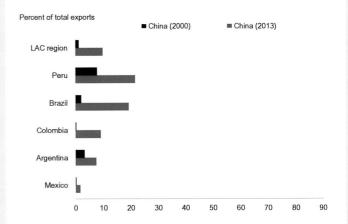

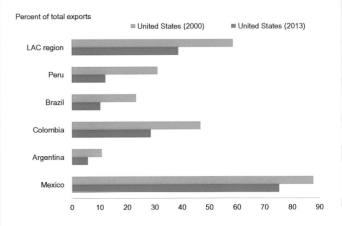

Source: World Bank calculations based on Comtrade (2014).
Note: LAC refers to low- and middle-income countries in Latin America and the Caribbean.

Growth in Latin America and the Caribbean (LAC) received a substantial boost from China in the first decade of the 2000s through growing trade, investment, and commodity market linkages. As linkages between China and LAC have strengthened, their business cycles have also become more correlated (Figure B2.2.1). During the same period, global commodity prices and activity have also become more closely aligned with Chinese growth dynamics. The carefully managed slowdown in China expected over the near term, however, may dampen growth and pose policy challenges for the LAC region.

This box briefly documents the growing linkages between LAC and China and analyzes the implications for the region of the slowdown in China.

Linkages between LAC and China

There are two main channels through which China's growth performance has spurred activity in LAC: (i) directly, as trade, and to some extent, foreign direct investment (FDI) from China to several LAC countries have increased; and (ii) indirectly, as

---

[1] The main authors of this box are Young Il Choi, Marcio Cruz, and Raju Huidrom.

BOX 2.2   *(continued)*

the economic expansion in China has contributed to higher global commodity prices, raising receipts for many LAC commodity exporters not only from exports to China, but also to the rest of the world.[2]

China's rapid growth has coincided with a sharp increase in its trade with LAC.[3] The share of the region's exports going to China increased by tenfold between 2000 and 2013 (Figure B2.2.2). China's impact on the export profile of Argentina, Brazil, Colombia, and Peru has been particularly large, although there is some distinction in the types of products China imports from these countries. Argentina, Uruguay, and Paraguay export predominantly agricultural products to China, whereas Chile and Peru export mostly metals and Colombia and República Bolivariana de Venezuela export mainly oil. Brazil exports a large share of both its agricultural and mineral production to China. While the region's trade linkages with the United States have weakened over time, they remain quite strong. Although FDI from China to the LAC region has risen, it remains relatively small.[4]

Since the early 2000s, rapid expansion of the Chinese economy has played an important role in the steady growth of global commodity prices (World Bank, 2014e). China's imports of some commodities have risen significantly, and many of these are produced in LAC (Figure B2.2.3).[5] A slowdown in China could reduce demand for commodities and soften their prices, especially of metals that are heavily used in industrial production. This could weaken growth in commodity-exporting countries, including those in LAC.

Near-term effects of slowdown in China

To better understand the possible short- and medium-term effects that a slowdown in China could have on the LAC region, a simple structural vector auto regression (SVAR) model is estimated using data over 1992Q2–2014Q2 with the following variables: rest of world's gross domestic product (GDP) growth, world interest rate (proxied by the U.S. federal funds rate),

___

[2] There are other direct and indirect linkages between LAC and China (World Bank, 2011). For example, low cost production of labor-intensive goods in China may have contributed to global disinflationary pressures over the 2000s.

[3] Trade between LAC and China has picked up from a low base, after the accession of China as a member of the World Trade Organization, in 2001.

[4] FDI from China is significant in República Bolivariana de Venezuela (accounting for an average of more than 11 percent of total FDI between 2010 and 2012). There is little evidence that FDI from China has a significant impact on overall FDI to LAC (Garcia-Herrero et. al. 2008).

[5] Baffes and Savescu (2014) and Roache (2012) documented that China plays a key role in global base metal markets.

FIGURE B2.2.3   Shares of global commodity trade, 2012

LAC countries account for a significant share of global commodity exports.

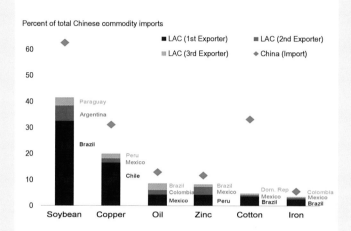

Source: World Bank calculations based on Comtrade (2014).
Note: The green diamonds refer to China's share of global imports and the bars refer to the shares of the top three Latin America and Caribbean exporters in global exports with respect to soybean, copper, oil, zinc, cotton and iron.

FIGURE B2.2.4   Growth response of a 1 percentage point decline in China's growth

A growth slowdown in China would sharply reduce growth in some LAC countries.

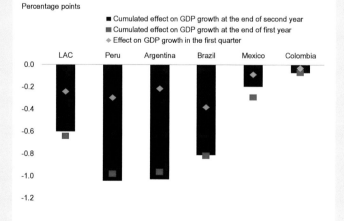

Source: World Bank estimations.
Note: Results for the cumulated effect on GDP growth at the end of first and second years are statistically significant at the 16th–84th percentile range based on 2000 draws for LAC, Peru, Argentina, and Brazil.

BOX 2.2   *(continued)*

China's GDP growth, LAC's GDP growth; world trade, and commodity prices (proxied by an index of metal prices).[6]

A slowdown in China is indeed associated with slower growth in the LAC region, which experiences a 0.6 percentage point reduction in GDP over a horizon of two years in response to a 1 percentage point reduction in China's growth (Figure B2.2.4).[7] A slowdown in China, by reducing demand for commodities, also adversely affects commodity prices: they decline by as much as 5 percentage points over two years when growth in China slows by 1 percentage point. The findings related to commodities suggest that commodity markets are an important channel for the transmission of a slowdown in China to the region.

Additional models are estimated to analyze the impact of a slowdown in China on select Latin American economies: Argentina, Brazil, Colombia, Mexico, and Peru.[8] The results indicate that a 1 percentage point decline in China's GDP tends to have a strong, statistically significant impact on Argentina, Brazil, and Peru whereas the impact on Colombia and Mexico is much weaker and not statistically significant (Figure B2.2.4). These results point to a complementary economic relationship between some of the largest Latin American commodity exporters and China and a potentially competitive relationship between Mexico and China for export markets, especially for manufactured goods going to the United States (Hanson, 2012).

Long-term challenges and opportunities

Growth in China has slowed since 2010, and this trend is expected to continue in the long term as a rebalancing away from credit-fueled investment toward consumption and services proceeds (World Bank, 2014f; Eichengreen et. al., 2012). Over a longer time horizon than that considered in the models here, the projected rebalancing of China's economy toward consumption and services is also likely to lower the growth of global demand for some commodities, such as copper, lead, tin, and aluminum (Roache, 2012; Ahuja and Nabar, 2012; Baffes and Savescu, 2014) proportionately more than for others, such as soybeans, corn, and meat (Westcott and Trostle, 2014). As a result, countries that are heavily dependent on metal exports will likely experience sharper growth headwinds than those that rely more on agricultural exports.

At the same time, structural changes underway in China's economy may provide opportunities for the region, regarding commodities, manufacturing, tradable services, and FDI (World Bank, 2014f). These include the potential increase in food prices if growing per capita incomes in China raises food demand, a potential increase in demand for services as China's population

ages, improving relative competitiveness of LAC countries as Chinese labor cost rise, and possibly rising FDI from China.

Conclusions

With the slowing of China's economy likely to have negative effects on LAC economies in the short and medium term, pushing forward with reforms aimed at increasing productivity and ensuring sustainable growth, as well as raising the odds that countries in the region benefit from new opportunities that may come with structural changes in China, becomes more urgent (World Bank, 2011a). First, it is critical to consolidate the improvements in macroeconomic management achieved in the last two decades. Second, supply-side measures are needed to increase savings and enable greater investment in infrastructure (World Bank, 2014g). Third, although LAC countries have made significant advances over the last few decades in raising access to education, as measured by years of schooling, the region needs to address lags in the quality of education (Barro and Lee, 2010; Programme for International Student Assessment, 2012). Ensuring continued improvements in human capital will be critical to seizing opportunities related to trade in services. Finally, there is substantial potential to improve the business environment as LAC economies still exhibit among the longest times needed to comply with tax obligations, obtain construction permits, and start a new business (World Bank, 2014h).

---

[6] All variables are seasonally adjusted and transformed into log differences (Q-o-Q). The identification is based on a Cholesky decomposition with the variables ordered as listed, which is based on the presumed exogeneity or predetermination of variables. For instance, global GDP and global interest rates are presumably more exogenous than China's GDP in the VAR system, and hence ordered before China's GDP. Rest of world real GDP refers to global GDP minus the combined GDP of China and LAC countries. World trade volume is estimated using import data. LAC's GDP corresponds to the summed GDP of 10 countries in the region (Argentina, Bolivia, Brazil, Colombia, Costa Rica, Ecuador, Guatemala, Mexico, Peru and Paraguay) for which quarterly data over the 1992Q2-2014Q2 period are available; these economies represent close to 90 percent of total GDP (in 2013 U.S. dollars) of low- and middle- income countries (according to the World Bank's classification) in the Latin America and Caribbean region.

[7] This result is broadly in line with those of other studies using different types of models. Gruss (2014), for example, reports that a 1 percentage point reduction in China's growth rate is associated with a growth decline of 1/2 percentage point over the following three years on average for commodity exporters in Latin America. In addition, the Inter-American Development Bank (2014) considers the risk of a slowdown in China's growth, and projects a negative effect on the Latin America and Caribbean region's economic performance lasting more than 1.5 years.

[8] These five economies are the largest Latin America and the Caribbean economies for which quarterly data are available. The variables used to estimate the five country-specific SVARs are the same as those used to estimate the first SVAR except that the data for Latin America and Caribbean's GDP growth is replaced by GDP growth data for the individual country being considered.

CHAPTER 2

MIDDLE EAST
& NORTH AFRICA

Following years of turmoil, some economies in the Middle East and North Africa appear to be stabilizing, although growth remains fragile and uneven. Growth in oil-importing countries was broadly flat in 2014, while activity in oil-exporting countries recovered slightly after contracting in 2013. Fiscal and external imbalances remain significant. Growth is expected to pick up gradually to 3.5 percent in 2017. Risks from regional turmoil and from the volatile price of oil are considerable; political transitions and security challenges persist. Measures to address long-standing structural challenges have been repeatedly delayed and high unemployment remains a key challenge. Lower oil prices offer an opportunity to remove the region's heavy energy subsidies both in oil-importing and oil-exporting countries alike.

Recent Developments

Growth in the developing countries of the Middle East and North Africa recovered in 2014 to 1.2 percent (Table 2.7).[1] The preceding year had been marked by domestic and regional turmoil, weak external demand, and stagnant activity. Improvements in confidence (Arab Republic of Egypt, Tunisia), manufacturing and exports (Egypt, Morocco), as well as a bottoming out of oil production, contributed to the pick-up in growth. This modest upturn, however, remains fragile, and output still languishes well below the region's potential. Structural reforms needed to spur growth, reduce unemployment and alleviate poverty remain unaddressed. While there has been progress on the political transition in Tunisia and greater stability in Egypt, others remain mired in tensions. Security challenges and/or resulting spillovers in several countries are a key source of instability, with security risks affecting an estimated 20 percent of regional GDP (Iraq, Jordan, Lebanon, Libya, Syrian Arab Republic, Republic of Yemen), and political transition affecting another 20 percent (Egypt, Tunisia). Fiscal and external accounts

remain weak, even in countries that have received exceptional official support from the high-income Gulf Cooperation Council (GCC) countries.

In *oil-importing* developing countries, economic activity appears to be picking up (Figure 2.23) as a weak first quarter was followed by a rebound in the second and third quarters. Growth, on average, is estimated to have been flat at 2.6 percent in 2014. However, it has been fragile and uneven. Egypt especially benefited from greater stability and large-scale financial support from the

FIGURE 2.23 Oil importers, GDP growth

Growth has picked up in oil importers but is uneven.

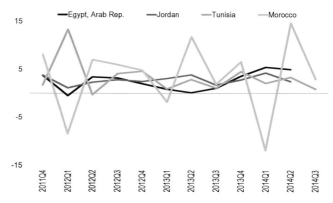

Sources: Haver Analytics and World Bank.
Note: Seasonally adjusted and annualized data.

---

[1]This chapter covers low- and middle-income countries of the Middle East and North Africa region while high-income Gulf Cooperation Council (GCC) countries are excluded. The developing countries are further divided into two groups; oil importers and oil exporters. Developing oil importers are: Djibouti, the Arab Republic of Egypt, Jordan, Lebanon, Morocco, Tunisia, and West Bank and Gaza. Developing oil exporters are: Algeria, the Islamic Republic of Iran, Iraq, Libya, the Syrian Arab Republic, and the Republic of Yemen.

FIGURE 2.24 Industrial production

Industrial production rebounded, especially in Egypt where it was supported by greater stability.

Percent change, 3-month moving average, annualized rate

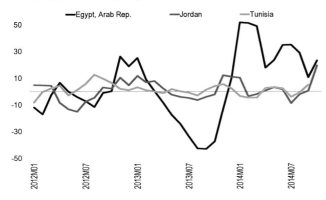

Sources: Haver Analytics and World Bank.

FIGURE 2.25 Oil production

Oil production has recovered but remains fragile given large security challenges.

Million barrels per day

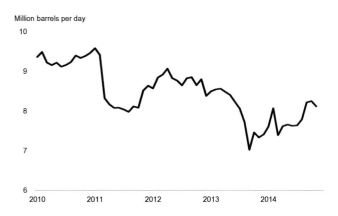

Source: International Energy Agency.

GCC for investment programs. As a result, industrial production rebounded sharply (Figure 2.24) and the purchasing managers' indexes (PMIs) indicated marked improvements in confidence.

The recovery has been less robust in Tunisia, Jordan, and Lebanon. Tunisia's political transition accelerated in 2014, with the adoption of the new constitution and general elections, but external demand, tourism and investment have yet to recover. In Morocco, nonagricultural output remained buoyant, driven by private consumption and a surge in exports of manufactured goods (including cars and electrical items) and phosphates. In Lebanon, however, despite some acceleration, activity, exports, and sentiment remain depressed, reflecting spillovers from the conflict in Syria, and political uncertainty. Lebanon's PMI pointed to a contraction in business activity for the 16th consecutive month, with security issues weighing heavily on tourist arrivals, and harming domestic wholesale and hospitality industries.

In *oil-exporting* developing countries, output has stopped contracting but remains highly volatile. After contracting by 0.8 percent in 2013, activity rebounded slightly by 0.3 percent in 2014. Oil production was disrupted in the first half of 2014, but has stabilized at around 8 million barrels per day (mb/d)—25 percent below the pre–Arab Spring average (Figure 2.25). Security setbacks have affected production in Iraq, Libya, and the Republic of Yemen while sanctions have limited output in the Islamic Republic of Iran. The Islamic State of Iraq and Levant (ISIL) insurgency captured large swaths of territory in Iraq, disrupting production in the north of the country. Production in

the country's larger oil fields in the south has not been affected. In fact, despite the insurgency, Iraq's production in 2014 increased, averaging 3.3 mb/d though November, up from 3.1 mb/d in 2013. Before the advance of ISIL, Iraq was expected to account for 60 percent of OPEC's additional capacity in the next five years. However, this may be set back by the unstable security situation. In Libya, oil output recovered in November to about 0.7 mb/d, up from 0.2 mb/d from the first half 2014 as the year-long blockade of the eastern oil export terminals has been lifted. However, political tensions have increased and the security situation has deteriorated as armed groups and two parliaments are vying for control of the country. The recovery remains tenuous as security risks persist.

Fiscal deficits have widened in the wake of the Arab Spring. In 2014, they reached 7.1 percent of regional GDP compared with 6 percent in 2013. Revenues were weak while expenditures on public sector wages and general subsidies—a large share of fiscal expenditures—have increased rapidly.

- Facing fiscal pressures and to sustain priority spending, *oil importers* have cut government investment and borrowed from domestic banks. Partly as a result of gradual subsidy reforms, fiscal deficits fell, on average, by 1 percentage point to 10 percent of GDP in 2014. These were partially funded by exceptional official financing from GCC countries (U.S. $22 billion).

- In virtually all *oil exporters*, fiscal deficits have emerged or widened as production declined or was disrupted in the first half of 2014, with some recovery in the second half. Especially in the last quarter of 2014, oil prices fell sharply and below fiscal break-even points (the prices at which budgets would be balanced) for most developing oil exporters (Figure 2.26). The fiscal deterioration was most acute in Libya and the Republic of Yemen as internal strife curtailed oil output and revenues compared to 2013.

Gross capital flows to the region slowed in 2014, as a sharp rise in bank lending only partially offset weak bond and equity flows. Four countries (Jordan, Lebanon, Morocco, and Tunisia) have been able to raise funds in international bond markets, although bond issuance from Jordan and Tunisia had to be guaranteed by the U.S. government and the Japan Bank of International Cooperation while Morocco benefited indirectly from having an active IMF program. Many of the region's economies lack access to international capital markets because of geopolitical risk and economic uncertainty. However, there are signs of a nascent increase in investor interest in Egypt, as the economy is recovering and as increased support from GCC countries has helped ease foreign-exchange shortages. Overall, however, net FDI remains well below pre-Arab Spring inflows and is projected to recover to those levels only late in the forecast period.

Remittances to the region increased in 2014 by about 3 percent. After the sharp fall in 2013, remittance flows to Egypt stabilized in 2014, in part because of heavy interest in purchasing investment certificates for the expansion of the Suez Canal available to Egyptian citizens only. Egyptian and Tunisian migrant workers began to return from Libya in 2014 as the security situation deteriorated, but in smaller numbers than in 2011.

Outlook

Growth in the developing countries of the region is projected to pick up gradually to 3.5 percent in 2017, helped by a rebound in oil production among oil exporters and a modest recovery among oil importing economies. Egypt, Jordan, and, to lesser extent, Lebanon and Tunisia, appear to be entering a steady recovery from a period of heightened volatility and uncertainty (Table 2.8). Other countries in the region, such as Iraq, Libya, and, the Republic of Yemen continue to be affected adversely by security challenges.

In the baseline scenario, only limited improvement is expected in the political uncertainty and lack of security

FIGURE 2.26 Oil producers' fiscal breakeven prices

Oil exporters in the region are under fiscal pressure because of volatile production and weak oil prices.

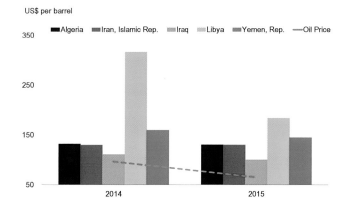

US$ per barrel

Source: IMF.
Note: Oil price is the average of West Texas Intermediate, Dubai, and Brent. Libya's fiscal break-even price spiked in 2014 because of output disruptions.

that has plagued the region for the past four years. As a result, although growth is expected to pick up, the recovery is not sufficient to make deep inroads into spare capacity and unemployment. The region needs to create 4 million jobs per year to keep the unemployment rate from rising (World Bank, 2014i). Historically, the region created jobs near this rate only when growth was in excess of 5 percent (World Bank, 2014i).

- Among *oil exporters*, growth is expected to firm to about 3.1 percent by 2017 as some improvements in security allow an increase in oil output. The baseline outlook for the Islamic Republic of Iran assumes a partial easing of the sanctions in line with steps taken to date. Following their sharp decline in 2014, oil prices are expected to remain soft in 2015 but rise modestly in the medium term. In turn, this will steady fiscal positions and support domestic demand.

- Among *oil importers*, the baseline outlook is for a gradual improvement in growth driven by increasing investment. Aggregate growth for the subregion is expected to pick up to about 4.1 percent by 2017, close to but still below the historical average. Consumption will be underpinned by large public outlays on wages and increased remittances. A reduction in and improved targeting of general subsidies will make room for increased public investment.

Risks

The outlook is subject to significant downside risks that are mostly internal to the region.

Violence in Syria could escalate and spill over to other countries (mainly Iraq, Jordan, and Lebanon). More than 3 million Syrian refugees are hosted in the neighboring countries, with officially registered refugees in Lebanon and Jordan amounting to about 25 percent and 10 percent of local populations. Actual numbers are likely to be even higher. In Iraq, the number of internally displaced persons because of ISIL's advance has reached 2 million in 2014 or 6 percent of the population. Social as well as external and fiscal pressures are high for these countries and could be exacerbated further should the civil war in Syria and its spillover to Iraq intensify. Setbacks in political transitions or an escalation of violence in Egypt, Iraq, Libya, Tunisia, and the Republic of Yemen would undermine confidence and delay necessary structural reforms as well as reduce oil output. On the upside, restoration of political stability and policy certainty that leads to sustained attention to structural reforms could substantially boost confidence and return growth to the long-run potential.

Debt rollover and refinancing risks are rising. Countries in political transition have benefited from large official financing from the Gulf economies. While these are expected to continue, the associated debt will become increasingly burdensome and presents a rollover risk for recipient countries. Public debt levels have increased in oil-importing countries from 73 to 88 percent of GDP during 2011–14. They may be approaching unsustainable levels as debt servicing costs account for an ever larger share of the expenditures.

External risks are also tilted to the downside. A weaker-than-expected recovery in the Euro Area could reduce exports, tourism, remittances, and capital flows in North Africa. In addition, sharply tightening or persistently volatile global financial conditions could raise risk premia for developing countries, raising borrowing costs and at the same time lowering FDI.

A sharper- or longer-than-projected decline in oil prices could lead to a significant deterioration in external and fiscal accounts of oil-exporting countries (although benefiting, more vulnerable, oil importers). This could be triggered by a return to the market of some 1.5 mb/d of idle capacity in the Islamic Republic of Iran and Libya, at a time of a surging unconventional North American production and moderating demand in Europe and Asia.

A permanent 10 percent oil price drop could cut GDP growth by 0.8–2.5 percentage points in the developing oil exporters of the region in the first year (World Bank, 2013b; Berument, Ceylan, and Dogan, 2010). Current account balances would deteriorate by 1.8 percent of GDP and fiscal balances would weaken by 1.0 percent of GDP (World Bank, 2013a). While this would benefit oil importers in the region, the impact would be limited. Their growth would improve by 0.3 percentage point on average, while current and fiscal accounts would improve by 0.3 percent and 0.1 percent of GDP, respectively (World Bank, 2013a).

Conversely, a sharp rise in geopolitical risk could disrupt oil supplies leading to a temporary oil price spike. Iraq is poised for a material increase in output in the forecast period, but the deteriorating security situation could spread to core production facilities so far unaffected. Intensifying turmoil in Libya could further disrupt oil production and exports, while deteriorating prospects for an international agreement with Iran could result in tighter sanctions that dent oil exports even further.

Policy Challenges

Since 2011, many developing countries of the region have been in political turmoil, in some cases associated with conflict, which has disrupted economic activity. Economies have stagnated, with growth averaging a mere 0.8 percent per year, a sharp slowdown compared to the average of 4.4 percent during the previous decade. Measures to address long-standing structural challenges, which predate the Arab Spring uprisings, have been repeatedly delayed. There has been progress on the political transition in Tunisia and greater stability in Egypt; however, Iraq, Libya, Syria, and the Republic of Yemen remain mired in internal strife.

Aside from the need to improve security and ease political tensions, the region faces a long list of economic challenges—slow growth, high unemployment, poor service delivery, barriers to competition, unequal access to economic opportunity (IMF, 2014a). Unless credible reform programs are implemented to tackle long-overdue structural problems, growth will remain weak and insufficient to reduce unemployment, the region's key economic challenge (Chapter 1 includes a discussion of structural reform priorities).

Subsidies in the region are large and inefficient. Historically, energy subsidies have been used to shield the population from price swings (in oil importers) or to share oil revenues (in oil exporters), but there is growing evidence that they are disproportionally benefiting the well-off segments of the population, while adding to both fiscal and current account pressures (IMF, 2014b). Large energy subsidies carry high fiscal cost and dampen growth, tilt production and FDI towards energy- and capital-intensive activities (World Bank, 2013b AfDB, 2014), discourage employment, contribute to higher road traffic volumes (and hence accidents and fatalities), lower air quality and encourage water-intense agriculture (World Bank, 2014j). Consequently, reform of the region's high energy subsidies should be a priority.

Some progress has been made, despite the political opposition to rising prices of basic goods and services. Efforts are underway in Egypt, the Islamic Republic of Iran, Jordan, Morocco, Tunisia, and the Republic of Yemen to reform fuel and energy subsidies, which amount to 5 percent of GDP in Tunisia, about 9 percent in Egypt and the Republic of Yemen, and 11 percent in Libya. Egypt has started to reform energy subsidies by raising electricity and fuel prices, which, together with revenue measures, should lower the fiscal deficit from 14 percent of GDP in the fiscal year ending June 2013, to 11 percent of GDP in two years. In the Republic of Yemen, fuel subsidies were removed in July 2014, but were partially restored in wake of significant political and even armed opposition. Nevertheless, the net reduction in untargeted subsidies remains substantial. Earlier efforts in Jordan, Morocco, and Tunisia are also beginning to reduce deficits. Recent declines in oil prices offer an opportunity to remove the region's heavy energy subsidies in oil-importing and oil-exporting countries alike.

TABLE 2.7   Middle East and North Africa forecast summary

(Annual percent change unless indicated otherwise)

	00-10[a]	2011	2012	2013	2014e	2015f	2016f	2017f
GDP at market prices, geographic region[b, c]	4.6	3.2	3.3	2.3	3.0	3.3	3.6	3.9
GDP at market prices, developing countries[c]	4.4	-0.1	1.4	0.5	1.2	2.5	3.0	3.5
(Average including countries with full national accounts and balance of payments data only)[d]								
GDP at market prices, developing countries[c,d]	4.7	2.7	-1.1	0.9	2.3	2.5	2.7	3.3
GDP per capita (units in US$)	3.1	1.1	-2.6	-0.5	0.8	1.1	1.4	2.0
PPP GDP[e]	4.7	2.6	-1.0	1.0	2.3	2.6	2.8	3.4
Private consumption	4.5	3.4	2.8	2.7	2.7	3.2	3.4	3.5
Public consumption	3.5	4.0	4.0	-0.4	3.3	2.2	2.3	3.2
Fixed investment	7.0	1.9	-0.5	-1.8	-2.0	3.0	2.9	4.3
Exports, GNFS[f]	5.1	-1.7	-7.1	0.3	3.6	4.6	4.7	4.9
Imports, GNFS[f]	8.1	1.2	4.4	-3.3	4.1	5.7	5.7	5.9
Net exports, contribution to growth	-0.5	-0.9	-3.4	1.1	-0.3	-0.5	-0.5	-0.6
Current account balance (percent of GDP)	3.8	4.4	1.3	0.6	-1.0	-4.3	-4.1	-3.9
Consumer prices (annual average)[g]	7.1	11.9	14.4	18.6	10.3	...	...	...
Fiscal balance (percent of GDP)[h]	0.1	-4.0	-3.8	-6.0	-7.1	-6.1	-5.3	-4.4
Memo items: GDP								
Developing countries, ex. Libya	4.4	3.1	-0.6	1.1	2.0	2.5	2.9	3.4
High-income oil exporters[i]	4.8	7.0	5.4	4.1	4.7	4.1	4.2	4.3
Developing oil exporters	4.2	-1.7	0.5	-0.8	0.3	1.8	2.4	3.1
Developing oil importers	4.9	2.6	2.6	2.6	2.6	3.6	3.8	4.1
Egypt	4.8	2.0	2.2	2.1	2.9	3.6	3.9	4.0
Fiscal year basis	4.8	1.8	2.2	2.1	2.2	3.5	3.8	4.0
Iran	5.0	3.9	-6.6	-1.9	1.5	0.9	1.0	2.2
Algeria	3.9	2.8	3.3	2.8	3.0	3.3	3.5	3.5

Source: World Bank.

World Bank forecasts are frequently updated based on new information and changing (global) circumstances. Consequently, projections presented here may differ from those contained in other Bank documents, even if basic assessments of countries' prospects do not differ at any given moment in time.

a. Growth rates over intervals are compound weighted averages; average growth contributions, ratios and deflators are calculated as simple averages of the annual weighted averages for the region.

b. Geographic region includes the following high-income countries: Bahrain, Kuwait, Oman, Qatar, Saudi Arabia, and United Arab Emirates.

c. GDP at market prices and expenditure components are measured in constant 2010 U.S. dollars.

d. Sub-region aggregate excludes Djibouti, Iraq, Libya, Syria and West Bank and Gaza, for which data limitations prevent the forecasting of GDP components or balance of payments details.

e. GDP measured at PPP exchange rates.

f. Exports and imports of goods and non factor services (GNFS).

g. Latest observation for 2014 is Sepember.

h. Includes all developing countries, except Syria for which data is not available.

i. High-income oil exporting countries: Bahrain, Kuwait, Oman, Qatar, Saudi Arabia and United Arab Emirates.

TABLE 2.8 Middle East and North Africa country forecast

(Real GDP growth at market prices in percent and current account balance in percent of GDP, unless indicated otherwise)

	00-10[a]	2011	2012	2013	2014e	2015f	2016f	2017f
Algeria								
GDP	3.9	2.8	3.3	2.8	3.0	3.3	3.5	3.5
Current account balance	13.3	10.0	6.1	0.5	-3.3	-9.1	-9.3	-9.5
Djibouti								
GDP	3.9	4.5	4.8	5.0	5.5	5.5	6.0	6.0
Current account balance	..	-14.1	-18.4	-23.7	-33.0	-36.6	-40.6	-47.4
Egypt, Arab Rep.								
GDP	4.8	2.0	2.2	2.1	2.9	3.6	3.9	4.0
Fiscal year basis	4.8	1.8	2.2	2.1	2.2	3.5	3.8	4.0
Current account balance	0.8	-2.6	-3.9	-2.7	-0.9	-1.7	-1.8	-2.0
Iran, Islamic Rep.								
GDP	5.0	3.9	-6.6	-1.9	1.5	0.9	1.0	2.2
Current account balance	6.3	11.0	6.6	7.5	3.6	-2.6	-2.2	-1.9
Iraq								
GDP	-0.4	10.2	10.3	4.2	-2.7	0.9	7.0	5.9
Current account balance	..	12.0	6.7	-0.8	2.0	-5.3	-2.2	-1.5
Jordan								
GDP	6.3	2.6	2.7	2.8	3.0	3.4	3.9	4.0
Current account balance	-4.6	-10.2	-15.2	-10.0	-11.3	-9.4	-7.9	-6.0
Lebanon								
GDP	5.9	2.0	2.2	0.9	1.5	2.0	3.4	3.6
Current account balance	-17.1	-10.9	-8.1	-8.5	-8.3	-8.0	-7.3	-7.1
Libya								
GDP	4.3	-62.1	104.5	-13.7	-21.8	4.3	4.4	6.5
Current account balance	..	9.2	29.1	-3.5	-24.3	-12.5	-11.2	-9.8
Morocco								
GDP	4.9	5.0	2.7	4.4	3.0	4.6	4.0	4.5
Current account balance	0.1	-8.0	-9.7	-7.6	-5.9	-4.2	-3.6	-2.9
Tunisia								
GDP	4.4	-0.5	4.7	2.5	2.3	2.7	3.5	4.0
Current account balance	-3.0	-7.4	-8.2	-8.4	-9.1	-8.6	-7.3	-6.6
Yemen, Rep.								
GDP	3.0	-12.7	2.4	4.8	1.9	3.7	3.8	5.2
Current account balance	0.4	-3.2	-1.9	-3.3	-3.6	-6.5	-6.1	-5.5
West Bank and Gaza								
GDP	3.3	12.2	5.9	1.9	-3.7	4.4	4.0	4.0
Current account balance	..	-32.0	-36.4	-29.1	-37.5	-39.7	-36.9	-34.1

	00-10[a]	2011	2012	2013	2014e	2015f	2016f	2017f
Recently transitioned to high-income economies[b]								
Oman								
GDP	4.9	4.5	5.0	5.1	4.4	5.0	3.9	4.0
Current account balance	8.5	15.3	11.4	9.2	3.0	-4.9	-5.9	-7.9
Saudi Arabia								
GDP	5.4	8.6	5.8	4.0	5.2	4.1	4.4	4.6
Current account balance	15.0	23.7	22.4	18.4	12.8	2.4	-2.4	-2.3

Source: World Bank.

World Bank forecasts are frequently updated based on new information and changing (global) circumstances. Consequently, projections presented here may differ from those contained in other Bank documents, even if basic assessments of countries' prospects do not significantly differ at any given moment in time. Data for Syria are excluded due to uncertain political situation.

a. GDP growth rates over intervals are compound average; current account balance shares are simple averages over the period.

b. The recently high-income countries are based on World Bank's country reclassification from 2004 to 2014.

CHAPTER 2
SOUTH ASIA

Growth in South Asia rose to an estimated 5.5 percent in 2014 from a 10-year low of 4.9 percent in 2013. The upturn was driven by India, the region's largest economy, which emerged from two years of modest growth. Regional growth is projected to rise to 6.8 percent by 2017, as reforms ease supply constraints in India, political tensions subside in Pakistan, remittances remain robust in Bangladesh and Nepal, and demand for the region's exports firms. Past adjustments have reduced vulnerability to financial market volatility. Risks are mainly domestic and of a political nature. Sustaining the pace of reform and maintaining political stability are key to maintaining the recent growth momentum.

Recent Developments

Economic activity in South Asia began to revive in 2014 as India, the largest economy in the region, emerged from two years of modest growth. Growth in the region is estimated to have accelerated to 5.5 percent in 2014 from 4.9 percent in 2013, the slowest in a decade (Table 2.9). In India, a slow economic recovery is underway, helped by a sharp slide in inflation to multiyear lows and improving export momentum in line with rising demand from the US, a major trading partner. With the reform agenda building momentum and current account vulnerabilities considerably diminished compared to 2013, currency and equity markets came under some pressure but were less affected than other emerging market peers during an episode of global financial volatility in December 2014. The improvement follows a sharp slowdown in the previous two years—to the weakest growth in nearly a quarter of a century—during which high inflation and a perception of policy paralysis had depressed domestic investment, while growing macroeconomic imbalances increased vulnerability to volatility in global financial markets.

Improved political stability supported activity elsewhere in the region, except in Afghanistan and, in the second half of the year, in Pakistan. Activity in Bangladesh began to normalize in 2014 as social unrest abated from a spike in the run-up to national elections in January 2014 (Table 2.10). With government spending offsetting softness in private demand, the economy is (officially)

estimated to have grown by 6.1 percent in FY2013–14, ostensibly because increased agriculture and service sector growth outweighed the decrease in industrial growth. Reconstruction efforts in Sri Lanka since the end of the civil war in 2009 have raised growth to an average of 7.5 percent. Growth was further bolstered by robust exports and strong FDI and remittance inflows especially in the first half of 2014. In Afghanistan, a difficult political transition following presidential elections in 2014 has weighed on activity and undermined fiscal resource mobilization amidst a challenging security environment. Growth in Pakistan,

FIGURE 2.27   Inflation

Inflation is easing across the region, in part because of favorable base effects.

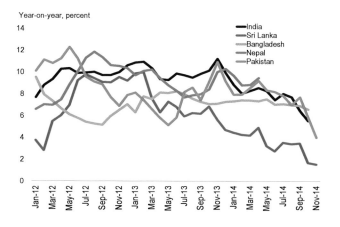

Sources: Haver and World Bank.

FIGURE 2.28 Remittances, 2013

Remittance inflows are large in some countries.

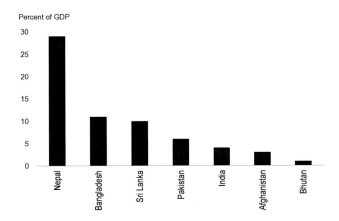

Source: World Bank Remittances Database.

FIGURE 2.29 Industrial output

Industrial output has grown more slowly in India and Pakistan than in Bangladesh.

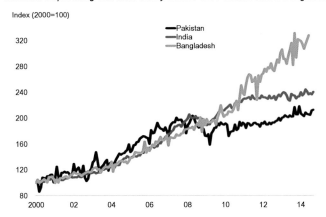

Sources: Haver and World Bank.
Note: Based on seasonally adjusted data.

the region's second largest economy, accelerated to 5.4 percent in FY2013-14 from 4.4 percent the previous year, reflecting a lull in political turmoil and increased macroeconomic stability under an IMF support program. However, a spike in political unrest in the second half of 2014 has taken a toll on confidence and activity.

With inflation easing, room for central banks to loosen policy is growing. Weakening global oil prices, fading pass-through from currency depreciations in 2013 (India, Pakistan and Sri Lanka) and the lagged effect of monetary tightening in 2013 (India and Pakistan) made for lower headline inflation in the region (Figure 2.27). In India and Pakistan, part of the decline in inflation also stems from favorable base effects, which drove the moderation in food price pressures in the second half of the year despite poor monsoons in India and Pakistan and drought in Sri Lanka. Nevertheless food inflation, which tends to have large second round effects on core inflation (Anand et al., 2014) remains elevated, particularly in India and Bangladesh.

With inflation falling to an 11-year low in Pakistan, the central bank lowered its benchmark rate in November. In India, a revised monetary policy framework, with an implicit objective of 6 percent inflation by 2016, is gaining credibility. The Indian central bank has held policy rates constant following a slight increase in early 2014, but has eased reserve requirements to boost credit growth and indicated that rate cuts could be possible if inflation momentum eases further.

A recovery in exports, declining oil import bills and strong remittance inflows are helping to narrow current account deficits. A particularly sharp compression

occurred in India where the deficit printed at 2.2 percent of GDP in Q3 2014, a 4.7 percentage point decline relative to its peak in Q4 2012. Some two-fifths of this improvement was due to stronger exports, and another two-fifths due to a decline in gold imports as a result of administrative restrictions. With the trade balance continuing to improve in line with falling global energy prices, restrictions on gold imports have been recently eased. In Pakistan, concessional inflows, and migrant remittances, helped shore up the currency, rebuild reserves, and reduce external financing pressures. Sustained remittance inflows in 2014—which are a sizeable share of GDP in several countries—helped offset large trade deficits in Bangladesh, Nepal and, to a lesser degree, Sri Lanka (Figure 2.28). In Afghanistan, aid flows continued to offset the large trade deficit, and help sustain a current account surplus. In Sri Lanka, the current account deficit narrowed in the first half of 2014, supported by robust exports, strong remittances and tourism receipts. Current account deficits in Bhutan have exceeded 20 percent of GDP in recent years, owing to large imports related to the construction of hydropower projects and some domestic overheating pressures, but have been comfortably financed by robust aid inflows.

Capital inflows rose across the board in 2014. Several countries tapped international bond markets, including Pakistan, which issued US$2 billion of international bonds in April and US$1 billion in *sukuk* bonds in November, and Sri Lanka which raised US$ 1billion and US$500 million, respectively, in January and April. In India, cumulative foreign portfolio investments crossed US$30 billion by the end of Q3 2014 (up from less than US$4 billion in 2013 and the highest since 2010), enabling the central bank to steadily rebuild reserves.

FIGURE 2.30 Share of manufacturing in GDP, 2013

The share of manufacturing in India and Pakistan is lower than in peers.

Percent of GDP

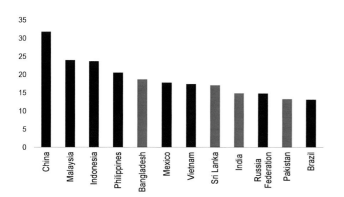

FIGURE 2.31 Fiscal balances

Fiscal consolidation is a priority for several countries in the region.

Percent of GDP

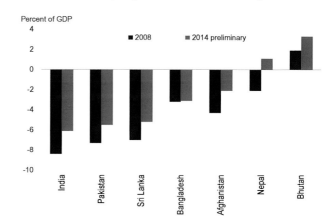

Sources: Haver and World Bank.
Note: Data for China is for 2012, the latest available.

Source: World Bank.

Indian financial markets came under some pressure in December amid heightened global risk aversion. However despite the correction, stock indices remain close to multiyear highs, while the Indian rupee has held up much better than other major emerging market economies. The resilience of capital flows and asset markets has partly reflected improved (India) or healthy (Bangladesh) current account balances, robust growth prospects (India, Bangladesh), and ample global liquidity as a result of accommodative monetary policies in the Euro Area and Japan.

Stagnant or declining shares of manufacturing in GDP in the region's two largest economies are symptomatic of substantial supply-side bottlenecks and lagging reforms. Onerous labor regulations, cumbersome bureaucracies, underinvestment in human capital, and large infrastructure deficits have undermined the region's competitiveness, making it hard for low-cost labor-intensive manufacturing to thrive and to compete against the more flexible economies of East Asia. Added to this, cyclical weakness in recent years has meant that industrial output has expanded slowly in the post-crisis period (Figure 2.29), posing challenges of coping with a rapidly growing labor force.[1]

As a consequence, manufacturing's share of economic output in India has stagnated over the past decade while in Pakistan it has trended down to near the bottom of the range for major developing or emerging market economies (Figure 2.30). In contrast, in Bangladesh the

share of manufacturing in GDP has gradually increased, reflecting the impact of a program of reforms (notably investments in human capital), begun over a decade ago, which have enabled a successful integration into global supply chains. Despite civil conflict, a similar trend is visible in Sri Lanka, the result of a liberalization started in 1977. There is evidence too that the labor intensity of manufacturing has increased over time in Sri Lanka (Chandrasiri, 2009).

Reform momentum has picked up in India. After several years of stalled progress, the newly elected government has begun to implement measures to cut red tape, raise infrastructure investment, deregulate key parts of the economy, and shrink the role of government. If successfully implemented, these reforms should support the recovery currently underway by bolstering confidence and private investment. Implementation stepped up during the fourth quarter, with the opening up of the coal industry to private investors, a deregulation of diesel prices to reduce the fiscal subsidy bill, a relaxation of labor market laws, and a linking of cash transfers with efforts to increase financial inclusion. Financial sector reforms, started in 2013, included efforts to increase private sector participation in a banking sector dominated by state owned banks, and to improve the monitoring of systemic risks. The positive effects should last over the medium term, through easing supply-side constraints.

Fiscal deficits remain large in the region (Figure 2.31) and government debt ratios are high in some countries (Bhutan, India, and Pakistan), constraining policy space. Successful fiscal consolidation will require long-term reforms to expenditure management notably subsidies, as well as tax reforms given extremely low tax to GDP

---

[1]India's working-age population is projected to rise by 127 million between 2010 and 2020, Pakistan's by 26 million, and Bangladesh's by 19 million (UN Population Statistics, 2014).

ratios relative to peers. The latter in particular will be necessary to ensure fiscal sustainability and increase the resource envelope for critically needed poverty reducing expenditures (Box 2.3). Fiscal reforms are underway in Bangladesh and Pakistan (as part of ongoing IMF-supported programs) and in India and Sri Lanka. Bhutan's public debt ratios exceed 90 percent of GDP; mainly external (denominated in Indian rupees), these are related to major hydropower projects financed by India and should decline once these projects start to produce and Bhutan's electricity exports to India increase. Deficits in India should gradually decline as revenues improve in line with activity, and as the government rationalizes subsidies and reduces its stakes in major public corporations. Political deadlock in Afghanistan during most of 2014 led to a deteriorating fiscal situation, with declining revenues and an unfinanced fiscal gap. The country will likely need additional financing to fund government spending, while maintaining security.

Outlook

Supported by a recovery in domestic demand, especially investment, regional growth is expected to steadily accelerate toward 6.8 percent by 2017. The implementation of reforms and deregulation in India should lift FDI. Investment, which accounts for about 30 percent of GDP, should strengthen, and help raise growth to 7 percent by 2016, although this is contingent on strong and sustained progress on reforms. Any slackening in the reform momentum could result in a more modest or slower pace of recovery. In Pakistan, growth is expected to decelerate in FY2015 as a result of simmering political tensions. As these subside, the economy should begin to recover. However the pace of this recovery should remain slow on account of persistent energy shortages and a troubled security situation.

Soft oil prices will also raise real incomes and support consumption and help ease current account pressures across a region of energy importers. Meanwhile the region's smallest economies will be lifted by strengthening growth in India, which provides official financing flows to Afghanistan, Bhutan, and Maldives, remittances to Bangladesh and Nepal, and tourism to Maldives and Nepal.[2] In Bangladesh, growth will be

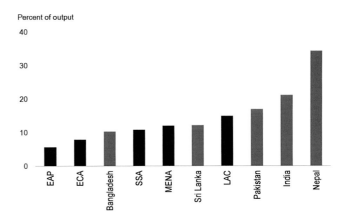

FIGURE 2.32 Electricity losses, 2011

Electricity transmission and distribution losses are substantial.

Percent of output

Sources: World Bank and World Development Indicators.
Note: Darker bars indicate GDP-weighted averages for developing country regions.

supported by continued robust remittances and recovery in private consumption demand if political stability is sustained in 2015. In Sri Lanka, with elections due in 2015, growth in the near term will be buoyed by higher investment and government spending, while continued strong remittance inflows should support private demand. Growth in Bhutan is expected to accelerate as the Dagacchu hydropower project goes into production and, in both Bhutan and Nepal, the construction of hydropower projects (as part of recent investment agreements with India) will support a positive outlook. In Afghanistan, stronger growth is conditional upon an easing of political uncertainties and stability following the withdrawal of international forces from the country.

Export momentum is expected to build in line with strengthening global import demand in high-income countries, particularly in the United States and the Euro Area, the two largest markets for South Asian exports. In Pakistan, preferential market access by the EU could boost export performance unless continued energy supply shortages hamper exporting companies. In Bangladesh, exports are projected to improve after transition to better enforcement of factory safety standards and working conditions. However, wage pressures in the absence of productivity gains could erode its competitiveness. Given the high obstacles to trading across borders, trade facilitation reforms in the region could significantly boost integration into global trade.[3]

---

[2]Trade and financial integration between India and South Asia's other large economies (Bangladesh, India, and Pakistan) is small compared to other developing regions. This limits the spillovers from India to these countries (Ding and Masha , 2012).

[3]South Asia ranks among regions with the highest costs of trading across borders after Sub-Saharan Africa. For instance, it takes about 33 days to comply with all procedures to export or import, versus an average of 21 days to export, and 7.5 days, to import in other developing regions (World Bank, 2014h).

Supply-side bottlenecks continue to hold back growth in the baseline forecast, particularly in Sri Lanka and Bangladesh where economies are operating at close to capacity. With power generation unlikely to keep pace with growing demand in the region, shortages are expected to persist in the near term, including in Bangladesh, India, Nepal, and Pakistan. In India, stagnating coal production has already resulted in repeated shortages in supplies to power plants. In both India and Pakistan, substantial transmission and distribution losses (Figure 2.32), insufficiently high user prices, and subsidies to special interest groups have resulted in repeated bailouts for the energy sector. In India, these represented a fiscal cost of 1 percent of GDP in 2001 and again in 2011 (Pargal and Banerjee, 2014); in Pakistan, 1.4 percent of GDP in 2013 (IMF, 2013b).

Risks

Risks are mainly domestic in nature, predominantly of a political nature, and are roughly balanced. Downside risks include mainly political tensions and slowing reform momentum that fails to address banking sector weakness, energy bottlenecks, and weak business environments. Improved growth prospects for South Asia are predicated on the implementation of structural reforms to ease supply side constraints, which are substantial, and put government finances on a sustainable footing. Disappointments could weaken confidence, depress investment, trigger a reappraisal of growth prospects and reversal of investor sentiment, and, in Pakistan, derail financing under the IMF-supported program. On the upside, faster implementation of reforms in India and elsewhere than assumed in the baseline scenario would improve the outlook.

Among external risks, slower growth in the Euro Area, an important trading partner for South Asia, would affect South Asia's exports. India's openness to global financial markets leaves it exposed to sustained increases in financial market volatility, which could be triggered by a reappraisal of growth prospects or by geopolitical risks. However, risks on this front have receded considerably with the narrowing of India's current account balances since 2013. Tensions in Ukraine or conflict in the Middle East could sharply raise global energy prices. Since the region is a heavy energy importer, and governments offer generous fuel subsidies, this could widen current account and fiscal deficits and push up inflation. In India, despite recent deregulation of diesel prices, restrictions on the pace at which state-run oil companies can pass on higher prices to consumers remain in place.

On the positive side, regional growth might surprise on the upside if global energy prices continue to decline further than projected. This would raise real household incomes and encourage consumption spending, and ease fiscal and current account pressures. The positive effects of this would, however, be tempered by softer migrant remittances from high income oil-exporting countries. Finally, there remains the potential for stronger than expected growth in the United States, where the recovery is looking increasingly healthy, and from the Euro Area if recently announced monetary measures successfully support growth.

Policy Challenges

The region has significant policy challenges, which include the following.

- Electricity supply remains unreliable. In India, electricity supply investment could become increasingly constrained by raw material shortages (notably of coal, used to generate about 70 percent of electricity needs). Although reforms to increase private-sector participation and to auction some 200 coal mines to the private sector are important first steps, coal output will likely rise only slowly given still substantial impediments before the bulk of these can be put up for auction. In Sri Lanka, progress on augmenting and diversifying power-generating capacity has eliminated power shortages, and enabled a reduction in electricity tariffs during 2014 (which were among the highest in the world). Nevertheless, the country remains heavily dependent on hydropower, which contributes between one-third to one-half toward the country's energy needs. Regional progress on energy sharing remains slow, although there have been positive steps, including about US$2 billion worth of agreements between India and Nepal in 2014 that would help develop the latter's hydropower resources and substantially raise electricity exports to India over the medium term.

- Weak bank balance sheets continue to impede financing for an upturn the investment cycle. Stressed bank loans (including restructured loans) exceed 10 percent of loans in Bangladesh, Bhutan, India, and Pakistan. Restructured and problem loans need to be recognized as nonperforming, even though this would impair capital (with possible need for fiscal support). Banking system reforms, in particular aimed at strengthening human resources, improving nonperforming loan management, and raising capital ratios would help to improve financial intermediation. Such reforms are especially needed in India, where state-owned banks account for close to three-quarters of banking assets.

Most countries in South Asia need to rebuild fiscal policy space, having used buffers since 2009 (Chapter 3). Successful budget consolidation in the near term, and sustainability over the longer term, hinge upon revenue mobilization, through tax policy reforms.

- Measures to simplify the tax system, broaden the tax base, and improve compliance will be critical for fiscal consolidation efforts (Box 2.3). Momentum on tax reform, notably the introduction of a value-added tax, has been weak, despite low revenue mobilization compared with other developing countries. Tax administrations systems are extremely weak in several countries in the region.

- If the benefits of tax reforms are to be fully realized, however, they will need to be complemented by

efforts to improve the quality and efficiency of public spending. Public financial management tends to be weak across the region. Both Nepal and Maldives face considerable challenges on the expenditure side (as opposed to revenue mobilization which is the case with the rest of the region) with Nepal struggling with budget under-execution (Nepal) and fiscal deficits growing in the Maldives, despite strong revenue growth, due to persistent and large expenditure overruns.

- The fiscal cost of food and fuel subsidies is also heavy. Energy subsidies alone amount to between 6-10 percent of revenues in India and Bangladesh, and 30 percent in Pakistan (IMF, 2013b). The decline in international crude oil prices over the past year has lowered fuel subsidy bills, making it easier to liberalize diesel prices. India has taken advantage of the window of opportunity to reduce and reform subsidies. Other governments in the region should follow.

TABLE 2.9   South Asia forecast summary

(Annual percent change unless indicated otherwise)

	00-10[a]	2011	2012	2013	2014e	2015f	2016f	2017f
GDP at market prices[b,e]	6.9	7.3	5.0	4.9	5.5	6.1	6.6	6.8
GDP per capita (units in US$)	5.2	5.8	3.5	3.4	4.1	4.7	5.3	5.5
PPP GDP[c]	6.8	7.3	4.9	4.8	5.5	6.1	6.6	6.8
Private consumption	5.9	9.0	5.5	4.1	5.3	5.9	6.2	6.2
Public consumption	6.3	6.0	7.2	4.8	6.1	5.6	5.3	5.3
Fixed investment	10.4	10.7	4.4	-0.2	6.5	9.6	9.8	8.8
Exports, GNFS[d]	12.9	18.0	7.2	5.2	5.8	6.4	6.9	6.9
Imports, GNFS[d]	11.0	16.3	9.4	-0.2	4.7	7.4	7.8	7.1
Net exports, contribution to growth	-0.3	-0.7	-1.2	1.3	0.0	-0.7	-0.7	-0.5
Current account balance (percent of GDP)	-0.8	-3.1	-4.1	-2.0	-1.1	-1.2	-1.3	-1.3
Consumer prices (annual average)	6.2	9.8	9.5	9.6	6.9	...	...	...
Fiscal balance (percent of GDP)	-7.4	-7.6	-7.2	-6.9	-6.7	-6.5	-6.1	-5.8
Memo items: GDP at market prices[e]								
South Asia excluding India	5.0	5.0	5.1	5.7	5.8	5.7	5.8	5.9
India (at factor cost)[f]	7.5	6.6	4.7	5.0	5.6	6.4	7.0	7.0
Pakistan (at factor cost)[f]	4.2	2.7	3.5	4.4	5.4	4.6	4.8	4.9
Bangladesh	6.1	6.5	6.5	6.0	6.1	6.2	6.5	7.0

Source: World Bank.

World Bank forecasts are frequently updated based on new information and changing (global) circumstances. Consequently, projections presented here may differ from those contained in other Bank documents, even if basic assessments of countries' prospects do not differ at any given moment in time.

a. Growth rates over intervals are compound weighted averages; average growth contributions, ratios and deflators are calculated as simple averages of the annual weighted averages for the region.

b. GDP at market prices and expenditure components are measured in constant 2010 U.S. dollars.

c. GDP measured at PPP exchange rates.

d. Exports and imports of goods and non-factor services (GNFS).

e. National income and product account data refer to fiscal years (FY) for the South Asian countries, while aggregates are presented in calendar year (CY) terms. The fiscal year runs from July 1 through June 30 in Bangladesh, Bhutan, and Pakistan, from July 16 through July 15 in Nepal, and April 1 through March 31 in India. Due to reporting practices, Bangladesh, Bhutan, Nepal, and Pakistan report FY2012/13 data in CY2013, while India reports FY2012/13 in CY2012.

f. Historical data is market price basis and forecasts are factor cost basis.

TABLE 2.10   South Asia country forecast

(Real GDP grow th at market prices in percent and current account balance in percent of GDP, unless indicated otherw ise)

	00-10ᵃ	2011	2012	2013	2014e	2015f	2016f	2017f
Calendar year basisᵇ								
Afghanistan								
GDP	12.8	6.1	14.4	3.7	1.5	4.0	5.0	5.1
Current account balance	0.0	3.1	3.9	3.7	4.1	0.3	-1.9	-1.9
Bangladesh								
GDP	6.2	6.5	6.3	6.0	6.1	6.4	6.8	7.0
Current account balance	0.6	-1.5	0.5	2.0	0.8	0.8	0.6	0.5
Bhutanᶜ								
GDP	8.7	7.9	5.1	2.0	5.5	7.9	8.4	8.6
Current account balance	-13.9	-32.6	-23.0	-25.0	-21.9	-26.2	-26.6	-27.9
India								
GDP at factor cost (% annual grow th)ᵈ	7.3	7.9	4.9	4.7	5.5	6.2	6.8	7.0
Current account balance	-0.8	-3.4	-5.0	-2.5	-1.3	-1.5	-1.6	-1.6
Maldives								
GDPᵉ	7.0	6.5	1.3	4.7	5.0	5.3	4.3	4.3
Current account balance	-12.6	-18.1	-10.6	-6.5	-8.1	-7.3	-8.1	-7.6
Nepal								
GDP	3.9	4.1	4.3	4.6	5.2	4.8	4.6	4.5
Current account balance	0.5	2.5	3.9	6.9	5.8	4.9	3.8	2.8
Pakistan								
GDP at factor cost (% annual grow th)ᵈ	4.2	3.1	4.0	4.9	5.0	4.7	4.9	4.9
Current account balance	-1.3	-1.0	-1.0	-1.9	-1.2	-1.1	-1.0	-0.9
Sri Lanka								
GDP	5.2	8.2	6.3	7.3	7.8	7.5	6.8	6.5
Current account balance	-3.3	-7.8	-6.7	-3.9	-3.6	-3.4	-3.1	-2.9
Fiscal year basisᵇ								
Bangladesh								
GDP	6.1	6.5	6.5	6.0	6.1	6.2	6.5	7.0
India								
GDP at factor cost (% annual grow th)ᵈ	7.5	6.6	4.7	5.0	5.6	6.4	7.0	7.0
Nepal								
GDP	3.9	3.4	4.9	3.8	5.5	5.0	4.7	4.5
Pakistan								
GDP at factor cost (% annual grow th)ᵈ	4.2	2.7	3.5	4.4	5.4	4.6	4.8	4.9

Source: World Bank.

World Bank forecasts are frequently updated based on new information and changing (global) circumstances. Consequently, projections presented here may differ from those contained in other Bank documents, even if basic assessments of countries' prospects do not significantly differ at any given moment in time.

a. GDP growth rates over intervals are compound average; current account balance shares are simple averages over the period.

b. Historical data is reported on a market price basis.National income and product account data refer to fiscal years (FY) for the South Asian countries with the exception of Afghanistan, Maldives and Sri Lanka, which report in calendar year (CY). The fiscal year runs from July 1through June 30 in Bangladesh, Bhutan, and Pakistan, from July 16 through July 15 in Nepal, and April 1through March 31in India. Due to reporting practices, Bangladesh, Bhutan, Nepal, and Pakistan report FY2012/13 data in CY2013, while India reports FY2012/13 in CY2012. GDP figures presented in calendar years (CY) terms for Bangladesh, Nepal, and Pakistan are calculated taking the average growth over the two fiscal year periods to provide an approximation of CY activity. Historical GDP data in CY terms for India are the sum of GDP in the four calendar quarters.

c. GDP data for Bhutan is on a CY basis, but Current Account data is on a FY basis.

d. Historical data is market price basis and forecasts are factor cost basis.

e. Data for Maldives is GDP data at basic prices (i.e excluding taxes and including subsidies).

BOX 2.3   Revenue Mobilization in South Asia: Policy Challenges and Recommendations[1]

Low tax-to-GDP ratios in South Asia reflect narrow tax bases, weak tax administrations, and structural factors. In several countries, efforts are under way to address these challenges.

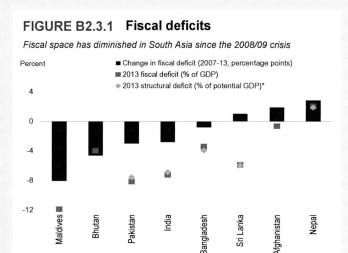

FIGURE B2.3.1   Fiscal deficits

Fiscal space has diminished in South Asia since the 2008/09 crisis

Source: World Bank calculations using data from the World Development Indicators, Government Financial Statistics, and IMF Country Reports.

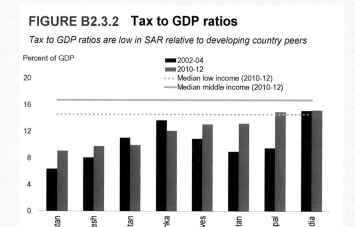

FIGURE B2.3.2   Tax to GDP ratios

Tax to GDP ratios are low in SAR relative to developing country peers

Source: World Bank calculations using data from the World Development Indicators, Government Financial Statistics, and IMF Country Reports.

Greater revenue mobilization in the South Asia region (SAR) is necessary to reduce macroeconomic vulnerabilities and promote long-term growth. First, fiscal space has diminished since the 2008/09 global financial crisis; average deficits in the region were some 2 percentage points higher than in the pre-crisis period in 2013 and in several countries reached over 6 percent or more of GDP in 2013 (Figure B2.3.1). This has left limited room to counter shocks that could arise from setbacks to global or domestic growth. Second, given extremely low tax-to-GDP ratios (Figure B2.3.2) and debt levels over 60 percent of GDP in some countries, successful fiscal consolidation, and long term fiscal sustainability hinge upon greater revenue mobilization. This has been recognized in consolidation plans by the new government in India and ongoing IMF-supported programs in Bangladesh and Pakistan.

In addition, lower levels of tax collection imply less spending for critical infrastructure and social sector needs than other developing countries at comparable levels of per capita income, despite significant infrastructure bottlenecks, pervasive poverty and lagging human development indicators.[2] A larger revenue envelope is also necessary to fund successful state building in

postconflict Afghanistan and strengthening public institutions and public service delivery in other parts of South Asia affected by low-intensity social conflict or unrest. Box 2.3 examines the reasons for poor revenue mobilization performance in South Asia and highlights key reform priorities.

Revenue trends

The larger SAR countries have struggled to increase their tax-to-GDP ratio over the past decade despite ongoing tax reforms. In fact, tax-to-GDP ratios have declined since the early 2000s in Pakistan and Sri Lanka, and stagnated in India. Among the smaller countries, there has been some improvement in revenue mobilization. This can partly be attributed to initial dividends associated with growth, tax reforms, and strengthened tax administration; it may taper off, unless the countries are able to overcome broader challenges in raising tax revenues.

Most governments in South Asia have lagged other developing countries in mobilizing revenues from direct and consumption taxes (Figures B2.3.3 and B2.3.4), despite a growing need for scaling up of such revenues to compensate for falling trade revenue taxes due to trade liberalization (Norregaard and Khan, 2007). India has been more successful than other countries in the region in raising its direct tax ratio, in part because of robust economic growth and improvements in tax administration (World Bank, 2012), but its tax revenues from consumption taxes has fallen over the past decade, as is also the case in Sri Pakistan and Sri Lanka. In India and Pakistan, constitutional restrictions originating in the pre-independence 1935

---

[1]The main authors of this box are Poonam Gupta and Tehmina Khan.

[2]The region needs to invest between US$ 1.7–2.5 trillion (at current prices) in infrastructure until 2020, part of which will need to be financed by governments through higher tax revenues (Andres, Biller, and Dappe, 2013). This implies an annual increase of up to 3 percentage points of GDP from the 6.9 percent of GDP invested in infrastructure by SAR countries in 2009 (See Andres et al., 2013).

BOX 2.3 *(continued)*

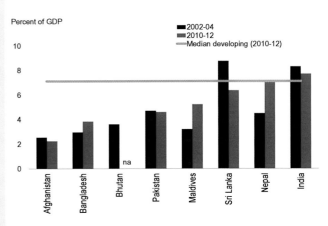

FIGURE B2.3.3   Direct tax revenues

SAR countries struggle to raise revenues from direct taxes.

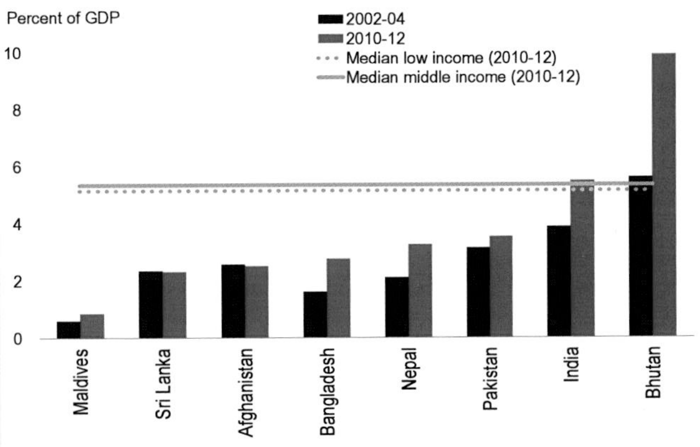

Percent of GDP

- 2002-04
- 2010-12
- ····· Median low income (2010-12)
- —— Median middle income (2010-12)

Source: World Bank calculations using data from the World Development Indicators, Government Financial Statistics, and IMF Country Reports.

FIGURE B2.3.4   Indirect tax revenues

Indirect tax ratios have fallen in most countries over the past decade.

Percent of GDP

- 2002-04
- 2010-12
- —— Median developing (2010-12)

Source: World Bank calculations using data from the World Development Indicators, Government Financial Statistics, and IMF Country Reports.

Government of India Act, that allocate the powers to tax goods and services to distinct levels of government (Keen, 2012), have held back the development and implementation of modern value added tax regimes.

Challenges in revenue mobilization

Weak revenue mobilization in SAR reflects a number of administrative and structural factors. The underperformance of SAR countries in tax revenue mobilization does not appear to be due to the paucity of tax policy reforms: several have undertaken considerable reforms in line with international best practice, transitioning their indirect taxes towards consumption taxes away from taxes on international trade and rationalizing their personal and corporate income taxes, although in the case of Bangladesh, progress even in this context has been small given limited rationalization of personal and corporate tax structures[3].[4] However, tax collection has been held back for several, interrelated reasons:

- *A narrow tax base.* Tax payments tend to be concentrated only among a few taxpayers in South Asian countries. In India, for instance, only 3 percent of the population in India pays the personal income tax, with the figure dropping to about 1 percent in Bangladesh, Nepal, and Pakistan (Figure

B2.3.5). Added to this, a plethora of exemptions exist. These have narrowed the tax base, with research indicating a sharp fall in average effective tax rates, and an even larger decline in marginal effective tax rates over the last decade in (Abbas and Klemm, 2012, also see Figure B2.3.6). They have also made tax systems more complex and may have contributed to the emergence of vested interests to resist further reforms. As a result, in most of South Asia, a large proportion of corporate income and trade taxation is collected from a few large corporations and on the import of a few commodities. (World Bank, 2012).

- *Inefficient tax administrations.* SAR countries rank low on some of the common yardsticks of efficient tax administration, typically in the bottom half or the last quartile among the 189 countries ranked in the World Bank's doing business indicators, which can hinder compliance. For instance, time spent preparing and paying taxes for a typical firm in South Asia is more than 300 hours, compared to 200 hours in East Asia and 175 hours in advanced countries (World Bank, 2014h).

- *Structural factors.* Higher shares of agriculture and service sectors in GDP are negatively correlated with revenue to GDP ratios in developing countries, as is poor governance (World Bank, 2012). This is particularly relevant for South Asia, where agriculture has historically been untaxed or undertaxed, while service sectors are also relatively large. Other factors that may impinge on low revenue mobilization include low literacy rates, large rural populations, large informal economies, and poor governance. These factors

---

[3]Bangladesh is an exception in that there has not been much rationalization of personal and corporate tax structures.

[4]The coverage of value-added tax in SAR remains narrow, and in many cases confined to the first point of sale, manufacturing or import, rather than extending to the whole value chain.

BOX 2.3 *(continued)*

FIGURE B2.3.5 Tax payers

Only a small share of the population pays income taxes in SAR countries

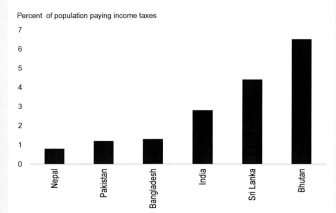

Percent of population paying income taxes

Sources: Asad, 2012; Bangladesh Budget Watch, 2009; Inland Revenue Department, Nepal, 2013; Ministry of Finance, Government of India, 2011; Ministry of Finance, Royal Government of Bhutan, 2010; Sri Lanka, 2012.

FIGURE B2.3.6 Tax rates

Tax incentives have eroded effective rates of corporate tax in South Asia, as elsewhere in the developing world.

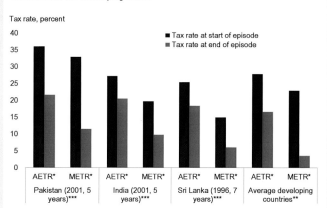

Tax rate, percent

Sources: Abbas and Klemm (2012).
Note: *AETR is the average effective rate of corporate tax and measures ratio of the present discounted value of taxes over the present discounted value of the profit of a project in the absence of taxation and affects the decision of where to locate investment (or the effective rate for a profitable project). The METR is the marginal effective rate of taxation and a special case of the AETR, where a project just breaks even, affecting firms' decisions on whether to invest more or not. Data in parentheses refer to the year in which episode of decline in the effective tax rate started, and its duration. Average developing countries data reflect average from a sample of 50 emerging and developing economies.

keep a large proportion of the population and economic transactions outside the tax net, thus lowering tax revenue. In addition, the financial sector is underdeveloped in SAR countries with the implication that financial transactions occur in cash, abetting tax evasion. The countries that have succeeded in increasing the size of their financial sector in the past decade, Bhutan, Maldives, and Nepal. have also managed to increase their tax ratios.

Reform priorities

A second generation of tax reforms is needed in the region given substantial benefits that the additional revenues can bring to the severely resource-constrained governments, and the moderate success of their past reforms. Indeed, empirical evidence indicates that even after taking into account structural factors such as per capita income levels, the share of agriculture and services in national output and integration into global trade, South Asia's revenue performance lags behind peers (World Bank, 2012, IMF 2014c), mainly due to extremely narrow tax bases (in part reflecting weak tax policy design) and weak tax administrations. Accordingly, reform efforts should be focused in the following areas.

Broadening the tax base and simplifying tax structures. By and large, income tax rate structures are relatively simple in South Asia, with the exception of Pakistan and Sri Lanka where both personal and corporate income taxes have complex/multiple rate structures (World Bank, 2012, Lopez-Calix and Touqeer, 2013). However, policy makers across SAR need to review extensive tax exemptions and widely employed tax holidays,

which significantly erode corporate, income, and indirect tax bases. Tax coverage should also be increased to sectors that are currently untaxed or undertaxed. For instance, extremely low taxation of the agriculture and service sectors in Pakistan, has raised the tax burden on industry: although industry accounts for only a quarter of GDP, tax revenues from industry are about 60 times more than for agriculture and 5 times more than for services (Lopez-Calix and Touqeer, 2013). More generally, tax policy should refrain from attempting to achieve multiple objectives such as the development of regions or industries, infrastructure creation or choice of technology as it complicates the tax system, increases compliance cost (and potentially the degree of informality), and distorts economic choices.

Strengthening tax administration and improving compliance. The institutional arrangements and organizations for tax administration should be granted more independence, insulated from political influences, and provided adequate financial and technical resources to enhance their data collection and assessment capacity. There has also been limited progress in SAR in moving to e-tax administration due to low literacy and e-literacy, and lack of financial and technical resources. In Pakistan, for instance, Lopez-Calix and Touqeer (2013) argue that the reason for poor outcomes vis-à-vis tax administration

BOX 2.3 *(continued)*

reforms in the last decade has been the limited uptake and integration of new information technology–based systems.[5] Reforms should be extended, and capacity strengthened, at the subnational and local government level to generate larger revenues at these levels of governments.

While "informality" is widely regarded as being a central challenge for revenue mobilization in developing countries, there is growing concern that the issue is being conflated with that of *noncompliance* (Keen, 2012). This is because to the extent that the administrative and compliance costs associated with bringing small and medium-sized enterprises and low-wage earners into the tax net outweighs the revenue forgone from excluding them, then the optimal tax remitted by them is likely zero. Instead, the challenge is one of ensuring that "hard to tax" professionals (e.g., doctors, lawyers, architects) are within the tax net. Policy recommendations accordingly depend on whether the problem is one of those who do not register to pay taxes at all, or those who are registered but underpay or both, as appears to be the case in South Asia. For instance, in India, the number of taxpayers who declare their incomes to be more than Rs.10 million is 42,800, while in Pakistan only 3.1 million people possess tax numbers. To address the first problem, tax authorities have to invest resources in the identification and registration of taxpayers; in the second case, audit and enforcement are key (Keen, 2012).

Country specific measures. Besides these common challenges for SAR countries, there are country-specific challenges. For Nepal, the sequencing of tax reforms will matter, with small initial changes in specific tax laws likely to yield relatively large improvements in tax revenues. Pakistan is already implementing comprehensive and multipronged reforms spanning tax administration, regulatory reforms, and governance reforms. In light of fiscal decentralization reforms in recent years, the tax administration capacity in the provinces needs to be strengthened to ease financing constraints. Most countries in the region would also likely benefit from considering a bigger role for the value-added tax (VAT) given its inherent advantages over other forms of indirect taxes and evidence that its adoption is likely to lead to greater revenue (Keen and Lockwood, 2010). Bangladesh is currently undertaking reforms to strengthen tax legislation and administration, but the implementation of a new value-added tax regime which would replace an existing non-uniform goods and services tax (GST), a critical element of tax reforms has been repeatedly delayed in the face of considerable public opposition. In Bhutan, where revenues depend to a large extent on hydropower, revenue sources must be diversified for stable and increased revenue generation. Similarly, in Maldives, tax collection relies on tourism, and for sustainable tax collection, revenue sources must be diversified. Finally, in India, the existing GST is fragmented with rates and administration varying by state. A new GST was announced in 2008, but has missed several implementation deadlines although there are signs of progress under the newly elected government. In particular, a constitutional amendment bill for introducing a uniform GST was tabled in the lower house of the Parliament in December 2014. If implemented, as expected in 2015, it is likely to boost revenues by reducing distortions and creating a single market for goods and services. In Afghanistan, delays in introducing a value-added tax have contributed to declining tax revenues alongside weak customs and tax compliance, undermining fiscal stability. In the medium term, extractive industries can make a significant contribution to revenue generation, but this requires legislative and regulatory progress to develop the sector.

---

[5]Other factors include continued political interference (reflected in high levels of turnover in senior management in the country's main tax agency), and poor audit systems (reflecting a lack of effective centralized, parameter-based risk-audit functions, Lopez-Calix and Touqeer 2013).

CHAPTER 2

SUB-SAHARAN AFRICA

Sub-Saharan Africa's growth improved, for the second consecutive year, to 4.5 percent in 2014. Despite headwinds, growth is projected to pick up to 5.1 percent by 2017, lifted by infrastructure investment, increased agriculture production, and buoyant services. The outlook is subject to downside risks arising from a renewed spread of the Ebola epidemic, violent insurgencies, lower commodity prices, and volatile global financial conditions. Policy priorities include a need for budget restraint for some countries in the region and a shift of spending to increasingly productive ends, as infrastructure constraints are acute. Project selection and management could be improved with greater transparency and accountability in the use of public resources.

Recent Developments

Growth picked up moderately in Sub-Saharan Africa in 2014, to an average of about 4.5 percent compared with 4.2 percent in 2013. GDP growth slowed markedly in South Africa, constrained by strikes in the mining sector, electricity shortages, and low investor confidence. Angola was set back by a decline in oil production. The Ebola outbreak severely disrupted economic activity in Guinea, Liberia, and Sierra Leone. By contrast, in Nigeria, the region's largest economy, activity expanded at a robust pace, supported by a buoyant non-oil sector. Growth was also strong in many of the region's low-income countries, including Côte d'Ivoire, Mozambique, and Tanzania. Excluding South Africa, the average growth for the rest of the region was 5.6 percent. This is a faster pace than other developing regions, excluding China (Figure 2.33). Extreme poverty remains high across the region, however.

Investment in public infrastructure, increased agriculture production, and buoyant services were key drivers of growth. Infrastructure investment across the region, for example, in ports, electricity capacity, and transportation, helped to sustain growth. Increased agricultural production also buoyed growth. A record maize harvest in Zambia more than offset the decline in copper production. A strong increase in cocoa production lifted output in Côte d'Ivoire, despite concerns that the Ebola outbreak might disrupt the industry. Services sector expansion, led by

transport, telecommunication and financial services, spearheaded growth in countries such as Nigeria, Tanzania, and Uganda.

However, FDI flows, an important source of financing of fixed capital formation in the region, declined in 2014, reflecting slower growth in emerging markets and soft commodity prices. Portfolio investment flows also slowed, driven by reduced flows to South Africa and Nigeria, as did official flows directed mainly at low-income countries. Meanwhile, several frontier market countries were able to tap international bond markets to finance infrastructure

FIGURE 2.33 GDP growth

Growth was steady in Sub-Saharan Africa in 2014.

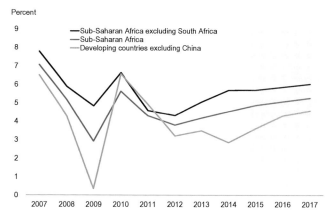

Source: World Bank.

FIGURE 2.34 Overall fiscal balance

Fiscal balances deteriorated in many countries in 2014.

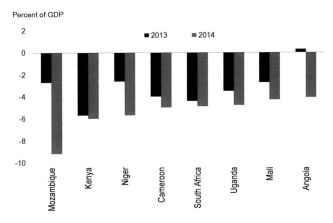

Source: World Bank.

FIGURE 2.35 Inflation

Inflation edged higher in the first half of the year.

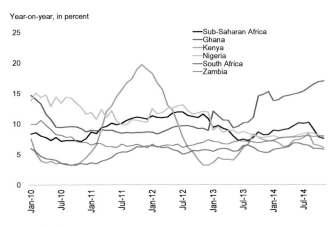

Source: World Bank.

projects. Bond issuances of Côte d'Ivoire, Kenya, and Senegal were highly oversubscribed as a result of accommodative international financial conditions.

The fiscal deficit for the region narrowed to 2.5 percent of GDP, as several countries took measures in 2014 to control expenditures. Nigeria's overall deficit fell thanks to higher non-oil revenues and reduced current spending. In Senegal, the authorities cut less productive expenditures, including those on wages and salaries. In Burkina Faso, improvements in the overall balance came from better revenue collection and tax policy reforms. At the same time, however, the fiscal position deteriorated in many countries (Figure 2.34). In some, it was due to increases in the wage bill (e.g., Kenya and Mozambique). In other countries, it was due to higher spending associated with the frontloading and scaling up of public investment (e.g., Mali, Niger, and Uganda). Elsewhere, the higher deficits reflected declining revenues, notably among oil-exporting countries because of declining production and lower oil prices (Angola).

The region's debt ratio remained moderate, at 30 percent of GDP. Robust growth and concessional interest rates have helped to keep debt burdens manageable. However, in a few countries, debt increased significantly in 2014, especially in Ghana (to 65 percent of GDP), Niger (to 42 percent of GDP), Mozambique, and Senegal (both above 50 percent of GDP). In some countries, particularly those that have newly accessed international bond markets, the share of nonconcessional loans rose, pushing up debt servicing costs.

Current account deficits stabilized at 2.9 percent of GDP in 2014, reflecting soft commodity prices and strong investment-related imports. Falling prices for oil, metals, and agricultural commodities weighed on the region's exports, which remain dominated by primary commodities. In contrast, spurred by infrastructure projects and private consumption growth, import demand was strong across the region. Several frontier market countries (Ghana, Kenya, Namibia) as well as South Africa—which relies heavily on portfolio capital flows to meet large financing needs—continued to have substantial twin fiscal and current account deficits.

Inflation edged up in the first half of 2014, due in part to higher food prices, but remained in single digits in most countries. The uptick was most visible among frontier market countries that sustained large currency depreciations—notably Ghana, where inflation was in double digits (Figure 2.35). In some countries (Ghana, South Africa), inflation rose above the upper limit of the central bank target range for 2014, prompting a tightening of monetary policy. Reduced real disposable income, due to inflation, and higher borrowing costs weighed on investor sentiment and kept household consumption subdued, slowing economic activity. However, low and declining commodity prices helped contain inflation in most countries in the region.

The low-interest-rate international environment and subdued volatility in global financial markets benefited Sub-Saharan Africa's capacity to issue bonds. Sovereign spreads fell across the region although they remained relatively high in Ghana and Zambia (Figure 2.36), suggesting that investors were differentiating between countries on the basis of macroeconomic imbalances and the pace of reforms. In recent months, reflecting concerns about low oil prices, sovereign spreads for oil

FIGURE 2.36   10-year sovereign bond spreads

Sovereign bond spreads fell across the region.

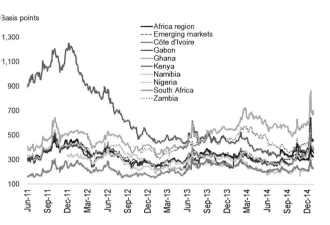

FIGURE 2.37   Exchange rates

The region's major currencies depreciated against the U.S. dollar.

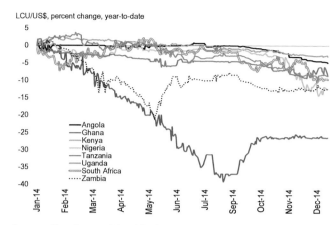

Sources: J.P. Morgan and World Bank.

Sources: Bloomberg and World Bank.

exporters (Gabon, Ghana, Nigeria) rose strongly and currencies of some oil exporters depreciated (Angola, Nigeria, Figure 2.37). The Nigerian naira weakened markedly against the U.S. dollar in November, prompting the central bank to raise interest rates and devalue the naira. In contrast, the Zambian kwacha rebounded from its slide in the first half of the year when it had weakened by more than 20 percent. The Ghanaian cedi also stabilized after concerns about loose fiscal stance and low external reserves had led to bouts of pressure and a depreciation of about 40 percent against the U.S. dollar in the first 9 months of the year. Meanwhile, the South African rand continued to fall on concerns about the country's larger-than-expected current account deficit.

Outlook

Regional GDP growth is projected to remain steady at 4.6 percent in 2015 and rise gradually to 5.1 percent in 2017 (Table 2.11), supported by sustained infrastructure investment, increased agricultural production, and expanding service sectors. Commodity prices and capital inflows are expected to provide less support, with demand and economic activity in emerging markets remaining subdued. FDI flows are projected to remain flat in 2015 and sovereign bond issuance will slow as global financial conditions gradually tighten. Sub-Saharan Africa would nevertheless remain one of the fastest growing regions.

In the baseline forecast, growth remains robust in most low-income countries, by virtue of infrastructure investment and agriculture expansion, although soft commodity prices dampen activity in commodity

exporters. South Africa is expected to experience slow but steady economic growth, helped by improving labor relations, gradually increasing net exports, and reforms to alleviate bottlenecks in the energy sector. Growth is expected to pick up moderately in Angola as oil production rebounds with the attenuation of maintenance problems in oil fields. In Nigeria, the devaluation of the naira will push up inflation and slow growth in 2015, but with continued expansion of non-oil sectors, particularly the services sector which now accounts for more than 50 percent of GDP as well as agriculture and manufacturing, growth is expected to pick up again in 2016 and beyond.

Among frontier market countries, growth is expected to increase in Kenya, boosted by higher public investment and the recovery of agriculture and tourism. Growth should remain robust in Zambia, as new large copper mining projects start producing and agriculture continues to recover. In contrast, high interest rates and inflation would weigh on consumer and investor sentiment in Ghana. Real GDP growth is expected to strengthen in fragile states, such as Madagascar, as investment rises on the back of improved political stability. Oil importers would benefit from low oil prices, especially as the prices of their agricultural commodities (including coffee, cocoa, and tobacco) remain stable.

The baseline forecast assumes that the economic impact of Ebola would be concentrated in Guinea, Liberia, and Sierra Leone, with limited spillovers to the rest of West Africa. Preliminary World Bank estimates indicate that with effective containment within the three most affected countries, the epidemic would cause a moderate economic loss in West Africa by the end of 2015 (World

Bank, 2014k). To date the epidemic has been successfully contained in Nigeria and Senegal, two of the region's major transportation hubs.

Private consumption growth in the region is expected to remain robust. Reduced imported inflation, aided by low commodity prices as well as stable exchange rates, and adequate local harvests should help contain inflationary pressures in most countries and boost real disposable incomes. Remittances are projected to rise by 5 percent annually during 2015–17, which would help support private consumption and underpin a strengthening of domestic demand. Monetary policy is expected to remain broadly accommodative. However, currency-induced price pressures, which could adversely affect private consumption growth, remain a concern for countries where inflation is high, including Ghana and South Africa.

Government consumption is projected to grow at a steady but robust pace, as governments across the region strive to consolidate budgets. Spending on goods and services is expected to continue to expand and support rising public investment. Demands on governments to increase wages and salaries will keep upward pressure on total current expenditures.

The sharp drop in 2014 in oil and metal prices as well as the prices of agricultural commodities is expected to persist in 2015, partly as a result of rising supply in countries in Sub-Saharan Africa. Weakening terms of trade will hold back exports and growth in commodity exporters. The demand for imported capital goods is projected to remain strong in 2015–16, as governments continue to frontload investment projects. Over time, as investment projects mature, import demand will soften and exports will rise. Reflecting these trends, the contribution of net exports to growth is expected to remain marginally negative through most of the forecast period. The improvement in the trade balance will not be sufficient to rein in current account deficits, which are projected to rise to 3.8 percent of GDP by 2017.

Risks

The risks to the region's outlook are mostly on the downside, stemming from both external and domestic factors. A range of idiosyncratic risks includes the Ebola epidemic, expansionary fiscal policy and currency weaknesses, and the precarious security situation in a number of countries. A sudden increase in volatility in international financial markets, and lower growth in export markets are among the major external risks to the region's outlook.

Domestic Risks

The Ebola outbreak continues to spread in West Africa with a recent surge of new cases in Liberia. Without a strengthened program for effective intervention, the virus could spread more widely than assumed in the baseline forecast, and could reach large urban centers and new countries. Public health infrastructures and institutional capacities are inadequate to deal with the outbreak. In addition to the loss of lives, affected countries would suffer a sharper decline in output. If the epidemic were to hit the transportation hubs in Ghana and Senegal, disruptions to cross-border trade and supply chains would hurt the entire sub-region. Heightened fears of Ebola would further undermine confidence, investment, and travel.

In various countries, government budgets are at risk from demands for increased spending (Ghana and Zambia). Large deficits are already a source of vulnerability for such countries. Monetary policy has to strike a balance between the need to contain inflationary pressures, which might in some cases stem from currency depreciation, and the risk that high real interest rates could hamper growth.

Conflicts in South Sudan and Central Africa Republic, and security concerns in northern Nigeria could deteriorate further with harmful regional spillovers. With the outlook for a political settlement still poor, the South Sudan conflict could escalate and disrupt trade in East Africa. The political and security conditions in Central Africa Republic remain explosive and could deteriorate into renewed fighting and violence that could spill over to the rest of Central Africa. An expansion of the Boko Haram insurgency could further disrupt agricultural production in northern Nigeria. Governments in the region might be forced to divert budgetary resources from infrastructure investment to security, which would have a negative impact on longer-term growth.

External Risks

A reemergence of volatility in global financial markets, with a jump in risk premiums from their current low levels, would hurt the region. A sudden deterioration in liquidity conditions would have a particularly hard impact on South Africa, which depends heavily on portfolio flows to finance its current account balance. It would also affect frontier market countries such as Ghana, Nigeria, and Zambia, which have increased their reliance on external financing. Recent episodes of capital market volatility suggest that countries with large macroeconomic imbalances would face strong downward pressure on the

FIGURE 2.38 **Changes in trade balance due to terms of trade effects, 2014–17**

A sharp decline in commodity prices would weaken trade balances across Sub-Saharan Africa.

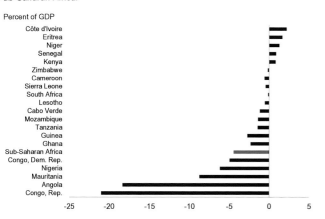

Source: World Bank.
Note: Effect of 30 percent decline in oil, 5 percent decline in agricultural prices and 10 percent decline in metal prices on the difference between exports and imports in percent of GDP, assuming no supply response.

exchange rate, and hence an increased risk of inflation. More generally, in a situation of deteriorating terms of trade, one can expect currency depreciations, and without monetary policy discipline, currency-depreciation-induced inflation would become a constant threat.

Lower growth in emerging economies, to which Sub-Saharan Africa exports, is the main external risk to the regional outlook (Box 2.4). A worse-than-expected slowdown in China especially would reduce demand for commodities, putting further downward pressure on prices, especially where supply is abundant. A further decline in the already depressed price of metals, in particular iron ore, gold, and copper, would severely affect a large number of countries in the region. In countries such as Mauritania, Mozambique, Niger, Tanzania, and Zambia, metals account for a large share of exports; and their exploitation involves large FDI flows. A protracted decline in metal prices would lead to a significant drop in export revenues. A scaling down of operations and new investments in these countries would reduce output in the short run, and reduce growth momentum over an extended period of years.

Simulation results suggest that the income effects of a sharp decline of commodity prices on Sub-Saharan African economies could be large. The scenario considered has a price decline from the baseline of 10 percent for metals (aluminum, copper, gold, iron ore, and silver), 5 percent for agricultural commodities (cocoa, coffee, tea, cotton, and tobacco), and 30 percent for crude oil. In the simulation, Sub-Saharan Africa is affected more than other parts of the developing world. Countries where

metals, agricultural products, or oil represent a large share of total exports see their terms of trade deteriorate sharply. A sharper-than-expected and sustained decline in the price of oil from the baseline would, on the whole, adversely affect the Sub-Saharan Africa region, even though non-oil importers would gain. Oil exporters with a narrow economic base such as Angola and the Republic of Congo would be affected the most. The positive effect on oil importers is reflected in large trade balance improvements for Côte d'Ivoire, Eritrea, Kenya, Niger, and Senegal and moderate trade balance deterioration in South Africa (Figure 2.38).

Policy Challenges

Governments in the region should pursue policies that preserve economic and financial stability. In view of the heightened risks in the outlook, the need for governments to act as a steadying force is paramount. Yet large fiscal deficits and inefficient government spending are sources of vulnerability in much of the region. The basic need is to strengthen fiscal positions, and restore fiscal buffers to increase resilience against exogenous shocks (Chapter 3). In Ghana, Senegal, and Zambia, governments have to resist pressures for public sector wage increases, and cut less productive spending. Widening budget deficits in the region have been linked systematically to excessive current expenditures, rather than to infrastructure and other capital spending. Budget consolidation should involve a shift that enhances the efficiency of public expenditures and encourages growth, for example, toward efficient infrastructure investment as described below.

On the monetary policy front, given the favorable inflation outlook, many countries appear to have the space to maintain an accommodative monetary policy stance. In some countries (e.g., Ghana and South Africa), policy tightening would help reduce vulnerabilities and contain the potential inflationary impact of any exchange rate depreciation. With terms of trade of commodity exporters deteriorating, some currency depreciation may be appropriate, but monetary policy has to be sufficiently tight to ward off any secondary rounds of wage and price increases that might follow the one-off impact on consumer prices of more expensive imports.

There is an urgent need across the region for structural reforms to increase potential output growth. An acute infrastructure deficit is evident, especially in energy and roads. Countries across the region are rightly increasing public investment in infrastructure, as they strive to boost potential growth and to broaden it to reduce poverty. It is critical that improvements in public investment management systems are accompanied by efforts to ensure that resources are allocated to the most productive ends. For most countries in the region, concerns about the quality of public investment, and the

capacity to maintain and operate infrastructure once it is installed, highlight the need for financial management reforms. Reform efforts should aim at strengthening project selection, execution, and monitoring, and encourage transparency and accountability in the use of public resources.

TABLE 2.11   Sub-Saharan Africa forecast summary

(Annual percent change unless indicated otherwise)

	00-10[a]	2011	2012	2013	2014e	2015f	2016f	2017f
GDP at market prices[b]	5.7	4.3	4.0	4.2	4.5	4.6	4.9	5.1
(Average including countries with full national accounts and balance of payments data only)[c]								
GDP at market prices[c]	5.7	4.3	4.0	4.2	4.5	4.6	4.9	5.1
GDP per capita (units in US$)	3.1	1.7	1.5	1.7	2.0	2.1	2.4	2.6
PPP GDP[c]	5.8	4.4	4.1	4.4	4.7	4.8	5.0	5.3
Private consumption[d]	5.6	3.6	2.2	12.1	4.4	4.4	4.5	4.7
Public consumption	7.2	7.9	5.2	3.7	3.9	4.4	4.4	4.4
Fixed investment	9.2	-0.6	7.1	4.1	5.1	6.0	6.1	6.2
Exports, GNFS[f]	5.0	10.7	0.8	-7.3	3.4	3.9	4.1	4.2
Imports, GNFS[f]	8.2	8.3	1.4	6.0	3.3	4.5	4.3	3.9
Net exports, contribution to growth	-0.6	0.8	-0.1	-4.1	-0.1	-0.3	-0.2	0.0
Current account balance (percent of GDP)	-0.3	-1.3	-2.4	-2.8	-2.9	-3.9	-4.0	-3.8
Consumer prices (annual average)	8.6	10.1	11.3	8.2	8.7	...	...	...
Fiscal balance (percent of GDP)	-0.6	-1.1	-1.7	-2.9	-2.5	-2.2	-2.2	-2.1
Memo items: GDP								
SSA excluding South Africa	6.6	4.6	4.6	5.1	5.6	5.4	5.7	5.9
Broader geographic region (incl. recently high income countries)[f]	5.7	4.3	4.0	4.2	4.4	4.5	4.8	5.0
Oil exporters[g]	7.7	3.5	3.8	4.8	5.8	5.5	5.6	5.9
CFA countries[h]	4.1	2.4	5.7	4.4	5.5	5.0	5.2	5.4
South Africa	3.5	3.6	2.5	1.9	1.4	2.2	2.5	2.7
Nigeria	8.9	4.9	4.3	5.4	6.3	5.5	5.8	6.2
Angola	11.3	3.9	8.4	6.8	4.4	5.3	5.0	5.2

Source: World Bank.

World Bank forecasts are frequently updated based on new information and changing (global) circumstances. Consequently, projections presented here may differ from those contained in other Bank documents, even if basic assessments of countries' prospects do not differ at any given moment in time.

a. Growth rates over intervals are compound weighted averages; average growth contributions, ratios and deflators are calculated as simple averages of the annual weighted averages for the region.

b. GDP at market prices and expenditure components are measured in constant 2010 U.S. dollars.

c. Sub-region aggregate excludes Liberia, Chad, Somalia, Central African Republic, and São Tomé and Principe. Data limitations prevent the forecasting of GDP components or Balance of Payments details for these countries.

d. The sudden surge in Private Consumption in the region in 2013 is driven by the revised and rebased NIA data of Nigeria in 2014.

e. Exports and imports of goods and non-factor services (GNFS).

f. Recently high-income countries include Equatorial Guinea.

g. Oil Exporters: Angola, Côte d'Ivoire, Cameroon, Congo, Rep., Gabon, Nigeria, Sudan, Chad, Congo, Dem. Rep.

h. CFA Countries: Benin, Burkina Faso, Central African Republic, Côte d'Ivoire, Cameroon, Congo, Rep., Gabon, Equatorial Guinea, Mali, Niger, Senegal, Chad, Togo.

TABLE 2.12   Sub-Saharan Africa country forecast

(Real GDP growth at market prices in percent and current account balance in percent of GDP, unless indicated otherwise)

	00-10ᵃ	2011	2012	2013	2014e	2015f	2016f	2017f
Angola								
GDP	11.3	3.9	8.4	6.8	4.4	5.3	5.0	5.2
Current account balance	5.3	12.6	11.9	5.8	2.8	-2.0	-5.5	-5.7
Benin								
GDP	3.9	3.5	5.4	5.6	5.2	5.0	4.7	4.7
Current account balance	-7.1	-7.1	-6.0	-14.4	-12.8	-12.5	-8.0	-2.2
Botswana								
GDP	4.2	5.2	5.1	5.2	4.5	4.6	4.9	5.0
Current account balance	7.1	-2.1	-7.1	9.5	7.6	6.1	5.1	3.9
Burkina Faso								
GDP	6.0	4.2	9.5	5.3	6.0	5.5	6.5	6.8
Current account balance	-8.8	-1.5	-4.5	-7.1	-7.5	-6.9	-5.9	-5.1
Cabo Verde								
GDP	5.3	4.0	1.2	0.5	2.1	2.8	3.0	3.1
Current account balance	-11.1	-17.3	-9.8	-4.2	-5.0	-6.3	-5.1	-4.6
Cameroon								
GDP	3.3	4.1	4.6	5.5	5.1	5.1	4.9	5.1
Current account balance	-2.2	-2.8	-3.6	-3.7	-3.6	-4.1	-4.6	-4.9
Comoros								
GDP	1.8	2.2	3.0	3.5	3.4	3.6	3.2	3.0
Current account balance	-13.5	-26.2	-29.4	-27.1	-26.6	-25.3	-25.5	-24.8
Congo, Dem. Rep.								
GDP	4.7	6.9	7.2	8.5	8.0	7.8	7.5	7.3
Current account balance	-0.7	-5.4	-6.2	-10.3	-9.4	-10.1	-10.6	-10.8
Côte d'Ivoire								
GDP	1.1	-4.7	9.5	8.7	9.1	8.5	8.2	8.0
Current account balance	1.8	13.0	-1.7	-3.0	-2.1	-2.5	-3.9	-5.0
Eritrea								
GDP	0.9	8.7	7.0	1.3	3.2	3.0	4.0	4.3
Current account balance	-19.5	4.9	12.8	2.5	-3.1	-4.3	-7.6	-6.8
Ethiopia								
GDP	8.6	11.2	8.7	10.4	6.7	6.9	6.6	6.7
Current account balance	-4.7	-2.0	-6.2	-6.0	-7.0	-7.5	-7.6	-7.5
Gabon								
GDP	2.0	7.1	5.6	5.9	5.0	5.5	5.6	5.7
Current account balance	14.1	11.3	9.1	5.4	3.8	1.4	-2.8	-2.1
Gambia, The								
GDP	3.8	-4.3	6.1	5.6	5.7	5.3	4.8	4.6
Current account balance	-1.6	12.2	6.4	3.3	-2.0	-1.9	-1.3	-1.3
Ghana								
GDP	5.8	15.0	8.8	7.1	4.7	4.5	5.5	6.0
Current account balance	-13.5	-10.9	-11.4	-12.0	-10.6	-10.9	-9.9	-8.8
Guinea								
GDP	2.6	3.9	3.9	2.5	0.5	-0.2	2.2	2.5
Current account balance	-6.9	-23.5	-19.4	-10.9	-11.5	-15.1	-15.4	-14.9

TABLE 2.12   *(continued)*

(Real GDP grow th at market prices in percent and current account balance in percent of GDP, unless indicated otherw ise)

	00-10[a]	2011	2012	2013	2014e	2015f	2016f	2017f
Guinea-Bissau								
GDP	2.2	5.3	-1.5	0.3	2.1	2.5	2.3	2.0
Current account balance	-0.7	2.6	-7.6	-8.1	-7.8	-7.0	-6.1	-6.3
Kenya								
GDP	4.4	6.1	4.5	5.7	5.4	6.0	6.6	6.5
Current account balance	-2.4	-9.1	-8.4	-8.3	-7.4	-6.7	-5.8	-4.7
Lesotho								
GDP	4.0	2.8	6.5	5.9	4.6	4.7	4.5	4.4
Current account balance	2.7	-18.5	-25.2	-5.5	-2.6	-2.0	-2.2	-2.8
Madagascar								
GDP	2.5	1.0	2.4	2.1	3.0	3.6	3.8	3.9
Current account balance	-11.5	-7.7	-8.4	-6.2	-8.5	-11.0	-0.7	1.8
Malaw i								
GDP	4.5	4.3	1.9	5.0	4.2	4.6	5.0	5.2
Current account balance	-10.8	-13.6	-18.9	-18.1	-17.8	-17.4	-15.8	-14.2
Mali								
GDP at market prices (% annual grow th)[b]	6.0	2.7	-0.4	2.1	5.0	4.3	4.6	4.8
Current account balance	-8.5	-6.2	-2.7	-5.4	-9.3	-9.4	-9.8	-9.9
Mauritania								
GDP	4.9	4.0	7.0	6.7	5.7	5.5	5.6	5.6
Current account balance	-10.6	-0.5	-25.8	-18.3	-20.7	-22.1	-24.2	-25.7
Mauritius								
GDP	3.8	3.9	3.2	3.2	3.4	3.9	3.7	3.7
Current account balance	-3.4	-13.4	-10.5	-12.5	-10.8	-10.0	-9.4	-8.7
Mozam bique								
GDP	7.8	7.3	7.2	7.1	7.2	8.0	8.1	8.2
Current account balance	-14.1	-23.9	-43.2	-36.3	-33.9	-31.4	-31.1	-31.2
Nam ibia								
GDP	4.6	5.1	5.2	5.1	4.2	4.3	4.1	4.0
Current account balance	4.4	-1.2	-2.2	-7.9	-6.5	-6.6	-5.2	-4.1
Niger								
GDP	4.6	2.3	10.8	3.9	5.7	6.0	6.2	6.3
Current account balance	-10.5	-18.7	-8.4	-8.2	-11.4	-12.0	-12.9	-13.4
Nigeria								
GDP	8.9	4.9	4.3	5.4	6.3	5.5	5.8	6.2
Current account balance	13.5	3.0	4.4	4.0	3.7	1.9	2.0	1.8
Rw anda								
GDP	7.9	7.5	7.3	4.6	6.0	6.5	7.0	7.1
Current account balance	-5.5	-7.5	-11.5	-7.1	-6.0	-4.9	-4.1	-4.5
Senegal								
GDP	4.1	2.1	3.5	4.0	4.5	4.8	4.7	4.7
Current account balance	-7.7	-7.9	-12.1	-10.6	-9.6	-8.2	-7.5	-6.4
Sierra Leone								
GDP	8.9	6.0	15.2	20.1	4.0	-2.0	2.5	2.7
Current account balance	-6.5	-66.6	-22.9	-10.3	-12.5	-15.0	-15.4	-15.7

TABLE 2.12   *(continued)*

(Real GDP grow th at market prices in percent and current account balance in percent of GDP, unless indicated otherw ise)

	00-10ᵃ	2011	2012	2013	2014e	2015f	2016f	2017f
South Africa								
GDP	3.5	3.6	2.5	1.9	1.4	2.2	2.5	2.7
Current account balance	-2.9	-2.3	-5.2	-5.8	-5.6	-5.2	-4.8	-4.5
Sudan								
GDP	6.3	-3.3	-10.1	-6.0	2.6	2.5	2.8	3.0
Current account balance	-7.2	-1.7	-9.7	-8.6	-11.2	-10.9	-10.7	-10.2
Sw aziland								
GDP	2.3	-0.7	1.9	2.8	2.0	2.2	2.6	2.8
Current account balance	-3.2	-8.2	3.8	3.8	1.8	-2.8	-3.2	-3.3
Tanzania								
GDP	7.0	6.4	6.9	7.0	7.0	7.2	6.8	7.0
Current account balance	-5.1	-16.7	-12.9	-11.4	-13.5	-13.1	-12.9	-12.6
Togo								
GDP	2.2	4.9	5.9	5.1	5.2	5.0	4.9	4.7
Current account balance	-9.0	-8.2	-8.1	-11.3	-12.6	-12.6	-13.2	-12.5
Uganda								
GDP	7.5	5.0	4.6	5.9	6.3	6.6	6.9	7.0
Current account balance	-4.2	-9.8	-6.8	-7.0	-8.7	-9.2	-10.3	-10.9
Zambia								
GDP	5.6	6.8	7.3	6.4	6.4	6.3	6.5	6.7
Current account balance	-6.1	9.2	5.2	1.5	0.6	0.1	0.4	1.2
Zimbabw e								
GDP	-4.7	11.9	10.6	4.5	3.1	3.2	3.7	3.4
Current account balance	-13.6	-29.9	-24.4	-25.4	-23.9	-24.2	-25.4	-25.4

	00-10ᵃ	2011	2012	2013	2014e	2015f	2016f	2017f
Recently transitioned to high-income countries [b]								
Equatorial Guinea								
GDP	14.7	5.0	3.2	-4.9	-2.2	-8.1	-7.3	-6.4
Current account balance	-26.9	-17.3	-9.3	-19.1	-13.9	-17.8	-20.0	-19.2

Source: World Bank.

World Bank forecasts are frequently updated based on new information and changing (global) circumstances. Consequently, projections presented here may differ from those contained in other Bank documents, even if basic assessments of countries' prospects do not significantly differ at any given moment in time.

Liberia, Somalia, Sao Tome and Principe are not forecast owing to data limitations.

a. GDP growth rates over intervals are compound average; current account balance shares are simple averages over the period.

b. The recently high-income countries are based on World Bank's reclassification from 2004 to 2014.

BOX 2.4   How Resilient Is Sub-Saharan Africa?[1]

Growth in Sub-Saharan Africa is fairly resilient to a variety of external shocks. In contrast, it is highly vulnerable to domestic shocks, such as drought or civil conflict.

FIGURE B2.4.1   GDP growth

Sub-Saharan Africa has been resilient to global recession and weak recovery.

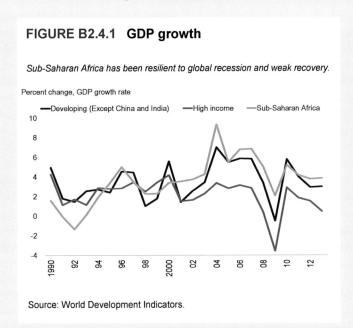

Source: World Development Indicators.

FIGURE B2.4.2   Deviations from the baseline GDP under various scenarios in 2025

The slowdown in BRICS and conflict scenarios have the largest impacts on GDP.

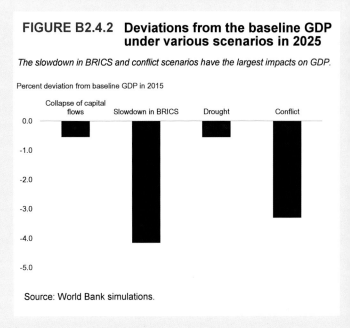

Source: World Bank simulations.

Despite weak global growth in recent years, Sub-Saharan Africa has recovered well (Figure B2.4.1). However, in light of the fragile medium-term global growth outlook, concerns remain about the resilience of Sub-Saharan African to future shocks. This box takes a long-term view and studies how Sub-Saharan African growth will react to various shocks through 2025 by employing a multicountry general equilibrium model.[2]

Baseline scenario and the shocks

The baseline scenario assumes a steady recovery in high-income countries and continued growth in developing countries. The supportive external environment, together with capital accumulation, technological catch-up, and within-region demographic change support growth in Sub-Saharan Africa of 5 percent a year through 2025. The baseline is perturbed by shocks that originate outside the region (a prolonged recession

in the high-income countries and an accompanying decline in global capital flows, and a prolonged recession in the BRICS countries (Brazil, Russian Federation, India, China, and South Africa) and within the region (drought in several countries, and civil conflict in key countries). Except for the cessation of global capital flows (which would be unprecedented), the shocks are of a duration and magnitude within the range of historical norms. The external shocks are assumed to last throughout the entire period under analysis, while droughts and conflicts are modeled to last three years followed by a swift recovery.

Slowdown in high-income countries and decline of global capital flows

Growth in several Sub-Saharan African economies that rely heavily on capital inflows would be dampened by a prolonged slowdown in high-income countries and accompanying disruption to global capital flows. Given that high-income countries account for almost 90 percent of the FDI flows to Africa, a collapse in capital flows is considered a worst-case scenario in order to illustrate their importance for the region. The growth slowdown and reduction in capital flows are modeled as halving the per capita growth rate of high-income countries to 0.7 percent over 2015—25 and a gradual withdrawal of capital flows to Sub-Saharan Africa by 2025.

---

[1] The main author of this box is Maryla Maliszewska.

[2] For details of the model here, see Devarajan, Go, Maliszewska, Osorio-Rodarte, and Timmer (2013) and World Bank (2013c). The framework involves a multicountry general equilibrium model and a microsimulation model that subjects the African economies to a series of shocks (van der Mensbrugghe, 2011 and 2013; Bourguignon and Bussolo, 2013).

BOX 2.4   *(continued)*

FIGURE B2.4.3   **Share of BRICS and HIC in SSA exports**

The importance of BRICS has been steadily growing.

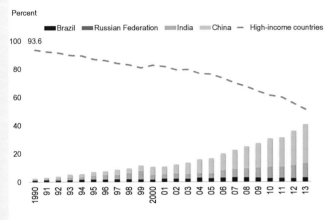

Source: World Integrated Trade Solution.

FIGURE B2.4.4   **Droughts in Sub-Saharan Africa**

Droughts are a recurrent event affecting millions of people.

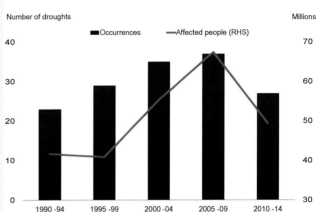

Source: The OFDA/CRED International Disaster.
Note: Occurrences are the number of droughts in a given 5-year period.

Without external financing, investment in several countries relying on capital inflows would drop significantly, while slower external demand would reduce the volume of exports. As a result, investment in countries such as Ghana and Malawi would fall by up to 10 percentage points of GDP in 2025 relative to the baseline. GDP in net capital importers as a group would decline almost 6 percent below the baseline level in 2025.

The effect of a downturn in capital inflows would be tempered by the fact that the number of resource-rich Sub-Saharan African countries, which are net exporters of capital, is rising. If large resource-rich economies, such as Botswana, Nigeria, or Zambia, are able to absorb and invest their excess capital domestically (which would otherwise flow to the rest of the world), expanding output accordingly, GDP in net capital exporters would rise 13.4 percent above the baseline by 2025.

The diverging effects of net importers versus net exporters of capital would offset one another. As a result, Sub-Saharan Africa's overall GDP would only fall 0.5 percent below the baseline in 2025 (Figure B2.4.2). If, however, resource-rich countries are not able to deploy their excess capital productively, the adverse impact on the regional output would be much larger.[3]

Slowdown in the BRICS

From negligible trade flows two decades ago, China has become Africa's major trading partner and, together with Brazil, India, and

the Russian Federation, buys 44 percent of Africa's exports, mainly commodities (Figure B2.4.3). This deepening trade link implies that African economies have become more vulnerable to lower growth rates in the BRICS countries. Indeed, recent research finds that Africa's business cycles are increasingly linked to the BRICS' business cycles (Diallo and Tapsoba, 2014). The importance of China's economic performance for Africa has also received attention: a 1 percentage point increase in China's investment growth is associated with a 0.6 percentage point increase in Sub-Saharan Africa export growth (Drummond and Liu, 2013).

Under the scenario of a persistent slowdown in the BRICS (with their average per capita growth rate at 2.3 percent over 2015-25, about 1.4 percentage points lower than in the baseline), Sub-Saharan African countries' exports would be 13 percentage points below the baseline, although the weaker global demand would dampen increases in commodity and agricultural and food prices over time.[4] Sub-Saharan African GDP would drop about 4 percent below the baseline by 2025. In contrast to the scenario of

---

[3]These findings confirm those from other recent studies. For example, a structural slowdown in high-income countries would have smaller negative spillover effects for developing countries than a cyclical slowdown, where monetary policy easing would lead to a depreciation of currencies of emerging markets, magnifying the impact on developing countries through lower imports (IMF, 2014d).

[4]This scenario does not incorporate the potential impact of rebalancing of China's growth.

BOX 2.4   *(continued)*

a slowdown in the high-income countries and an accompanying collapse of capital flows, activity in all Sub-Saharan African countries would be reduced by slowing growth in the BRICS.

Droughts

Droughts are recurrent events in Sub-Saharan Africa, with tragic repercussions for millions of people (Figure B2.4.4). As of 2012, more than 18 million people suffered food shortages and over 1 million children faced the risk of acute malnutrition.

Following historical patterns, the drought scenario assumes a temporary shock to productivity in agriculture that initially reduces agricultural output by around 10 percent and dissipates over the next two years. Prices of agricultural products and food would rise following the drop in output and Sub-Saharan imports would increase in this scenario, reducing GDP by almost 1 percent below the baseline. Households would bear the burden of higher prices. Given that agricultural and food expenditures constitute a high share of household budgets in Sub-Saharan African countries, real consumption would decrease substantially absent government or international intervention. The loss in household consumption for Sub-Saharan Africa as a whole would amount to 1.3 percent in 2015 and would be fairly persistent.

Other research also finds that in a typical developing country a drought leads to a reduction of agricultural and industrial annual growth rate of the order of 1.0 percentage point, resulting in a decline of GDP of 0.6 percentage points per year, or 3.0 percentage points over a period of five years (Loayza et al., 2009). These effects are expected to be considerably worse in the case of a severe drought.[5]

Conflict

Conflict is a significant contributor to growth collapses or decelerations among African countries (Arbache et al., 2008). In 2000, for example, one in five people in Sub-Saharan Africa lived in a country affected by conflict (World Bank, 2000; Figure B2.4.5).

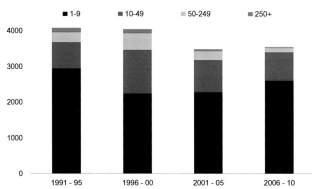

FIGURE B2.4.5   Conflicts in Sub-Sahara in Africa

The 2000s saw a decline in the number of state-related violent incidents.

Numbers of state-related violences

Source: UCDP GEP - Uppsala Conflict Data Program's Georeferenced Event Dataset
Note: State related violence is classified by the estimated number of deaths; for example, an event marked as 1-9 is a conflict with 1-9 deaths.

The conflict scenario models hypothetical civil unrest in three large countries lasting for a period of three years.[6] The destruction of capital is captured by doubling the depreciation rates over that period, while the investment-to-GDP ratio is halved. Conflict is also assumed to reduce productivity, with a larger reduction in manufacturing and services than in agriculture. Productivity is assumed to revert to the pre-conflict level two years after the end of the conflict.

The results of the scenario are consistent with historical experience. Investment quickly recovers to and rises above the pre-conflict level, and marginal returns to capital are much higher following the destruction of a large part of the capital stock. Even so, the capital stock in the countries hit by civil unrest would remain well below the baseline levels. GDP would take a significant hit in the countries affected by conflict, with declines of up to 15 percent below the baseline but it would recover quickly. Nonetheless, regional GDP would remain more than 3 percent below the baseline level in 2025 under the conflict scenario, mainly because the initial loss in capital stock would prevent it from returning to its reference trend level.

Other research finds a GDP loss from conflict of a similar magnitude. Although damages can vary, annual per capita growth during civil wars is estimated to be reduced by 2.2 percentage points below the baseline. The length of war, however, has an impact on the speed of post-war recovery (Collier, 1999). A

---

[5]For instance, in the case of Malawi, a severe drought (occurring on average every 25 years) could destroy more than 20 percent of agricultural GDP and reduce GDP by 10 percent (Pauw, Thurlow and van Seventer, 2010).

[6]These are Ethiopia, Nigeria, and South Africa. Ethiopia engaged in a border war with Eritrea in the late 1990s and bouts of violence resurface occasionally. Nigeria faces an ongoing insurgency, with Boko Haram controlling the Northern part of the country. South Africa faces recurring strikes of workers in gold mines resulting in a significant reduction of export revenues, investment, and growth.

BOX 2.4   *(continued)*

range of policies such as developing institutional resilience, good governance, building inclusive coalitions for policies or managing external stress have been recommended to prevent conflict in the region (World Bank, 2011b).

Conclusion

The results of the simulations paint a cautiously optimistic picture. Growth in Sub-Saharan Africa is fairly resilient to a prolonged recession in high-income countries, partly as a result of declining trade links. The region appears to be more vulnerable to persistently lower growth rates in the BRICS, but a slowdown of limited duration would not impact its long-term growth prospects. Further, Sub-Saharan African economies are sensitive to domestic shocks, such as drought or civil conflict, with strong negative and immediate impacts.

These adverse shocks also affect poverty in the region. Specifically, in the medium term, the domestic shocks would inflict greater damage in terms of forgone poverty reduction than the external shocks. The poverty headcount at PPP$1.25/day in the conflict and drought scenarios would be greater by 2.1 and 1.0 percentage points, respectively, relative to the baseline numbers in 2025, adding 26 million and 12 million more people in poverty, respectively. The external shocks would increase poverty by about 0.3 percentage points in the medium run, but due to their persistence, their long-term impact would be much more severe.

Because of the economic importance of agriculture and food in household budgets, Sub-Saharan Africa will need to increase the resilience and productivity of its agricultural sector against droughts. Diversifying exports and expanding regional integration and markets, as well as improving financial markets will also increase the region's resilience to negative shocks to external demand. However, as in the past, civil conflicts and violence could pose by far the greatest danger to the region's economic performance and poverty reduction.

References

Abbas, A., and A. Klemm. 2012. "A Partial Race to the Bottom: Corporate Tax Developments in Emerging and Developing Economies." Working Paper 12/28, International Monetary Fund, Washington, DC.

African Development Bank. 2014. Innovation and Productivity: Empirical Analysis for North African Countries, Tunis. Tunisia: African Development Bank.

Ahuja, A., and M. Nabar. 2012. "Investment-Led Growth in China: Global Spillovers." Working Paper 12/267, International Monetary Fund, Washington, DC.

Anand, R., D. Ding, and V. Tulin. 2014. "Food Inflation in India: The Role for Monetary Policy." Working Paper WP/14/178, International Monetary Fund, Washington, DC.

Andres, L., D. Biller, and M. H. Dappe. 2013. Reducing Poverty by Closing South Asia's Infrastructure Gap. Washington, DC: World Bank.

Arbache, J, D. S. Go, and J. Page. 2008. "Is Africa's Economy at a Turning Point?" In Africa at a Turning Point: Growth, Aid, and External Shocks, ed. Delfin Go and John Page, 13–85. Washington, DC: World Bank.

Baffes, J., and C. Savescu. 2014. "Causes of the Post-2000 Metal Super Cycle." Mimeo, World Bank, Washington, DC.

Bahar, D. R.Hausmann, and C.A. Hidalgo. 2014. "Neighbors and the Evolution of the Comparative Advantage of Nations: Evidence of International Knowledge Diffusion?" Journal of International Economics 92 (1): 111–23.

Barnett, A., B. Broadbent, A. Chiu, J. Franklin, and H. Miller. 2014. "Impaired Capital Reallocation and Productivity." National Institute Economic Review 228 (1): 35–41.

Barro, R.J., and J. Lee. 2013. "A New Data Set of Educational Attainment in the World, 1950–2010." Journal of Development Economics 104: 184–98.

Berument, H., M. Nildag, B. Ceylan, and N.Dogan. 2010. "The Impact of Oil Price Shocks on Economic Growth of Selected MENA Countries." The Energy Journal 31(1): 149-76.

Bourguignon, F., and M. Bussolo. 2013. "Income Distribution in Computable General Equilibrium Modeling." In Handbook of Computable General Equilibrium Modeling, ed. P.B. Dixon and D.W. Jorgenson, 1383–1437. North Holland: Elsevier B.V.

Caballero, R., J., Takeo Hoshi, and A.K. Kashyap. 2008. "Zombie Lending and Depressed Restructuring in Japan." American Economic Review 98 (5): 1943–77.

Chandrasiri, S. 2009. Promoting Employment-Intensive Growth in Sri Lanka: Policy Analysis of the Manufacturing and Service Sectors. Geneva: International Labour Organization.

Cheung, Y., M. D. Chinn, and X. Qian. 2014. "The Structural Behavior of China-U.S. Trade Flows." La Follette School Working Paper No. 2014-009, University of Wisconsin-Madison.

Collier, P. 1999. "On the Economic Consequences of Civil War." Oxford Economic Papers 51 (1): 168–83.

Devarajan, D., Delfin S. Go, M. Maliszewska, I. Osorio-Rodarte, and H. Timmer. 2013. "Stress-Testing Africa's Recent Growth and Poverty Performance." Policy Research Working Paper 6317, World Bank, Washington, DC.

Diallo, O., and S.J.-A. Tapsoba. 2014. "Rising BRICS and Changes in Sub-Saharan Africa's Business Cycle Patterns." IMF Working Paper 14/35, International Monetary Fund, Washington, DC.

Ding, D., and I. Masha. 2012. "India's Growth Spillovers to South Asia." Working Paper 12/56, International Monetary Fund, Washington, DC.

Drummond, P., and E. Xue Liu. 2013. "Africa's Rising Exposure to China: How Large Are Spillovers Through Trade?" IMF Working Paper 13/250, International Monetary Fund, Washington, DC.

ECLAC (United Nations Economic Commission for Latin America and the Caribbean). 2014. Latin America and the Caribbean in the World Economy: Regional Integration and Value Chains in a Challenging External Environment. Santiago: ECLAC.

Eichengreen, B., P. Donghyung, and S. Kwanho. 2012. "When Fast Growing Economies Slow Down: International Evidence and Implications for China." Asian Economic Papers 11 (1): 42–87.

Garcia-Herrero, A., and D. Santabárbara. 2008. "Does China Have an Impact on Foreign Direct Investment to Latin America?" China Economic Review 18 (2007): 266–86.

Gauvin, L., and C. Rebillard. 2014. "Towards Recoupling? Assessing the Impact of a Chinese Hard Landing on Commodity Exporters: Results from Conditional Forecast in a GVAR Model." Mimeo. Lyon Meeting.

Gruss, B. 2014. "After the Boom: Commodity Prices and Economic Growth in Latin America and the Caribbean." Working Paper 14/154, International Monetary Fund, Washington, DC.

Hanson, G. 2012. Understanding Mexico's Economic Underperformance. Washington, DC: Migration Policy Institute.

IDB (Inter-American Development Bank). 2014. "Global Recovery and Monetary Normalization: Escaping a Chronicle Foretold?" Organized by Andrew Powell. 2014 Latin American and Caribbean Macroeconomic Report, IDB, Washington, DC.

IMF (International Monetary Fund). 2013a. "Russian Federation: 2013 Article IV Consultation." Country Report 13/310, International Monetary Fund, Washington, DC.

———. 2013b. "Pakistan: Article IV Consultation and Request for an Extended Arrangement under the Extended Fund Facility." Country Report 13/287, IMF, Washington, DC.

———. 2014a. Toward New Horizons: Arab Economic Transformation Amid Political Transitions. Washington, DC: IMF.

———. 2014b. Subsidy Reforms in the Middle East and North Africa: Recent Progress and Challenges Ahead. Washington, DC: IMF.

———. 2014c. "India: Staff Report for 2014 Article IV Consultation." Country Report 14/57, IMF, Washington, DC.

———. 2014d. "Spillovers from a Potential Reversal of Fortune in Emerging Market Economies." In IMF Multilateral Policy Issues Report: 2014 Spillover Report, ed. IMF, 55–81. Washington, DC: IMF.

Jian, C., Y. Lingxiu, and H. Yiping. 2013. "How Big Is the Chinese Government Debt?" China Economic Journal 6 (2–3): 152–71.

Keen, M. 2012. "Taxation and Development: Again." Working Paper 12/220, International Monetary Fund, Washington, DC.

Keen, M., and B. Lockwood. 2010. "The Value Added Tax: Its Causes and Consequences." Journal of Development Economics 92 (2): 138–51.

Koopman, R., W. Powers, Z. Wang, and S. Wei. 2010. "Give Credit Where Credit is Due: Tracing Value Added in Global Production Chains." NBER Working Paper 16426.

———. 2014. "Tracing Value-Added and Double Counting in Gross Exports: Dataset." American Economic Review 104 (2): 459–94.

Loayza, N., E.Olaberria, J.Rigolini, and L.Christiaensen. 2009. "Natural Disasters and Growth: Going beyond the Averages." Policy Research Working Paper 4980, World Bank, Washington, DC.

Lopez-Calix, R. Jose, and Irum Touqeer. 2013. "Mobilizing Revenue." Pakistan Policy Note 16, World Bank, Washington, DC.

Norregaard, J., and T. Khan. 2007. "Tax Policy: Recent Trends and Coming Challenges." Working Paper 07/274, International Monetary Fund, Washington, DC.

Pargal, S., and S. Banerjee. 2014. More Power to India: The Challenge of Electricity Distribution. Washington, DC: World Bank. http://documents.worldbank.org/curated/en/2014/06/19703395/more-power-india-challenge-electricity-distribution.

Pauw, K., J. Thurlow, and D. van Seventer. 2010. "Droughts and Floods in Malawi." Discussion Paper 962, International Food Policy Research Institute, Washington, DC.

PISA (Programme for International Student Assessment). 2012. "OECD: Programme for International Student Assessment." Organisation for Economic Co-operation and Development, Paris. http://www.oecd.org.

Rahman, J., and T. Zhao. 2013. "Export Performance in Europe: What Do We Know from Supply Links?" Working Paper 13/62, International Monetary Fund, Washington, DC.

Roache, S. K. 2012. "China's Impact on World Commodity Markets." Working Paper 12/115, International Monetary Fund, Washington, DC.

Timmer, M., ed. 2012. "The World Input-Output Database (WIOD): Contents, Sources and Methods." Working Paper 10, World Input-Output Database.

UNODC (United Nations Office on Drugs and Crime). 2014. Global Study on Homicide 2013. Vienna: UNODC.

Van der Mensbrugghe, D. 2011. "Linkage Technical Reference Document." Version 7.1. World Bank, Washington, DC. http://siteresources.worldbank.org/INTPROSPECTS/Resources/334934-1314986341738/TechRef7.1_01Mar2011.pdf.

———. 2013. "Modeling the Global Economy: Forward Looking Scenarios for Agriculture." In Handbook of Computable General Equilibrium Modeling, ed. P.B. Dixon and D.W. Jorgenson, 933–94. North Holland: Elsevier B.V.

Westcott, P., and R. Trostle. 2014. "USDA Agricultural Projections to 2023." Economic Research Service, U.S. Department of Agriculture, Washington, DC.

World Bank. 2000. Can Africa Claim the 21st Century? Washington, DC: World Bank.

———. 2011a. "LAC's Long-Term Growth: Made in China?" Latin America and the Caribbean Region Report, World Bank, Washington, DC.

———. 2011b. World Development Report 2011: Conflict, Security, and Development. Washington, DC: World Bank.

———. 2012. "South Asia Economic Focus, June 2012: Creating Fiscal Space through Revenue Mobilization." World Bank, Washington, DC.

————. 2013a. "June 2013 Global Economic Prospects." World Bank, Washington, DC.

————. 2013b. Middle East and North Africa Economic Developments and Prospects: Investing in Turbulent Times. Washington, DC: World Bank.

————. 2013c. "An Analysis of Issues Shaping Africa's Economic Future." Africa's Pulse 8 (October 2013), World Bank, Washington, DC.

————. 2014a. "China Economic Update, June 2014." World Bank, Washington, DC.

————. 2014b. "Enhancing Competitiveness in an Uncertain World." East Asia Update, October, World Bank, Washington, DC.

————. 2014c. "Brittle Recovery." South East Europe Regular Economic Report, May, World Bank, Washington, DC.

————. 2014d. Diversified Development—Making the Most of Natural Resources in Eurasia. Washington, DC: World Bank.

————. 2014e. "Global Economic Prospects: Commodity Markets Outlook." World Bank, Washington, DC.

————. 2014f. "Implications of a Changing China for Brazil: A New Window of Opportunity." Economic Report, World Bank, Washington, DC.

————. 2014g. The Rise of the South: Challenges for Latin America and the Caribbean. Washington, DC: World Bank.

————. 2014h. Doing Business 2015. Washington, DC: World Bank.

————. 2014i. "Harnessing the Global Recovery: A Tough Road Ahead." MENA Regional Economic Update, April, World Bank, Washington, DC.

————. 2014j. "Corrosive Subsidies." MENA Economic Monitor, October, World Bank, Washington, DC.

————. 2014k. The Economic Impact of the 2014 Ebola Epidemic: Short and Medium-Term Estimates for West Africa. Washington, DC: World Bank.

World Bank and Development Research Center of the State Council, the People's Republic of China. 2014. Urban China: Toward Efficient, Inclusive, and Sustainable Urbanization. Washington, DC: World Bank.

Wang, S. 2011. "State Misallocation and Housing Prices: Theory and Evidence from China." American Economic Review 101 (5): 2081–107.

Xing, Y., and N. Detert. 2010. "How the iPhone Widens the United States Trade Deficit with the People's Republic of China." Working Paper 257, Asian Development Bank, Washington, DC.

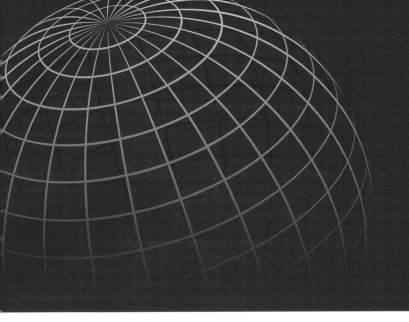

CHAPTER 3

HAVING SPACE AND USING IT:

Fiscal Policy Challenges in Developing Economies

Developing economies face downside risks to growth and prospects of rising financing costs. In the event that these cause a cyclical slowdown, policymakers may need to employ fiscal policy as a possible tool for stimulus. But will developing economies be able to use fiscal policy effectively? This chapter argues that fiscal space is essential for both the availability and the effectiveness of fiscal policy. Developing economies built fiscal space in the runup to the Great Recession of 2008–09, which was then used for stimulus. This reflects a more general trend over the past three decades, where availability of fiscal space has been associated with increasingly countercyclical (or less procyclical) fiscal policy. Wider fiscal space also appears to make fiscal policy more effective. However, fiscal space has shrunk since the Great Recession and has not returned to pre-crisis levels. Thus, developing economies need to rebuild buffers at a pace appropriate to country-specific conditions. For many countries, soft oil prices provide a window of opportunity to implement subsidy reforms that help build fiscal space while, at the same time, removing long-standing distortions. Over the medium-term, credible and well-designed institutional arrangements, such as fiscal rules, stabilization funds, and medium-term expenditure frameworks, can help build fiscal space and strengthen policy outcomes.[1]

Introduction

Growth in developing economies has slowed in recent years and significant downside risks remain, including slowdowns in major trading partners. In addition, financing costs are expected to rise from the current exceptionally low levels when monetary policy normalization gets under way in some advanced economies. Tightening of global financial conditions and bouts of financial market volatility might cause slowdowns or reversals of capital inflows.[2] Since the risk to capital flows can constrain monetary policy in developing economies, the option of fiscal policy as a countercyclical tool becomes particularly important.[3] How effective will fiscal policy be in supporting activity in developing economies in the event of a downturn? This question is the main focus of the chapter.

There are two related prerequisites for fiscal policy to be useful. First, *availability*: governments need to have the necessary fiscal space to implement countercyclical measures. Second, *effectiveness*: countercyclical fiscal policy has to be actually effective in raising the level of economic activity.[4] This chapter draws policy lessons by analyzing the historical experience of developing economies and answering the following questions:

- How has fiscal space evolved over time?
- Have developing economies "graduated" from the procyclicality of fiscal policy during the 1980s?
- Has greater fiscal space supported more effective fiscal policy?
- What institutional arrangements might strengthen fiscal space and policy outcomes, drawing lessons from country experiences?
- What objectives with respect to fiscal space should policymakers pursue in the current environment?

The focus here is on Emerging Market Economies (EMEs) and Frontier Market Economies (FMEs) that are able to tap international capital markets.[5] The chapter also briefly explores the role of fiscal policy in stimulating activity in Low Income Countries (LICs) that depend on concessional finance.

The chapter reports four main findings:

- During the 2000s, in the runup to the Great Recession of 2008–09, EMEs and FMEs built fiscal space by reducing debt and closing deficits (Figure 3.1). To support activity during the Great Recession, this space was used for fiscal stimulus. Deficits rose and have remained elevated as EMEs and FMEs have taken advantage of historically low interest rates.

- Fiscal policy in EMEs and FMEs has become more countercyclical (or less procyclical) since the 1980s, as most clearly demonstrated during the Great Recession.

- Wider fiscal space is associated with more effective fiscal policy in developing economies: fiscal multipliers tend to be larger in countries with greater fiscal space.

---

[1]This chapter is prepared by a team led by Ayhan Kose and Franziska Ohnsorge, and including S. Amer Ahmed, Raju Huidrom, Sergio Kurlat, and Jamus J. Lim, with contributions from Israel Osorio-Rodarte and Nao Sugawara, as well as consultancy support from Raphael Espinoza, Ugo Panizza, and Carlos Végh.

[2]For a discussion on the potential impact of monetary policy normalization on growth and capital inflows in developing economies, see World Bank (2014a) and IMF (2014a).

[3]Countercyclicality of fiscal policy refers to an increase in government consumption or cut in taxes during downturns to support economic activity. In the empirical analysis, countercyclicality is defined as a negative and statistically significant response of government consumption to exogenous movements in GDP, as inferred from an econometric model. The chapter also examines countercyclicality in terms of negative and statistically significant correlations between the cyclical components of government consumption and GDP. See Technical Annex for details.

---

[4]The changing nature of fiscal policy, its availability, and effectiveness in advanced and developing economies have received attention in recent research. Vegh and Vuletin (2013) show how fiscal policy has become increasingly countercyclical in Latin America. Ilzetzki et al (2013) and Auerbach and Gorodnichenko (2012a) explore the effectiveness of fiscal policy in various samples of advanced economies and large emerging markets. Kraay (2012) and Eden and Kraay (2014) examine the impact of fiscal policy in low-income countries.

[5]See Annex 3B for details on country classification.

FIGURE 3.1 Evolution of fiscal space and financing costs

Fiscal space used during the crisis has not been rebuilt and EMEs and FMEs are still taking advantage of historically low financing costs to run deficits.

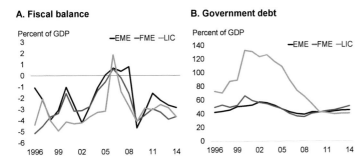

A. Fiscal balance

B. Government debt

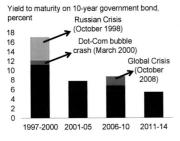

C. EME long-term interest rates

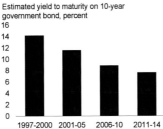

D. FME long-term interest rates

Source: World Bank estimates.
Note: All figures are based on unweighted averages across the country grouping or time period. The interest rates over a given time period are averages of daily rates. For EMEs, the nominal long-term interest rate is equal to the government 10-year bond yield. In the case of FMEs, the generic bond yield data were sparse for many economies and time periods. Hence, the nominal interest rate is estimated as the sum of 10-year U.S. Treasury yields plus the predicted spreads from a fixed-effect OLS regression of J.P. Morgan's EMBI on the Institutional Investor Rating. For the crisis periods, the interest rates refer to the average of daily rates in that month. EME: emerging market economies; FME: frontier market economies; LIC: low income countries. Details on the fiscal space data and market based country classifications are described in the Annex 3B. Orange and red bars indicate spikes in long-term interest rates during the relevant months.

- Well-designed and credible institutional frameworks, such as fiscal rules, stabilization funds, and medium-term expenditure frameworks, can help build fiscal space and strengthen policy outcomes.

In developing economies, debt stocks on average remain moderate despite being higher than expected immediately after the crisis. Fiscal deficits are substantial and have not yet returned to pre-crisis levels. Many economies will need to reduce their fiscal deficits to more sustainable levels. The appropriate speed of adjustment towards these medium-term goals, however, depends on a range of country-specific factors, in particular the cyclical position of the economy and constraints on monetary policy. With restored space, fiscal policy will be more effective in providing support to activity in developing economies than under the current fiscal conditions.

The rest of the chapter is organized as follows. The next section describes the conceptual framework for defining and measuring fiscal space. It also outlines the evolution of fiscal space and fiscal policy in EMEs and FMEs. Next, using an econometric model, the chapter estimates fiscal multipliers, which depend on fiscal space. It then discusses institutional arrangements designed to implement sound fiscal policy. The next section assesses current risks, and appropriate medium-term operational goals. The chapter concludes with a brief summary of the main findings and policy recommendations.

How Has Fiscal Space Evolved?

Definition of Fiscal Space

A range of definitions for fiscal space is used in the literature. This chapter follows the definition of Ley (2009): "availability of budgetary resources for a specific purpose...without jeopardizing the sustainability of the government's financial position or the sustainability of the economy." This broad definition allows fiscal space to be considered along multiple dimensions.[6] The first is fiscal solvency risk. The second delineates balance sheet vulnerabilities, such as maturity profile and nonresident shares of government debt, which could generate rollover or liquidity risk for sovereign debt. The third dimension involves factors that could stress private sector balance sheets, and eventually lead to the buildup of contingent fiscal liabilities—such as the ratio of external debt-to-GDP or to foreign reserves, the share of short-term debt in external debt, and domestic credit to the private sector relative to gross domestic product (GDP).

In line with the literature, this chapter tracks fiscal space mainly in terms of fiscal solvency. Fiscal solvency risk is measured in three alternative ways to capture different elements: first, the government debt-to-GDP ratio (a stock measure of current debt sustainability); second, the fiscal balance-to-GDP ratio (a flow measure of debt accumulation, indicating future debt sustainability, and also one of the measures of rollover risk); and third, the sustainability gap. The sustainability gap is defined as the difference between the actual primary balance and the

---

[6]This multidimensional definition helps address the ambiguity of how fiscal space is defined in much of the literature (Perotti, 2007). Heller (2005) describes fiscal space more broadly as the budgetary room that allows a government to provide financial resources for a specific activity without affecting its financial sustainability while Ostry et al. (2010) defines fiscal space specifically as the difference between the current public debt and their estimate of the debt limit implied by the economy's history of fiscal adjustments.

debt-stabilizing primary balance, which depends on the target debt-to-GDP ratio to be achieved in the long run, the interest rate, and growth.[7] This last measure recognizes that debt sustainability depends on output growth and interest rates, as well as on outstanding debt and deficits. In addition to these measures of fiscal solvency risk, the chapter briefly discusses some aspects of balance-sheet vulnerabilities and private-sector debt.

Evolution of Space during the 2000s

Between 2001 and 2007, in the runup to the Great Recession, fiscal space widened for much of the developing world, with government debt ratios falling and fiscal deficits closing (Figures 3.1 and 3.2). Three factors contributed to these changes. First, there was rapid growth, with government revenues in commodity exporting economies bolstered by high and rising prices (Figure 3.3). This coincided with a period of increasing graduation of developing economies' fiscal policy from earlier procyclicality to more recent countercyclicality. Second, debt relief initiatives, such as the Heavily Indebted Poor Countries (HIPC) Initiative and Multilateral Debt Relief Initiative (MDRI), helped to reduce debt sharply in many FMEs and LICs.[8] As a result, most developing economies consolidated their finances in the early 2000s. Third, institutional arrangements in developing economies allowed for improvements in debt management, which also contributed to the reduction in debt-to-GDP ratios (Anderson, Silva and Valendia-Rubiano, 2011; Frankel, Vegh, and Vuletin, 2013).

During the Great Recession, fiscal space narrowed as economies implemented fiscal stimulus.[9] For example, the Republic of Korea boasted wide fiscal space in 2007, when government debt was a third of GDP, and fiscal balance was in surplus. In response to the crisis, the government implemented two fiscal stimulus packages, amounting to

3.6 percent of GDP in 2009 and 1.2 percent of GDP in 2010. Korea's surplus has diminished since then and debt is now almost 38 percent of GDP. Similarly, China had a fiscal surplus in 2007, and government debt that was just one-fifth of GDP. Following a stimulus package equivalent to 12.5 percent of GDP in 2008, China ran fiscal deficits from 2008 to 2010. Government debt rose to more than 50 percent of GDP by 2010.[10] Both economies succeeded in preventing a contraction in real GDP, despite the sharp downturn in the global economy.

Space and Policy during Contractions

China and Korea were particularly pronounced examples of a broader pattern among EMEs and FMEs. Many implemented countercyclical fiscal policy during the Great Recession, but not all avoided GDP contractions. To analyze fiscal policy responses during the Great Recession as well as in past crises, the chapter conducts an event study that identifies 101 episodes of sharp annual GDP contractions in 157 advanced and developing economies since 1990 (see Annex 3A for details). A country is considered to have experienced a contraction event if its GDP growth in a given year fulfills two conditions: first, growth is negative (i.e., a contraction), and second, growth is more than one standard deviation below the average growth that the economy experienced over 1990–2013. These criteria yielded 51 economies in the sample that experienced a contraction during the Great Recession, of which 21 were EMEs or FMEs.[11]

During the Great Recession, EMEs and FMEs used the wider fiscal space they had accumulated during the preceding years to allow automatic stabilizers to operate and to implement larger fiscal stimulus than in earlier contractions. Structural balances, which measure the fiscal policy stance, declined sharply as economies entered severe contractions (Figure 3.4).[12] During both event samples, fiscal space deteriorated following the stimulus, reflected in an increase in government debt. Government debt evolved differently across the two samples, likely as a result of different exchange rate movements and financial sector support programs.

---

[7]The debt stabilizing primary balance is defined as the primary balance that allows debt to converge to a target debt-to-GDP ratio. This is assumed to be the median stock of public debt as a share of a GDP for a given country grouping. The primary balance is the fiscal balance net of interest expense. Throughout this chapter, government debt refers to gross general government debt unless otherwise specified. See Annex 3B for additional details.

[8]As of 2014, 35 countries have reached the HIPC completion point and are eligible for assistance under the initiative, of which six are FMEs and 22 are LICs (IMF, 2014b). The most recent assessment of debt relief costs by the IMF (2013) determined that $126 billion has been committed under these initiatives to the 35 HIPC completion point countries, with another $442 million committed to Chad (an interim HIPC country), Cambodia, and Tajikistan. The latter two countries are non-HIPC.

[9]See Eskesen (2009), Arbatli et al. (2010), and Fardoust, Lin, and Luo (2012) for a detailed discussion.

---

[10]The buildup of general government debt reflected a substantial expansion in local government off-balance sheet lending (World Bank, 2013a, 2014b).

[11]More than 80 percent of advanced market countries (AMEs), a third of EMEs and FMEs, and less than a tenth of LICs experienced a contraction in 2008-09 in the sample of countries considered.

[12]In this chapter, the structural balance is defined as the difference between cyclically-adjusted revenues and cyclically-adjusted expenditures. It thus removes the cycle-induced component of taxes and expenditures, such as social safety nets. See Statistical Annex for additional details.

FIGURE 3.2   Government debt in 2001 and 2007

The combination of strong growth, high commodity prices, and debt relief initiatives helped developing economies gain fiscal space in the runup to the Great Recession.

A. 2001

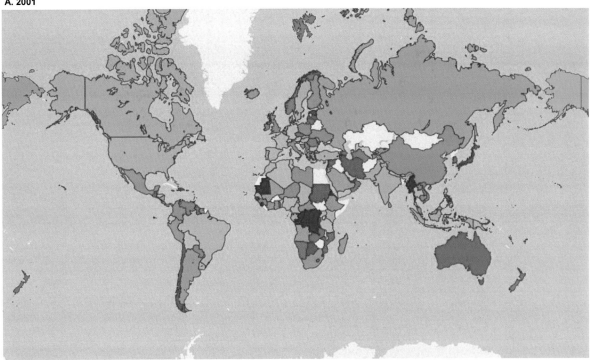

B. 2007

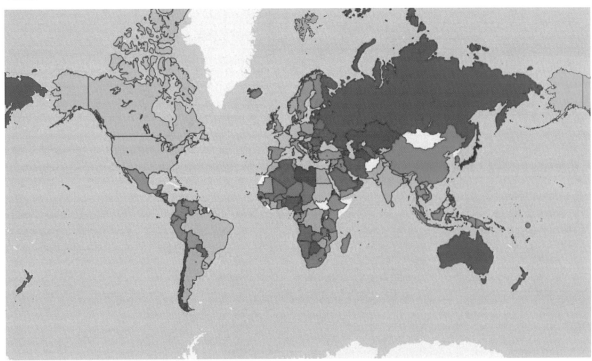

Source: World Bank estimates.
Note: A greener color indicates lower government debt as a percentage of GDP and a redder color indicates higher government debt as a percentage of GDP.

FIGURE 3.3 Fiscal space in commodity exporters and importers

The gains in fiscal space were more pronounced for commodity exporters.

A. Government debt

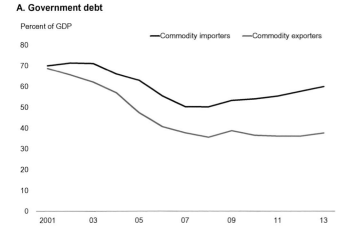

B. Fiscal balance

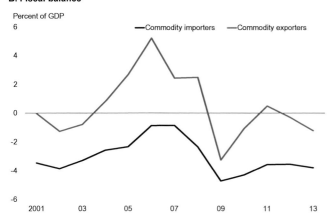

Source: World Bank estimates.
Note: Commodity exporters include all oil and mineral exporting economies that are identified as such by the Global Economic Prospects. Commodity importers are all economies that are not classified as exporters. Figures refer to un-weighted averages of commodity importers' and exporters' data.

FIGURE 3.4 Fiscal policy and space during contractions

EMEs and FMEs made greater use of fiscal stimulus during the Great Recession than during earlier contractions.

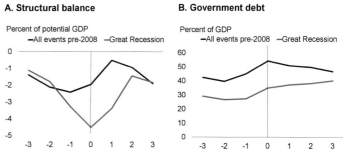

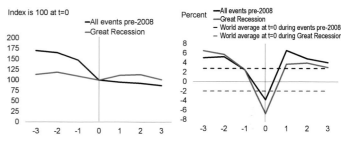

Source: World Bank estimates.
Note: 't=0' is the year of the trough of the contraction episode. All variables refer to the unweighted sample mean. The structural balance is defined as the difference between cyclically adjusted revenues and cyclically adjusted expenditures. The exchange rate index is set to be 100 at 't=0' and shows how exchange rates depreciated in pre-2008 contraction episodes but not during the Great Recession. The world average growth during pre-2008 contraction episodes was much higher than during the Great Recession, and so economies experiencing contractions in 2008-09 did so under more difficult global conditions than in previous contractions.

In particular, in pre-2008 contractions, sharp exchange rate depreciations raised the cost of holding foreign currency debt and contributed to steep increases in the debt ratio. Cases in point are the Asian crisis and the Russian crisis of the late 1990s.[13] In comparison, during 2008–09, EME and FME currencies dropped less and rebounded to pre-crisis levels before the Great Recession

was over. This partly reflected a different, more difficult, global environment—with a somewhat deeper contraction and weaker global recovery. The risks posed by exchange rate depreciation may be smaller for emerging economies now than in the past, due to deeper domestic financial markets and a policy decision to borrow in domestic currency, thus reducing "original sin."[14]

In addition, before 2008, some EMEs suffered systemic banking crises which required governments to provide heavy financial support. Though typically not fully reflected in deficits, such outlays substantially increased public debt above and beyond the increases attributable to the fiscal deficit (Laeven and Valencia, 2013). As these cross-country experiences illustrate, the fiscal space implicit in low debt can shrink rapidly especially during periods of elevated financial stress (Figure 3.5).

---

[13]Kohler (2010) documents the differences in exchange rate depreciations between the 2008–09 crisis and the Asian and Russian crises. Didier, Hevia, and Schmukler (2012) show that there were structural breaks in policy in EMEs, based on a comparison between policies in the Asian and Russian crises and the Great Recession. EMEs experienced smaller depreciations during the Great Recession. Moreover, EMEs lost substantially less reserves during the 2008–2009 crisis than during the Asian and Russian crises.

---

[14]Original sin refers to the inability of some developing countries to borrow internationally in their own currency (Eichengreen and Hausmann, 1999). Hausmann and Panizza (2011) analyze the risks posed by original sin.

FIGURE 3.5 Government debt in select crises

Debt can rise very quickly during a crisis episode.

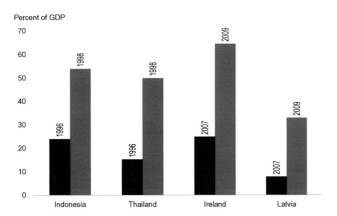

Percent of GDP

Source: World Bank estimates.
Note: Central government debt is used for Indonesia. The others refer to general government debt.

Have Developing Economies Graduated from Procyclicality?

There are several measures of the stance of fiscal policy. This chapter employs two that are commonly used in the literature: the structural balance and government consumption. The structural balance strips from the overall balance the rise and fall of revenues (such as the cycle-induced component of income taxes) and expenditures (especially social benefits) that can be attributed to the business cycle. The other measure, government consumption expenditures, which are mainly government wages and outlays on goods and services, provides a narrower definition of the fiscal policy stance, but one that is more readily comparable across economies and not subject to the uncertainty surrounding the accuracy of cyclical adjustments, for example the uncertainty about the cyclical income elasticity of tax revenues or the size of the output gap. On either measure, fiscal policy was significantly more expansionary during the Great Recession than during earlier contraction episodes. Structural balances widened, on average among EMEs and FMEs, by 4 percentage points of GDP during the Great Recession, whereas they tightened in earlier contractions.

The buildup of fiscal space during the global expansion of the early 2000s, and its use during the Great Recession suggest that fiscal policy has become less procyclical in developing economies. Estimated responses of government consumption to GDP shocks indeed show that fiscal policy has become less procyclical since the 1990s, and more countercyclical since the Great Recession (Figure 3.6).[15]

While the sample is too small to compute estimates for EMEs and FMEs separately, correlations between real GDP and real government consumption also suggest a similarity between the two groups. High procyclicality between 1980 and 1999, broadly turned to acyclicality in EMEs in the early 2000s, and to countercyclicality after the Great Recession. This evolution of fiscal cyclicality can be attributed to several factors, including improvements in policies, institutions, and enhanced financial market access.[16]

The move to less procyclical fiscal policy has also been associated with greater fiscal space. Throughout the 2000s, procyclicality was less pronounced in economies with wide fiscal space (Figure 3.7). During the Great Recession, economies with government debt below 40 percent of GDP (implying wider fiscal space) were able to implement greater fiscal stimulus than more indebted governments (with narrower space) (Figure 3.8). Fiscal policy in LICs has remained mostly acyclical reflecting the severe budgetary constraints they often face (Box 3.1).[17]

Overall, the evidence presented in this section suggests that fiscal space matters for a government's ability to implement countercyclical fiscal policy. The next section explores the importance of space for policy effectiveness.

Does Greater Space Tend to Support More Effective Fiscal Outcomes?

Countries with more ample fiscal space have used stimulus more extensively during the Great Recession than those with tighter space. But has this stimulus been more effective at meeting the goal of supporting activity? Space may affect the effectiveness of fiscal policy through two channels.

- *Interest rate channel:* When fiscal space is narrow, expansionary policy can increase lenders' perceptions

---

[15]These responses are estimated using a vector autoregressive model (VAR) with a pooled sample of EMEs and FMEs. See Technical Annex for details of the VAR model.

[16]Frankel, Végh, and Vuletin (2013) emphasize the importance of improvements in institutional quality for the changes in cyclicality. Calderon and Schmidt-Hebbel (2008) and World Bank (2013b) discuss the importance of greater credibility of fiscal policies and deepening domestic financial markets.

[17]World Bank (2013b) offers explanations of the procyclical bias of fiscal policy in developing countries. Developing countries have generally procyclical access to capital markets, and governments must therefore make spending cuts during downturns, when they are less able or unable to borrow. During upswings, governments are often under political pressure to spend the higher revenues.

FIGURE 3.6   Changing stance of fiscal policy

Fiscal policy has become countercyclical (or less procyclical) in EMEs and FMEs since the 1980s.

A. Impulse responses of government consumption to GDP shocks

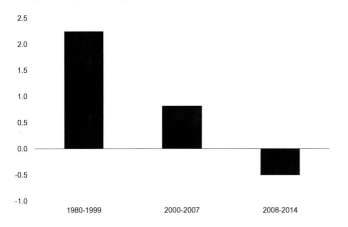

B. Correlations between government consumption and GDP

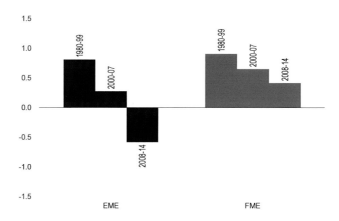

Source: World Bank estimates.
Note: The cumulative impulse responses of government consumption (in percent) at the one-year horizon following a 1 percent positive shock to GDP. The impulse responses are estimated using a panel SVAR model with a sample of 15 EMEs and FMEs (see Annex 3A for details of the model and Table 3B.2 in Annex 3B for the list of countries).

Source: World Bank estimates.
Note: Presents correlations between the cyclical components of government consumption and GDP from an unbalanced panel of annual data for 31 EMEs and 29 FMEs. All correlations are statistically significantly different from zero and differences in correlations across time are also statistically significant. Positive responses (Panel A) and positive correlations (Panel B) suggest procyclicality, while negative responses (Panel A) and negative correlations (Panel B) suggest countercyclicality.

FIGURE 3.7   Cyclicality of fiscal policy and fiscal space

In the 2000s, fiscal policy was countercyclical (or less procyclical) in countries with wider fiscal space.

Correlation between government consumption and GDP

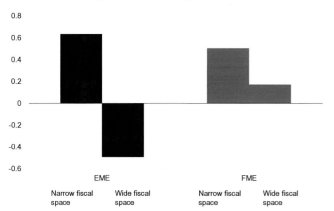

FIGURE 3.8   Structural balance during the Great Recession

Countries with wider fiscal space implemented larger stimulus packages during the Great Recession.

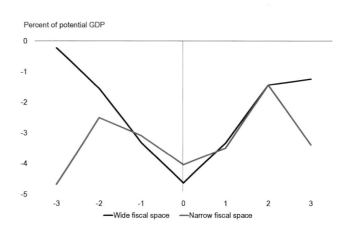

Source: World Bank estimates.
Note: The correlations are between the cyclical components of government consumption and GDP with samples divided based on fiscal space from an unbalanced panel of annual data for 31 EMEs and 29 FMEs. The median debt-to-GDP ratio in the full sample is 44 percent. Countries with debt-to-GDP ratios above the median are considered to have narrow fiscal space, while those with debt-to-GDP ratios below the median are considered to have wide fiscal space. All correlations are statistically significantly different from zero and across time. Positive correlations suggest procyclicality, while negative correlations suggest countercyclicality.

Source: World Bank estimates.
Note: 't=0' is the year of the trough of the contraction episode. All variables refer to the unweighted sample mean. These results are based on the data sample of the event study which includes the 21 EMEs and FMEs that experienced contractions during the Great Recession. The median debt-to-GDP ratio in the full sample of 63 EMEs and FMEs is 44 percent. Countries with debt-to-GDP ratios above the median are considered to have narrow fiscal space, while those with debt-to-GDP ratios below the median are considered to have wide fiscal space.

BOX 3.1   Fiscal Policy in Low-Income Countries[1]

Fiscal policy in low-income countries (LICs) has been largely acyclical over the past two decades as shown by very low correlations between the cyclical components of government consumption and GDP during this period (Figure B3.1.1, panel A). This suggests that LICs do not systematically use fiscal policy to stabilize the business cycle. But when they do, how effective is fiscal policy? Empirical estimates of the multipliers in LICs are few, partly because the identification of an exogenous fiscal shock imposes stringent data requirements.

One approach, used in Kraay (2012, 2014), is to identify a fiscal shock using World Bank loan disbursements. First, loans disbursed by the World Bank are a major source of finance for government spending in LICs. Second, the timings of approval and disbursement of such loans are not systematically related to cyclical macroeconomic conditions in recipient countries. This makes World Bank loans a good instrument for exogenous government spending, unrelated to cyclical macroeconomic conditions in LICs. Using this approach, the average (one-year) fiscal multipliers in LICs are estimated to be small at about 0.5.

The second approach is to apply a panel structural vector auto regression (SVAR) model to annual data—the only frequency available for LICs on a comparable cross-country basis—for government consumption and GDP. A fiscal shock is identified by a similar timing assumption used in Blanchard and Perotti (2002) except that now it is assumed that discretionary fiscal policy takes at least a year (and not a quarter) to respond to macroeconomic conditions. Such a prolonged lag in the response of discretionary fiscal policy may be justified in LICs on two grounds. First, LICs often rely on concessional loans to finance government spending and these are disbursed less frequently than every quarter and may discount macroeconomic conditions. Second, GDP data is extensively revised in these economies so that the government would likely take more than just one quarter to gather reliable GDP data (Ley and Misch, 2014). This then implies that discretionary fiscal policy aimed at stabilizing the economy would take more than just one quarter to implement. Fiscal multipliers are estimated using annual data for 34 low income-economies and a panel SVAR following the methodology of Ilzetzki, Mendoza, and Vegh (2013). The multiplier estimates are just above 0.6 (Figure B3.1.1, panel B), closely in line with the results from Kraay (2012, 2014).

Government financing in LICs is mostly concessional and not market based. Hence, market concerns about government solvency that underpin the relationship between fiscal space and

FIGURE B3.1.1 Cyclicality and multipliers in LICs

Fiscal policy is acyclical in LICs and multipliers are relatively small.

A. Cyclicality of fiscal policy

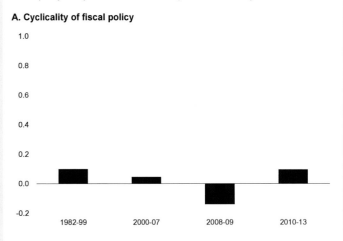

B. Fiscal multipliers

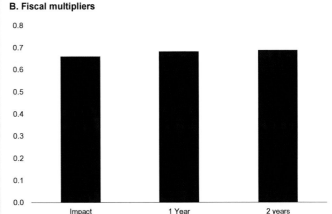

Source: World Bank estimates.
Note: Panel A shows the correlation between the cyclical components of government consumption and GDP. The correlations are all statistically insignificant which suggest that fiscal policy is acyclical in LICs. Panel B shows the fiscal multipliers based on a panel SVAR model. See Annex 3A for the details.

multipliers are expected to be less relevant in LICs than in EMEs and FMEs. Therefore, fiscal multipliers likely do not vary significantly with fiscal space in LICs. That said, fiscal space remains important in LICs, because it ensures that countercyclical fiscal policy is available when needed.

---

[1]The main author of this box is Raju Huidrom.

of sovereign credit risk. This raises sovereign bond yields and hence, borrowing costs across the whole economy (Corsetti et al., 2013; Bi, Shen, and Yang, 2014). This, in turn, crowds out private investment and consumption. If the crowding out is sufficiently strong, the net effect of expansionary fiscal policy on output, that is, the size of the fiscal multiplier, may be negligible or even negative.

- *Ricardian channel:* When a government with narrow fiscal space conducts a fiscal expansion, households expect tax increases sooner than in an economy with wide fiscal space (Perotti, 1999; Sutherland, 1997). The perceived negative wealth effect encourages households to cut consumption and save, thereby weakening the impact of the policy on output.[18]

The effectiveness of fiscal policy is usually evaluated in terms of the fiscal multiplier–the change in output for a dollar increase in government consumption. The more positive the multiplier, the more effective is policy. For developing economies, the literature reports multipliers that are small in size, and variable, ranging from -0.4 to 0.9 (Box 3.2). These estimates often refer to average multipliers, over a whole range of macroeconomic conditions. Recent work in the context of advanced economies has found that multipliers vary significantly depending on macroeconomic conditions and country characteristics: they tend to be larger during recessions (Auerbach and Gorodnichenko, 2012a, 2012b), for economies using a fixed exchange rate regime, and for economies with low debt (Ilzetzki, Mendoza, and Vegh, 2013, based on pre-crisis data; Nickel and Tudyka, 2013, for OECD economies).

To estimate fiscal multipliers for developing economies that depend on fiscal space, this section employs an Interacted Panel VAR (IPVAR) model (Towbin and Weber, 2013). This allows model parameters, and hence estimated fiscal multipliers, to interact with fiscal space. Fiscal shocks are identified by assuming that discretionary policy takes at least one quarter to respond to macroeconomic conditions (Blanchard and Perotti, 2002). The variables included in the model are government consumption, GDP, current account balance, and real

effective exchange rates.[19] The baseline results are based on an unbalanced panel for 15 EMEs and FMEs (augmented by 19 advanced economies in robustness exercises). The data are quarterly, 1980:1–2014:1. Fiscal policy is proxied by government consumption.[20] The model estimates fiscal multipliers as a function of fiscal space, which is proxied by fiscal balances as percent of GDP, corresponding to a flow measure. To control for endogeneity and to ensure that fiscal balances do not systematically pick up business cycle effects, lagged moving averages of fiscal balances are employed.[21]

The results (Figure 3.9) suggest that the multipliers at the one-year horizon are not much above zero when pre-existing fiscal deficits leading up to the stimulus have been high (narrow fiscal space), but are positive and significant when there have been surpluses (wide fiscal space).[22] The multipliers at the two-year horizon are generally greater than at the one-year horizon, suggesting that the effects peak with some lag. At longer horizons, multipliers remain near zero and statistically insignificant when fiscal space is narrow, but can be as high as 1.8 when fiscal space is wide.

This result is qualitatively robust to alternative measures of fiscal space. For example, the results for the multipliers that use the sustainability gap as the gauge of fiscal space also point to these conclusions (Figure 3.10). The results are similar when government debt as percent of GDP is used as the measure of fiscal space (see Annex 3A).

In addition to the baseline model above, two alternative econometric models are used to examine robustness: a panel Structural VAR (SVAR) as in Ilzetzki, Mendoza, and Vegh (2013), and a local projections model as in Riera-Crichton, Vegh,

---

[18]While crowding-out effects of fiscal policy, that operate via higher interest rates or future increase in taxes, have long been discussed in the literature, the emphasis in this chapter is that such crowding-out effects can be nonlinear and can depend on fiscal space. In particular, the nonlinearity pertains to investors' perception of sovereign credit risk (interest rate channel) and households' expectation of future tax increases as fiscal space becomes narrow (Ricardian channel). The interest rate channel is less relevant for large advanced economies that are able to issue debt in their own currency (Krugman, 2011).

[19]This follows Ilzetzki, Mendoza, and Vegh (2013).

[20]Since data availability and comparability is limited for the EMEs and FMEs included here, the analysis does not address the issue of spending composition, although this may be important. For instance, government spending on infrastructure and health has been shown to protect and strengthen social safety net programs, and result in long-run growth benefits (Berg et al., 2009; Kraay and Serven, 2013). Public infrastructure investment multipliers are often much larger than the public consumption multipliers (IMF, 2014c). The analysis here also does not cover automatic stabilizers which, at least in the case of OECD countries, has played a strong role in stabilizing output (Fatás and Mihov, 2012).

[21]Indeed, this fiscal space measure is not systematically wider during recessions than expansions in the sample of EMEs and FMEs. For example, the average fiscal deficit during recessions is 2.7 percent of GDP, which is very close to the deficits during expansions, 2.8 percent of GDP. Alternatively, the regression coefficients could be interacted with an additional dummy for recessions. However, this reduces the degrees of freedom significantly and results in imprecise estimates. The fiscal space measure also does not reflect exchange rate regimes—the proportion of fixed and flexible exchange rate regimes in the sample is roughly the same during periods of wide and narrow fiscal space.

[22]The multipliers presented here are the cumulative multipliers that take into account the persistence in the response of government consumption due to a fiscal shock. See Annex 3A for details.

BOX 3.2   What Affects the Size of Fiscal Multipliers?[1]

The size of fiscal multipliers depends on macroeconomic conditions and country-specific features. While the chapter examines how fiscal multipliers depend on fiscal space, especially in the context of developing economies, this box reviews additional aspects that have been important in explaining the size of multipliers.

Conditions affecting multipliers

Fiscal multipliers depend on the phase of the business cycle: they tend to be larger during recessions than during expansions (Auerbach and Gorodnichenko, 2012a, 2012b). In theory, this is attributed to a higher level of economic slack (Rendahl, 2012) and a greater share of liquidity-constrained households (Canzoneri et al., 2012) during economic downturns. The effectiveness of fiscal policy also depends on monetary policy. Monetary contraction, in response to expansionary fiscal policy that increases inflation and output, blunts the effects of the fiscal policy on output. Similarly, the effects of fiscal policy on output are more pronounced when monetary policy is more accommodative, especially when interest rates are at the zero lower bound (Christiano, Eichenbaum, and Rebelo, 2011).

The effectiveness of fiscal policy also depends on country-specific features. Fiscal multipliers tend to be larger in economies with fixed exchange rates than in economies with flexible exchange rates (Ilzetzki, Mendoza, and Vegh, 2013) because, in fixed regimes, expansionary fiscal policy tends to trigger some monetary accommodation. Fiscal multipliers are also larger in less open economies because of lower leakages into import demand.

Finally, the choice of the fiscal instrument matters. Revenue-based fiscal multipliers tend to be lower (especially in the short term) than expenditure-based multipliers. Expenditures tend to affect aggregate demand directly, whereas changes in revenues operate only indirectly and are subject to leakage. For example, households may save a portion of tax cuts intended to stimulate aggregate demand. Some caution is warranted here as recent work has shown that cyclically adjusted tax revenues are not a good proxy for tax policy. Riera-Crichton, Vegh and Vuletin (2012) argue that using tax rates instead of tax revenues yields considerably higher tax multipliers.

Empirical estimates

Empirical estimation of fiscal multipliers requires a strategy to identify exogenous fiscal shocks. The one deployed in the chapter relies on a timing assumption that discretionary fiscal policy takes at least a quarter to respond to macroeconomic conditions (Blanchard and Perotti, 2002). There are alternative identification strategies deployed in the literature: the narrative approach as in Ramey and Shapiro (1998) or Guajardo, Leigh, and Pescatori (2014); forecast errors as in Blanchard and Leigh (2013); or fluctuations in aid-related financing approval used as instruments in Kraay (2012, 2014). Fiscal multipliers can also be obtained from estimated dynamic stochastic general equilibrium (DSGE) models (Coenen et al., 2012). While empirical approaches yield reduced-form estimates of fiscal multipliers, DSGE-based estimates can capture deep structural features of the economy, in particular the interactions between private-sector behavior and policy parameters.

The vast majority of the estimates fall between zero and unity. Multipliers, on average, tend to be somewhat larger in advanced economies relative to developing ones. Recent work, although mostly in the context of advanced economies, has shown that multipliers depend on macroeconomic conditions consistent with the theoretical predictions above. For instance, the size of multipliers tends to be significantly larger during recessions. Estimates place the long-term fiscal multiplier during recessions between 0.6 and 2.7, which is generally several times larger than multipliers during more tranquil economic conditions. These effects are even larger when interest rates are at the zero lower bound. In addition to the phase of the business cycle, evidence for advanced economies suggests that fiscal multipliers are smaller in the presence of narrow fiscal space, and can even turn negative (Table B3.2.1).

---

[1]The main author of this box is Jamus J. Lim.

[2]Using tax revenues as the fiscal instrument first involves adjusting for the cyclical or the automatic stabilizer component via elasticity estimates. One reason the chapter does not discuss revenue-based multipliers is that elasticity estimates tend to be unreliable for EMEs and FMEs.

BOX 3.2 *(continued)*

TABLE B3.2.1 Fiscal multipliers: A review of studies

Groups/Features	Short-term multiplier	Long-term multiplier
Income group		
Advanced economies	-0.1 – 1.2	-1.1 – 1.8
Developing economies	-0.4 – 0.6	-0.4 – 0.9
Upper-middle income[1]	0.0 – 0.6	-0.3 – 0.9
Lower-middle income	-0.4 – 0.4	-0.4 – 0.0
Low income	0.2 – 0.5	-0.3 – 0.8
Business cycle		
Expansion	-0.9 – 1.4	-0.5 – 1.1
Recession	0.3 – 2.5	0.6 – 2.7
Zero lower bound[2]	2.3 – 3.7	1.0 – 4.0
Fiscal space		
Wide space[3]	0.0 – 1.1	-0.4 – 1.8
Narrow space	-0.2 – 0.9	-3.0 – 1.3

Sources: World Bank compilation; Batini et al., (2014); Ilzetzki, Mendoza, and Vegh (2013); Mineshima, Poplawski-Ribeiro, and Weber (2014); and Ramey (2011).
Notes: Estimates are for both government consumption and expenditure multipliers. Minimum and maximum estimates may refer to distinct studies and/or economies. Where available, short-term multipliers report the impact multiplier; otherwise the multiplier at the one-year horizon is used. Where available, long-term multipliers report the cumulative multiplier at the horizon of five years; otherwise the longest (generally three-year) horizon is used. The high-income and developing multipliers report linear estimates without state dependency.
[1]The upper-middle income estimates are skewed by the unusually large multiplier of China (2.8). Hence, China was excluded from the computation of the upper bound.
[2]Applies to zero lower bound for monetary policy rates. Multipliers depend heavily on the duration of the period in which the zero lower bound is binding; short-term (long-term) estimates reported here correspond to a zero lower bound of one (twelve) quarters.
[3]Fiscal space in these studies is usually measured in terms of the debt-to-GDP ratio: a high (low) debt-GDP ratio indicates fiscal space is narrow (wide).

FIGURE 3.9   Fiscal multipliers by fiscal space

Fiscal policy in EMEs and FMEs tends to be more effective when fiscal space is wider.

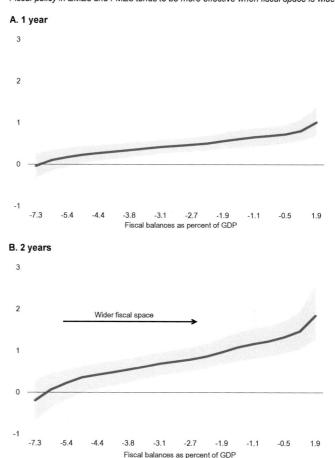

A. 1 year

B. 2 years

Source: World Bank estimates.
Note: The graphs show fiscal multipliers for different levels of fiscal space at horizons of one and two years. These are based on the estimates from the IPVAR model using a sample of 15 EMEs and FMEs. Fiscal balance as a percentage of GDP is the measure of fiscal space and the values shown on the x-axis correspond to the percentiles from the sample. Fiscal space is narrow (wide) when fiscal balances are low (high). Solid lines represent the median, and shaded areas around the solid lines are the 16-84 percent confidence bands.

and Vuletin (2014).[23] Although the precise estimates of the multipliers differ, the results from the alternative models also suggest that fiscal policy is more effective—fiscal multipliers are higher—when pre-existing fiscal space leading up to the stimulus is wide than when it is narrow (see Annex 3A).

In sum, the empirical evidence presented here suggests that wider fiscal space is associated with more effective fiscal policy in developing economies. This result holds for different types of fiscal space measures using various empirical approaches.

---

[23]Details of these two models are provided in Annex 3A.

FIGURE 3.10 Fiscal multipliers and sustainability gap

A. 1 year

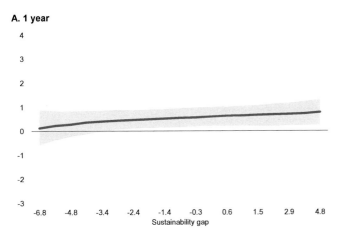

B. 2 years

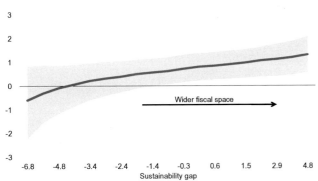

Source: World Bank estimates.
Note: The graphs show fiscal multipliers for different levels of fiscal space at horizons of one and two years. These are based on the estimates from the IPVAR model using a sample of 15 EMEs and FMEs. The sustainability gap, the difference between the actual primary balance and the debt-stabilizing primary balance at current interest and growth rates, is the measure of fiscal space. The values shown on the x-axis correspond to the percentiles from the sample. Fiscal space is narrow (wide) when the sustainability gap is low (high). Solid lines represent the median, and shaded areas around the solid lines are the 16-84 percent confidence bands.

Institutional Arrangements: How Can Fiscal Space Be Strengthened?

The past procyclicality of fiscal policy in developing economies has been attributed in part to political economy pressures.[24] This section discusses how credible and well-designed institutional mechanisms can help

mitigate these pressures and support fiscal discipline. In particular, it highlights best practices for three institutional mechanisms—fiscal rules, stabilization funds, and medium-term expenditure frameworks (MTEFs)— along with empirical evidence on the relative success of these institutions in strengthening fiscal space and supporting countercyclical fiscal policy.[25]

Fiscal Rules

Fiscal rules impose lasting numerical constraints on budgetary aggregates—debt, overall balance, expenditures, or revenues. Rules often allow for flexibility in meeting budget targets by taking into account temporary cyclical deviations—such as a large output gap—or structural adjustments, such as changes in the medium-term price of a key export.

Fiscal rules, and in particular cyclically-adjusted or structural balance rules, have become increasingly popular in developing economies (Figure 3.11), especially since the Great Recession (Schaechter et al., 2012). Balanced budget rules have become common in Africa and Eastern Europe, often adopted alongside debt rules.

The adoption of rules, *per se*, has had mixed success in limiting procyclicality. Indeed, balanced budget rules that target headline fiscal balances can lead not only to more volatile business cycles but they also tend to be associated with more procyclical fiscal stances (Bova, Carcenac, and Guerguil, 2014). In contrast, budget balance rules that target structural balances tend to be more closely associated with countercyclical fiscal stances. Many countries with budget rules have been transitioning to targeting cyclically-adjusted balance.

Other possible factors that explain the limited success of balanced budget rules to reduce procyclicality include challenges to enforcement such as the off-budget government guarantees (World Bank, 2014b), insufficient flexibility (Snudden, 2013), and the need for greater

---

[24]See World Bank (2013a) for a more detailed discussion. Volatile foreign capital market access is another constraint discussed in the literature (Cuadra, Sanchez, and Sapriza, 2010).

[25]Broadly speaking, the design of an effective budgeting process that ensures that macroeconomic fiscal targets are met depends on the type of governing approaches. A delegation approach, based on clear hierarchical layers between decision makers, tends to be more effective in countries where governments are formed by a single party, or the electoral process is not competitive. A contract approach, based on agreement between decision makers along largely horizontal relation-ships, tends to be more effective in countries where coalition govern-ments are the norm, and elections are competitive (Buttiglione et al., 2014). Within these two broad approaches, fiscal rules, stabilization funds, and medium-term budgeting frameworks can appropriately constrain discretion, and ensure that budgets are in line with longer-run macroeconomic goals.

FIGURE 3.11 Fiscal rules: Trends and distribution

A. Trends, 1952–2013

Number of countries with balance budget rules

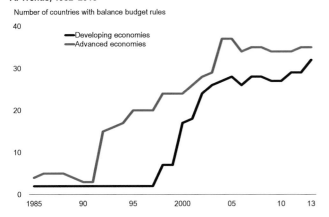

FIGURE 3.12 Stabilization funds: Trends and distribution

A. Trends, 1952–2013

Number of funds   Dollars per barrel

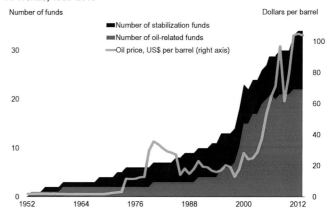

B. Distribution across developing economies, 2013

Number of rules

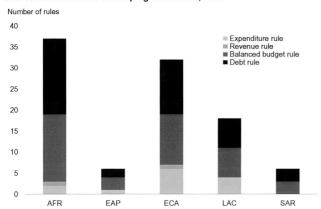

Source: World Bank estimates.
Notes: The database includes 87 economies. AFR: Sub-Saharan Africa; EAP: East Asia and Pacific; ECA: Europe and Central Asia; LAC: Latin America and Caribbean; SAR: South Asia. There is no reported fiscal rule for the Middle East and North Africa.

B. Distribution across developing economies, 2013

Number of funds   ■ Pre-1980 ■ 1980-89 ■ 1990-99 ■ Post-2000

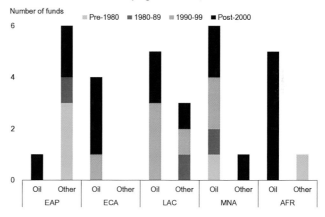

Source: World Bank estimates.
Notes: Stabilization funds here are all those listed in Sugawara (2014), together with Panama's fund (established in 2012), but excluding Norway. Oil-related stabilization funds are those whose funding sources include petroleum, the rest are referred to as "Other" in the graph. Only the first fund each country created is included if multiple funds exist (or existed) in a country. AFR: Sub-Saharan Africa; EAP: East Asia and Pacific; ECA: Europe and Central Asia; LAC: Latin America and Caribbean; MNA: Middle East and North Africa.

transparency and improved measurement in the estimation of structural balances. Rules are best when simply defined and supported by surveillance arrangements, respected by the government, yet operated by a non-government agency (Frankel, 2011). Chile's use of a technical fiscal council and a fiscal rule that targets a fixed structural balance is a good example of a well-designed, credible, and successfully operated fiscal rule (Box 3.3). Such agencies have legal guarantees for independence, highly qualified professional staff, and assured financing (Debrun and Schaechter, 2014).

Stabilization Funds

Stabilization funds set aside receipts from significant natural resource revenues such as oil and natural gas.

Funds saved during favorable times are released to cushion potential revenue shortfalls and to mitigate negative shocks to government expenditure. Stabilization funds were first set up in Kuwait in 1953, and were adopted widely in the 2000s, when high international oil prices—along with the discovery of oil in a number of economies—facilitated their establishment (Figure 3.12). Many stabilization funds are integrated with the budget, with clear rules to guide the accumulation and withdrawal of fund resources (Bagnall and Truman, 2013).[26] Since

---

[26]For example, Trinidad and Tobago's Heritage and Stabilization Fund requires that at least 60 percent of total excess petroleum revenues must be deposited into the stabilization fund. Similarly, Timor-Leste's Petroleum Fund Law of 2005 requires all receipts from petroleum-related activities to be transferred to its stabilization fund.

BOX 3.3   Chile's Fiscal Rule—An Example of Success[1]

Political pressures that underlie procyclicality of fiscal policy can be partly mitigated by the design of mechanisms (such as fiscal rules or stabilization funds) that are supported by technically sound and credible institutions (such as fiscal councils) (World Bank, 2013c). Chile presents an example of a well-designed mechanism in an enabling institutional environment.

Chile is the world's largest exporter of copper. It has experienced significant macroeconomic volatility for much of its history due to terms-of-trade shocks associated with fluctuations in global copper prices. In 2001, Chile adopted a fiscal regime that was designed to break this pattern. The regime was based on a target for the structurally-adjusted fiscal balance, which adjusted the overall balance for the output gap and commodity prices. Importantly, the determination of both the output gap and the medium-term price of copper is entrusted to two expert panels, comprising representatives from both the private sector and academia, which serve the crucial role of providing unbiased projections of these key variables (Frankel, 2011). The role of the government is limited to adjusting expenditures to meet the structural balance target. The Fiscal Responsibility Law that Chile enacted in 2006 provides an institutional framework that strengthens the link between the fiscal rule, government savings, and two sovereign wealth funds—the Pension Reserve Fund and the Economic and Social Stabilization Fund (Schmidt-Hebbel, 2012a; 2012b). The law also facilitates greater transparency and disclosure in the conduct of fiscal policy.

The introduction of the fiscal regime coincided with a global copper boom, which led to steadily increasing fiscal surpluses, peaking at 7.4 percent of GDP on the eve of the global crisis (Figure B3.3.1). By the end of 2007, the government debt-to-GDP ratio had fallen to single digits. As surpluses rose, the council of technical experts stood firm against political pressures to assume that copper prices would remain permanently high and to maintain higher spending levels. Copper prices fell sharply during the Great Recession. The significant fiscal space built up over the preceding years allowed Chile to implement a stimulus package amounting to 2.9 percent of GDP. It included increases in public investment; temporary reductions in a range of taxes; and subsidies for housing, transportation, and low-income households (IMF, 2009). In part because of this fiscal stimulus, growth resumed the following year. While the recovery of the global economy was also accompanied by a rebound in copper prices, they did not return to pre-crisis levels.

Chile's fiscal rule and its use of fiscal policy during the crisis illustrate an important limitation of the rule. Chile's rule specifically calls for a zero structural balance, and thus does not

FIGURE B3.3.1 Chile's fiscal indicators and economic performance

A. Fiscal balance, 1990-2014

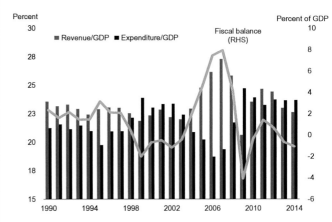

B. Structural fiscal balance, government debt, and growth 2001-14

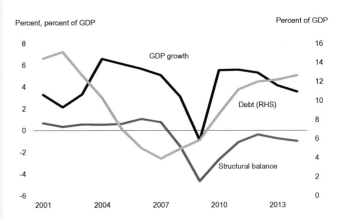

Source: World Bank estimates.
Notes: Fiscal and structural balance data are from the database described in Annex 3B. GDP data are from the World Development Indicators.

allow the implementation of countercyclical fiscal stimulus. The stimulus of 2009 was only implemented with a change in the rule after much deliberation by country authorities. Escape clauses in fiscal rules that accommodate such circumstances can thus provide valuable flexibility in dealing with low probability events and are included in recent fiscal rules (Schaechter et al., 2012).

[1]The main author for this box is Jamus J. Lim.

stabilization funds separate government expenditure from fluctuations in the availability of revenues, they can be important institutional mechanisms for improving fiscal space, while mitigating fiscal procyclicality.

Although the empirical evidence is somewhat mixed, a number of studies find that stabilization funds can help improve fiscal discipline (Fasano, 2000) and expand fiscal space (Bagattini, 2011). Stabilization funds do appear to smooth government expenditure, reducing their volatility by as much as 13 percent compared to economies without such funds (Sugawara, 2014).

While a stabilization fund can be a powerful fiscal tool to manage fiscal resources and create fiscal space, the establishment itself does not guarantee its success. Cross-country evidence even suggests that the effectiveness of a particular stabilization fund in shielding the domestic economy from commodity price volatility depends largely on government commitment to fiscal discipline and macroeconomic management, rather than on just the existence of the instrument itself (Gill et al., 2014). Proper designs and strong institutional environments that support their operations are crucial factors for the success of stabilization funds.

Among resource-rich economies, Norway and Chile are often treated as examples of economies with stabilization funds that are based on specific resource revenues and associated with good fiscal management (Schmidt-Hebbel, 2012a, 2012b). Norway's Government Pension Fund and Chile's Economic and Social Stabilization Fund are ranked highest and third, respectively, in a scoring of 58 sovereign wealth funds and government pension funds (Bagnall and Truman, 2013). The main characteristics that distinguish Norway's and Chile's funds from those with lower scores are governance and transparency and accountability of fund operations.

Medium-Term Expenditure Frameworks (MTEF)

MTEFs were first introduced to facilitate modern public financial management in pursuit of long-run policy priorities in OECD economies. Among developing economies, they gained prominence in the late 1990s, as annual budgets were perceived to create uncertainty about future budgetary commitments. International financial agencies, such as the World Bank, have also sought to encourage stable allocations toward poverty reduction targets. More than two-thirds of all economies have adopted MTEFs of some form (World Bank, 2013c).

The objective of MTEFs is to establish or improve credibility in the budgetary process. They seek to ensure a transparent budgetary process, where government agencies establish credible contracts for the allocation of public resources toward agreed strategic priorities, over an average of three years. The most common design of MTEFs translates macroeconomic objectives into budget aggregates and detailed spending plans; less sophisticated approaches target either aggregate fiscal goals, or micro-level costs and outcomes.

Empirical evidence suggests that credible MTEFs can significantly improve fiscal discipline (World Bank, 2013c). Furthermore, the results tend to be more positive for more sophisticated frameworks (Grigoli et al., 2012). Significant heterogeneity exists, however, and certain studies limited to smaller regional samples have been unable to find conclusive evidence, possibly reflecting shortcomings in the practical implementation of MTEFs.[27]

Keys to robust implementation are coordination with broader public sector reform, and sensitivity to country characteristics (World Bank, 2013c). For example, Jordan's MTEF was a component of major public financial management reforms in 2004 and part of the national development strategy. The MTEF's specific objective was to improve fiscal discipline through realistic revenue projections, followed by better expenditure prioritization and the identification of fiscal space. In the case of South Africa, the MTEF was introduced in the context of high government debt and a combination of underspending by the central government and overspending by provincial governments. Underspending and overspending were both reduced following the introduction of the MTEF. One of the lessons from the experiences of South Africa, Tanzania, and Uganda is the need for realistic expectations during the preparation of the budget, without which even well-designed MTEFs cannot succeed (Holmes and Evans, 2003).

Risks and Medium-Term Objectives

While debt stocks in many developing economies remain moderate, primary deficits are wider than they were before the crisis. Although debt has grown slowly under the current benign market conditions, especially low interest rates, the debt-to-GDP ratios could increase much more rapidly if domestic growth slows and global interest rates rise (Figure

---

[27]For example, Le Houerou and Taliercio (2002) examine the design and implementation of MTEFs in a sample of African economies.

FIGURE 3.13 Sustainability gaps under different conditions in 2013

In some EMEs and FMEs, fiscal risks would increase under historic market conditions.

A. Current market conditions

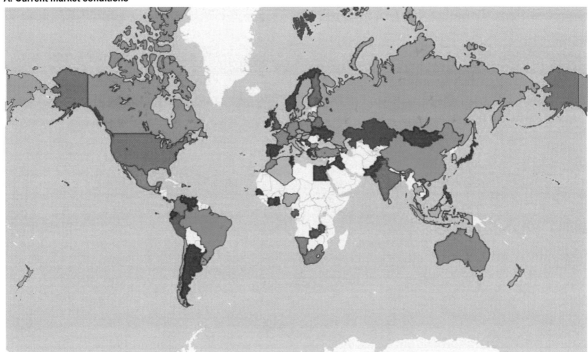

B. Historic market conditions

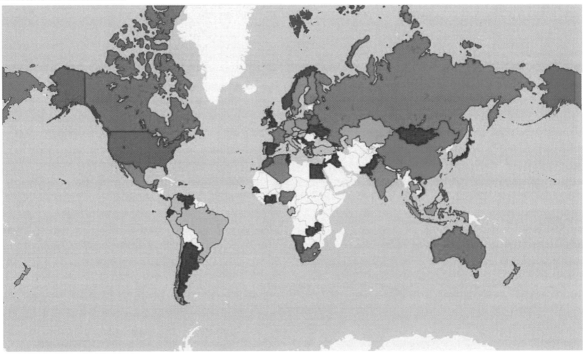

Source: World Bank estimates.
Note: The sustainability gap is the difference between the primary balance and an estimated debt-stabilizing primary balance, which depends on as-sumptions about interest rates and growth rates. For a given country, current market conditions refer to 2013 interest and growth rates, while historic conditions refer to the sample average during 1980–2013. A negative value suggests that the balance is debt-increasing, a value of zero suggests that the balance holds debt constant, and positive values suggest that the balance is debt-reducing. A redder color indicates a more negative sustainability gap; a greener color a more positive gap. If the data was updated to 2014, some countries would show more benign sustainability gaps (e.g. Spain) while others would show lower ones.

3.13).[28] This is especially relevant for some FMEs that have placed sovereign bonds in international markets recently and have increased their exposure to risks linked to global financing conditions.[29] Some economies could thus become more vulnerable to sharp increases in borrowing cost. The historical experience discussed earlier also highlights several instances in recent decades when debt ratios rose sharply.

Private sector vulnerabilities are another source of risk that EMEs and FMEs should monitor since they have been associated with debt crises in the past (Box 3.4). Corporate and household debt in EMEs and FMEs has risen since the crisis (Figure 3.14). This rise has been substantial in some EMEs, with aggregate non-financial corporate debt growing by 39 percent over 2007–13. Moreover, in some countries, rising private sector debt has been accompanied by deteriorating fiscal sustainability. Some countries have already taken measures to restrain private credit growth.[30] Rapid currency depreciations can be another source of risk in some countries, where nonfinancial firms have been borrowing substantially in international markets in foreign currencies, but depositing the proceeds in local currencies in domestic financial systems (IDB, 2014). Sharp depreciations could thus strain the solvency of domestic firms and weaken the soundness of domestic financial sectors.

The recent slump in oil prices presents both risks and opportunities for developing countries. For oil exporters, the slump could result in loss of oil revenues, eroding their fiscal space. At the same time, many countries have substantial food and fuel subsidies. Continued soft commodity prices (as projected for 2015-16) would offer an opportunity to implement subsidy reform which would both help rebuild fiscal space and lessen distortions associated with these subsidies.

Over the medium term, in view of these risks as well as the desirability of strengthening fiscal space, developing economies will need to return their fiscal positions to more sustainable levels. The appropriate speed of adjustment, however, depends on a host of country-specific factors, including the cyclical position of the economy and constraints on monetary policy. If monetary policy normalization in advanced economies results in higher

FIGURE 3.14 Private sector vulnerabilities

Credit to the private sector has expanded since 2007 in EMEs and FMEs. In some countries this expansion has been rapid and also associated with fiscal sustainability challenges.

A. Private sector credit evolution

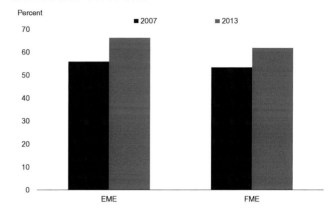

B. Credit growth and sustainability gaps in 2013

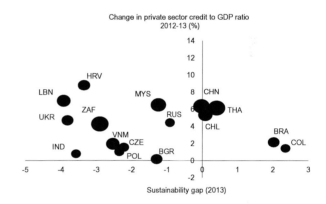

Source: World Bank estimates.
Note: Panel A shows domestic private sector credit as percent of GDP in EMEs and FMEs. In Panel B, the size of the circle is proportional to domestic private credit-to–GDP ratio. The sustainability gap is the difference between the primary balance and an estimated debt-stabilizing primary balance based on interest rates and growth rates in 2013. A negative value suggests that the balance is debt increasing, a value of zero suggests that the balance holds debt constant, and positive values suggest that the balance is debt reducing. All economies in the figure are EMEs and FMEs with domestic private credit-to-GDP ratios greater than 50 percent. Sustainability gap data are from the database described in Annex 3B; private-sector credit data from World Development Indicators.

interest rates, a sharp drop in or reversal of capital flows could constrain monetary policy responses to weakening growth. Fiscal space would help ensure that fiscal policy remains available as a countercyclical policy tool. A wider fiscal space would not only increase the likelihood that fiscal stimulus is a feasibly policy option, but would also improve its effectiveness. This implies that adhering to an appropriate medium-term program of deficit reduction offers the prospect of a much more effective fiscal policy when it is needed most. For instance, the estimates from the baseline model suggest that fiscal multipliers would be reduced by one-third from pre-crisis levels (Figure 3.15).

---

[28]The relationship between primary balances and debt is characterized by the sustainability gap. The sustainability gap measure here is based on long rates, and as such does not take into account the fact that developing economies also hold short term debt. However, to the extent that the average maturity of bond issuances in developing economies is lengthening (Chapter 1), the bias from using the long rates is likely small.

[29]See Chapter 1 for discussion on Cote d'Ivoire and Kenya, and IMF (2104d) for the cases of Ghana and Zambia.

[30]World Bank (2014b) describes recent efforts to reduce vulnerabilities in China, Malaysia, Thailand, and Vietnam.

BOX 3.4   Narrow Fiscal Space and the Risk of a Debt Crisis[1]

This chapter has examined how fiscal space had been built and used in the course of the Great Recession. Although in most countries it remains significantly wider than in the early 2000s, it has yet to be rebuilt to pre-crisis levels. Severely depleted fiscal space may become a contributor to possible future stresses, such as a debt crisis. This box reviews some of the key indicators that have been associated with debt crises.[2]

The implications of high public debt or high external debt have been extensively explored in the debt intolerance literature. Debt intolerance is often associated with the extreme stress that developing economies experience at levels of external debt that would be easily managed by advanced economies. Empirical studies of debt intolerance and serial default suggest that the likelihood of an external debt crisis rises substantially when external debt of an emerging economy is above 30-35 percent of GDP (Reinhart and Rogoff, 2009; Reinhart, Rogoff, and Savastano, 2003). Later estimates building on the early warning systems literature find a somewhat higher threshold: external debt as a share of GDP in emerging markets could be as high as 50 percent before a debt crisis becomes likely (Bandiera, Cuaresma, and Vinclette., 2010; Manasse and Roubini, 2009).

The literature on the determinants of debt crises has considered a range of different indicators.[3] However, for liquidity crisis-prone and solvency crisis-prone economies, four indicators can be identified as being particularly relevant: total external debt-to-GDP ratios, inflation, short-term external debt-to-reserve ratios, and public external debt-to-revenue ratios. These variables have threshold values (although always conditional on other factors) at which they indicate elevated debt crisis likelihoods.

The threshold values are 31–50 percent for external-debt-to GDP ratios; 11 percent for inflation rates; 134 percent for short-term external debt-to reserve ratios; and 300 percent for public external debt-to-revenue ratios.[4] With these thresholds in mind, most emerging market economies (EMEs), frontier market economies (FMEs), and low-income countries (LICs) do not appear to be at imminent risk of a debt crisis (Figure B3.4.1).

FIGURE 3.4.1   Indicators of resilience in 2013

A. Total external debt-to-GDP and inflation

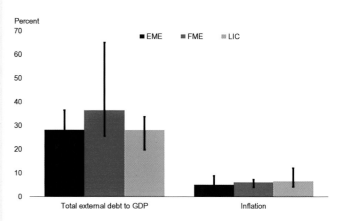

B. Short-term external debt to reserve and government external debt to revenue

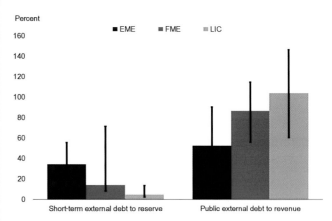

Source: World Bank estimates.
Note: All statistics refer to the sample medians. Error bars indicate the range from the 25th to the 75th percentile within each country sample.

---

[1]This main author of this box is S. Amer Ahmed.

[2]Aside from the broader macroeconomic environment, the composition of debt can also matter, as excessive amounts of short-term debt can threaten liquidity (Detragiache and Spilimbergo, 2004). Eichengreen, Hausmann, and Panizza (2009) and Dell'Erba, Hausmann, and Panizza (2013) also show that foreign currency debt and large foreign liabilities can exacerbate debt vulnerabilities. For example, EMEs with low levels of foreign currency debt are characterized by lower correlations between debt levels and spreads.

[3]Jedidi (2013), Reinhart and Rogoff (2011) and Bandiera, Cuaresma, and Vinclette (2010) offer extensive reviews of the literature, describing the ranges of methodologies and variables considered.

[4]IMF (2002) reports that the relevant threshold for external debt-to-GDP ratios (excluding heavily indebted poor countries) was between 31 and 39 percent. Similarly, Reinhart, Rogoff, and Savastano (2003) find that, on average, an external debt-to-GDP ratio of 35 percent increases the likelihood of a debt crisis, although they caution that this threshold could be lower if the economy has a poor institutional investor rating. Manasse and Roubini (2009) and Bandiera, Cuaresma, and Vinclette (2010) find an elevated likelihood of debt crisis risk if total external debt is greater than 50 percent of GDP. Manasse and Roubini (2009) note that external debt-to-GDP ratios greater than 50 percent can contribute to debt crisis risk especially if inflation rates are greater than 11 percent and public external debt-to-revenue ratios are greater than 300 percent. If external-debt-to-GDP ratios are less than 50 percent, then other key indicators must reach threshold values for a crisis to become likely: short-term external debt-to-reserve ratios must be greater than 134 percent, public external debt-to-revenue ratios must be greater than 215 percent and inflation must be greater than 11 percent. Kraay and Nehru (2006) also find that inflation rates in excess of 40 percent could contribute to greater debt crisis risk while a cross-country event study of debt crises between 1980 and 2002 (Ciarlone and Trebeschi, 2006) finds that short-term external debt-to-reserve ratios surge from 220 percent to 383 percent in the year before a crisis.

Conclusions

This chapter has examined whether fiscal policy in emerging and frontier market economies will be able to provide effective support to activity in the event of a renewed global contractionary shock. Two conditions—fiscal space and policy effectiveness—are crucial. Fiscal space implies a lack of binding constraints from financing requirements, such as a large pre-existing deficit, a heavy debt burden, or excessive short-term liabilities.

Over the past two decades, a growing number of EMEs and FMEs have graduated from procyclical policies, towards more countercyclical policies. In large part, the earlier procyclicality had been the result of weak fiscal sustainability, which constrained policymakers' options, and political pressures to spend during times of good revenues.

The chapter has presented evidence that fiscal policy is more effective when supported by wider space. In EMEs and FMEs, estimated fiscal policy multipliers—the increase in GDP for a given exogenous increase in government spending—are considerably larger from a starting point with a strong budget position than from a starting point with a weak one. Since 2009, deficits have remained unexpectedly large, and fiscal space has not been restored to its pre-crisis level. While the technical analysis in this chapter, due to data constraints, has focused on fiscal debt and deficits, other dimensions of fiscal space, including a small share of short-term or foreign-currency debt, can add to fiscal space by reducing rollover or other risks.

Three institutional mechanisms for strengthening fiscal governance have been examined: fiscal rules, stabilization funds, and medium-term expenditure frameworks. Developing economies have increasingly adopted these institutions over recent decades. While the experience has been mixed, each mechanism has seen success in cases where the mechanism has been well-designed and credible and its implementation steadfast.

While the chapter has discussed fiscal space and policy from the perspective of short-term output stabilization, they both have important implications for poverty reduction. Diminished fiscal space in the aftermath of the Great Recession has been associated with constrained social spending, which directly affects poverty reduction and equity (UN, 2011). Restoring fiscal space would allow more budgetary resources for these programs. Fiscal policy also has significance for poverty reduction and greater equity. First, an increase in growth due to fiscal stimulus can imply a positive mean shift in a

FIGURE 3.15 Fiscal multipliers – prospects

Fiscal policy in EMEs and FMEs would be more effective with restored space.

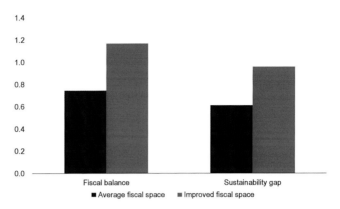

Source: World Bank estimates.
Note: The graph shows the fiscal multipliers at the two-year horizon for an average fiscal space and a (hypothetical) wide fiscal space. The average fiscal space corresponds to the cross-sectional median in 2013 from a sample of EMEs and FMEs while the wide fiscal space corresponds to the 75th percentile which is close to the pre-crisis level. These are based on the estimates from the IPVAR model using the sample of EMEs and FMEs. The results are shown for two alternative measures of fiscal space: fiscal balance as percent of GDP and the sustainability gap.

county's income distribution. Second, fiscal policy targeted to increase or preserve social spending (such as social safety net and conditional cash transfer programs) can reduce inequality, i.e., the shape of the income distribution. These changes in the mean and the shape of the income distribution are key dimensions of poverty reduction (World Bank, 2014c, 2014d).

Even under the current global environment, with historically low interest rates, fiscal deficits in some developing economies seem sizeable. Under a less benign environment, with domestic growth and world interest rates at historical norms, the picture could worsen. Given the risks, there is a need to rebuild fiscal space over the medium term. For many developing countries, the expected soft commodity prices are an opportunity to implement subsidy reforms to help rebuild fiscal space while, at the same time, removing longstanding distortions to economic activity. The appropriate path of deficit reduction would depend on a variety of factors, notably the phase of the domestic business cycle and country-specific characteristics. For example, it would not be appropriate to aim inflexibly at reduced deficits during years of recession. The pace at which fiscal space is restored would also depend on the degree to which monetary stimulus is constrained by concerns over financial system soundness. At the end of the process, with restored space, fiscal policy would be a more reliable and effective countercyclical tool.

Annex 3A: Technical Information[1]

A. Fiscal Multipliers

This annex provides further details regarding the methodology used in the estimation of the fiscal multipliers as discussed in the main text. In particular, it describes the econometric models, identification strategies, estimation, and database. It also presents additional results that serve as robustness checks.

Models

1. *Interacted Panel VAR:* The model is written as:

$$\begin{bmatrix} 1 & 0 & 0 & 0 \\ \alpha_{0,it}^{21} & 1 & 0 & 0 \\ \alpha_{0,it}^{31} & \alpha_{0,it}^{32} & 1 & 0 \\ \alpha_{0,it}^{41} & \alpha_{0,it}^{42} & \alpha_{0,it}^{43} & 1 \end{bmatrix} \begin{bmatrix} gc_{i,t} \\ gdp_{i,t} \\ ca_{i,t} \\ reer_{i,t} \end{bmatrix} = \gamma X_{i,t}$$

$$+ \sum_{l=1}^{L} \begin{bmatrix} \alpha_{l,it}^{11} & \alpha_{l,it}^{12} & \alpha_{l,it}^{13} & \alpha_{l,it}^{14} \\ \alpha_{l,it}^{21} & \alpha_{l,it}^{22} & \alpha_{l,it}^{23} & \alpha_{l,it}^{24} \\ \alpha_{l,it}^{31} & \alpha_{l,it}^{32} & \alpha_{l,it}^{33} & \alpha_{l,it}^{34} \\ \alpha_{l,it}^{41} & \alpha_{l,it}^{42} & \alpha_{l,it}^{43} & \alpha_{l,it}^{44} \end{bmatrix} \begin{bmatrix} gc_{i,t-l} \\ gdp_{i,t-l} \\ ca_{i,t-l} \\ reer_{i,t-l} \end{bmatrix} + U_{i,t} \quad (1)$$

where *gc* represents real government consumption; *gdp*, real gross domestic product (GDP), *ca*, current account as percent of GDP; *reer*, real effective exchange rates. Real government consumption and real GDP (in logs) are detrended. Real effective exchange rates are in growth rates while the current account is in levels. Details of the database are described in Section B of Annex 3B.

Note the panel structure of the model where the variables are indexed for each country by *i*. The vector $U_{i,t}$ represents uncorrelated independent, identically distributed "structural" shocks. The shock corresponding to the equation of government consumption is the fiscal shock and is the main shock of interest in the context of the chapter. The vector $X_{i,t}$ denotes controls which are the country-specific intercepts. *L* denotes the maximum lag length in the vector auto regression (VAR), set at 4 in line with Ilzetzki, Mendoza, and Vegh (2013).

The impact matrix, that is, the matrix of coefficients on the left-hand side of Equation 1, is lower-triangular. This, along with the ordering of the variables in the VAR, is related to the recursive identification scheme used in the chapter, which is that government consumption does not react to GDP within the quarter.[2] The impact matrix and the corresponding matrices in the right-hand side of the equation determine the effects of structural shocks on

the dynamics of endogenous variables in the VAR system. The coefficients in these matrices are time varying, and hence indexed by time *t*. The coefficients evolve according to a measure of fiscal space. That is,

$$\alpha_{l,it}^{jk} = \beta_{l,1}^{jk} + \beta_{l,2}^{jk} fspace_{i,t} \quad (2)$$

where *fspace* denotes fiscal space, which in the baseline scenario is taken to be the fiscal balance. As noted in the main text, the section takes lagged moving averages of fiscal balance to control for any endogeneity issues. The model is estimated equation by equation using ordinary least squares (OLS). The coefficients are then evaluated at specific values of fiscal space (taken to be the percentiles in the sample) for computing the impulse responses and the fiscal multipliers. Confidence bands are calculated by bootstrapping methods with 300 samples. The section reports the medians and the 16-84 percent confidence bands.

The cumulative fiscal multiplier at horizon *T* is defined as the discounted cumulative change in output until horizon *T* when the discounted cumulative government consumption increases by 1$. That is,

$$Cumulative\ multiplier(T) = \frac{\sum_{t=0}^{T}(1+r)^{-t}\Delta gdp_t}{\sum_{t=0}^{T}(1+r)^{-t}\Delta gc_t}$$

where, *r* denotes the interest rate which is taken to be the median short-term nominal rate in the sample.

From the multiplier equation above, the impact multiplier is obtained when $T = 0$ and the long-run multiplier when *T* is some large number that is taken to be 5 years. In the text, the multipliers are reported for $T = 1$ year and $T = 2$ years that are the horizons when fiscal policy generally has maximum effects on the economy. To calculate the fiscal multiplier from the estimates from the IPVAR, the discounted impulses of output and government

---

[1]The main authors of this Annex are Raju Huidrom and S. Amer Ahmed.

[2]In addition, the ordering implies that GDP does not respond to the current account within one quarter and that the current account does not move within one quarter when the real effective exchange rate is shocked.

consumption are cumulated at different horizons. Then, the ratio of the two impulses is scaled by the average government consumption to GDP ratio.

2. Panel SVAR: The model is written as:

$$\begin{bmatrix} 1 & 0 & 0 & 0 \\ \alpha_0^{21} & 1 & 0 & 0 \\ \alpha_0^{31} & \alpha_0^{32} & 1 & 0 \\ \alpha_0^{41} & \alpha_0^{42} & \alpha_0^{43} & 1 \end{bmatrix} \begin{bmatrix} gc_{i,t} \\ gdp_{i,t} \\ ca_{i,t} \\ reer_{i,t} \end{bmatrix} = C_0 +$$

$$\Sigma_{l=1}^{L} \begin{bmatrix} \alpha_l^{11} & \alpha_l^{12} & \alpha_l^{13} & \alpha_l^{14} \\ \alpha_l^{21} & \alpha_l^{22} & \alpha_l^{23} & \alpha_l^{24} \\ \alpha_l^{31} & \alpha_l^{32} & \alpha_l^{33} & \alpha_l^{34} \\ \alpha_l^{41} & \alpha_l^{42} & \alpha_l^{43} & \alpha_l^{44} \end{bmatrix} \begin{bmatrix} gc_{i,t-l} \\ gdp_{i,t-l} \\ ca_{i,t-l} \\ reer_{i,t-l} \end{bmatrix} + U_{i,t}$$

where the notations closely follow the IPVAR. The vector C_0 captures the intercept terms. The set of variables included in the VAR is also the same as before, and so is the identification scheme. Thus, the impact matrix retains the lower triangular structure. Unlike the IPVAR, the law of motion of the coefficients in Equation (2) is absent in this model. Accordingly, the VAR coefficients are no longer indexed by country i and time t. In other words, the panel SVAR (structural vector auto regression) only estimates a single set of coefficients from the pooled sample. The sample is split by episodes of wide and narrow fiscal space at an exogenous cut-off point, determined by judgment, to calculate estimates that vary by fiscal space. The IPVAR, on the other hand, estimates fiscal multipliers for continuous levels of fiscal space, thereby avoiding the cut-off choice. The confidence bands are based on 1000 Monte Carlo draws. Country fixed effects are taken into account by removing means and trends country by country. As in the IPVAR, a maximum lag length of 4 is used.

The model is also used to infer the evolution of the cyclicality of fiscal policy in developing economies. To that end, the model is estimated during three sub-samples (1980–1999, 2000–2007, and 2008–2014) and the response of government consumption to GDP shocks is calculated for each sub-sample. Fiscal policy is procyclical when that response is positive and statistically significant.

3. Local Projections Model: The model is written as:

$$\Delta Y_{i,t+h}$$
$$= \alpha_{i,h} + \left(1 - I(x_{i,t})\right)\beta_{surplus,h}FE_{i,t}^{G}$$
$$+ I(x_{i,t})\beta_{deficit,h}FE_{i,t}^{G}$$
$$+ \left(1 - I(x_{i,t})\right)\lambda_{surplus,h}(L)\Delta Y_{i,t-1}$$
$$+ I(x_{i,t})\lambda_{deficit,h}(L)\Delta Y_{i,t-1}$$
$$+ \left(1 - I(x_{i,t})\right)\Psi_{surplus,h}(L)\Delta G_{i,t-1}$$
$$+ I(x_{i,t})\Psi_{deficit,h}(L)\Delta G_{i,t-1} + \varphi_1 T_{t,h} + \varphi_2 T_{t,h}^2 + \mu_{i,t},$$

with

$$I(x_{i,t}) = \frac{\exp(-\gamma x_{i,t})}{1 + \exp(-\gamma x_{i,t})}, \gamma > 0$$

where x indicates fiscal space normalized to have zero mean and unit variance. Like the previous models, fiscal space is measured by lagged moving averages of fiscal balances as percent of GDP. The parameter γ is calibrated as 2.5. $\Delta Y_{i,t+h}$ denotes the growth rate of output of country i at horizon h, FE^G is the forecast error of government consumption. The parameter captures country fixed effects and the time trend. The indicator function I pins down the probability that the economy is in a regime of narrow fiscal space.

The local projections model is a single equation model unlike the multivariate framework of the IPVAR and the panel SVAR. In this model, fiscal shocks are defined as fiscal surprises constructed outside the model as the forecast errors of government consumption. The forecast errors proxy unanticipated fiscal shocks in that they represent any surprises in government consumption over and above what private agents expect them to be given their available information set. The forecast errors of government consumption (in growth rates) are compiled from various OECD publications.[3]

The effects of fiscal policy on output are then traced out by regressing output on the fiscal surprises, taking into account country fixed effects. Those effects are dependent on whether the economy is in a regime of wide or narrow fiscal space, as pinned down by the indicator function. Lags of government consumption and GDP are included as controls to purge any effects that they may have had on the forecasts of government consumption. The model is separately estimated for each horizon, which is then used to *project* the dynamic effects of fiscal shocks on output.

Additional results

This section presents additional results that serve as robustness checks.

• Fiscal multipliers during recessions and expansions: Annex 3A.1 shows that fiscal multipliers are larger during periods of recessions than expansions – a result consistent with standard macroeconomic

---

[3] The forecast error series is only available at the semi-annual frequency and accordingly, the model is estimated only at that frequency. The series is available for only 29 countries (22 AMEs and 7 EMEs and FMEs) and during the period 1987-2013. See Section B of the Annex 3B for the details of this database.

FIGURE 3A.1   Fiscal multipliers by business cycle phase

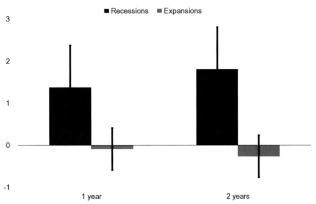

Source: World Bank estimates.
Note: The graph shows fiscal multipliers during recessions at different horizons. Recessions are defined as the peak-to-trough periods as determined by the Harding-Pagan (2002) business cycle dating algorithm. Solid bars represent the median and error bars represent the 16-84 percent confidence bands. These are from the baseline model with the pooled sample.

FIGURE 3A.2   Fiscal multipliers in EMEs and FMEs by government debt

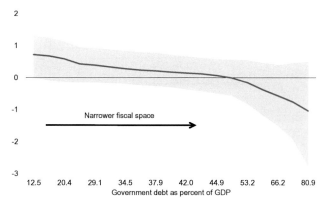

Source: World Bank estimates.
Note: The graph shows long run fiscal multipliers (i.e. at the five-year horizon) for different levels of fiscal space. These are based on the estimates from the IPVAR model using a sample of EMEs and FMEs. Government debt as percent of GDP is used as the measure of fiscal space. The values shown on the x axis correspond to the percentiles from the sample. Fiscal space is narrow (wide) when government debt is high (low). Solid lines represent the median, and shaded areas around the solid line are the 16-84 percent confidence bands.

theory. For this, the IPVAR model is estimated by conditioning on the phase of the business cycles, as determined by the Harding-Pagan (2002) business cycle dating algorithm.

- Fiscal multipliers by government debt: Figure 3A.2 shows that the result in the main text—fiscal multipliers are larger with a wider fiscal space—is robust when the government debt-to-GDP ratio is used as an alternative measure of fiscal space. The graph underlines that fiscal policy can be counterproductive, especially in the long run (i.e. at the five-year horizon), when fiscal space is narrow.

- Alternative methodologies yield results that are similar to the baseline (Figure 3A.3). In the panel SVAR model as in Ilzetzki, Mendoza and Vegh (2013), the multiplier at the two-year horizon is about 0.5 during episodes of high fiscal balance, whereas it is very close to zero during episodes of low fiscal balance. In the local projections model as in Riera-Crichton, Vegh, and Vuletin (2014), the output responses to a positive fiscal shock are again larger during periods of high fiscal balance than low balance. The differences between the estimates for the narrowest and widest fiscal space are statistically significant.

FIGURE 3A.3   Fiscal multipliers: Alternative econometric models

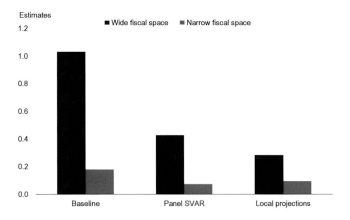

Source: World Bank estimates.
Note: The graph shows fiscal multipliers at the two-year horizon across alternative econometric models: IPVAR model of Towbin and Weber (2013) which is the baseline, a panel SVAR model as in Ilzetzki, Mendoza, and Vegh (2013), and a local projections model as in Riera-Crichton, Vegh, and Vuletin (2014). To maintain enough degrees of freedom, the latter two models are estimated from a pooled sample of AMEs, EMEs, and FMEs. Fiscal balance as a percentage of GDP is the measure of fiscal space. For the baseline model, the fiscal multipliers are averaged over fiscal deficits below and above 4 percent of GDP cutoff. In the sample, 4 percent of GDP for deficits roughly corresponds to the percentile position of a 60 percent of GDP cutoff for debt used in Ilzetzki, Mendoza, and Vegh (2013) to define episodes of wide and narrow fiscal space. Wide (narrow) fiscal space refers to episodes where fiscal deficits are above (below) this cutoff. The figures shown for the local projections model are the output responses (growth rates, in percent) to a fiscal shock.

B. Identifying Contraction Events

This chapter uses an event study to examine how fiscal space and fiscal policy in EMEs and FMEs changes in the runup to, during, and immediately after a contraction episode. Three sets of comparisons are made. The first set is between EMEs and FMEs in a particular contraction episode to highlight their differences within the same episode. The second set is between economies with differing levels of fiscal space within the same contraction episode. The third set is between economies' contraction episodes during the Great Recession and during pre-2008 contraction episodes.

A country is considered here to have experienced a contraction event if its growth in a given year fulfills two conditions. The first is that the growth is negative (i.e., a contraction), and the second is that the growth is more than one standard deviation below the average that the country experienced in the 1990–2013 period. The year of the event, as defined, is then 't=0.' If there are two or more contractionary episodes within a five-year period, the year with the greatest growth contraction is taken as 't=0.' This is a variation of the censoring rule applied by IMF (2012a) in its application of the Harding and Pagan (2002) quarterly business cycle dating methodology to annual data. If key fiscal space data, such as gross government debt, are not available in the database for the country in the event year, then the event is dropped.[4] This approach identifies 101 contraction events, 50 in the pre-2008 period and 51 in 2008–09 for the full sample of all countries including AMEs, EMEs, and FMEs. These events, along with their associated real GDP contraction can be seen in Annex Tables 3A.1 and 3A.2 for EMEs and FMEs. Episodes identified as crises but not included in the event study because of data constraints are noted in Annex Table 3A.3.

This definition of events considers output contractions only. The comprehensive financial crisis database of Laeven and Valencia (2013) has been considered a source for event dates. However, it focuses on financial crises, and thereby excludes episodes in many economies, such as those in Sub-Saharan Africa. Also, some of the episodes it considers do not necessarily have output contractions associated with them.

[4]To ensure that the crisis of 1995 in Mexico is included, the database is augmented the IMF's Global Data Source.

TABLE 3A.1 Contraction events between 1990 and 2007

Country	Year	Country Group	Real GDP Growth (%)
Argentina	2002	EME	-10.9
Bahrain	1994	EME	-0.3
Chile	1999	EME	-0.8
Côte d'Ivoire	2000	FME	-3.7
Colombia	1999	EME	-4.2
Korea, Rep.	1998	EME	-5.7
Sri Lanka	2001	EME	-1.5
Morocco	1993	EME	-1.0
Malaysia	1998	EME	-7.4
Oman	1999	EME	-0.1
Philippines	1998	EME	-0.6
Mexico	1995	EME	-5.8

Note: EME: Emerging Market Economy.

TABLE 3A.2 Contraction events in 2008 and 2009

Country	Year	Country Group	Real GDP Growth (%)
Bulgaria	2009	FME	-5.5
Botswana	2009	FME	-7.8
Chile	2009	EME	-1.0
Cyprus	2009	FME	-1.7
Czech Republic	2009	EME	-4.5
Estonia	2009	FME	-14.1
Honduras	2009	FME	-2.4
Hungary	2009	EME	-6.8
Latvia	2009	FME	-18.0
Mexico	2009	EME	-4.7
Malaysia	2009	EME	-1.5
Romania	2009	FME	-6.8
Russian Federation	2009	EME	-7.8
Slovak Republic	2009	EME	-4.9
Slovenia	2009	FME	-8.0
Thailand	2009	EME	-2.3
Trinidad and Tobago	2009	FME	-4.4
Turkey	2009	EME	-4.8
Ukraine	2009	FME	-14.8
South Africa	2009	EME	-1.5
Zimbabwe	2008	EME	-17.7

Note: EME: Emerging Market Economy; FME: Frontier Market Economy.

TABLE 3A.3   Contraction events between 1990 and 2007 excluded because of data constraints

Country	Year	Country Group	Real GDP Growth (%)
Bulgaria	1992	FME	-7.3
Bulgaria	1996	FME	-9.0
Brazil	1990	EME	-4.3
Czech Republic	1991	EME	-11.6
Ecuador	1999	FME	-4.7
Estonia	1994	FME	-1.6
Honduras	1994	FME	-1.3
Honduras	1999	FME	-1.9
Hungary	1992	EME	-3.1
Indonesia	1998	EME	-13.1
Israel	2002	EME	-0.6
Kenya	1992	FME	-0.8
Latvia	1992	FME	-32.1
Macedonia, FYR	1993	FME	-7.5
Macedonia, FYR	2001	FME	-4.5
Mongolia	1993	FME	-3.2
Mongolia	2009	FME	-1.3
Peru	1990	EME	-5.1
Philippines	1991	EME	-0.6
Poland	1991	EME	-7.0
Romania	1992	FME	-8.8
Romania	1998	FME	-4.8
Russian Federation	1994	EME	-12.6
Rwanda	1994	FME	-50.2
Senegal	1990	FME	-0.7
Senegal	1994	FME	0.0
Serbia	1993	FME	-30.5
Serbia	1999	FME	-11.2
Slovak Republic	1993	EME	-3.7
Slovenia	1992	FME	-5.5
Thailand	1998	EME	-10.5
Turkey	1994	EME	-4.7
Turkey	2001	EME	-5.7
Venezuela, RB	2003	EME	-7.8
South Africa	1992	EME	-2.1
Zambia	1992	FME	-1.7
Zambia	1998	FME	-1.9
Zimbabwe	1992	EME	-9.0
Zimbabwe	2003	EME	-17.0

Note: EME = emerging market economy; FME = frontier market economy.

Annex 3B: Statistical Information[1]

A. Database for Fiscal Space

The database contains annual data for up to 196 countries from 1980 to the present, with greater coverage starting from 1990s.[2] Economies are classified according to gross national income (GNI) per capita (as in the World Bank's official documents) as well as according to market access. Following this classification, economies are divided into Advanced Market Economies (AMEs), Emerging Market Economies (EMEs), Frontier Market Economies (FMEs), Other Developing Countries (ODs), and Other Low Income Countries (LICs). This grouping captures financial market participants' perceptions of fiscal vulnerabilities, and aligns well with standard definitions used by financial market investors for index construction and portfolio allocation. EMEs include economies that currently are, or have been for most of their recent history, middle-income countries with a long-established record of access to international financial markets. FMEs include economies that are usually smaller and less developed than EMEs and, in the view of investors, considerably riskier (although economies undergoing extreme economic or political instability are excluded). Technically, the EME and FME lists consolidate the ones independently developed by FTSE and S&P. The AME category follows the IMF classification.

Data sources

In order to address quality and consistency concerns, most series are sourced from databases maintained by international organizations, in cooperation with national statistical agencies using harmonized methodologies. World Bank and IMF staff also perform adjustments and contribute their own estimates, so data series may ultimately differ slightly across and also within organizations. Much of the data are drawn from the IMF's most recent World Economic Outlook database, the World Bank's World Development Indicators (WDI) and International Debt Statistics (IDS), and the Quarterly External Debt Statistics (QEDS). For a few specific data series, information is gathered from the Joint External

Debt Hub (JEDH, a joint initiative by the World Bank, BIS, IMF, and the Organisation for Economic Co-operation and Developement), the Bank for International Settlements (BIS), and from Bloomberg.

Debt sustainability indicators

Two variables within this group are readily available in or can be computed from WEO data: general government gross debt and general government (primary and overall) net lending/borrowing in percent of GDP.

The structural balance is defined here as the difference between cyclically-adjusted revenues (assuming an output-gap elasticity of one for revenues) and cyclically-adjusted expenditures (assuming an elasticity close to zero).

$$Structural\ balance = revenues(1 + output\ gap)^{-1}$$
$$-expenditures(1 + output\ gap)^{0.1}$$

This definition typically defines the cyclically adjusted balance. The more commonly used definition of structural balance takes into account one-off, discretionary expenditures and changes in commodity and assets prices (IMF, 2012; Bornhorst et al., 2011). Since the goal of the database is to provide comparable definitions for as broad a set of countries as possible, these country-specific, one-off adjustments are not taken into account.

Fiscal sustainability gaps are calculated following Ley (2009) to capture the pressures on sustainability that emerge from large fiscal balances accumulating over time to unsustainable debt stocks, even when initial debt stocks are modest. The overall balance sustainability gap is given by:

$$overall\ sustainability\ gap = b - \left(\frac{-\gamma}{1 + \gamma}\right)d^*$$

where γ represents the nominal GDP growth rate, b the overall fiscal balance (in percent of GDP), and the last term the overall fiscal balance that stabilizes the stock of debt (in percentage of GDP) at d^*. The stock of debt d^* is the target debt-to-GDP ratio that is taken to the median in a given country group.[3]

The primary balance sustainability gap is the difference between the primary balance and the debt-stabilizing primary balance:

---

[1]The main authors of this Annex are Sergio Kurlat, Raju Huidrom, and S. Amer Ahmed.

[2]Fifty-seven small countries (defined as those with a population of less than a million) and dependent territories were excluded from most samples in the analytical sections. This chapter uses the term country interchangeably with economy, referring to territories for which authorities report separate statistics.

TABLE 3B.1   Descriptive statistics

Variable	Quartile		
	0.25	0.5	0.75
Government debt (percent of GDP)			
AMEs	42	59	84
EMEs, FMEs, ODs	25	43	68
LICs	35	56	106
Primary balance (percent of GDP)	-2.5	-0.3	2.1
Structural balance (percent of potential GDP)	-4.4	-2.2	0
Overall fiscal balance (percent of potential GDP)	-4.6	-2.3	0.2
Government debt (percent of revenues)			
AMEs	91	137	208
EMEs, FMEs, ODs	87	163	259
LICs	203	331	575
Overall deficit (percent of revenue)	-17.8	-8.2	0.6
Sustainability gap (overall balance)	-3.5	1	5.7
Sustainability gap (primary balance)	-3.6	-1	1.5
Sustainability gap under current conditions (primary balance)	-3.6	-0.6	2.2
Total external debt/GDP (%)			
AMEs	117	183	282
EMEs, FMEs, ODs	28	45	73
LICs	34	66	98
External private debt/GDP (%)			
AMEs	76	132	244
EMEs, FMEs, ODs	0	1	6
LICs	0	0	0.1
Domestic credit to private Sector/GDP (%)			
AMEs	84	106	148
EMEs, FMEs, ODs	17	30	51
LICs	6	11	17
Short-term external debt/ Total external debt (%)			
AMEs	31	39	58
EMEs, FMEs, ODs	5	12	20
LICs	2	5	10
Short-term external debt/reserves (%)			
AMEs	527	1029	2349
EMEs, FMEs, ODs	11	37	87
LICs	12	32	88
Total external debt/reserves (%)	212	421	1261
Total external debt/reserves (without gold) (%)	216	440	1397

$$primary\ balance\ sustainability\ gap = p - \frac{i - \gamma}{1 + \gamma}d^*$$
$$= p - \frac{r - g}{1 + g}d^*$$

where p is the primary balance (in percent of GDP), i is the nominal long-term interest rate[4], γ is the nominal GDP growth, r is the real interest rate (defined as the nominal interest rate deflated by the U.S. GDP deflator), g is the real growth rate, and d^* is the target stock of debt. The primary balance sustainability gap is calculated using (i) average growth and interest rates over the entire sample period, and (ii) current growth and interest rates.

Private sector debt indicators

Private-sector debt has the potential to impact fiscal sustainability if governments respond to a shock by assuming some of the private sector liabilities. The costs associated with such interventions rise with the overall size of the private sector obligations and maturity or currency mismatches.

The share of total external debt over GDP is calculated using QEDS and WEO data. Gaps in the series are filled with IDS data. The share of external private debt over GDP is calculated using QEDS and WEO data in the case of AMEs, and IDS and WEO for all other countries. The share of short-term over total external debt is drawn from QEDS. Gaps in the series are filled with IDS data.

Reserve adequacy is calculated as the ratio of short-term external debt over reserves and the ratio of total external debt over reserves (from QEDS and WDI; gaps in the series are filled with IDS data; see Bianchi et al., 2013).[5]

---

[3]The median debt levels are 58 percent of GDP for AMEs; 43 percent of GDP for the combined EMEs, FMEs, and ODs; and 56 percent for LICs. If only the post-2001 sample is considered the median for LICs would be lower. As such, the sustainability gap estimated in this chapter is more optimistic for LICs than would be suggested if the post-2001 median debt were considered.

[4]The nominal long-term interest rate is proxied by the 10-year government bond yield for a group of 42 economies that have data available (through Bloomberg) over a reasonably long period. For another group of 43 countries, the rate is estimated as the sum of U.S. dollar Libor plus the predicted spreads from a fixed-effect OLS regression of J. P. Morgan's EMBI on the Institutional Investor Rating.

[5]The Greenspan-Guidotti rule prescribes, as a rule of thumb, full short-term debt coverage for Emerging Markets (IMF, 2011).

TABLE 3B.2 List of economies in quarterly database

Advanced		Emerging and Frontier	
Code	Economy	Code	Economy
AUS	Australia	ARG	Argentina
BEL	Belgium	BGR	Bulgaria
CAN	Canada	BRA	Brazil
DEU	Germany	CHL	Chile
DNK	Denmark	COL	Colombia
ESP	Spain	CZE	Czech Republic
FIN	Finland	HRV	Croatia
FRA	France	HUN	Hungary
GBR	United Kingdom	ISR	Israel
ISL	Iceland	MEX	Mexico
ITA	Italy	POL	Poland
LTU	Lithuania	ROM	Romania
NLD	Netherlands	SVK	Slovak Republic
NOR	Norway	ZAF	South Africa
PRT	Puerto Rico	TUR	Turkey
SVN	Slovenia		
SWE	Sweden		
USA	United States		

The share of domestic credit to the private sector in percentage of GDP is available through WDI. It refers to the sum of financial corporations' claims on the non-financial private sector (and, for some countries, on public enterprises too).

B. Database for Fiscal Multipliers

The main database is an unbalanced panel that covers 34 economies (19 AMEs, and 15 EMEs and FMEs) at the quarterly frequency during the period 1980:1–2014:1 (Annex Table 3B.2). Real government consumption and real GDP are based on the quarterly database in Ilzetzki, Mendoza, and Vegh (2013), which ends around 2008. These two series are extended until 2014:1 by splicing from the OECD Economic Outlook database and Haver Analytics. Real effective exchange rates are the narrow (wherever available) and the broad indices from BIS at the end of each quarter. The current account to GDP series is drawn from the WEO.

Government consumption and GDP series are in logs and detrended using a linear quadratic trend as in Ilzetzki, Mendoza, and Vegh (2013). The real effective rate is transformed into quarter-to-quarter growth rates. The current account-to-GDP ratio series is seasonally-adjusted using the X11 routine. All four series are detrended and demeaned on a country by country basis so as to control for country fixed effects in the regressions. The median short term interest rate used for discounting in the multiplier calculation is computed from the original Ilzetzki, Mendoza, and Vegh (2013) database.

A second database is an unbalanced panel with the same cross sectional and time series coverage as before but at an annual frequency. This includes variables that are not explicitly required for the identification scheme to be valid in the IPVAR and Panel SVAR models but are necessary for the conditioning and the multiplier calculation. Annual data are used for fiscal balance, government debt-to-GDP ratio, and government consumption-to-GDP—all drawn from the October 2014 World Economic Outlook database.

A third database is for the Local Projections model. The crucial variable here is the forecast error of government consumption. This is constructed using OECD forecasts, publicly available at a semi-annual frequency. Forecast errors of government consumption were constructed for 29 economies (22 advanced and 7 developing economies), during the period 1988-2013. The list of economies is in Annex Table 3B.3. This database has a much smaller sample than those in the IPVAR and Panel SVAR models.

TABLE 3B.3   List of economies in semiannual database

Advanced		Emerging and Frontier
Australia	Japan	Chile
Austria	Luxembourg	Czech Republic
Belgium	Netherlands	Hungary
Canada	New Zealand	Korea, Rep
Denmark	Norway	Mexico
Finland	Portugal	Poland
France	Spain	Slovak Republic
Germany	Sweden	Turkey
Greece	United Kingdom	
Ireland	United States	
Italy		

C. Database for the Event Study

Structural balances and sustainability gaps are taken from the database described in Section A, while other macroeconomic variables are taken from publicly available databases shown in Annex Table 3B.4.

The aggregated database for the event study covers up to 196 economies, spanning 1990–2013, although coverage for any given variable varies by country. First, starting in 1990 prevents the results from being driven by the transition in former centrally planning economies. Second, starting in 1990 allows for the capture of complete time series for the largest number of economies and key variables while also allowing for time series long enough to include multiple events.

TABLE 3B.4   Data sources and variables

Source	Variables
GDP (constant 2005 USD)	WDI, WBG
GDP (current USD);	WDI, WBG
GDP (current LCU);	WDI, WBG
Government consumption (constant 2005 USD)	WDI, WBG
Private household consumption (constant 2005 USD)	WDI, WBG
Domestic credit to the private sector (as share of GDP)	WDI, WBG
Gross capital formation (constant 2005 USD)	WDI, WBG
Gross government debt as a share of GDP	WEO, IMF
Exchange rate index (1995=100)	IFS, IMF
Brent crude oil price per barrel (2010 USD)	GEM Commodities Database, WBG

References

Anderson, P. R. D., C. S. Silva, and A. Velandia-Rubiano. 2010. "Public Debt Management in Emerging Economies: Has This Time Been Different?" Policy Research Working Paper 5399, World Bank, Washington, DC.

Arbatli, E., T. Baunsgaard, A. Guerson, and K-S. Min. 2010. "Fiscal Policy Response in Advanced and Emerging Economies." In Post-Crisis Fiscal Policy, ed. C. Cottarelli, P. Gerson, and A. Senhadji. Cambridge, MA: MIT Press.

Auerbach, A. J., and Y. Gorodnichenko. 2012a. "Fiscal Multipliers in Recession and Expansion." In Fiscal Policy after the Financial Crisis, ed. A. Alesina and F. Giavazzi, 63–98. Chicago, IL: University of Chicago Press.

———. 2012b. "Measuring the Output Responses to Fiscal Policy." American Economic Journal: Economic Policy 4 (2): 1–27.

Bagattini, G. Y. 2011. "The Political Economy of Stabilisation Funds: Measuring Their Success in Resource-Dependent Countries." Working Paper 356, Institute of Development Studies, Brighton.

Bagnall, A. E., and E. M. Truman. 2013. "Progress on Sovereign Wealth Fund Transparency and Accountability: An Updated SWF Scoreboard." Policy Brief 13-19, Peterson Institute for International Economics, Washington, DC.

Bandiera, L., J. C. Cuaresma, and G. A. Vinclette. 2010. "Unpleasant Surprises: Determinants and Risks of Sovereign Default." In Sovereign Debt and the Financial Crisis: Will This Time Be Different?, edited by C. A. Primo and G. A. Vincelette. Washington, DC: World Bank.

Batini, N. L., and A. Weber. 2014. "A Simple Method to Compute Fiscal Multipliers." Working Paper 14/93, International Monetary Fund, Washington, DC.

Berg, A., N. Funke, A. Hajdenberg, and V. Lledo. 2009. "Fiscal Policy in Sub-Saharan Africa in Response to the Impact of the Global Crisis." Staff Position Note 09/10, International Monetary Fund, Washington, DC.

Bi, H., W. Shen, and S. Yang. 2014. "Fiscal Limits, External Debt, and Fiscal Policy in Developing Countries." Working Paper 14/49, International Monetary Fund, Washington, DC.

Bianchi, J., Carlos J. Hatchondo, and L. Martinez. 2013. "International Reserves and Rollover Risk." Working Paper 13/33, International Monetary Fund, Washington, DC.

Blanchard, O., and D. Leigh. 2013. "Growth Forecast Errors and Fiscal Multipliers." American Economic Review 103 (3): 117–20.

Blanchard, O., and R. Perotti. 2002. "An Empirical Characterization of the Dynamic Effects of Changes in Government Spending and Taxes on Output." Quarterly Journal of Economics 117 (4): 1329–68.

Bornhorst, F., G. Dobrescu, G. J. Fedelino, and T. Nakata. 2011. "When and How to Adjust beyond the Business Cycle: A Guide to Structural Fiscal Balances." Technical Notes and Manuals 11/02, International Monetary Fund, Washington, DC.

Bova, E., N. Carcenac, and M. Guerguil. 2014. "Fiscal Rules and the Procyclicality of Fiscal Policy in the Developing World." Working Paper 14/122, International Monetary Fund, Washington, DC.

Buttiglione, L., P. R. Lane, L. Reichlin, and V. Reinhart. 2014. "Deleveraging? What Develeveraging?" Geneva Reports on the World Economy 16, International Center for Monetary and Banking Studies, Geneva.

Calderon, C., and K. Schmidt-Hebbel. 2008. "Business Cycles and Fiscal Policies: the Role of Institutions and Financial Markets." Working Paper 481, Central Bank of Chile, Santiago.

Canzoneri, M., F. Collard, H. Dellas, B. Diba. 2012. "Fiscal Multipliers in Recessions." Universität Bern Diskussionsschriften 1204, University of Bern.

Christiano, L., M. Eichenbaum, and S. Rebelo. 2011. "When Is the Government Spending Multiplier Large?" Journal of Political Economy 119 (1): 78–21.

Ciarlone, A., and G. Trebeschi. 2006. "Designing an Early Warning System for Debt Crises." Emerging Markets Review 6 (2005): 376–95.

Coenen, Günter, Christopher J. Erceg, Charles Freedman, Davide Furceri, Michael Kumhof, René Lalonde, Douglas Laxton, Jesper Lindé, Annabelle Mourougane, Dirk Muir, Susanna Mursula, Carlos de Resende, John Roberts, Werner Roeger, Stephen Snudden, Mathias Trabandt, and Jan in't Veld. 2012. "Effects of Fiscal Stimulus in Structural Models." American Economic Journal: Macroeconomics 4 (1): 22–68.

Corsetti, G., K. Kuester, A. Meier, and G. J. Müller. 2013. "Sovereign Risk, Fiscal Policy, and Macroeconomics." Economic Journal 123 (566): F99–F132.

Cuadra, G., J. M. Sanchez, and H. Sapriza. 2010. "Fiscal Policy and Default Risk in Emerging Markets." Review of Economic Dynamics 13 (2): 305–73.

Debrun, X., and A. Schaechte. 2014. "Institutional Reforms and Fiscal Adjustment." In Post-Crisis Fiscal Policy, ed. C. Cottarelli, P. Gerson, and A. Senhadji, 485–514. Cambridge, MA: MIT Press.

Dell'Erba, S., R. Hausmann, and U. Panizza. 2013. "Debt Levels, Debt Composition, and Sovereign Spreads in Emerging and Advanced Economies." Oxford Review of Economic Policy 29 (3): 518–47.

Detragiache, E., and A. Spilibergo. 2004. "Empirical Models of Short-Term Debt and Crises: Do They Rest the Creditor Run Hypothesis?" European Economic Review 48 (2): 379–89.

Didier, T., C. Hevia, and S. L. Schmukler. 2012. "How Resilient and Countercyclical Were Emerging Economies during the Global Financial Crisis?" Journal of International Money and Finance 31 (8): 2052–77.

Eden, M., and A. C. Kraay. 2014. "'Crowding in' and the Returns to Government Investment in Low-Income Countries." Policy Research Working Paper 6781, World Bank, Washington DC.

Eichengreen, B., and R. Hausmann. 1999. "Exchange Rates and Financial Fragility." Proceedings from the Economic Policy Symposium, Federal Reserve Bank of Kansas City, Jackson Hole, WY, August 26–28.

Eichengreen, B., R. Hausmann, and U. Panizza. 2009. "Currency Mismatches, Debt Intolerance, and Original Sin: Why They Are Not the Same and Why It Matters." In Capital Controls and Capital Flows in Emerging Markets: Policies, Practices, and Consequences, edited by S. Edwards. National Bureau of Economic Research, Cambridge, MA.

Eskesen, L. L. 2009. "Countering the Cycle—The Effectiveness of Fiscal Policy in Korea." Working Paper 09/249, International Monetary Fund, Washington, DC.

Fardoust, S., J. Y. Lin, and X. Luo. 2012. "Demystifying China's Fiscal Stimulus." Policy Research Working Paper 6221, World Bank, Washington, DC.

Fasano, U. 2000. "Review of the Experience with Oil Stabilization and Savings Funds in Selected Countries." Working Paper 00/112, International Monetary Fund, Washington, DC.

Fatás, A. and I. Mihov. 2012. "Fiscal Policy as a Stabilization Tool." Discussion Paper, Center for Economic Policy Research.

Frankel, J. 2011. "A Solution to Fiscal Procyclicality: The Structural Budget Institutions Pioneered by Chile." Journal Economía Chilena 14 (2): 39–78.

Frankel, J. A., C. A. Végh, and G. Vuletin. 2013. "On Graduation from Fiscal Procyclicality." Journal of Development Economics 100 (1): 32–47.

Gill, I. S., I. Izviorski, W. van Eeghen, and D. De Rosa. 2014. Diversified Development: Making the Most of Natural Resources in Eurasia. Washington, DC: World Bank.

Grigoli, F., Z. Mills, M. Verhoeven, and R. Vlaicu. 2012. "MTEFs and Fiscal Performance: Panel Data Evidence." Policy Research Working Paper 6186, World Bank, Washington, DC.

Guajardo, J. C., D. Leigh, and A. Pescatori. 2014. "Expansionary Austerity? International Evidence." Journal of the European Economic Association 12 (4): 949–68.

Harding, D., and A. Pagan. 2002. "Dissecting the Cycle: A Methodological Investigation." Journal of Monetary Economics 49 (2): 365–81.

Hausmann, R., and U. Panizza. 2011. "Redemption or Abstinence? Original Sin, Currency Mismatches, and Counter Cyclical Policies in the New Millennium." Journal of Globalization and Development 2 (1): 1–35.

Heller, P. S. 2005. "Understanding Fiscal Space." Policy Discussion Paper 05/04, International Monetary Fund, Washington, DC.

Holmes, M., and A. Evans. 2003. A Review of Experience in Implementing Medium Term Expenditure Frameworks in a PRSP Context: A Synthesis of Eight Country Studies. London: Overseas Development Institute.

IDB (Inter-American Development Bank) 2014. 2014 Latin America and Caribbean Macroeconomic Report. Washington, DC: IDB.

Ilzetzki, E., E. Mendoza, and C. Végh. 2013. "How Big (Small?) Are Fiscal Multipliers?" Journal of Monetary Economics 60 (2): 239–54.

IMF (International Monetary Fund). 2002. Assessing Sustainability. Washington, DC: IMF.

———. 2009. "Chile: 2009 Article IV Consultation." Country Report 09/271, IMF, Washington, DC.

———. 2010. "World Economic Outlook." October, IMF, Washington, DC.

———. 2011. Assessing Reserve Adequacy. Washington, DC: IMF.

———. 2012. "World Economic Outlook." October, IMF, Washington, DC.

———. 2013. "Heavily Indebted Poor Countries (HIPC) Initiative and Multilateral Debt Relief Initiative (MDRI): Statistical Update." IMF, Washington, DC.

———. 2014a. "2014 Spillover Report." Policy Paper, IMF, Washington, DC.

———. 2014b. "Debt Relief under the Heavily Indebted Poor Countries (HIPC) Initiatives Factsheet." IMF, Washington, DC. https://www.imf.org/external/np/exr/facts/pdf/hipc.pdf.

————. 2014c. "World Economic Outlook." October, IMF, Washington, DC.

————. 2014d. "Fiscal Monitor." October, IMF, Washington, DC.

Jedidi, O. 2013. "Predicting Sovereign Debt Crises: A Panel Data Approach Using Composite Indices." Mimeo, University of Rennes.

JP Morgan. 2014. "EMBI Global and EMBI Global Diversified: Rules and Methodology." Methodology Brief, JP Morgan.

Kohler, M. 2010. "Exchange Rates during Financial Crises." BIS Quarterly Review 2010(March).

Kraay, A. C. 2012. "How Large Is the Government Spending Multiplier? Evidence from World Bank Lending." Quarterly Journal of Economics 127 (2): 829–87.

————. 2014. "Government Spending Multipliers in Developing Countries: Evidence from Lending by Official Creditors." American Economic Journal: Macroeconomics 6 (4): 170–208.

Kraay, A. C., and V. Nehru. 2006. "When Is External Debt Sustainable?" World Bank Economic Review 20 (3): 341–65.

Kraay, A. C., and L. Serven. 2013. "Fiscal Policy as Tool for Stabilization in Developing Countries." Background Note for 2014 World Development Report: Managing Risks for Development, Washington, DC, World Bank.

Krugman, P., 2013. "Currency Regimes, Capital Flows, and Crises," Paper presented at the 14th Jacques Polak Annual Research Conference, IMF.

Laeven, L., and F. Valencia. 2013. "Systemic Banking Crises Database." IMF Economic Review 2013 (61): 225–70.

Le Houerou, P., and Taliercio. 2002. "Medium Term Expenditure Frameworks: From Concept to Practice, Preliminary Lessons from Africa." Africa Region Working Paper 28, World Bank, Washington, DC.

Ley, E. 2009. "Fiscal Policy for Growth." PREM Note131, World Bank, Washington, DC.

Ley, E., and F. Misch. 2014. "Output Data Revisions in Low-Income Countries." Paper presented at the joint RES-SPR conference on "Macroeconomic Challenges Facing Low-Income Countries," Washington, DC, January 30–31.

Manasse, P., and N. Roubini. 2009. "'Rules of Thumb' for Sovereign Debt Crises." Journal of International Economics 78 (2): 192–205.

Mineshima, A., M. Poplawski-Ribeiro, and A. Weber. 2014. "Size of Fiscal Multipliers." In Post-Crisis Fiscal Policy, ed. C. Cottarelli, P. Gerson, and A. Senhadji, 315–72. Cambridge, MA: MIT Press.

Nickel, R., and A. Tudyka. 2013. "Fiscal Stimulus in Times of High Debt: Reconsidering Multipliers and Twin Deficits." Working Paper 1513, European Central Bank, Frankfurt.

Ostry, J. D., A. R. Ghosh, J. I. Kim, and M. S. Qureshi. 2010. "Fiscal Space." Staff Position Note 10/11, International Monetary Fund, Washington, DC.

Perotti, R. 1999. "Fiscal Policy in Good Times and Bad." Quarterly Journal of Economics 114 (4): 1399–1436.

————. 2007. "Fiscal Policy in Developing Countries: A Framework and Some Questions." Policy Research Working Paper 4365, World Bank, Washington, DC.

Primiceri, G. E. 2005. "Time Varying Structural Vector Autoregressions and Monetary Policy." Review of Economic Studies 72 (3): 821–52.

Ramey, V. 2011. "Identifying Government Spending Shocks: It's All in the Timing." Quarterly Journal of Economics 126 (1): 1–50.

Ramey, V., and M. D. Shapiro. 1998. "Costly Capital Reallocation and the Effects of Government Spending." Carnegie-Rochester Conference Series on Public Policy 48 (1998): 145–94.

Reinhart, C.M and K.S. Rogoff. 2009. This Time is Different: Eight Centuries of Financial Folly. Princeton, NJ: Princeton University Press.

———. 2011. "From Financial Crash to Debt Crash." American Economic Review 101 (5): 1676–1706.

Reinhart, C. M., K. S. Rogoff, and M. A. Savastano. 2003. "Debt Intolerance." Working Paper 9908, National Bureau of Economic Research, Cambridge, MA.

Rendahl, P. 2012. "Fiscal Policy in an Unemployment Crisis." Working Papers in Economics 1211, University of Cambridge.

Riera-Crichton, D., C. A. Végh, and G. Vuletin. 2012. "Tax Multipliers: Pitfalls in Measurement and Identification." Working Paper 18497, National Bureau of Economic Research, Cambridge, MA.

———. 2014. "Fiscal Multipliers in Recessions and Expansions: Does It Matter Whether Government Spending Is Increasing or Decreasing?" Policy Research Working Paper 6993, World Bank, Washington, DC.

Schaechter, A., T. Kinda, N. Budina, and A. Weber. 2012. "Fiscal Rules in Response to the Crisis—Toward the "Next-Generation" Rules: A New Dataset. Working Paper 12/187, International Monetary Fund, Washington, DC.

Schmidt-Hebbel, K. 2012a. "The Political Economy of Distribution and Growth in Chile." Working Paper 417, Instituto de Economía, Pontificia Universidad Católica de Chile.

———. 2012b. "Fiscal Institutions in Resource-Rich Economies: Lessons from Chile and Norway." Working Paper 416, Instituto de Economía, Pontificia Universidad Católica de Chile, Santiago, Chile.

Snudden, S. 2013. "Countercyclical Fiscal Rules for Oil Exporting Countries." Working Paper 13/229, International Monetary Fund, Washington, DC.

Sugawara, N. 2014. "From Volatility to Stability in Expenditure: Stabilization Funds in Resource-Rich Countries." Working Paper 14/43, International Monetary Fund, Washington, DC.

Sutherland, A. J. 1997. "Fiscal Crises and Aggregate Demand: Can High Public Debt Reverse the Effects of Fiscal Policy?" Journal of Public Economics 65 (2): 147–62.

Towbin, P., and S. Weber. 2013. "Limits of Floats: The Role of Foreign Currency Debt and Import Structure." Journal of Development Economics 101 (March 2013): 179–94.

UN. 2011. The Global Social Crisis: Report on the World Social Situation 2011. New York: United Nations.

Végh, C., and G. Vuletin. 2013. The Road to Redemption: Policy Response to Crises in Latin America. Washington, DC: International Monetary Fund.

World Bank. 2013a. Global Economic Prospects June 2013: Less Volatile, but Slower Growth. Washington, DC: World

Bank.

————. 2013b. World Development Report 2014: Risk and Opportunity—Managing Risk for Development. Washington, DC: World Bank.

————. 2013c. Beyond the Annual Budget. Washington, DC: World Bank.

————. 2014a. Global Economic Prospects January 2014: Coping with Policy Normalization in High-Income Countries. Washington, DC: World Bank.

————. 2014b. East Asia Economic Update October 2014: Enhancing Competitiveness in an Uncertain World. Washington, DC: World Bank.

————. 2014c. Global Monitoring Report 2014/2015: Ending Poverty and Sharing Prosperity. Washington, DC: World Bank.

————. 2014d. A Measured Approach to Ending Poverty and Boosting Shared Prosperity: Concepts, Data, and the Twin Goals. Washington, DC: World Bank.

CHAPTER 4

THREE TOPICAL ISSUES:

Oil Price Developments, Global Trade
Slowdown, and Stability of Remittances

Introduction

This chapter includes three essays on topical issues relevant for developing countries. The first essay presents an analysis of the causes and implications of the recent decline in oil prices. It argues that supply-related factors appear to have played a dominant role in explaining the plunge in oil prices. If sustained, lower oil prices would support global activity and reduce inflationary, external, and fiscal pressures in oil-importing countries but affect oil-exporting countries adversely by weakening growth prospects, and fiscal and external positions. The second essay explores the cyclical and structural reasons for the slowdown in global trade since the global financial crisis. It reports that both the weak recovery in advanced economies and structural factors, including changes in the global production process, have played important roles in explaining the slow growth in global trade. The third essay highlights the exceptional resilience of remittance flows compared with other types of capital flows, and finds that the stable nature of remittance flows can help stabilize consumption in recipient countries.

Plunging oil prices. Following four years of stability at around $105/bbl, oil prices have declined sharply since June 2014. Compared to the early 2011 commodity price peaks, the decline in oil prices was much larger than those in other commodity price indices. There are a number of drivers behind the recent plunge in oil prices: several years of upward surprises in oil supply and downward surprises in demand, unwinding of some geopolitical risks that had threatened production, changing OPEC policy objectives, and appreciation of the U.S. dollar. Although it is difficult to pin down the relative importance of these factors, supply-related factors appear to have played a dominant role. The decline in oil prices has significant macroeconomic, financial, and policy implications. If sustained, lower oil prices will contribute to global growth and lead to sizeable real income shifts to oil importers from oil exporters. For oil-importing countries, weak oil prices will support activity and reduce inflationary, external, and fiscal pressures. On the other hand, oil-exporting countries will be adversely impacted by weakening fiscal and external positions and slowing economic activity. Low oil prices will also affect investor sentiment about oil-exporting emerging market economies and can lead to substantial volatility in financial markets by triggering capital outflows, reserve losses, sharp depreciations, or rising sovereign spreads, as happened in some countries during the last quarter of 2014. However, soft oil prices present a significant window of opportunity to reform fuel subsidies or energy taxes in several developing countries.

Weak global trade. Since the financial crisis, activity in many developing countries has been adversely affected by weak global trade. In 2012 and 2013, global trade grew less than 3.5 percent, well below the pre-crisis average of 7 percent. Part of this slowdown can be attributed to cyclical forces—in particular, the slowdown in import demand that reflects weak growth in advanced economies. However, structural forces were also at work. In particular, the sensitivity of trade flows to changes in global activity between the pre-crisis 2000s and the post-crisis period halved. Two factors have been important in driving this change. First, global value chains expanded rapidly during the pre-crisis decade (although they now appear to be maturing). The contribution to global trade of the import and export of intermediate goods along global value chains has slowed as the fragmentation of production processes has settled. Second, the composition of global demand shifted away from trade-intensive goods. Indeed, among the components of aggregate demand, the recovery in investment, the most trade-intensive component, has been slowest, thereby further contributing to the weakening sensitivity of trade to gross domestic product (GDP). As a result of these factors, the expected recovery in growth is unlikely to be accompanied by the rapid growth in global trade that prevailed prior to the crisis.

Resilient remittances. Many developing countries rely heavily on remittances. For low- and lower-middle-income countries as a group, remittance flows exceed foreign direct investment (FDI) flows and on average accounted for almost 5 percent of GDP in 2013. Across developing countries more broadly, remittances have amounted to 60 percent of FDI flows since 2000. At the household level, these flows help support spending on consumption, education, and health services. At the macroeconomic level, remittances are a resilient source of financial flows that continue to grow even during episodes of sudden stops when other capital flows reverse. The third essay finds that remittances are substantially less volatile than all other external flows, including FDI and official development assistance. As a result, remittances can help smooth consumption.

Understanding the Plunge in Oil Prices: Sources and Implications[1]

Oil prices fell sharply in the second half of 2014, bringing to an end a four-year period of stability around $105 per barrel.[2] The decline, which is much larger than that of the non-oil commodity price indices compared to early-2011 peaks, may signal an end to a price "supercycle".[3] Oil prices are expected to remain low in 2015 and rise only marginally in 2016 (Chapter 1). The sources and implications of the sharp decline in oil prices have led to intensive debate.

This essay presents a brief assessment of the magnitude, drivers, and implications of the recent oil price drop. Specifically, it addresses four major questions:

- How does the recent decline in oil prices compare with previous episodes?

- What are the causes of the sharp drop?

- What are the macroeconomic and financial implications of a sustained decline in oil prices?

- What are the main policy implications?

How Does the Recent Decline in Oil Prices Compare with Previous Episodes?

Compared to previous episodes of price declines during the past thirty years, the fall in oil prices in the second half of 2014 qualifies as a significant event (Figure 4.1). Between 1984-2013, five other episodes of oil price declines of 30 percent or more in a six-month period occurred, coinciding with major changes in the global economy and oil markets: an increase in the supply of oil and change in OPEC policy (1985-86); U.S. recessions (1990–91 and 2001); the Asian crisis (1997–98); and the global financial crisis (2007–09).

There are particularly interesting parallels between the recent episode and the collapse in oil prices in 1985-86. After the sharp increase in oil prices in the 1970s, technological developments made possible to reduce the intensity of oil consumption and to extract oil from various

---

[1]This essay was produced by a team led by John Baffes, Ayhan Kose, Franziska Ohnsorge, and Marc Stocker, and including Derek Chen, Damir Cosic, Xinghao Gong, Raju Huidrom, Ekaterine Vashakmadze, Jiayi Zhang, and Tianli Zhao.

[2]During the period 2011:1-2014:6, monthly average oil prices fluctuated between $93 and $118 per barrel. Since 2000, monthly average oil prices touched an all-time high of $133 (July 2008) prior to going down to $61 per barrel (December 2014).

[3]For additional information about the commodity price supercycle, see World Bank (2009); Canuto (2014); Erten and Ocampo (2013); and Cuddington and Jerrett (2008).

FIGURE 4.1 Changes in commodity prices

Oil prices dropped sharply between June and December 2014, bringing to an end a four-year period of relative price stability. The decline, which was much larger than that of other commodity prices from their early-2011 peaks, may signal an end to a price supercycle.

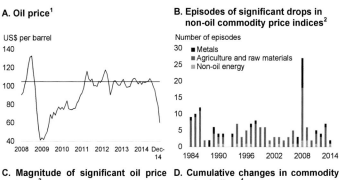

A. Oil price[1]

B. Episodes of significant drops in non-oil commodity price indices[2]

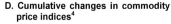

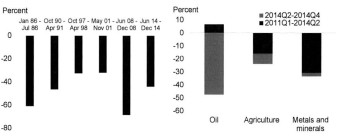

C. Magnitude of significant oil price drops[3]

D. Cumulative changes in commodity price indices[4]

Source: World Bank.
1. Monthly average of WTI, Dubai, and Brent oil prices. Horizontal line denotes $105 per barrel, the average for January 2011-June 2014. Latest data for December 2014.
2. Non-consecutive episodes of six-months for which commodity prices dropped by more than 30 percent (31 agricultural and raw materials, 4 non-oil energy commodities, 7 industrial and 2 precious metals and minerals).
3. Non-consecutive episodes of six-months for which the unweighted average of WTI, Dubai, and Brent oil prices dropped by more than 30 percent.
4. Includes unweighted average of WTI, Brent, and Dubai oil prices, 21 agricultural goods, and 7 metal and mineral commodities.

offshore fields, including the North Sea and Alaska. After Saudi Arabia changed policy in December 1985 to increase its market share, the price of oil declined by 61 percent, from $24.68 to $9.62 per barrel between January-July 1986. Following this episode, low oil prices prevailed for more than fifteen years.

In other commodity markets, episodes of large price declines have mostly been observed in agriculture, typically associated with specific weather conditions. After reaching deep lows during the global financial crisis, most commodity prices peaked in the first quarter of 2011. Since then, prices of metals and agricultural and raw materials have declined steadily as a result of weak global demand and robust supplies. In contrast, oil prices fluctuated within

FIGURE 4.2   Short-term drivers of oil price decline

Despite concerns about geopolitical risk, oil supply has repeatedly surprised on the upside, especially in the United States, while oil demand has surprised on the downside, partly reflecting weaker-than-expected global growth. Oil prices declines have coincided with a strengthening U.S. dollar.

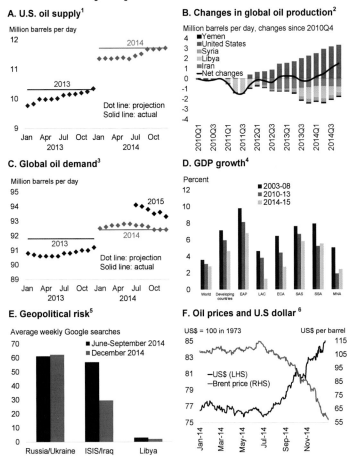

A. U.S. oil supply[1]

B. Changes in global oil production[2]

C. Global oil demand[3]

D. GDP growth[4]

E. Geopolitical risk[5]

F. Oil prices and U.S dollar[6]

Sources: World Bank, IEA, Bloomberg, FRED, and Google Trends.
1. Oil supply includes supply of crude oil, biofuels and liquids.
2. Crude oil supply only.
3. Oil demand includes demand for crude oil, biofuels, and liquids.
4. Weighted average of real GDP growth rates for developing countries in each region.
5. Average weekly Google searches for the words Russia, Ukraine, ISIS, Iraq, and Libya.
6. "US$" is the nominal effective exchange rate of the U.S. dollar against a trade-weighted basket of major currencies. Latest data for December 26, 2014.

a narrow band around $105/barrel (bbl) until June 2014. Softness in the global economy was offset by concerns about geopolitical risks, supply disruptions, and production controls exercised by OPEC (led by Saudi Arabia, its largest oil producer). The last factor in part reflected the willingness of Saudi Arabia and other low-cost producers to withhold output in support of OPEC price objectives. The steep decline in the second half of 2014 intensified after a change in policy at the OPEC meeting in late November. By the end of 2014, the cumulative fall in oil prices from the 2011 peak was much larger than that in non-oil commodity price indices.

What are the Causes of the Sharp Drop?

As for any storable commodity, underlying demand and supply conditions for oil determine the long-run trend in prices, while in the short-run movements in market sentiment and expectations (in some cases driven by geopolitical developments and OPEC decisions) exert an influence too. Prices may respond rapidly to surprises in the news even before actual changes occur. In 2014, relevant events included geopolitical conflicts in some oil-producing regions, OPEC announcements, and the appreciation of the U.S. dollar (Figure 4.2). Long-term developments in supply and demand have also played important roles in driving the recent decline in oil prices (Figure 4.3).

- *Trends in supply and demand.* Recent developments in global oil markets have occurred against a long-term trend of greater-than-anticipated supply and less-than-anticipated demand. Since 2011, U.S. shale oil production has persistently surprised on the upside, by some 0.9 million barrels per day (mb/d, about 1 percent of global supply) in 2014.[4] Expectations of global oil demand have been revised downwards on several occasions during the same period as economic growth disappointed. Between July and December 2014 alone, the projected oil demand for 2015 has been revised downwards by 0.8 mb/d (IEA, 2014a and 2014b). Global growth in 2015 is expected to remain much weaker than it was during the 2003-08 period when oil prices rose substantially. Further, the oil-intensity of global GDP has almost halved since the 1970s as a result of increasing energy efficiency and declining oil-intensity of energy consumption.

- *Changes in OPEC objectives.* Saudi Arabia has traditionally acted as the cartel's swing producer, often using its spare capacity to either increase or reduce OPEC's oil supply and stabilize prices within a desired band. This changed dramatically in late November 2014 after OPEC failed to agree on production cuts. The OPEC decision to maintain its production level of 30 mb/d signaled a significant change in the cartel's policy objectives from targeting an oil price band to maintaining market share.[5]

---

[4]The high oil prices of recent years made technologies of extracting oil from tight rock formations and tar sands profitable. These technologies employ hydraulic fracturing and horizontal drilling. Two key characteristics of the projects which use these new technologies are their very short lifecycle (2.5-3 years from development to full extraction) and relatively low capital costs. Shale (or tight) oil is among so-called unconventional oils. Other types of unconventional oil include oil sands (produced in Canada), deep sea oil and biofuels.

- *Receding geopolitical concerns about supply disruptions.* In the second half of 2014, it became apparent that supply disruptions from conflict in the Middle East had unwound, or did not materialize as expected. In Libya, despite the internal conflict, production recovered by 0.5 million barrels per day (about ½ percent of global production) in the third quarter of 2014. In Iraq, as the advance of ISIS stalled, it became apparent that oil output could be maintained. In addition, the sanctions and counter-sanctions imposed after June 2014 as a result of the conflict in Ukraine have had little effect on oil and natural gas markets thus far.

- *U.S. dollar appreciation.* In the second half of 2014, the U.S. dollar appreciated by 10 percent against major currencies in trade-weighted nominal terms. A U.S. dollar appreciation tends to have a negative impact on the price of oil as demand can decline in countries that experience an erosion in the purchasing power of their currencies. Empirical estimates of the size of the U.S. dollar effect cover a wide range: the high estimates suggest that a 10 percent appreciation is associated with a decline of about 10 percent in the oil price, whereas the low estimates suggest 3 percent or less.[6]

Although the exact contribution of each of these factors cannot be quantified with precision, it is clear that the dominant factor in the price fall has been changes in supply conditions, stemming from the expansion of oil output in the United States, receding concerns on supply disruptions, and OPEC's switch to a policy of maintaining market share.

What are the Macroeconomic and Financial Implications?

Oil prices feed into growth and inflation mainly through three channels (see Box 4.1 for a brief review of the literature on the analytical and empirical linkages between oil prices, output, and inflation).

- *Input costs.* Lower oil prices reduce energy costs generally, as prices of competing energy materials are forced down too, and oil-fired electrical power is

FIGURE 4.3   Long-term drivers of oil price decline

OPEC's share of global oil supply has fallen, partly as a result of rising unconventional oil production in the United States and biofuel production. Meanwhile, the oil intensity of global activity has steadily declined.

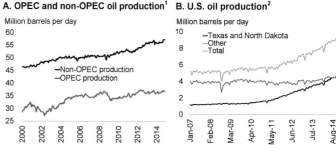

A. OPEC and non-OPEC oil production[1]   B. U.S. oil production[2]

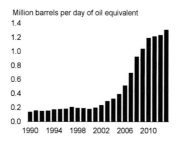

C. Global production of biofuels[3]

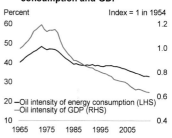

D. Oil intensity of energy consumption and GDP[4]

Source: IEA, BP Statistical Review, U.S. Energy Information Agency, and World Bank.
1. Production includes crude, biofuel-based, and liquid-based oil. Latest observation for November, 2014.
2. Crude oil production only. Texas and North Dakota are the U.S. states with the largest shale oil production. Latest observation for October, 2014.
3. Most biofuels are accounted by maize-based ethanol in the United States, sugar cane-based ethanol in Brazil, and edible oil-based bio diesel in Europe.
4. Oil intensity of real GDP is measured as oil consumption relative to real GDP, indexed at 1 in 1954. Oil intensity of energy consumption is measured as oil consumption in percent of total energy consumption. Latest observation for 2013.

cheaper to produce. In addition, since oil is feedstock for various sectors, including petrochemicals, paper, and aluminum, the decline in price directly impacts a wide range of processed or semi-processed inputs. The transportation, petrochemicals, and agricultural sectors, and some manufacturing industries, would be major beneficiaries from lower prices.

- *Real income shifts.* Oil price declines generate changes in real income benefiting oil-importers and losses hurting oil-exporters. The shift in income from oil exporting economies with higher average saving rates to net importers with a higher propensity to spend should generally result in stronger global demand over the medium-term. However, the effects could vary significantly across countries and over time: some exporting economies may be forced by financial constraints to adjust both government spending and

---

[5]OPEC's "desired" range was set to $100-110/bbl during the early 2010s. OPEC produces about 36 mb/d, of which 30 mb/d comes from crude oil (subject to quotas) and 6 from liquids (not subject to quotas). Non-OPEC countries produce about 55 mb/d. Even before the November 27 decision, Saudi Arabia has signaled its intention to maintain its market share by aggressively cutting prices for East Asian buyers.

[6]Zhang et al. (2008) and Akram (2009) present estimates. Frankel (2014) argues that U.S. dollar appreciation, triggered by diverging monetary policies in the United States, Euro Area, and Japan, played an important role in the general decline of commodity prices.

BOX 4.1   What do we know about the impact of oil prices on output and inflation? A Brief Survey[1]

Movements in oil prices have often been associated with changes in output and inflation. Although the effects of oil price movements on output and inflation have declined over time, they tend to be larger when prices go up (rather than down) and when they are driven by changes in oil supply (rather than demand).

Large jumps in oil prices have historically been followed by rising inflation and recessions in many countries.[2] This basic observation led to a voluminous literature analyzing the complex linkages between movements in oil prices and activity and inflation. This box presents a brief review of this literature to address the following questions:

- Which key channels transmit changes in oil prices to activity and inflation?

- How large is the impact of oil price movements on activity?

- How large is the pass-through of changes in oil prices to inflation?

Which key channels transmit oil price changes to activity and inflation?

Falling oil prices often affect activity and inflation by shifting aggregate demand and supply and triggering policy responses. On the supply side, lower oil prices lead to a decline in the cost of production (Finn, 2000). The lower cost of production across a whole range of energy-intensive goods may be passed on to consumers and hence, indirectly, reduce inflation (Blanchard and Gali 2008). The lower cost of production can also translate in higher investment. On the demand side, by reducing energy bills, a decline in oil prices raises consumers' real income and leads to an increase in consumption (Edelstein and Kilian, 2008; Kilian, 2014; Hamilton, 2009).[3]

If falling oil prices ease inflation—especially, core inflation or inflation expectations (Alvarez et al., 2011)—central banks may respond with monetary loosening which, in turn, can boost

activity (Bernanke, Watson and Gertler, 1997).[4] However, if core inflation or inflation expectations do not ease with falling oil prices, central banks may refrain from a monetary policy response such that the impact on real activity could be small (Hunt, Isard and Laxton, 2001). Lower oil prices can also lead to adjustments in fiscal policies that can in turn affect activity.

How large is the impact of oil price movements on activity?

The literature mostly focuses on estimating the impact of oil price *increases* on real activity in major economies.[5] These estimates vary widely, depending on the oil intensity of the economy, oil exporter status, data samples, and methodology. For example, for OECD countries, a 10 percent increase in oil prices has been associated with a decline in real activity of 0.3-0.6 percent in the United States and 0.1-0.3 percent for the Euro Area (Jimenez-Rodriguez and Sanchez, 2005).[6] Similar results have also been found for developing countries.[7]

Recent literature has established that the effects of oil prices on activity and inflation depend on the underlying source and direction of the changes in prices. Also, the impact has declined over the years.[8]

Source of the oil price movements. The impact of oil prices on activity depends critically on their source. Oil supply shocks would be expected to generate an independent impact on activity. In contrast, oil demand shocks would themselves be the outcome of changing real activity with limited second-round effects (Kilian, 2009). Indeed, oil price changes driven by oil supply shocks are often associated with significant changes in global output and income shifts between oil-exporters and importers. Changes in prices driven by demand shocks, on the other hand,

---

[1]The main authors of this box are Derek Chen, Raju Huidrom and Tianli Zhao.

[2]Hamilton (2005) documents that nine out of ten recessions in the U.S. were preceded by sharp oil price increases. De Gregorio, Landerretche, and Neilson (2007) show the strong correlation between oil price shocks and subsequent high inflation in many countries.

[3]For example, a $10 per barrel oil price decline may reduce U.S. consumers' gasoline bills by as much as $30 billion (0.2 percent of GDP; Gault, 2011). However, the uncertainty associated with oil price swings can have a negative impact on investment (Elder and Serletis, 2010).

[4]The impact of endogenous monetary responses to oil price movements on aggregate activity is contested in the literature. For instance, Kilian and Lewis (2011) argue that, once the endogeneity of oil price movements is taken into account, there is no empirical support for a significant role of the monetary policy in amplifying the effects of oil price shocks on the U.S. economy.

[5]For the global economy, as mentioned in the text, Arezki and Blanchard (2014) report estimates of model simulations that the current oil price slump could increase global output by 0.3 – 0.7 percentage points. Similar estimates based on such large scale- macroeconomic models are also available from other sources (World Bank, 2013; IMF, 2014; OECD, 2014).

[6]Jimenez-Rodriguez and Sanchez (2005) derive these estimates from a variety of different methodologies. Their results are broadly in line with Abeysinghe (2001), Reifschneider, Tetlow and Williams (1999), and Mork (1994), Cashin, Mohaddes and Raissi (2014), and Peersman and Van Robays (2012).

[7]See Tang, Wu, and Zhang (2010) and Allegret, Couharde and Guillaumin (2012). In addition to changes in the level of oil prices, their volatility has been associated with a decline in investment in some developing countries, for example in Thailand (Shuddhasawtta, Salim, Bloch, 2010).

[8]Hamilton (2005), Kilian (2008, 2014) provide comprehensive surveys of the literature on these issues.

BOX 4.1 *(continued)*

tend to lead to weaker and, in some studies, insignificant effects (Cashin, Mohaddin, and Raissi, 2014; Kilian, 2009; Peersman and Van Robays, 2012).

Asymmetric effects. The failure of the 1986 oil price collapse to produce an economic boom has sparked a literature on the asymmetric impact of oil price movements on activity. Such an asymmetric effect may result from costly factor reallocation, uncertainty, and an asymmetric monetary policy response. In particular, the U.S. Federal Reserve has typically chosen to respond vigorously to inflation increases triggered by higher oil prices but has responded less to unexpected declines in inflation following oil price declines (Kilian, 2014; Bernanke, Gertler, and Watson, 1997).[9] Hence, while oil price increases—especially large ones—have been associated with significantly lower output in the United States, oil price declines have been followed by much smaller, and statistically insignificant, benefits to activity (Hamilton, 2003; Jimenez-Rodriguez and Sanchez, 2005).[10]

Declining impact. Several studies have documented that the impact of oil prices on output has fallen over time. For example, Hamilton (2005) estimates that a 10 percent oil price spike would reduce U.S. output by almost 3 percent below the baseline over four quarters in 1949-80 but less than 1 percent in a sample that extends to 2005. The literature has offered a variety of reasons for the declining impact of oil prices on the economy (Blanchard and Gali, 2008): structural changes such as falling energy-intensity of activity, and more flexible labor markets which lowered rigidities associated with price-markups.[11] In addition, stronger monetary policy frameworks have reduced the impact of oil price shocks by better anchoring inflation expectations, thus dampening firm pricing power

(Taylor, 2000) and helping create a regime where inflation is less sensitive to price shocks.

How large is the pass-through of changes in oil prices to inflation?

Historically, oil price swings and inflation have been positively correlated, even though this relationship has varied widely across countries (as documented in Figure 4.5 in the main text). Large increases in oil prices during the past forty years were often followed by episodes of high inflation in many countries (De Gregorio, Landerretche, and Neilson, 2007). As in the case of output, the impact of oil price swings on inflation has, however, declined over the years. For instance, Hooker (2002) showed that oil prices contributed substantially to U.S. inflation before 1981, but since that time the pass-through has been much smaller. Similar results have been found for other advanced economies (Cologni and Manera 2006; Alvarez et.al, 2011) and for some emerging market economies (De Gregorio, Landerretche, and Neilson, 2007; Cunado and Gracia, 2005). The decline in pass-through is attributable to the reasons above that explain the decline in the impact on activity, in particular improvements in monetary policy frameworks that resulted in better anchoring of long-run inflation expectations.

---

[9]Kilian and Vigfusson (2011) presents a survey of the literature on the nonlinearities and asymmetries in oil price-output relationship.

[10]Similar estimates are also found in the earlier literature (Mork et. al., 1994; Smyth, 1993; Mory, 1993).

[11]Barsky and Kilian (2004) and Blanchard and Gali (2008) argue that the impact of oil prices on the U.S. stagnation in the 1970s is overestimated in the earlier literature.

imports abruptly in the short-term, while benefits for importing countries could be diffuse and offset by higher precautionary savings if confidence in recovery remains low.

- *Monetary and fiscal policies.* In oil-importing countries where declining oil prices may reduce medium-term inflation expectations below target, central banks could respond with additional monetary policy loosening, which, in turn, can support growth. The combination of lower inflation and higher output implies a favorable short-run policy outcome. In oil-exporting countries, however, lower oil prices might trigger contractionary fiscal policy measures, unless

buffers are available to protect expenditures from the decline in tax revenues from the oil sector.

These channels operate with different strengths and lags across countries. However, it seems clear that oil price declines generally have smaller output effects on oil-importing economies than oil price increases.[7] This asymmetry could be caused by the frictions and adjustment costs associated with oil price changes.

---

[7]See Jimenez-Rodriguo and Sanchez (2005) for details on these findings. Hoffman (2012) provides a summary of the results in the literature.

The impacts of oil price changes on output may also vary between developing and developed countries. Output in developing countries may be relatively more energy intensive and, hence, may benefit more from a decline in energy input costs. Household inflation expectations in developing economies may also be more responsive to changes in fuel prices than in developed countries, partly as a result of a greater weight of fuel and food in consumption baskets. This is reflected in stronger effects of commodity price shocks on inflation in developing countries than in advanced economies (Gelos and Ustyugova, 2012; IMF, 2011).

Global growth

The upward surprises in oil supply, the unwinding of some geopolitical risks, and the changes in OPEC's policy objectives all indicate that supply-related factors have played a major role in the recent price drop.[8] Historical estimates suggest that a 30 percent oil price decline (as expected, on an annual average basis, between 2014 and 2015) driven by a supply shock would be associated with an increase in world GDP of about 0.5 percent in the medium-term (World Bank, 2013; IMF, 2014; OECD, 2014).

Because of the confluence of various types of demand, supply, and policy-related factors, growth outcomes following the five episodes of significant declines in oil prices listed above differed widely. However, most episodes were preceded by a period of weakening global growth and many were followed by relatively slow recoveries in the year after the oil price decline, particularly after 1990-91, 1997-98, and 2008-09. During the post-2001 recession, global growth picked up more rapidly in 2002 against the background of an aggressive easing of monetary policy by the major central banks. After the 1985-86 episode, global growth remained steady while the U.S. Federal Reserve embarked on a series of interest rate cuts in 1986.

Like previous declines, the current fall in oil prices takes place against the backdrop of both cyclical and structural developments that might affect the growth impact in 2015-16:

- *Weak growth.* Disappointing global growth prospects and weak oil demand are likely to be responsible in

some part for the price drop (Hamilton, 2014a and 2014b).[9] Demand shocks driven changes in oil prices tend to have a smaller impact on growth.

- *Limited support from monetary policy.* The monetary policy loosening that was typically associated with demand shocks driven oil price declines in the past is unlikely to materialize. Specifically, with policy interest rates of major central banks already at or near the zero lower bound, the room for additional monetary policy easing is limited should declining oil prices lead to a persistent undershooting of inflation expectations.

- *Small response of demand.* Post-crisis uncertainties associated with financial vulnerabilities, rapid household debt growth, elevated unemployment, and slowing long-term growth potential may encourage households and corporations to save real income gains from falling oil prices, rather than to consume and invest.

- *Changing nature of the relationship between oil and activity.* Recent research suggests that the impact of oil prices on overall activity has significantly declined since the mid-1980s as a result of the falling oil-intensity of GDP, increasing labor market flexibility, and better-anchored inflation expectations. The weakened income effect would reduce the responsiveness of demand to price changes.[10]

- *Reduced investment in new exploration or development.* Lower oil prices would especially put at risk oil investment projects in low-income countries (e.g., Mozambique, Uganda) or in unconventional sources such as shale oil, tar sands, deep sea oil fields (especially in Brazil, Mexico, Canada and the United States), and oil in the Arctic zone.

Income shifts, current accounts, and fiscal balances

Developments in global oil markets are accompanied by significant real income shifts from oil-exporting to oil-importing countries. The ultimate impact of lower oil prices on individual countries depends on a wide range of factors, including the amount of oil in their exports or imports, their cyclical positions, and the (monetary and fiscal) policy room they have to react (Figures 4.5).

---

[8]In simulations using the IMF's large-scale macroeconomic model, Arezki and Blanchard (2014) posit that three-fifths of the oil price drop in the second half of 2014 was caused by expanding supply, and argue that this should raise global activity between 0.3 and 0.7 percent in 2015.

[9]Hamilton (2014a) attributes about two-fifths of the decline in oil prices in the second half of 2014 to weak global demand.

[10]For the changing nature of the relationship between oil prices, and activity and inflation, see Blanchard and Galí (2008), Blanchard and Riggi (2013), and Baumeister and Peersman (2013).

Oil-exporting countries. Empirical estimates suggest that output in some oil-exporting countries, including Russia and some in the Middle East and North Africa, could contract by 0.8–2.5 percentage points in the year following a 10 percent decline in the annual average oil price.[11]

The slowdown would compound fiscal revenue losses in oil-exporting countries. Fiscal break-even prices, which range from $54 per barrel for Kuwait to $184 for Libya, exceed current oil prices for most oil exporters (Figure 4.6). In some countries, the fiscal pressures can partly be mitigated by large sovereign wealth fund or reserve assets. In contrast, several fragile oil exporters, such as Libya and the Republic of Yemen, do not have significant buffers, and a sustained oil price decline may require substantial fiscal and external adjustment, including through depreciation or import compression. Recent developments in oil markets will also require adjustments in macroeconomic and financial policies in other oil-exporting countries, including Russia, Venezuela, and Nigeria.

Oil-importing countries. A 10 percent decrease in oil prices would raise growth in oil-importing economies by some 0.1–0.5 percentage points, depending on the share of oil imports in GDP (World Bank, 2013; Rasmussen and Roitman, 2011). Their fiscal and current accounts could see substantial improvements (Kilian, Rebucci, and Spatafora, 2009).

In China, for example, the impact of lower oil prices on growth is expected to boost activity by 0.1-0.2 percent because oil accounts for only 18 percent of energy consumption, whereas 68 percent is accounted for by coal (Figure 4.4). The sectors most dependent on oil consumption—half of which is satisfied by domestic production—are transportation, petrochemicals, and agriculture. Since regulated fuel costs are adjusted with global prices (albeit with a lag), CPI inflation could fall over several quarters. The overall effect would be small, however, given that the weight of energy and transportation in the consumption basket is less than one-fifth. The fiscal impact is also expected to be limited since fuel subsidies are only 0.1 percent of GDP. Despite significant domestic oil production and the heavy use of coal, China remains the second-largest oil importer. Therefore, the sustained low oil prices of 2015 are expected to widen the current account surplus by some 0.4-0.7 percentage points of GDP.

Several other large oil-importing emerging market economies also stand to benefit from lower oil prices. In

FIGURE 4.4   Oil production and consumption for selected countries

The importance of oil production in GDP varies significantly across countries. While some countries rely heavily on oil for their energy consumption, some others have diverse sources of energy. Shares of oil in exports and imports also differ substantially across countries.

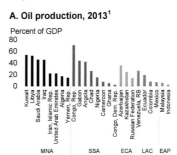

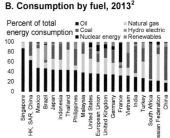

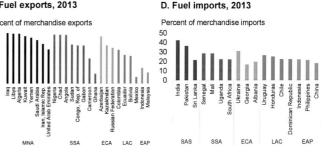

Sources: World Development Indicators, BP Statistical Review, CEIC, U.S. Energy Information Agency.
1. Oil production is estimated as oil rents which are defined as the difference between the value of crude oil production at world prices and total costs of production. Estimates based on sources and methods described in "The Changing Wealth of Nations: Measuring Sustainable Development in the New Millennium" (World Bank, 2011).
2. Oil consumption is measured in million tons; other fuels in million tons of oil equivalent.

Brazil, India, Indonesia, South Africa and Turkey, the fall in oil prices will help lower inflation and reduce current account deficits—a major source of vulnerability for many of these countries.

Some oil importers would also be affected by a slowdown in oil-exporting countries. Sustained low oil prices will weaken activity in exporting countries, with adverse spillovers to trading partners and recipient countries of remittances or official support. A sharp recession in Russia would dampen growth in Central Asia, while weakening external accounts in Venezuela or the Gulf Cooperation Council (GCC) countries may put at risk external financing support they provide to neighboring countries (see Chapter 2 for region- and country-specific details).

Inflation

Lower oil prices will temporarily reduce global inflation. The impact across countries will vary significantly, reflecting in particular the importance of oil in consumer

[11]For details, see World Bank (2013), Berument, Ceylan, and Dogan (2010), and Feldkirchner and Korhonen (2012).

FIGURE 4.5   Oil prices and inflation

The projected 30 percent decline in average oil prices in average annual oil prices between 2014 and 2015 is likely to lower global inflation temporarily by up to 0.9 percentage point, but the impact will dissipate by 2016.

A. Weights of energy in national CPI baskets[1]

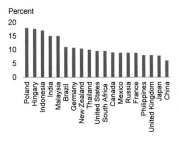

B. Correlation between oil price growth and inflation[2]

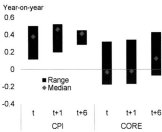

C. Impulse response of inflation to 10 percent oil price increase[3]

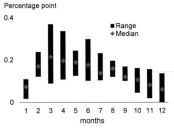

D. Evolution of oil price and inflation, 2010-16[4]

Sources: OECD, Morgan Stanley, IMF, Capital Economics, and World Bank.
1. Sourced from OECD (for high-income countries, Hungary, Mexico and South Africa); Morgan Stanley (for China); IMF for (India, Indonesia, Malaysia, Thailand and the Philippines); and Capital Economics (Brazil and Russia). Excludes transport.
2. Correlation computed for headline and core-CPI inflation on a monthly frequency over the period 2001-14 across 16 members of the G20. "t+1" and "t+6" refer to correlation of annual oil price changes with the first and sixth lead of inflation indicators (one month and six months ahead), respectively.
3. Impulse response of year-on-year CPI inflation to a 10 percent shock in year-on-year oil price changes, estimated from individual monthly Vector Auto-Regression (VAR) models for 16 countries (same sample as above) including year-on-year growth in consumer prices, producer prices, oil prices (in local currency), the nominal effective exchange rate and the deviation of industrial production from its Hodrick-Prescott-filtered trend. VAR models were estimated with 8 lags (based on a selection of information criteria) and impulse responses derived from a Choleski decomposition, with CPI inflation last in the ordering and therefore affected contemporaneously by shocks to all other variables. The range of impulse responses across countries is defined by the first and third quartiles of the distribution of individual country responses.
4. Inflation indicates a consumption weighted average of inflation rates of 16 members of the G20. Inflation projection is based on country specific VAR models.

baskets, exchange rate developments, stance of monetary policy, the extent of fuel subsidies and other price regulations (Figures 4.4 and 4.5). Historically, the correlation between oil price swings and headline inflation has varied widely across countries.

In order to gauge the likely impact of changes in oil prices on inflation, two simple econometric models are estimated using data for G20 countries.[12] First, the change in the price of oil is added to a standard Phillips curve model, in which inflation is a function of inflation

expectations and economic slack. Second, a simple Vector Auto Regression (VAR) model is estimated to study the dynamic interactions between headline consumer prices, producer prices, output gap, exchange rate and the price of oil.[13]

Results indicate that the pass-through to headline inflation in most cases is modest, with a 10 percent increase in the oil price raising inflation by up to 0.3 percentage point at its peak impact. This is in line with other estimates in the literature.[14] The impact is essentially one-off, peaking after three to five months, before fading gradually. These results suggest that a 30 percent decline in oil prices, if sustained, would reduce global inflation by about 0.4-0.9 percentage point through 2015. However, in the course of 2016, inflation would return to levels prior to the plunge in oil prices. Country-specific circumstances will in some cases influence the impact of oil prices on domestic inflation. For economies that import large volumes of oil, currency appreciation (depreciation) would reinforce (mitigate) the inflationary impact of the oil price decline. In countries where the government subsidizes household energy consumption, the pass-through of global oil prices to local energy prices will be dampened (Jongwanich and Park, 2009).

Financial markets

The sharp decline in oil prices has been accompanied by substantial volatility in foreign exchange and equity markets of a number of emerging economies since October (Figure 4.7). Low oil prices have already led investors to reassess growth prospects of oil-exporting countries. This has contributed to capital outflows, reserve losses, sharp depreciations, or rising sovereign CDS spreads in many oil-exporting countries, including

[12]The approach here closely follows the one in De Gregorio, Landerretche and Nielson (2007). The sample consists of sixteen members of the G20 (Brazil, Canada, China, Germany, Euro Area, Spain, France, United Kingdom, India, Indonesia, Italy, Japan, Mexico, Turkey, United States, and South Africa). All regressions are country-specific and estimated at a monthly frequency over the period 2001-14. Oil prices are measured in local currency to account for potentially offsetting exchange rate movements. Economic slack is proxied by the deviation of industrial production from its Hodrick-Prescott-filtered trend.
[13]The sample is the same as for the Phillips curve model estimations. Variables included are the year-on-year growth rate of the consumer price index, the producer price index, the nominal effective exchange rate, the oil price (denominated in local currency), and the deviation of industrial production from its Hodrick-Prescott-filtered trend.
[14]De Gregorio, Landerretche, and Nielson (2007) find, in a sample of 23 countries for 1980-2005, that a 10 percent increase in oil prices (in local currency) would raise inflation by somewhat less than 0.2 percentage point, on average.

in Russia, Venezuela, Colombia, Nigeria, and Angola. Growth slowdowns in oil-exporting countries could also strain corporate balance sheets (of especially large oil companies) and raise nonperforming loans. Financial problems in large oil-exporting emerging markets could have adverse contagion effects on other emerging and frontier economies.

In addition, oil-exporters have channeled surplus savings from oil revenues into a broad array of foreign assets, including government bonds, corporate bonds, equities, and real estate. The flow of so-called "petro-dollars" has boosted financial market liquidity, and helped keep borrowing costs down over the past decade. If oil prices remain low, repatriation of foreign assets could generate capital outflows, and potential financial strains, for countries that have become reliant on "petro-dollar" inflows.

What are the main policy implications?

Fiscal policy. A number of developing countries provide large fuel subsidies, in some cases exceeding 5 percent of GDP (Figure 4.6, IEA, 2014c). However, subsidies tend to benefit middle-income households disproportionately and to tilt consumption and production towards energy-intensive activities (World Bank, 2014). Falling oil prices reduce the need for fuel subsidies, and provide an opportunity for subsidy reform with limited impact on the prices paid by consumers. The Arab Republic of Egypt, India, Indonesia, the Islamic Republic of Iran, and Malaysia implemented such reforms in 2013 and 2014, removing some of the distortions and inefficiencies associated with subsidies. Fiscal resources released by lower fuel subsidies could either be saved to rebuild fiscal space lost after the global financial crisis or reallocated towards better-targeted programs to assist poor households, and critical infrastructure and human capital investments.

Monetary policy. Oil prices are expected to remain low over the 2015-16 period, implying that their impact on inflation is expected to be mostly temporary, dissipating by the end of 2016. In most cases, central banks would not need to respond to the temporary fall in inflation—unless there is a risk that inflation expectations become de-anchored. In some parts of Europe, where inflation is already uncomfortably low, several months of outright deflation could de-anchor inflation expectations. In this situation, central banks could help keep inflation expectations anchored by loosening monetary policy or providing forward guidance. In oil-exporting countries with flexible exchange rates, central banks will have to balance the need to support growth against the need to maintain stable inflation and investor confidence in the currency.

FIGURE 4.6   Fiscal balances and oil prices for selected countries

Revenues from commodity related sources account for a substantial fraction of fiscal revenues in a number of countries. For many oil producers, fiscal break-even price is higher than the current price of oil. In some oil exporters, large sovereign wealth fund assets can be deployed to mitigate the fiscal impact of oil prices. Declining oil prices will ease fiscal pressures from high energy subsidies.

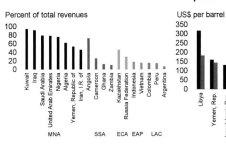

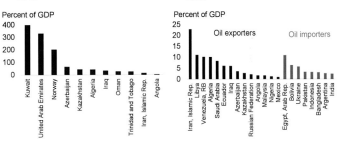

Source: IMF World Economic Outlook, The Economist Magazine, Bloomberg, JP Morgan Chase, IMF, IEA Fossil Fuel Database.
1. Includes revenues from all commodities, including oil.
2. Fiscal break-even prices are oil prices associated with a balanced budget.
3. Countries with sovereign wealth fund assets below 5 percent of GDP not shown.
4. Countries where the fiscal cost of fossil fuel subsidies is below 1 percent of GDP are not shown.

FIGURE 4.7   Exchange rates and equity prices for selected countries

Currencies have depreciated against the U.S. dollar and stock markets have declined in oil-exporting countries in the last quarter of 2014.

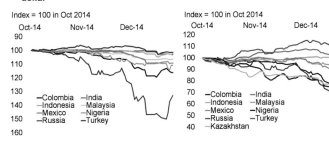

Sources: Haver Analytics.
1. U.S. dollars per local currency unit. An decrease denotes depreciation against the U.S. dollar. Latest observation for December 26, 2014.
2. Stock market index in national currency. Latest observation for December 23, 2014.

Structural policies. If sustained over the medium-term, low oil prices may encourage a move towards production which is more intensive in fossil fuels or energy more generally. This runs counter to broader environmental goals in many countries. To offset the medium-term incentives for increased oil consumption, while at the same time building fiscal space, policymakers could modify tax policies on the use of energy, especially in countries where fuel taxes are low.

For oil-exporters, the sharp decline in oil prices is also a reminder of the vulnerabilities inherent in a highly concentrated reliance on oil exports and an opportunity to reinvigorate their efforts to diversify. These efforts should focus on proactive measures to move incentives away from activities in the non-tradable sector and employment in the public sector, including encouraging high-value added activities, exports in non-resource intensive sectors, and development of skills that are important for private sector employment (Gill et. al, 2014; Cherif and Hasanof, 2014a and 2014b).

Conclusion

Following four years of stability at around $105/bbl, oil prices fell sharply in the second half of 2014. Compared to the early 2011 commodity price peaks, the decline in oil prices was much larger than that in non-oil commodity price indices. The decline in oil prices was quite significant compared with the previous episodes of oil price drops during the past three decades.

There have been a number of long- and short-term drivers behind the recent plunge in oil prices: several years of large upward surprises in oil supply; some downward surprises in demand; unwinding of some geopolitical risks that had threatened production; change in OPEC policy objectives; and appreciation of U.S. dollar. Supply related factors have clearly played a dominant role, with the new OPEC strategy aimed at market share triggering a further sharp decline since November.

The decline in oil prices has significant macroeconomic, financial and policy implications. If sustained, it will support activity and reduce inflationary, external, and fiscal pressures in oil-importing countries. On the other hand, it would affect oil-exporting countries adversely by weakening fiscal and external positions and reducing economic activity. Low oil prices affect investor sentiment about oil-exporting emerging market economies, and can lead to substantial volatility in financial markets, as already occurred in some countries in the last quarter of 2014. However, declining oil prices also present a significant window of opportunity to reform energy taxes and fuel subsidies, which are substantial in several developing countries, and reinvigorate reforms to diversify oil-reliant economies.

What Lies Behind the Global Trade Slowdown?[1]

Global trade performance has been disappointing in recent years. Except for a solid post-recession rebound in 2010, when global trade rose 13 percent, it has been relatively subdued in recent years, averaging 3.4 percent annual growth rate between 2012 and 2014. This rate is well below the pre-boom average growth of about 7 percent per annum. If global trade had continued to expand in accordance with the historical trend, it would have been some 20 percent above its actual level in 2014 (Figure 4.8). This essay reviews the key cyclical and structural factors that are likely to have contributed to the slowdown in global trade. Specifically, the essay addresses two questions:

- What has been the role of weak demand in the recent trade slowdown?
- Is the weakness in global trade a reflection of a weakening sensitivity of trade to GDP, and if so, what are the underlying reasons?

A Cyclical Factor: Weak Demand

Weak demand was one of the main reasons for the dramatic collapse of trade in 2009, with some studies reporting that it accounted for up to 90 percent of the contraction[2]. Historically, the negative effect of a crisis on trade performance is not limited to the crisis period, but persists through the medium term (Freund, 2009; IMF, 2010). In fact, five years after a crisis, import demand is typically 19 percent below its predicted level in the absence of a crisis.

This weakness in import demand is symptomatic of overall weakness in aggregate demand. Some five years after the global financial crisis, global GDP is about 4.5 percent below what it would have been had post-crisis growth rates been equivalent to the pre-crisis long-term average. Not surprisingly, weakness in demand has been most pronounced at the epicenter of the crisis, in high-income countries: GDP levels in the United States and the Euro Area are some 8 percent and 13 percent, respectively, below levels that would be suggested by historical average growth rates (Figure 4.9). Though other factors are at play, the implication of soft demand in high-income countries is reflected in the weakness of their import volumes, which deviates from trend by more than 20 percent in both the United States and the Euro Area. With high-income economies accounting for some 65 percent of global imports, their lingering weakness inevitably impacts the recovery in global trade.[3]

FIGURE 4.8   World trade: Actual and trend

World trade growth has been significantly subdued in recent years.

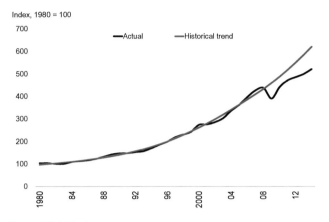

Source: World Bank.
Note: World trade refers to total world imports. The historical trend is computed over the 1970-2014 period, smoothed using a Hodrick-Prescott filter.

FIGURE 4.9   GDP and imports

Global demand remains well below trend levels.

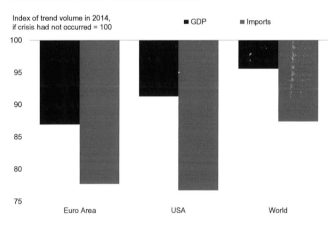

Source: World Bank.
Note: The post-crisis trend growth is assumed to be equivalent to the average growth rate during 1980-2008. Using this, the trend level for 2014 is rebased to 100. The 100 mark reflects where GDP and imports would have been in 2014 if pre-crisis trends continued into the post-crisis period. Hence, bars below 100 show deviations from trends in 2014.

---

[1]The main authors of this essay are Ileana-Cristina Constantinescu, Allen Dennis, Aaditya Mattoo and Michele Ruta.

[2]An extensive literature has examined the sources of trade collapse in 2009 (Baldwin, 2009; Borchert and Mattoo, 2009; Levchenko, 2010; Eaton et al., 2010; Bems et al .2010; Amiti and Weinstein, 2011; and Bussiere et al., 2013).

[3]There are differences across economies (see Chapter 1). The recoveries in the United States and the United Kingdom are on a much more solid footing than that in the Euro Area.

FIGURE 4.10 Contributions to world trade growth, 1970–2013

Both short-run and long-run factors have contributed to the recent slowdown in trade.

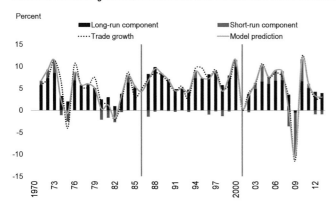

Source: Constantinescu, Mattoo and Ruta (2014).
Note: The model-predicted series are from an error correction model. The short-run component of import growth is obtained by subtracting the predicted long-run growth of imports from the total import growth predicted by the model.

FIGURE 4.11 Estimates of long-run trade elasticity

The decline in the long-run trade elasticity has contributed to the weakness in world trade

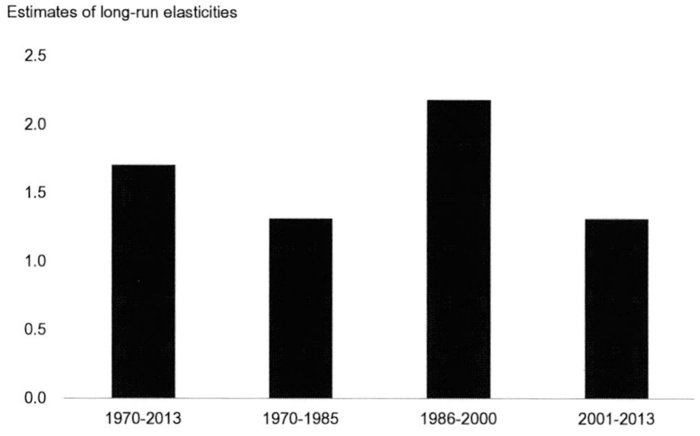

Estimates of long-run elasticities

Source: Constantinescu, Mattoo and Ruta (2014).
Note: Each bar represents the long-run elasticity estimate from an error correction model, retrieved from the residual of the cointegration equation between imports and GDP. See the Technical Annex for details of the estimation methodology.

It is unlikely, however, that weak demand alone explains the slow growth of global trade. Indeed, a decomposition analysis using an error correction model, estimated over the period 1970–2013, suggests that while short-term factors (including weak demand) were dominant during the crisis and the first year of the recovery, their contribution has subsided in recent years.[4] Short-term factors account for a shortfall in global trade growth of about 1 percentage point (Figure 4.10). This brings to the fore the importance of long-term factors. Indeed, the decomposition analysis shows that the contribution of the long-term component to global trade growth over 2012–13 was about 2 percentage points lower than its contribution in the two preceding decades.

A Structural Factor: Changing Relationship Between Trade and Income

In recent years, world trade has become less sensitive to changes in global income. Estimates from an error correction model for the period 1970–2013 yield a long-run elasticity of 1.7, although the response of trade to income differs considerably across decades. For the period 1986–2000, a 1 percent increase in world real GDP is associated with a 2.2 percent increase in the volume of world trade (Figure 4.11). This "elasticity" of 2.2 is substantially higher than that in preceding (1970–85) and subsequent (2001–13) years; for both of these

periods, the trade elasticity was about 1.3. Formal tests confirm that there was a significant structural break in the trade-income relationship in the period 1986–2000 relative to the preceding and subsequent periods.[5] These results suggest that global trade is growing more slowly not only because world income growth is lower, but also because trade has become less responsive to income growth.

What Explains the Lower Elasticity of Trade?

Four possible reasons for the decline in trade elasticities are examined: the changing structure of global value chains, changes in the composition of demand, weak trade finance, and increased trade protection.

Evolution of global value chains. The rise in trade elasticities in the 1990s has been explained by an acceleration of the international fragmentation of production processes.[6] This process was triggered by trade liberalization and sharp declines in shipping times and costs (due to the container revolution and bigger shipping vessels) and further boosted by the information and communication technology revolution and the spread of just-in-time production techniques. As a result, the production process increasingly involved a number of intermediate stages in various countries along the production chain, increasing the importance of

---

[4]See the Technical Annex for details of the error correction model specification. The results of the model are taken from Constantinescu et al. (2014).

[5]These results are broadly consistent with those from other studies, e.g., Irwin (2002); Freund (2009); and Escaith, Lindenberg and Miroudot (2010).

[6]For details on this, see Freund (2009) and Escaith et al. (2010).

international trade compared to previously, when the domestic value-added of a final good was relatively high.[7]

Just as the growing fragmentation of production across countries supported the rise in the elasticity of trade, the maturation of global value chains, at least among some of the major countries involved in the process, could help explain the weaker responsiveness of trade to GDP. An estimation of trade elasticity by major trading blocs over time suggests that much of the contribution to the decline in global trade elasticity has come from China and the United States. This is in contrast to the trade-income relationship in the European Union, which has remained fairly stable over the past decade.

The decline in China's trade elasticity can be explained by the rising amount of domestic value added in its exports. For instance, the share of Chinese imports of parts and components in China's total exports has declined from a peak of 60 percent in the mid-1990s to the current share of approximately 35 percent, implying a diminished fragmentation of the production process (Figure 4.12a). Further evidence of this change is the substitution of domestic inputs for foreign inputs by Chinese firms, which underpins the rise in domestic value added to trade (Kee and Tang, 2014).

The experience of the United States mirrors that of China along several dimensions. The United States was the primary source of the boom in Chinese and other emerging economies' imports of parts and components. At the same time, the United States was the major destination for China's exports of assembled goods. Since 2000, however, U.S. manufacturing imports as a share of GDP have been stable at about 8 percent, after nearly doubling over the prior decade and one-half (Figure 4.12b).

The changing patterns of trade in both China and the United States tentatively suggest that global value chains have played a role in the rise and subsequent decline in trade elasticities.

Changes in the composition of demand. Overall trade-income elasticity may be viewed as the weighted average of import elasticities of individual aggregate demand components. To the extent that different components of aggregate demand have different import elasticities, a change in the composition of aggregate demand would

FIGURE 4.12 Changing structure of imports in China and the United States

Growth of imports supportive of the international fragmentation of production in China and the United States is not expanding as rapidly as before.

A. China's imports of parts and components as a share of total exports of merchandise

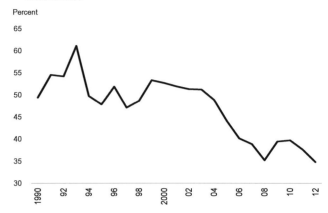

B. U.S. manufacturing imports

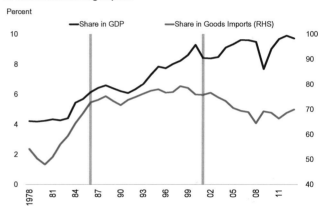

Source: Constantinescu, Mattoo and Ruta (2014).
Note: Parts and components are the sum of three UN Comtrade broad economic categories: 42 (parts and accessories of capital goods, except transport equipment), 53 (parts and accessories of transport equipment), and 22 (processed industrial supplies not elsewhere specified).

shift the overall elasticity.[8] In general, investment spending is the most import-intensive component of domestic demand, followed by consumption, with government spending being the least import intensive.[9] Hence, the weak recovery in the post-crisis period in the components of aggregate demand that have a higher import intensity could help explain the relatively weak post-crisis elasticity.[10]

---

[7]While there is an economic aspect to the amplification of trade due to changes in production processes, part of the amplification can be attributed to how trade flows are recorded. In particular, trade is typically measured on a gross basis (hence intermediate goods are double counted), whereas GDP is measured on a net or value-added basis.

[8]For detailed discussions about the linkages between international trade and the components aggregate demand, see Bems, Johnson and Yi (2013,) Anderton and Tewolde (2011), and Bussiere et al. (2013).

[9]This is mainly because the bulk of government spending is on services (which are in large part nontradeable). Exports have high import intensities because of the increased importance of global value chains.

[10]Boz et al. (2014) argue that most of the weakness in global trade has been due to cyclical factors, although structural factors, including global value chains and trade protectionism, may have played a role as well.

FIGURE 4.13   Recovery in aggregate demand and imports

Globally, the recovery in investment, which has a high import intensity, has been weak. This is reflected in the subdued capital goods import recovery.

A. Recovery in aggregate demand components[1]

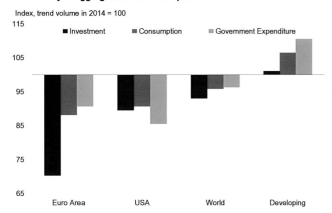

Index, trend volume in 2014 = 100

B. Recovery in imports by product[2]

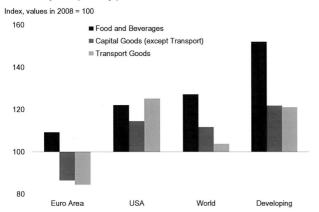

Index, values in 2008 = 100

Source: World Bank, using UN Comtrade data.
1. The post-crisis trend level growth is assumed to be equivalent to the average growth rate during 1980-2008. Using this, the trend level for 2014 is rebased to 100. Hence, bars below or above 100 show deviations from trends in 2014.
2. The 100 mark reflects the 2008 (or pre-crisis) level of imports. Hence bars below 100 show that import levels had not fully recovered to their pre-crisis (2008) level by 2013, while those above 100 show that import levels had more than fully recovered by 2013.

During the post-crisis recovery, investment (the component of aggregate demand that is most import intensive) has been particularly weak, most notably in the Euro Area (Figure 4.13a). This weakness in investment demand is mirrored in the relatively low imports of capital goods and transport equipment compared to pre-crisis levels. Further, given the high internationally traded value-added content of capital goods as compared to other products (e.g., food and beverages), the weak recovery of investment also impinges on the pick-up in global trade (Figure 4.13b). Thus, the uneven composition of the recovery in demand has also contributed to the decline in the trade elasticity.

Weak trade finance. Although not necessarily independent from the role of weak demand, impaired credit channels could be another important driver of trade performance, given that trade finance becomes costlier and less available during financial crises and their aftermath (Martin 2012; Chor and Manova 2012). Financial institutions facing deleveraging pressures are forced to cut back on credit growth in order to boost their liquid assets. Trade finance instruments, which are often short-term and self-liquidating in nature, tend to be among the most susceptible to credit crunches. Indeed, exporters and importers, particularly small- and medium-sized firms, faced serious funding challenges during the most recent crisis (Amiti and Weinstein, 2011; Ahn, Amiti, and Weinstein, 2011).

Large-scale injections of central bank liquidity into banking systems after the crisis and the loose monetary policy stance of several major high-income economies helped ease trade finance constraints. Nonetheless, new or proposed regulations may be having a long-term dampening effect on trade finance. These include, prominently, the higher capital requirements for banks under the Basel III regulations, which are scheduled to come into force by 2019. For example, a survey by International Chamber of Commerce (2014) shows that some 71 percent of banks consider higher capital requirements to be negative for export finance, and another 84 percent indicate that such requirements have caused them to become more selective in lending. Further, recent financial crime regulations (e.g. Anti-Money Laundering and Know Your Customer—i.e, AML/KYC regulations) led 68 percent of leading banks to decline a transaction, and 31 percent of banks to terminate relationships, with counterparties with whom they are less familiar. There is however, little hard evidence on how much the dearth of trade finance may be weighing down on global trade performance.

Increased trade protection. If the dismantling of trade barriers supported the acceleration of trade in earlier decades, then conversely, a rise in trade barriers, or even a slowdown in the rate of liberalization, could contribute to a deceleration. In the case of the trade collapse in 2009, the general consensus suggests that it is unlikely that increased protection was a major factor (Bown, 2009; Kee, Neagu, and Nicita, 2013).

There are signs that protection continued to rise even after 2009. For instance, in the year leading to May 2014, Group of Twenty (G-20) members put in place 228 new trade restrictive measures (WTO, 2014). Worryingly, while the measures imposed since 2009 were meant to be temporary ones, the vast majority of trade restrictive measures taken since the global financial crisis have remained in place: of 1,185 recorded since October 2008, only 251 (roughly one-fifth) of these had been removed by May 2014. The low removal rate and the continuing addition of new restrictions have resulted in an upward trend in the stock of trade-restricting measures (Figure 4.14).

However, according to the World Trade Organization (WTO), the net increase in import restrictive measures since October 2008 is estimated to affect only about 4.1 percent of world merchandise imports (Figure 4.13), so it is unlikely that increased protection has been the cause of weaker trade performance and the decline in the elasticity of trade. But the slower pace of liberalization in the 2000s, compared to the 1990s, may have contributed to the lower growth in trade and, hence, dampened trade elasticity.

Conclusion

The brief review of the evidence presented here suggests that both cyclical and structural factors have been important in explaining the recent slowdown in global trade. With high-income countries accounting for some 65 percent of global imports, the lingering weakness of their economies five years into the recovery suggests that weak demand is still impacting the recovery in global trade.[11] However, weak demand is not the only reason as trade had become much less responsive to income growth, even prior to the crisis. There is some evidence to suggest that part of the explanation may lie in shifts in the structure of value chains, in particular between China and the United States, with a higher proportion of the value of final goods being added domestically—that is, with less border crossing for intermediate goods. In addition, the post-crisis composition of demand has shifted from capital equipment to less import-intensive spending, such as consumption and government services.

As the world economy continues to recover, global trade growth can be expected to pick up. However, given the continued weak recovery projected (as discussed in Chapter 1), the contribution of demand to the pick-up in global trade is not likely to be substantial over the short and medium term. Assuming elasticity estimates over the past decade persist, global trade growth over the medium term would rise by less than 1 percentage point to about 5 percent, from the current rate, and considerably lower than the 7 percent rate typical of the pre-crisis expansion.[12]

FIGURE 4.14   World trade affected by new import-restrictive measures

New import restrictive measures have been continually imposed since 2008.

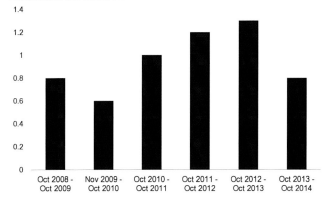

Source: World Trade Organization.
Note: Each bar represents the percent of world trade (in value terms) affected by new import restrictive measures imposed by G-20 WTO members during the respective time period. The analysis does not taken into account measures that were eliminated during the period.

Over the long term, even if the recovery accelerates and global growth returns to its trend, based on the diminished sensitivity of trade to income, global trade growth may not return to pre-crisis trend levels unless global trade relationships change. For instance, trade elasticities could pick up on account of a relatively robust pick-up in components of aggregate demand with stronger import intensities (e.g., investment) or on account of further changes in the organization of supply chains. Just as the high responsiveness of trade to growth in the 1990s reflected the increasing fragmentation of production driven primarily by developments in China and the United States, the scope for increasing international division of labor could reassert itself, especially in regions that have not yet made the most of global supply chains, such as South Asia, Sub-Saharan Africa, and South America. Drawing these parts of the world into a finer division of labor could lend renewed dynamism to trade.

---

[11]The strength of the recovery differs across countries. For example, the recoveries in the United Kingdom and the United States are on a much more solid footing than those in the Euro Area and Japan.

[12]This computation does not factor in any potential increase in elasticity resulting from compositional changes in domestic demand such as an acceleration of import-intensive investment.

Can Remittances Help Promote Consumption Stability?[1]

Remittance flows are projected to continue their upward climb over the medium term (Figure 4.15). The relative importance of remittances as a source of external resources is also expected to increase further, as growth in private capital flows to developing countries may moderate when interest rates begin rising in advanced economies, or if growth in developing economies remains weak.

Remittances are associated with significant development impacts such as accelerated poverty alleviation, improved access to education and health services, and enhanced financial development, as well as multiplier effects through higher household expenditures.[2] A small set of studies has also investigated the behavior of remittances over the business cycle, but knowledge on the issue has so far been limited.[3] This essay examines cyclical characteristics of remittances and explores the counterbalancing and consumption-smoothing potential of remittances. Specifically, the essay focuses on three questions:

- How do remittance flows behave over the business cycle, especially compared to other financial inflows?

- Can remittances act as a counterbalance during episodes of sudden stops in capital flows?

- Do remittances support consumption stability over time?

Magnitude, Drivers, and Cyclical Features

Magnitude. Remittances to developing countries (low- and middle-income economies) have been significant both as a share of GDP and compared to FDI and official development assistance (ODA).[4] Since 2000, total

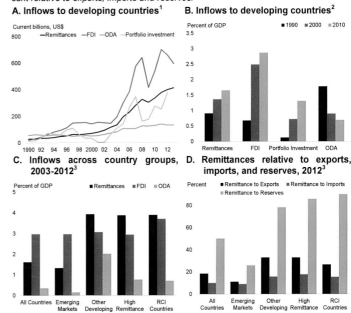

FIGURE 4.15   Magnitude of remittances and other flows

Remittances to developing countries have risen steadily over time and are now larger than FDI and ODA for developing and high remittance countries, and significant relative to exports, imports and reserves.

A. Inflows to developing countries[1]

B. Inflows to developing countries[2]

C. Inflows across country groups, 2003-2012[3]

D. Remittances relative to exports, imports, and reserves, 2012[3]

Sources: World Development Indicators, IMF Balance of Payments data, and World Bank estimates.

1. Remittances are based on IMF Balance of Payments Accounts; FDI is foreign direct investment, net inflows; Portfolio Investment is private debt and portfolio equity; ODA is net official development assistance and official aid received.
2. Values represent total flows as percentage of total GDP of low-income and middle-income countries in World Development Indicators.
3. All Countries includes all countries in the sample. High Remittance refers to a set of countries for which remittances have been above 1% during the period under consideration. RCI refers to a set of countries for which remittances have been above 1% and either FDI or equity flows have been above 3.5% and 1%, respectively, during the 2003-2012 time period. FDI measures foreign direct investment and ODA covers official development assistance and aid.

---

[1]This essay is produced by a team led by Ayhan Kose and Dilip Ratha, and including Supriyo De, Ergys Islamaj, and Seyed Reza Yousefi.

[2]Adams and Page (2005) and Acosta, et al., (2008) show that remittances are associated with lower poverty and inequality. Aggarwal, Demirgüç-Kunt, and Peria (2011) report that remittances help enhance financial development by increasing deposits and credit intermediated by local banks. Giuliano and Ruiz-Arranz (2009) find that remittances can substitute for a lack of financial development. The empirical literature on the impact of remittances on growth, however, remains inconclusive (Chami et al, 2008; Clemens and McKenzie, 2014). Drawbacks associated with migration may include the risk of "brain drain," which may dampen productivity of the migrant-sending countries and affect their tax base. On the positive side, however, migrants may find better opportunities to enhance earnings and skills in host countries than in their home countries, and can facilitate stronger international trade and commercial links over the long run.

[3]Some of these studies report mixed results about the cyclical features of remittances partly because they employ different samples and methodologies. Chami et al, (2008), Constantinescu and Schiff (2014) and Frankel (2011) find that remittances are countercyclical and less volatile than capital flows while Freund and Spatafora (2008) and Sayan (2006) report that remittances are procyclical.

[4]The dataset used for the analysis in this essay covers the period 1980-2012 and includes 109 countries, including emerging markets, developing economies, and countries that receive a large volume of remittances, Remittance and Capital Flow Intensive (RCI) countries. Specifically, the RCI group includes countries that have experienced, on average, ratios of remittances to GDP higher than 1 percent and either FDI inflows greater than 3.5 percent of GDP or equity inflows greater than 1 percent of GDP, on average, between 2003 and 2012 (the cut-offs correspond to median values for the full sample). Official remittance data (in U.S. dollars) is from the IMF's Balance of Payments Statistics. The overall size of remittances is likely to be even larger, since migrants also send money through informal channels. Freund and Spatafora (2005) conjecture that informal remittances amount to 35-75 percent of official remittances to developing countries.

FIGURE 4.16 Remittances, business cycles, and capital inflows

Remittances are acyclical in most countries, uncorrelated with capital inflows, and less volatile and less correlated with economic fundamentals than other inflows.

A. Remittances and business cycles[1]

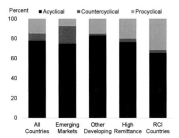

B. Remittances and capital inflows[1]

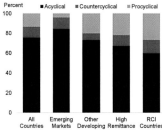

C. Volatility of inflows[2]

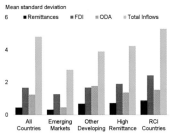

D. Correlation of remittances with GDP[3]

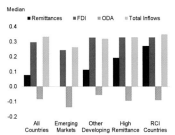

Source: World Bank estimates.
1. Remittances are considered: (i) procyclical if the correlation between the cyclical components of remittances and output is positive and statistically different from zero, (ii) countercyclical if it is negative and statistically different from zero and (iii) acyclical if the correlation is not statistically different from zero.
2. Volatility is defined as the standard deviation of the detrended ratio of the relevant inflow to GDP.
3. Cyclicality is defined as the correlation between the detrended real series of GDP and foreign direct investment, official development assistance (ODA), and total inflows (the sum of FDI, portfolio investment including equity and debt, financial derivatives, and other investments). RCI refers to a set of countries for which remittances were above 1% and either FDI or equity flows have been above 3.5% and 1%, respectively, during 2003-12. High remittance refers to a set of countries for which remittances have been above 1% during the period under consideration. Each time series is decomposed into trend and cyclical components using Hodrick-Prescott (HP) filter and the sample period is 1980-2012.

---

[5]For example, during 2013 remittances as a percentage of GDP were high for Kyrgyz Republic (32), Nepal (29), Moldova (25), Haiti (21) and many other countries (all numbers in parenthesis refer to percentage of GDP). They were also large as percentage of goods exports for Tajikistan (308), Nepal (646), and Haiti (201). Remittances as a percentage of reserves were high for Tajikistan (542), Pakistan (191), El Salvador (144), the Arab Republic of Egypt (108), Honduras (104), and Kyrgyz Republic (102), among others. Developing countries have also become sources of remittances in recent years; for example, Kazakhstan is an important source of remittance flows to Azerbaijan, the Russian Federation, Tajikistan, and Ukraine.

[6]The results are broadly similar when volatility is defined as the coefficient of variation (standard deviation of the series over the sample period normalized by the mean of the corresponding flow). These findings are also in line with previous studies in the literature, including Chami et al. (2008) and Constantinescu and Schiff (2014).

[7]Kaminsky, Reinhart, and Végh (2005) show that capital flows are highly procyclical. Contessi, De Pace, and Francis (2013) document that the components of inward capital flows are also procyclical for Group of Seven economies. Islamaj (2014) reports that capital flows may increase the volatility of output by increasing specialization of production.

remittances have averaged about 60 percent of the size of total FDI (Figure 4.15). A large and growing number of emerging and developing markets—the Remittance and Capital Flow Intensive countries (RCI)—have received substantial inflows of capital as well as remittances over the past decade. For developing economies, remittances amount, on average, to close to 80 percent of reserves. For a large number of countries, remittances constitute the single largest source of foreign exchange.[5] The rising trend of remittances is likely to persist given the large and growing stock of international migrants worldwide (more than 232 million at present).

Motives and Drivers. There is considerable overlap between individuals' motives to remit and other longer term and institutional drivers of remittances. Factors that affect migration decisions, the economic and policy environment in the origin and recipient countries, and transactions costs associated with intermediation of remittances all influence the volume and frequency of remittances. Remittances are closely related to migration patterns at the macroeconomic level, driven by a host of factors, including economic opportunities in the migrants' host and home countries, existing migrant stocks and networks, cost of emigration, and barriers to immigration. Such economic factors in empirical studies are typically captured by home and world output growth, employment in home and host country, and other global variables like London Interbank Offered Rate (LIBOR) and oil prices. Institutional factors that would discourage remittance flows include policies like exchange rate restrictions and black market premia. The diversity of motivations and drivers makes it difficult to predict *a priori* the business cycle features of remittance flows and their implications for macroeconomic stability.

Cyclical Features. Foreign currency inflows can be classified as: (i) *procyclical* if the correlation between output and the cyclical component of flows is positive and statistically different from zero; (ii) *countercyclical* if it is negative and statistically different from zero; and (iii) *acyclical* if the correlation is not statistically different from zero. Figure 4.16 summarizes these correlations for various country groups, demonstrating that remittances are *acyclical* in approximately 80 percent of countries (this holds across country groups). Remittances are not strongly correlated with capital flows either. However, remittances appear to be a more stable source of external finance than other inflows, including ODA.[6] They are also less correlated with the business cycle than FDI and total inflows.

Because capital flows such as FDI and debt flows are often procyclical, they can exacerbate output fluctuations and contribute to the volatility of consumption in developing countries when abruptly leaving the country.[7] Although remittances are not necessarily countercyclical, they have the potential to at least provide some stability for the balance of payments, and hence for economic activity more generally, when capital inflows decline.

Behavior of Remittances during Sudden Stops

A sudden stop, defined as a sharp decrease in gross capital inflows, is often associated with increased risk of macroeconomic volatility and financial crises in emerging markets and developing economies. The timing of sudden stops can be identified using a variety of methodologies. The methodology of Forbes and Warnock (2012) is followed here to identify sudden stops over the period 1990–2012, and a plethora of sudden stops in capital inflows is found to have coincided with the global financial crisis that began in 2008. In contrast, remittances showed slight above-trend growth during the financial crisis (Figure 4.17). The same pattern is observed during previous, less severe and less synchronized crisis episodes, with remittances generally displaying resilience, while capital inflows gyrate.[8]

While capital flows on average decline about 14.8 percent during the initial year of a sudden stop episode and continue to fall by another 10 percent the year after, remittances tend to increase by 6.6 percent during the first year and another 5.7 percent in the subsequent year. Moreover, remittances are resilient in emerging markets and RCI economies taken separately, even though the decline in capital inflows for these country groups is often sharper than for other groups. During the first year of a sudden stop, capital inflows to emerging markets fall 25.2 percent, on average, whereas remittances increase by 6.8 percent.

Also important to note is that countries differ substantially in terms of geographical dispersion of their migrant stocks: those with more geographically dispersed migrant stocks tend to receive relatively more stable remittance flows during sudden stops than those with more concentrated migrant stocks. Following sudden stops, remittances continued to increase at a faster pace in countries with more dispersed migrant stocks (Figure 4.18). These results broadly speak to a supporting role of remittances during periods of large capital flow reversals.

Promoting Consumption Stability

In principle, remittances, like capital flows can help buffer consumption from short-run fluctuations in income. The ability to reduce fluctuations in consumption is an important determinant of economic welfare. In the case of capital flows, short-term foreign

FIGURE 4.17 Remittances and capital inflows during sudden stops

Remittances have been resilient during sudden stops. On average, the decline in capital flows was greater in 2008 than during other sudden stops.
(Index numbers)

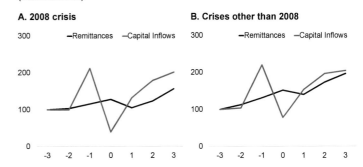

Source: World Bank calculations using data from World Development Indicators and World Bank's Global Capital Flows.
Notes: Values are averages of remittances and net capital inflows for emerging markets and developing economies that have experienced sudden stop episodes. Index numbers are calculated with a base of 100 for the period three years before the sudden stop year (-3). Capital inflows are net, that is, the difference between the amounts brought in by nonresidents and the amounts sent out by residents. The horizontal axis denotes years. Zero (0) refers to the year of the sudden stop episode.

FIGURE 4.18 Remittances and capital inflows in countries with more and less dispersed diasporas

Countries with more dispersed migrant stocks showed greater remittance resilience during the sudden stops.
(Index numbers)

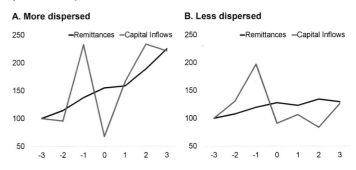

Source: World Bank calculations using data from World Development Indicators and World Bank's Global Capital Flows.
Notes: Values are averages of remittances and net capital inflows for emerging markets and developing economies that have experienced sudden stop episodes. Index numbers are calculated with a base of 100 for the period three years before the sudden stop year (-3). Capital inflows are net, that is, the difference between the amounts brought in by non-residents and the amounts sent out by residents. The horizontal axis denotes years. Zero (0) refers to the year of the sudden stop episode. More dispersed (less dispersed) refers to countries with migrant concentrations below (above) the sample median. Migrant concentration is defined as the percentage of migrants in the top destination to the total migrant population. Calculations are based on the 2013 bilateral migration matrix provided by the United Nations Population Division (UNPD).

---

[8]Remittances have also been more stable than FDI flows during sudden stop episodes. For details about the behavior of FDI flows during sudden stops, see Levchenko and Mauro (2007).

FIGURE 4.19 Remittances and consumption stability

Remittances help improve consumption stability.

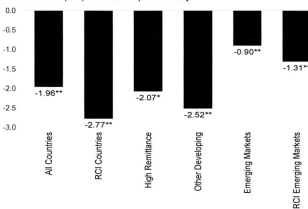

Source: World Bank estimates.
Note: The figure shows panel ordinary least squares estimates for the effect of remittances on consumption stability (β_2). The symbols * and ** indicate statistical
significance at the 10% and 5% levels, respectively. High Remittance refers to a set
of countries for which remittances have been above 1% during the time period
under consideration. RCI (Remittance and Capital Flow Intensive) countries refer to
a set of countries for which remittances have been above 1% and either FDI or
equity flows have been above 3.5% and 1%, respectively, during 2003-12.

borrowing, or sales of foreign liquid assets, can be used
to finance consumption during bad times. Provided that
fluctuations in income are not fully synchronized across
countries, and financial markets are operating effectively,
output uncertainty can be shared across borders through
capital flows.

There has been a growing literature studying the effects
of financial flows on consumption stability at the macro
level. This literature finds only minimal impacts of equity
flows on consumption smoothing in developing
countries. Although the relative stability of remittances
over the business cycle suggests that large-scale recipients
may be less prone to consumption volatility, little is
devoted in the literature to the stabilizing effects of
remittances on consumption fluctuations. To estimate
the quantitative effect, we follow a standard approach in
the risk sharing literature and consider the impact of
remittances on the comovement between domestic
consumption and output.[9] In particular, we regress
country-specific consumption growth on country-specific
output growth:

$$\Delta c_{it} - \Delta c_t^* = \beta_0 + \gamma_1 R_{it} + \beta_1\left(\Delta y_{it} - \Delta y_t^*\right) + \beta_2 R_{it}\left(\Delta y_{it} - \Delta y_t^*\right) + \Delta \varepsilon_{it}$$

where $\Delta c_{it} (\Delta c_t^*)$ is country (world) consumption growth
at time t; $\Delta y_{it} (\Delta y_t^*)$ is country (world) GDP growth at
time t; and R_{it} is remittance inflow as a ratio to GDP at
time t. The coefficient β_2 estimates the extent to which
domestic consumption growth is dependent on output
fluctuations. An interaction term between remittances

and output growth is added to the regression, and
measures the extent to which remittance flows help de-
link domestic consumption from domestic output
growth. A negative β_2 suggests that remittances help
lower the correlation between country-specific
consumption and output growth.

Estimates of the interaction coefficient β_2 for different
country groups are presented in Figure 4.19. Estimated β_2
is negative and statistically significant for all country
groups. The coefficients for RCI countries and countries
with large remittance inflows are even higher (in absolute
value) than those for most other groups, suggesting that
countries that receive a larger amount of remittances
have, on average, a lower correlation between output and
consumption growth.[10] These findings imply relatively
larger benefits of remittances for consumption stability in
counties that have (a) sizable remittance receipts and (b)
high exposure to interruptions in capital flows.[11]

Through what channels can remittances help stabilize
consumption fluctuations? First, remittances can help
stabilize consumption intertemporally by supporting
saving. Some studies based on microeconomic data
document that remittances are an important resource to
enable households to smooth consumption over time, as
they help improve access to financial services and ease
liquidity constraints.[12] Second, even if overall remittances
do not increase substantially during economic downturns,
a greater proportion of remittance receipts is likely to be

---

[9]The baseline regression model uses deviations from world aggregates because common risks cannot be eliminated completely, but can
only be shared more efficiently. Seminal contributions include Obstfeld
(1994) and Lewis (1996). Kose, Prasad, and Terrones (2009) provide a
review of the literature.

[10]All regressions include time- and country-fixed effects. The results
are robust to controlling for various de jure and de facto measures of
financial integration. The findings hold when using system generalized
method of moments (GMM) estimates, which, following the literature,
use lagged values of consumption and output growth as instruments.

[11]The stabilizing effect of remittances may also depend on the exchange rate system. During sudden stops and recessions, flexible exchange rates tend to depreciate. Given relative stability in terms of U.S.
dollars, the value of remittances in local currencies then tends to increase,
thereby acting as an automatic stabilizer for the purchasing power of
consumers. In fact, the stabilizing effects of remittances on consumption
tend to be much more pronounced under flexible exchange rate regimes.

[12]World Bank (2006), Adams and Cuecuecha (2013), Osili (2004), and
Aga and Martinez-Peria (2014) document that remittances improve financial inclusion for the poor households by increasing access to savings,
bank deposits, and bank credit. Giuliano and Ruiz-Arranz (2009) find that
remittances help ease liquidity constraints faced by the poor. Our findings
also complement others reported in the literature. For example, Craigwell,
Jackman, and Moore (2010) find that remittances reduce the impact of
negative output shocks. Bugamelli and Paterno (2011) and Acosta et al.
(2008) also report that remittances are negatively correlated with output
volatility. IMF (2005) also finds that remittances are associated with lower
volatility of output, consumption, and investment.

used for consumption purposes during such periods.[13] Given that remittances, unlike capital flows, are unrequited transfers that do not have to be paid back and target the portion of consumers that are more likely to be liquidity constrained, they may have substantial effects on consumption stability.

In addition, at the individual level, access to remittances enables consumers to maintain their consumption levels despite illness or some other calamity, which may be critical for people with very low levels of income. Some studies find that remittances support household consumption following natural disasters or other economic shocks. For example, Yang and Choi (2007), find that overseas remittances serve almost like insurance following rainfall shocks in the Philippines, while analysis of household survey data from Ethiopia shows that households that receive international remittances seem to rely more on cash reserves and less on selling household assets or livestock to cope with drought (Mohapatra, Joseph and Ratha, 2012).

Conclusion

The main findings are as follows:

- *Remittances are relatively stable, and acyclical.* In a substantial proportion of the countries, remittance receipts are not significantly related to the domestic business cycle. In contrast, debt flows and foreign direct investment are procyclical. Stability and acyclicality imply that remittances have the potential to make a critical contribution in supporting consumption in the face of economic adversity. This is particularly important in developing countries, where remittances are used to finance household consumption directly.

- *Remittances have also been stable during episodes of financial volatility when capital flows fell sharply.* This stabilizing effect tends to be greater for remittance-receiving countries with a more dispersed migrant population.

- *Remittances are associated with more stable domestic consumption growth.* Countries with large remittance receipts tend to display less correlation between output and consumption growth over the business cycle. Such consumption behavior often enhances welfare.

These findings provide additional evidence of the beneficial effects of remittances. While household members may not themselves base their decisions to work abroad mainly on a desire to send stable remittances back home, these benefits provide a rationale to implement policies in recipient countries to reduce impediments to remittances, like lowering the costs of sending remittances, avoiding the taxation of remittances, and doing away with multiple exchange rate regimes. These impediments often discourage remittances as well as drive them into informal channels. Specific policy areas to be considered are as follows:

- *Costs of Remittances.* While the average price of retail cross-border money transfers has been falling, it remains high. The average cost of sending about US $200 fell from 9.8 percent in 2008 to 7.9 percent in the third quarter of 2014.[14] It will be important to reduce such costs further by ensuring competition in money transfer services, establishing an appropriate regulatory regime for electronic transfers, and supporting improvements in retail payments services.

- *Taxes on Remittances.* Governments may be tempted to tax remittances in an effort to increase revenue. In general, this would discourage remittances and is likely to have a direct negative effect on household welfare. From the viewpoint of tax equity, one might note in addition that these transfers are made from after-tax income earned in source countries.

- *Exchange Rate Regime.* Exchange rate flexibility provides an automatic stabilizer to recipients of remittances, in that the domestic currency value of remittances increases when the U.S.-dollar value of the currency drops, as it usually does during an adverse event. Dual exchange rate systems, in contrast, may deter remittance inflows, by artificially lowering the local currency proceeds of remittances and creating uncertainty about the U.S.-dollar cost of the domestic currency. This undermines the automatic stabilizer role that remittances can play during periods of exchange rate depreciation.

---

[13]While consumption stability obviously promotes welfare, the use of remittances for consumption instead of investment purposes may have consequences for long-term growth.

[14]The average cost of sending $200 to Sub-Saharan Africa is almost twice the cost of sending the same amount to Latin America or South Asia. These costs have a direct negative impact on the amount received, as well as the volume of remittance flows. Freund and Spatafora (2008) find that a 1 percentage point reduction in transaction costs raises recorded remittances by 14–23 percent. Evidence from micro studies confirms the negative impacts of costs for remittance flows (Ashraf et al., 2011; Ambler et al., 2014; Gibson et al., 2006).

Technical Annex: Estimation Methodology

The analysis here uses an error correction model to estimate the relationship between world trade volumes and real GDP. These models have been widely used in time series analysis, as they address the issue of non-stationarity (common for most macroeconomic variables), and hence the problem of spurious correlation (Box and Jenkins, 1970; Granger and Newbold, 1974; Nelson and Plosser, 1982).

In the specific context considered here, the error correction model allows both the long-run elasticity of trade with respect to income (which captures trend, or structural, factors) and the short-run elasticity (which is relevant to short run or cyclical developments). In addition, an estimate of the speed of convergence back to the long-run steady state relationship, following a deviation, can also be derived.

To provide some intuition for the model estimated in the text, the analysis commences with the simple relationship:[27]

$$M_t = QY_t$$

where M_t and Y_t are world imports and GDP, respectively, and Q is the share of imports in GDP.

Taking natural logs, the relationship may be restated as:

$$m_t = q + y_t$$

Lagged imports and GDP variables are added to the above equation to obtain the following expression:

$$m_t = a_0 + a_1 m_{t-1} + \beta_1 y_t + \beta_2 y_{t-1} + \mu_t$$

Where m_t is the volume of world imports, y_t is real global GDP, and μ_t is the error term: all variables are in logarithms, and the t subscript denotes time t.

In a steady-state equilibrium, the error term is zero and, where m^* and y^* are steady state equilibrium values, equation (1) becomes,

$$m^* = a_0 + a_1 m^* + \beta_1 y^* + \beta_2 y^*$$

Rewriting, this becomes:

$$m^* = a_0 / (1 - a_1) + [(\beta_1 + \beta_2) / (1 - a_1)] y^*$$

where $[(\beta_1 + \beta_2) / (1 - a_1)]$ is the long-run trade elasticity.

To model short-run deviations from the equilibrium in the presence of stochastic shocks, first differences of m_t are taken and both $\beta_1 y_{t-1}$ and $(a_1-1) y_{t-1}$ are added and subtracted from the right hand side to get the error correction model below:

$$\Delta m_t = a_0 + (a_1-1)(m_{t-1} - y_{t-1}) + \beta_1 \Delta y_t + (\beta_1 + \beta_2 + a_1 - 1) y_{t-1} + \mu_t$$

which is equivalent to:

$$\Delta m_t = a_0 + (a_1 - 1) m_{t-1} + \beta_1 \Delta y_t + (\beta_1 + \beta_2) y_{t-1} + \mu_t$$

The above equation can be presented in the reduced form:

$$\Delta m_t = a + \beta \Delta y_t + \gamma m_t - 1 + \delta y_{t-1} + \varepsilon_t$$

where $\beta = \beta_1$ is the short-term trade elasticity, and the long-run trade elasticity is $-\delta/\gamma$. The reduced form coefficient $\gamma = (\alpha_1 - 1)$ captures lagged adjustment: a value of γ equal to zero implies instantaneous adjustment, a value approaching unity implies very long lags. In other words, $-\gamma$, the negative value, represents the speed of adjustment.

One limitation of this approach is that it treats GDP as exogenous to trade outcomes, whereas the two variables are endogenous. The results of the estimation should thus be interpreted with caution as the model does not capture the structural complexity of the trade-GDP nexus.

The model is estimated using annual data and the regression results are presented in Table 4A.1. For the entire sample, the long-run elasticity $(-\delta/\gamma)$ is 1.7, but the response of trade with respect to income differs considerably across the three periods. In the period 1986–2000, a 1 percent increase in world GDP at a steady rate is associated with an eventual 2.2 percent increase in the volume of world trade. This elasticity is substantially higher than in both the preceding (1970–85) and the later period (2001–2013), for both of which the trade elasticity is 1.3. There is a statistically significant structural break in the long-run trade-income relationship in the 1990s relative to the preceding and subsequent periods.

---

[27]This model is similar to that of Irwin, (2002), and Escaith et al. (2010)

TABLE 4A.1 Summary of regression results

	Without dummy variables[1]	With dummy variables for separate periods[2]		
	1970-2013	1970-1985	1986-2000	2001-2013
	(1)	(2)	(3)	(4)
α	-0.43**	-0.35	-3.17***	-0.52**
	(0.17)	(0.53)	(0.64)	(0.19)
Short-run elasticity (β)	2.82***	2.13***	2.77***	3.43***
	(0.36)	(0.60)	(0.35)	(0.21)
Speed of adjustment (-γ)	0.12**	0.18	0.58***	0.31**
	(0.05)	(0.31)	(0.13)	(0.13)
Coefficient of lagged GDP (δ)	0.20**	0.23	1.26***	0.40**
	(0.09)	(0.39)	(0.26)	(0.17)
Long-run elasticity[3] (-δ/γ)	1.70***	1.31***	2.18***	1.31***
Breusch-Godfrey LM test for serial correlation[4]	9.67**	10.52**	9.19*	7.43
Stationarity of the residual	yes	yes	yes	yes
		(2) vs (3)	(2) vs (4)	(3) vs (4)
Test that long-run elasticity differs across periods[3]		8.68***	0.00	291.21***
R-squared	0.740	0.957	0.957	0.957
N	43	43	43	43

Note: Standard errors in paranthesis; *** indicates a significance level of 1%, ** of 5%, and * of 10%.

[1] $d\ln(\text{total imports})_t = \alpha + \beta^*d\ln(\text{gdp})_t + \gamma^*\ln(\text{total imports})_{t-1} + \delta^*\ln(\text{gdp})_{t-1} + \varepsilon_t$, where total imports includes imports of goods and services

[2] $d\ln(\text{total imports})_t = \alpha_1 + \beta_1^*d\ln(\text{gdp})_t^*DV_1 + \gamma_1^*\ln(\text{total imports})_{t-1}^*DV_1 + \delta_1^*\ln(\text{gdp})_{t-1}^*DV_1 + \alpha_2 + \beta_2^*d\ln(\text{gdp})_t^*DV_2 + \gamma_2^*\ln(\text{total imports})_{t-1}^*DV_2 + \delta_2^*\ln(\text{gdp})_{t-1}^*DV_2 + \alpha_3 + \beta_3^*d\ln(\text{gdp})_t^*DV_3 + \gamma_3^*\ln(\text{total imports})_{t-1}^*DV_3 + \delta_3^*\ln(\text{gdp})_{t-1}^*DV_3 + \varepsilon_t$, where total imports includes imports of goods and services, and DV represents the period dummy variables.

[3] Significance established using non linear Wald test

[4] Null hypothesis states that there is no serial correlation in the residuals of the linear regression.

Source: Constantinescu, Mattoo and Ruta (2014)

References

Abeysinghe, T. 2001. "Estimation of direct and indirect impact of oil price on growth." Economic Letters 73: 147-153.

Acosta, P. A., C. Calderon, P. Fajnzylber, and J. H. Lopez. 2008. "Do Remittances Lower Poverty Levels in Latin America?" In Remittances and Development: Lessons from Latin America, ed. P. Fajnzylber and J. H. Lopez, 87–134. World Bank, Washington, DC.

Adams Jr, R. H., and A. Cuecuecha. 2013. "The Impact of Remittances on Investment and Poverty in Ghana." World Development 50: 24–40.

Adams Jr, R. H., and J. Page. 2005. "Do International Migration and Remittances Reduce Poverty in Developing Countries?" World Development 33 (10): 1645–69.

Aga, G. A., and M. S. Martinez Pería. 2014. "International Remittances and Financial Inclusion in Sub-Saharan Africa." Policy Research Working Paper 6991, World Bank, Washington, DC.

Aggarwal, R., A. Demirgüç-Kunt, and M. S. Martinex Pería. 2011. "Do Remittances Promote Financial Development?" Journal of Development Economics 96 (2): 255–64.

Ahn, J. 2011. "A Theory of Domestic and International Trade Finance." Working Paper 11/262, International Monetary Fund, Washington, DC.

Ahn, J., M Amiti, and D. E. Weinstein. 2011. "Trade Finance and the Great Trade Collapse." American Economic Review 101 (3): 298–302.

Akram, Q. F. 2009. "Commodity prices, interest rates and the dollar." Energy Economics 31: 838–851.

Allegret, J., C. Couharde, and C. Guillaumin. 2012. "The Impact of External Shocks in East Asia: Lessons from a Structural VAR Model with Block Exogeneity." Working Paper, University of Paris Ouest – Nanterre.

Alvarez, L., S. Hurtado, I. Sanchez, and C. Thomas. 2011. "The Impact of Oil Price Changes on Spanish and Euro Area Consumer Price Inflation." Economic Modeling 28: 422-431.

Ambler, K., D. Aycinena, and D. Yang. 2014. "Channeling Remittances to Education: A Field Experiment among Migrants from El Salvador." Working Paper 20262, National Bureau of Economic Research, Cambridge, MA.

Amiti, M., and D. E. Weinstein. 2011. "Exports and Financial Shocks." Quarterly Journal of Economics 126 (4): 1841–77.

Anderton, R., and T. Tewolde. 2011. "The Global Financial Crisis: Understanding the Global Trade Downturn and Recovery." The World Economy 34 (5): 741–63.

Ashraf, N., D. Aycinena, C. Martinez, and D. Yang. 2011. "Remittances and the Problem of Control: A Field Experiment among Migrants from El Salvador." Working Paper, Innovations for Poverty Action, Washington, DC.

Arezki, R. and O. Blanchard, 2014. "Seven Questions about the Recent Oil Price Slump." IMFdirect - The IMF Blog, December 22, 2014.

Baldwin, R., ed. 2009. The Great Trade Collapse: Causes, Consequences and Prospects. London: Centre for Economic Policy Research.

Barsky, R.B and Kilian, L. 2004. "Oil and the Macroeconomy Since the 1970s. " Journal of Economic Perspectives. 18 (4): 115-134.

Baumeister, C. and G. Peersman, 2013 "The Role of Time-Varying Price Elasticities in Accounting for Volatility Changes in the Crude Oil Market." Bank of Canada Working Paper 2011-28.

Bems, R., Robert C. J., and K. Yi. 2010. "Demand Spillovers and the Collapse of Trade in the Global Recession." IMF Economic Review 58 (2): 295–326.

————. 2013. "The Great Trade Collapse." Annual Review of Economics 5 (1): 375–400.

Bernanke, B., M. Gertler, and M. Watson. 1997. "Systematic Monetary Policy and the Effects of Oil Price Shocks." Brookings Papers on Economic Activity 28(1): 91-157.

Berument, H. M., N. B. Ceylan, and N. Dogan. 2010. "The impact of oil price shocks on the economic growth of selected MENA countries," The Energy Journal 31: 149-176.

Blanchard, O. J. and J. Galí. 2008. "The Macroeconomic Effects of Oil Price Shocks: Why are the 2000s so different from the 1970s?" NBER Working Paper No. 13368.

Blanchard, O. J. and M. Riggi. 2013. "Why are the 2000s so different from the 1970s? A structural interpretation of changes in the macroeconomic effects of oil prices." Journal of the European Economic Association, vol. 11, pp. 1032–1052.

Borchet, I., and A. Mattoo. 2009. "The Crisis-Resilience of Services Trade." Policy Research Working Paper 4917, World Bank, Washington, DC.

Bown, C. P. 2009. "The Global Resort to Antidumping, Safeguards, and Other Trade Remedies Amidst the Economic Crisis." In Effective Crisis Response and Openness: Implications for the Trading System, edited by Simon J. Evenett, Bernard M. Hoekman, and Olivier Cattaneo, 91–118. London: Centre for Economic Policy Research and World Bank.

Box, G. E. P., and G. M Jenkins. 1970. Time Series Analysis: Forecasting and Control. San Francisco: Holden Day.

Boz, E., M. Bussiere, and C. Marsili. 2014. "Recent Slowdown in Global Trade: Cyclical or Structural." Centre for Economic Policy Research. http://www.voxeu.org/article/recent-slowdown-global-trade.

Bugamelli, M., and F. Paterno. 2011. "Output Growth Volatility and Remittances." Economica 78 (311): 480–500.

Bussiere, M., G. Callegeri, F. Ghironi, G. Sestieri, and N. Yamano. 2013. "Estimating Trade Elasticities: Demand Composition and the Trade Collapse of 2008–2009." American Economic Journal: Macroeconomics 5 (3): 118–51.

Chami, R., A. Barajas, T. Cosimano, C. Fullenkamp, M. Gapen, and P. Montiel. 2008. "Macroeconomic Consequences of Remittances." Occasional Paper 259, International Monetary Fund, Washington, DC.

Canuto, O. 2014. "The commodity supercycle: Is this time different?" Economic Premise, no. 150. World Bank, Washington, DC.

Cashin, P., K. Mohaddes, M. Raissi, and M. Raissi. 2014. "The differential effects of oil demand and supply shocks on the global economy." Energy Economics 44: 113-134.

Cherif, R. and F. Hasanov. 2014a. "Oil Exporters at the Cross Roads: It is High Time to Diversify." IMF Research Bulleting. December 2014.

Cherif, R. and F. Hasanov. 2014b. "Soaring of the Gulf Falcons: Diversification in the GCC Oil Exporters in Seven Propositions" IMF Working Paper 14/177. International Monetary Fund, Washington, DC.

Chor, D., and K. Manova. 2012. "Off the Cliff and Back? Credit Conditions and International Trade during the Global Financial Crisis." Journal of International Economics 87 (2): 117–33.

Clemens, M. A., and D. McKenzie. 2014. "Why Don't Remittances Appear to Affect Growth?" Policy Research Working Paper 6856, World Bank, Washington, DC.

Cologni, A., and M. Manera. 2006. "Oil Prices, Inflation, and Interest Rates in a Structural Cointegrated VAR Model for the G-7 Economies." Energy Economics 30: 856-888.

Constantinescu, C., A. Mattoo, and M. Ruta. 2014. "Global Trade Slowdown: Cyclical or Structural?" Paper presented at Third International Monetary Fund/World Bank/World Trade Organization Workshop, Washington, DC, November 6–7.

Constantinescu, I. C., and M. Schiff. 2014. "Remittances, FDI and ODA: Stability, Cyclicality and Stabilising Impact in Developing Countries." International Journal of Migration and Residential Mobility 1 (1): 84–106.

Contessi, S., P. De Pace, and J. L. Francis. 2013. "The Cyclical Properties of Disaggregated Capital Flows." Journal of International Money and Finance 32: 528–55.

Craigwell, R., M. Jackman, and W. Moore. 2010. "Economic Volatility and Remittances." International Journal of Development Issues 9 (1): 25–42.

Cuddington, J. and D. Jerrett. 2008. "Supercycles in real metals prices?" IMF Staff Papers 55: 541-565. International Monetary Fund, Washington, DC.

Cunado, J. and P. De Gracia. 2005. "Oil Prices, Economic Activity and Inflation: Evidence for Some Asian Countries." The Quarterly Review of Economics and Finance. 45: 65-83.

De Gregorio, J., O. Landerretche, and C. Neilson. 2007. "Another Pass-Through Bites the Dust? Oil Prices and Inflation." Economia, 7, 155–96.

Eaton, J., S. Kortum, B. Neiman, and J. Romalis. 2011. "Trade and the Global Recession." Working Paper 16666, National Bureau of Economic Research, Cambridge, MA.

Edelstein, P. and L. Kilian, 2007. "Retail Energy Prices and Consumer Expenditures." CEPR Discussion Papers 6255.

Elder J, and A. Serletis. 2010. "Oil Price Uncertainty." Journal of Money, Credit and Banking 42: 1137-1159.

Erten, B. and J. A. Ocampo. 2013. "Super cycles of commodity prices since the mid-nineteenth century." World Development 44: 14-30.

Escaith, H., N. Lindenberg, and S. Miroudot. 2010. "International Supply Chains and Trade Elasticity in Times of Global Crisis." Staff working paper 2010-08, Economic Research and Statistics Division, World Trade Organization, Geneva.

Feldkirchner, M. and I. Korhonen. 2012. "The Rise of China and its Implications for Emerging Markets - Evidence from a GVAR model" Institute for Economies in Transition Discussion Papers 2012-20, Bank of Finland.

Finn, M. G. 2000. "Perfect Competition and the Effects of Energy Price Increases on Economic Activity," Journal of Money, Credit, and Banking 32: 400-416.

Forbes, K. J., and F. E. Warnock. 2012. "Capital Flow Waves: Surges, Stops, Flight, and Retrenchment." Journal of International Economics 88 (2): 235–51.

Frankel, J. 2011. "Are Bilateral Remittances Counter-Cyclical?" Open Economy Review 22: 1–16.

————. 2014. "Why are commodity prices falling?" Project Syndicate. December 15, 2014.

Freund, C.. 2009. "The Trade Response to Global Downturns: Historical Evidence." Policy Research Working Paper 5015, World Bank, Washington, DC.

Freund, C., and N. Spatafora. 2005. "Remittances: Transaction Costs, Determinants and Informal Flows." Policy Research Working Paper 3704, World Bank, Washington, DC.

————. 2008. "Remittances, Transaction Costs, and Informality." Journal of Development Economics 86 (2): 356–66.

Gault, N. 2011. "Oil Prices and the U.S. Economy: Some Rules of Thumb", published in HIS Global Insight Bulletins-Perspective Article.

Gelos, G. and Y. Ustyugova 2012. "Inflation Responses to Commodity Price Shocks–

How and Why Do Countries Differ?" IMF Working Paper 12/225. International Monetary Fund, Washington, DC.

Gibson, J., D. McKenzie, and H. T. A. S. Rohorua. 2006. "How Cost Elastic Are Remittances? Estimates from Tongan Migrants in New Zealand." World Bank, Washington, DC. http://siteresources.worldbank.org/DEC/Resources/PEBGibsonMcKenzieRohorua.pdf.

Gill, I. S., I. Izvorski, W. van Eeghen, D. D. Rosa. 2014. Diversified development : making the most of natural resources in Eurasia. Europe and Central Asia Studies. World Bank, Washington, DC.

Giuliano, P., and M. Ruiz-Arranz. 2009. "Remittances, Financial Development, and Growth." Journal of Development Economics 90 (1): 144–52.

Gordon, R. J. 2013. "The Philipps Curve is Alive and Well: Inflation and the NAIRU during the Slow Recovery." NBER Working Paper No. 19390.

————. 2011. "The History of the Phillips Curve: Consensus and Bifurcation," Economica 78, no. 1, pp. 10-50.

Granger, C., and P. Newbold. 1974. "Spurious Regressions in Econometrics." Journal of Econometrics 2: 111–20.

Hamilton, J. 2014a. "Oil prices as an indicator of global economic conditions." Econbrowser Blog entry, December 14, 2014, available at http://econbrowser.com/archives/2014/12/oil-prices-as-an-indicator-of-global-economic-conditions.

————. 2014b. "The Changing Face of World Oil Markets." IAEE Energy Forum Newsletter, Fourth Quarter 2014

————. 1983. "Oil and the Macroeconomy since World War II," Journal of Political Economy 91, pp. 228-248

————. 2003. "What is an Oil Shock?" Journal of Econometrics, 113(2): 363-398.

————. 2009. "The Causes and Consequences of the Oil Shock of 2007-08", Brookings Papers on Economic Activity 1: 215-261

————. 2005. "Oil and the Macroeconomy." in The New Palgrave Dictionary of Economics, ed. by S. Durlauf and L. Blume, (London: MacMillan, 2006, 2nd ed).

Hoffman, R. 2012. "Estimates of Oil Price Elasticities," IAEE Energy Forum Newsletter, 1st Quarter 2012, International Association for Energy Economics.

Hooker, M. A. 2002. "Are Oil Shocks Inflationary? Asymmetric and Nonlinear Specifications versus Changes in Regime." Journal of Money, Credit, and Banking 34 (May): 540-561.

Hunt, B., P. Isard, and D. Laxton. 2001. "The Macroeconomic Effects of Higher Oil Prices." IMF Working Paper 01/14. International Monetary Fund, Washington, DC.

ICC (International Chamber of Commerce). 2014. "Global Survey on Trade Finance." http://www.iccwbo.org/ Products-and-Services/Trade-facilitation/ICC-Global-Survey-on-Trade-Finance.

IEA, International Energy Agency. 2014a. Oil Market Report, June 13, Paris.

———. 2014b. Oil Market Report, December 12, Paris.

———. 2014c. Fossil Fuel Database, Paris.

IMF (International Monetary Fund). 2005. "World Economic Outlook, April 2005." International Monetary Fund, Washington, DC.

———. 2010. World Economic Outlook – October: Do Financial Crises Have Lasting Effects on Trade? International Monetary Fund, Washington, DC.

———. 2014. World Economic Outlook – October: Legacies, Clouds, Uncertainties. International Monetary Fund, Washington, DC.

———. 2011. World Economic Outlook – April: Tensions from the Two-Speed Recovery Unemployment, Commodities, and Capital Flows. International Monetary Fund, Washington, DC.

Islamaj, E. 2014. "Industrial Specialization, Financial Integration and International Consumption Risk Sharing." BE Journal of Macroeconomics 14 (1).

Jimenez-Rodriguez, R., and M. Sanchez. 2005. "Oil Price Shocks and Real GDP Growth:

Empirical Evidence for Some OECD Countries." Applied Economics. 37 (2): 201-228.

Jongwanich, J. and D. Park, 2009. "Inflation in developing Asia." Journal of Asian Economics 5: 507-518.

Kaminsky, G. L., C. M. Reinhart, and C. A. Végh. 2005. "When It Rains, It Pours: Procyclical Capital Flows and Macroeconomic Policies." In NBER Macroeconomics Annual 2004, vol. 19, edited by Kenneth Rogoff, 11–82. Cambridge, MA: MIT Press.

Kee, H. L., C. Neagu, and A. Nicita. 2013. "Is Protectionism on the Rise? Assessing National Trade Policies during the Crisis of 2008." Review of Economics and Statistics 95 (1): 342–46.

Kee, H. L., and H. Tang. 2014. "Domestic Value-Added in Exports: Theory and Firm Evidence from China." Mimeo, Word Bank, Washington, DC.

Kilian, L. 2014. "Oil Price Shocks: Causes and Consequences." Annual Review of Resource Economics, Annual Reviews, vol. 6(1): 133-154.

———. 2008. "The Economic Effects of Energy Price Shocks" Journal of Economic Literature, American Economic Association, vol. 46(4): 871-909.

————. 2009. "Not All Oil Price Shocks Are Alike: Disentangling Demand and Supply Shocks in the Crude Oil Market." American Economic Review 99(3): 1053-69.

Kilian, L., A. Rebucci and N. Spatafora. 2009. "Oil shocks and external balances" Journal of International Economics 77 (2): 181-194.

Kilian, L. & Lewis, L.T., 2011. "Does the Fed Respond to Oil Price Shocks?" Economic Journal, Royal Economic Society, vol. 121(555): 1047-1072.

Kilian, L. & Vigfusson, R. J., 2011. "Nonlinearities In The Oil Price–Output Relationship," Macroeconomic Dynamics, Cambridge University Press, vol. 15(S3): 337-363

Kose, Ayhan M., Eswar S. Prasad, and Marco E. Terrones. 2009. "Does Financial Globalization Promote Risk Sharing?" Journal of Development Economics 89 (2): 258–70.

Levchenko, A., L. Lewis, and L. Tesar. 2010. "The Collapse of International Trade during the 2008–09 Crisis: In Search of the Smoking Gun." IMF Economic Review 58 (2): 214–53.

Levchenko, A., and P. Mauro. 2007. "Do Some Forms of Financial Flows Protect from Sudden Stops?" World Bank Economic Review 21 (3): 389–411.

Lewis, K. K. 1996. "What Can Explain the Apparent Lack of International Consumption Risk Sharing?" Journal of Political Economy 104 (2): 267–97.

Mohapatra, Sa., G. Joseph, and D. Ratha. 2012. "Remittances and Natural Disasters: Ex-Post Response and Contribution to Ex-Ante Preparedness." Environment, Development and Sustainability 14 (3): 365–87.

Mork, K. A., Ø. Olsen, and H. T. Mysen. 1994. "Macroeconomic Responses to Oil Price Increases and Decreases in OECD Countries." Energy Journal 15(4): 19-35.

Mory, J. F. 1993. "Oil Prices and Economic Activity: Is the Relationship Symmetric?" Energy Journal 14(4): 151-161.

Nelson, C. R, and C. I. Plosser. 1982. "Trends and Random Walks in Macroeconomic Time Series." Journal of Monetary Economics 10 (982): 139–62.

Obstfeld, M.. 1994. "Are Industrial-Country Consumption Risks Globally Diversified?" In Capital Mobility: The Impact of Consumption, Investment and Growth, ed. L. Leiderman, L. and A. Razin, 13–47. New York: Cambridge University Press .

OECD. 2011. "The Effects of Oil Price Hikes on Economic Activity and Inflation." OECD Economics Department Policy Notes No. 4.

Osili, U. O. 2004. "Migrants and Housing Investments: Theory and Evidence from Nigeria." Economic Development and Cultural Change 52 (4): 821–49.

Peersman, G. and I. Van Robays. 2012. "Cross-country differences in the effects of oil shocks." Energy Economics. 34 (5): 1532-1547.

Rasmussen, T. N. and A. Roitman. 2011. "Oil Shocks in a Global Perspective: Are they Really that Bad?" IMF Working Paper WP/11/194. International Monetary Fund, Washington, DC.

Reifschneider, D., R. Tetlow, and J. Williams. 1999. "Aggregate disturbances, monetary policy, and the macroeconomy: the FRB/US perspective." Federal Reserve Bulletin, Board of Governors of the Federal Reserve System (U.S.): 1-19.

Sayan, S. 2006. "Business Cycles and Worker's Remittances: How Do Migrant Workers Respond to Cyclical Movements of GDP at Home?" Working Paper 06/52, International Monetary Fund, Washington, DC.

Shuddhasawtta, R., R. Salim, and H. Bloch. 2010. "Impact of crude oil price volatility on economic activities: An empirical investigation in the Thai economy." Resources Policy 121–132.

Smyth, D. J., 1993. "Energy Prices and the Aggregate Production Function." Energy Economics 15: 105-110.

Tang, W., L. Wu, and Z. Zhang. 2010. "Oil price shocks and their short- and long-term effects on the Chinese economy." Energy Economics 32: S3–S14.

Taylor, J. 2000. "Low Inflation, Pass-through, and the Pricing Power of Firms." European Economic Review 44: 1389-1408.

World Bank. 2006. Global Economic Prospects 2006: Economic Implications of Remittances and Migration. World Bank, Washington, DC.

————.2009. Global Economic Prospects 2009: Commodities at the Crossroads. World Bank, Washington, DC.

————. 2013. Global Economic Prospects –June 2013: Less Volatile, but Slower Growth. World Bank, Washington, DC.

————. 2014. MENA Economic Monitor October 2014: Corrosive Subsidies. World Bank, Washington, DC.

————.2011. The Changing Wealth of Nations: Measuring Sustainable Development in the New Millennium. World Bank, Washington, DC.

WTO (World Trade Organization). 2014. "Report to the TPRB from the Director-General on Trade-Related Developments." Report WT/TPR/ov/w/8, World Trade Organization, Geneva.

Yang, D., and H. Choi. 2007. "Are Remittances Insurance? Evidence from Rainfall Shocks in the Philippines." World Bank Economic Review 21 (2): 219–48.

Zhang, Y., Y. Fan, H. Tsai, and Y. Wei. 2008. "Spillover effect of US dollar exchange rate on oil prices." Journal of Policy Modeling 30: 973–991.

STATISTICAL
APPENDIX

Additional statistical data can be found online at
www.worldbank.org/gep

TABLE A.1   GDP Growth

(Constant 2010 U.S. Dollars)

| | Annual estimates and forecasts[a] | | | | | | | | Quarterly growth[b] | | | | | | |
| | | | | | | | | | 2013 | | | | 2014 | | |
	00-10[c]	2011	2012	2013	2014e	2015f	2016f	2017f	Q1	Q2	Q3	Q4	Q1	Q2	Q3
World	**2.8**	**3.1**	**2.4**	**2.5**	**2.6**	**3.0**	**3.3**	**3.2**	**2.6**	**2.9**	**3.3**	**2.8**	**1.7**	**2.3**	**3.0**
High-Income Countries	1.8	1.9	1.4	1.4	1.8	2.2	2.4	2.2	1.7	2.1	2.6	2.0	0.9	1.4	2.2
Euro Area	1.2	1.7	-0.7	-0.4	0.8	1.1	1.6	1.6	-1.5	1.4	0.7	0.9	1.2	0.3	0.6
OECD Countries (All)	1.6	1.8	1.3	1.4	1.7	2.2	2.4	2.2	1.8	1.9	2.7	1.9	1.0	1.4	2.3
Non-OECD Countries (High-income only)	4.6	5.1	3.5	2.4	2.5	0.9	2.4	2.9	1.6	3.0	2.3	4.1	0.9	1.0	1.5
Developing Countries	**6.1**	**6.3**	**4.7**	**4.9**	**4.5**	**4.8**	**5.3**	**5.4**	**5.1**	**5.1**	**5.1**	**5.0**	**3.8**	**4.6**	**5.0**
East Asia and the Pacific	**9.0**	**8.3**	**7.4**	**7.2**	**6.9**	**6.7**	**6.7**	**6.7**	**6.1**	**7.1**	**8.2**	**6.9**	**5.2**	**7.4**	**7.8**
Cambodia	8.0	7.1	7.3	7.4	7.2	7.5	7.2	7.0	..	..	..	..	..	..	..
China	10.5	9.3	7.7	7.7	7.4	7.1	7.0	6.9	6.8	7.7	8.8	7.2	6.0	7.7	8.6
Fiji	1.6	2.7	1.7	3.5	3.7	2.5	2.5	2.6	..	..	..	..	..	..	..
Indonesia	5.2	6.5	6.3	5.8	5.1	5.2	5.5	5.5	5.9	5.3	5.4	6.1	4.0	4.9	5.0
Lao PDR	7.1	8.0	8.0	8.5	7.5	6.4	7.0	6.9	..	..	..	..	..	..	..
Malaysia	4.6	5.2	5.6	4.7	5.7	4.7	5.1	5.2	-1.2	6.8	7.1	7.6	3.5	7.8	3.6
Mongolia	6.5	17.5	12.4	11.7	6.3	6.0	6.1	6.3	11.1	20.4	14.5	4.4	-6.9	2.8	..
Myanmar	10.3	5.9	7.3	8.3	8.5	8.5	8.2	8.0	..	..	..	..	..	..	..
Papua New Guinea	3.5	10.7	8.1	5.5	7.5	16.0	5.1	5.4	..	..	..	..	..	..	..
Philippines	4.8	3.6	6.8	7.2	6.0	6.5	6.5	6.3	10.0	5.3	5.7	4.8	6.5	8.6	1.7
Solomon Islands	2.9	10.7	4.9	3.0	0.1	3.5	3.5	3.5	..	..	..	..	..	..	..
Thailand	4.3	0.1	6.5	2.9	0.5	3.5	4.0	4.5	-5.2	1.1	3.7	2.7	-8.6	4.3	4.4
Timor-Leste	4.3	14.7	7.8	5.6	7.1	7.0	7.0	7.0	..	..	..	..	..	..	..
Vietnam	6.6	6.2	5.2	5.4	5.6	5.6	5.8	6.0	..	..	..	..	..	..	..
Europe and Central Asia	**4.6**	**6.3**	**1.9**	**3.6**	**2.4**	**3.0**	**3.6**	**3.9**	**5.8**	**5.5**	**2.3**	**4.1**	**3.9**	**-2.0**	**1.6**
Albania	5.5	2.5	1.6	1.4	2.1	3.0	4.0	4.5	2.0	5.1	-6.0	5.7	0.5	1.5	..
Armenia	7.9	4.7	7.2	3.5	2.6	3.3	3.7	4.1	..	..	..	..	..	..	..
Azerbaijan	14.9	0.1	2.2	5.8	4.5	4.4	4.1	3.8	..	..	..	..	..	..	..
Belarus	7.4	5.5	1.7	0.9	1.5	1.8	2.0	2.0	9.0	-3.9	-2.4	-3.5	15.3	-1.7	2.8
Bosnia and Herzegovina	4.1	1.0	-1.2	2.5	0.4	1.5	2.5	3.0	..	..	..	..	..	..	..
Bulgaria	4.1	1.8	0.6	1.1	1.4	1.1	2.0	2.7	2.0	0.4	2.7	2.6	0.5	1.2	1.8
Georgia	6.2	7.2	6.2	3.3	5.0	5.0	5.0	5.5	6.3	7.3	3.1	17.3	3.0	-3.2	4.5
Hungary	1.9	1.6	-1.7	1.5	3.2	2.0	2.5	2.7	3.6	2.7	4.1	3.5	3.7	3.4	1.9
Kazakhstan	8.3	7.5	5.0	6.0	4.1	1.8	3.2	4.7	1.4	9.8	10.1	5.2	..	..	..
Kosovo	6.2	4.5	2.8	3.4	2.5	3.0	3.5	3.5	..	..	..	..	..	..	..
Kyrgyz Republic	4.1	6.0	-0.1	10.9	3.0	2.0	4.0	5.0	..	..	..	..	..	..	..
Macedonia, FYR	3.0	2.3	-0.5	2.7	3.3	3.5	3.8	4.0	..	..	..	..	..	..	..
Moldova	5.1	6.8	-0.7	8.9	2.0	3.0	3.5	5.0	..	..	..	..	..	..	..
Montenegro	3.6	3.2	-2.5	3.3	1.5	3.4	2.9	3.0	..	..	..	..	..	..	..
Romania	4.1	2.3	0.6	3.5	2.6	2.9	3.2	3.9	5.2	5.7	3.7	3.6	3.0	-1.5	7.2
Serbia	3.7	1.6	-1.5	2.5	-2.0	-0.5	1.5	2.0	..	..	..	..	..	..	..
Tajikistan	8.3	7.4	7.5	7.4	6.4	4.2	5.3	6.2	..	..	..	..	..	..	..
Turkey	3.9	8.8	2.1	4.1	3.1	3.5	3.7	3.9	7.3	6.7	1.9	3.2	7.3	-1.8	1.8
Turkmenistan	13.6	14.7	11.1	10.2	10.1	10.0	10.4	10.6	..	..	..	..	..	..	..
Ukraine	4.3	5.2	0.3	0.0	-8.2	-2.3	3.5	3.8	4.4	2.3	-5.8	14.8	-13.9	-11.0	-8.3
Uzbekistan	6.9	8.3	8.2	8.0	7.9	7.4	8.2	8.1	..	..	..	..	..	..	..
Latin America and the Caribbean	**3.3**	**4.2**	**2.6**	**2.5**	**0.8**	**1.7**	**2.9**	**3.3**	**2.2**	**4.7**	**0.9**	**2.0**	**0.5**	**0.1**	**0.9**
Argentina[e]	3.8	8.6	0.9	2.9	-1.5	-0.3	1.6	3.1	2.0	4.4	1.3	-1.2	-2.7	3.1	-2.1
Belize	4.0	2.1	4.0	0.7	2.6	2.6	2.7	2.8	..	..	..	..	..	..	..
Bolivia	3.8	5.2	5.2	6.8	5.3	4.5	4.3	4.0	5.5	5.7	6.4	9.6	0.9	2.4	..
Brazil	3.6	2.7	1.0	2.5	0.1	1.0	2.5	2.7	0.7	8.4	-2.0	1.9	-0.7	-2.4	0.3
Colombia	4.1	6.6	4.0	4.7	4.7	4.4	4.3	4.3	6.3	8.4	3.0	4.4	10.6	-0.5	2.6
Costa Rica	4.4	4.5	5.1	3.5	3.7	4.1	4.2	4.5	-0.4	7.6	7.2	2.0	-1.3	6.8	7.3
Dominica	2.6	0.2	-1.1	0.8	1.5	1.3	1.5	1.6	..	..	..	..	..	..	..
Dominican Republic	4.9	2.9	2.6	4.6	5.9	4.9	4.7	4.7	..	..	..	..	..	..	..
Ecuador	4.1	7.8	5.1	4.5	4.0	3.8	4.3	5.0	3.3	8.7	6.4	2.6	0.9	4.0	..
El Salvador	1.9	2.2	1.9	1.7	1.9	2.4	2.7	2.9	..	..	..	..	..	..	..
Guatemala	3.3	4.2	3.0	3.7	3.5	3.6	3.6	3.5	3.7	6.3	1.7	0.7	5.2	9.9	..
Guyana	2.4	5.4	4.8	5.2	3.6	3.7	3.8	4.0	..	..	..	..	..	..	..
Haiti	0.1	5.5	2.9	4.3	3.6	3.8	4.1	4.1	..	..	..	..	..	..	..
Honduras	4.1	3.8	4.1	2.6	3.0	3.0	3.3	3.5	..	..	..	..	..	..	..
Jamaica[d]	0.7	1.7	-0.6	0.6	0.9	1.1	2.2	2.5	..	..	..	..	..	..	..
Mexico	1.8	4.0	4.0	1.1	2.1	3.3	3.8	3.8	2.6	-4.3	4.7	1.5	1.4	3.6	2.0
Nicaragua[e]	2.8	5.7	5.0	4.6	4.2	4.4	4.5	4.3	..	..	..	..	..	..	..
Panama	6.3	10.9	10.8	8.4	6.5	6.1	5.8	5.6	..	..	..	..	..	..	..
Paraguay	3.4	4.3	-1.2	14.2	4.0	4.3	4.3	4.6	66.4	0.6	2.8	-1.0	14.8	-2.9	7.3
Peru[e]	5.6	6.5	6.0	5.8	2.4	4.8	5.5	5.9	4.5	11.0	3.6	9.4	-2.6	-2.9	3.4
St. Lucia	1.8	1.2	-1.6	-0.4	-1.0	-0.6	0.8	1.4	..	..	..	..	..	..	..
St. Vincent and the Grenadines	2.9	-0.5	1.2	1.7	1.5	2.6	2.9	3.4	..	..	..	..	..	..	..
Venezuela, RB	3.1	4.2	5.6	1.3	-3.0	-2.0	0.5	1.5	..	..	..	..	..	..	..

	Annual estimates and forecasts[a]								Quarterly growth[b] 2013				2014		
	00-10[c]	2011	2012	2013	2014e	2015f	2016f	2017f	Q1	Q2	Q3	Q4	Q1	Q2	Q3
Middle East and North Africa	**4.7**	**2.7**	**-1.1**	**0.9**	**2.3**	**2.5**	**2.7**	**3.3**	**11.2**	**-11.9**	**1.0**	**4.5**	**6.5**	**3.3**	**..**
Algeria	3.9	2.8	3.3	2.8	3.0	3.3	3.5	3.5	..	..	..	..	..	..	..
Djibouti	3.9	4.5	4.8	5.0	5.5	5.5	6.0	6.0	..	..	..	..	..	..	..
Egypt, Arab Rep.[d]	4.8	1.8	2.2	2.1	2.2	3.5	3.8	4.0	0.8	0.1	1.1	3.6	5.4	5.0	..
Iran, Islamic Rep.	5.0	3.9	-6.6	-1.9	1.5	0.9	1.0	2.2	23.2	-25.2	0.6	4.6	13.3	-0.4	..
Iraq	-0.4	10.2	10.3	4.2	-2.7	0.9	7.0	5.9	..	..	..	..	..	..	..
Jordan	6.3	2.6	2.7	2.8	3.0	3.4	3.9	4.0	3.1	3.8	1.7	2.8	4.3	2.5	..
Lebanon	5.9	2.0	2.2	0.9	1.5	2.0	3.4	3.6	..	..	..	..	..	..	..
Libya	4.3	-62.1	104.5	-13.7	-21.8	4.3	4.4	6.5	..	..	..	..	..	..	..
Morocco	4.9	5.0	2.7	4.4	3.0	4.6	4.0	4.5	-1.8	11.7	1.9	6.5	-11.9	14.6	2.9
Tunisia	4.4	-0.5	4.7	2.5	2.3	2.7	3.5	4.0	0.9	2.9	1.1	4.5	2.1	3.4	0.9
Yemen, Rep.	3.0	-12.7	2.4	4.8	1.9	3.7	3.8	5.2	..	..	..	..	..	..	..
West Bank and Gaza	3.3	12.2	5.9	1.9	-3.7	4.4	4.0	4.0	..	..	..	..	..	..	..
South Asia	**6.8**	**7.3**	**5.0**	**4.9**	**5.5**	**6.1**	**6.6**	**6.8**	**4.8**	**3.8**	**6.5**	**3.6**	**5.0**	**8.1**	**4.9**
Afghanistan	12.8	6.1	14.4	3.7	1.5	4.0	5.0	5.1	..	..	..	..	..	..	..
Bangladesh[d]	6.1	6.5	6.5	6.0	6.1	6.2	6.5	7.0	..	..	..	..	..	..	..
India[d]	7.5	6.6	4.7	5.0	5.6	6.4	7.0	7.0	4.8	3.7	6.4	3.4	5.0	8.2	4.8
Maldives	7.0	6.5	1.3	4.7	5.0	5.3	4.3	4.3	..	..	..	..	..	..	..
Nepal[d]	3.9	3.4	4.9	3.8	5.5	5.0	4.7	4.5	..	..	..	..	..	..	..
Pakistan[d]	4.2	2.7	3.5	4.4	5.4	4.6	4.8	4.9	..	..	..	..	..	..	..
Sri Lanka	5.2	8.2	6.3	7.3	7.8	7.5	6.8	6.5	6.5	7.0	8.7	10.1	4.8	7.8	8.3
Sub-Saharan Africa	**5.7**	**4.3**	**4.0**	**4.2**	**4.5**	**4.6**	**4.9**	**5.1**	**3.8**	**5.9**	**3.5**	**6.0**	**1.2**	**5.3**	**2.9**
Angola	11.3	3.9	8.4	6.8	4.4	5.3	5.0	5.2	..	..	..	..	..	..	..
Benin	3.9	3.5	5.4	5.6	5.2	5.0	4.7	4.7	..	..	..	..	..	..	..
Botswana	4.2	5.2	5.1	5.2	4.5	4.6	4.9	5.0	3.5	8.9	-0.3	4.5	7.2	6.5	4.4
Burkina Faso	6.0	4.2	9.5	5.3	6.0	5.5	6.5	6.8	..	..	..	..	..	..	..
Cameroon	3.3	4.1	4.6	5.5	5.1	5.1	4.9	5.1	..	..	..	..	..	..	..
Cabo Verde	5.3	4.0	1.2	0.5	2.1	2.8	3.0	3.1	..	..	..	..	..	..	..
Comoros	1.8	2.2	3.0	3.5	3.4	3.6	3.2	3.0	..	..	..	..	..	..	..
Congo, Dem. Rep.	4.7	6.9	7.2	8.5	8.0	7.8	7.5	7.3	..	..	..	..	..	..	..
Côte d'Ivoire	1.1	-4.7	9.5	8.7	9.1	8.5	8.2	8.0	..	..	..	..	..	..	..
Eritrea	0.9	8.7	7.0	1.3	3.2	3.0	4.0	4.3	..	..	..	..	..	..	..
Ethiopia	8.6	11.2	8.7	10.4	6.7	6.9	6.6	6.7	..	..	..	..	..	..	..
Gabon	2.0	7.1	5.6	5.9	5.0	5.5	5.6	5.7	..	..	..	..	..	..	..
Gambia, The	3.8	-4.3	6.1	5.6	5.7	5.3	4.8	4.6	..	..	..	..	..	..	..
Ghana	5.8	15.0	8.8	7.1	4.7	4.5	5.5	6.0	..	..	..	..	..	..	..
Guinea	2.6	3.9	3.9	2.5	0.5	-0.2	2.2	2.5	..	..	..	..	..	..	..
Guinea-Bissau	2.2	5.3	-1.5	0.3	2.1	2.5	2.3	2.0	..	..	..	..	..	..	..
Kenya	4.4	6.1	4.5	5.7	5.4	6.0	6.6	6.5	..	..	..	..	..	..	..
Lesotho	4.0	2.8	6.5	5.9	4.6	4.7	4.5	4.4	..	..	..	..	..	..	..
Madagascar	2.5	1.0	2.4	2.1	3.0	3.6	3.8	3.9	..	..	..	..	..	..	..
Malawi	4.5	4.3	1.9	5.0	4.2	4.6	5.0	5.2	..	..	..	..	..	..	..
Mali	6.0	2.7	-0.4	2.1	5.0	4.3	4.6	4.8	..	..	..	..	..	..	..
Mauritania	4.9	4.0	7.0	6.7	5.7	5.5	5.6	5.6	..	..	..	..	..	..	..
Mauritius	3.8	3.9	3.2	3.2	3.4	3.9	3.7	3.7	..	..	..	..	..	..	..
Mozambique	7.8	7.3	7.2	7.1	7.2	8.0	8.1	8.2	..	..	..	..	..	..	..
Namibia	4.6	5.1	5.2	5.1	4.2	4.3	4.1	4.0	..	..	..	..	..	..	..
Niger	4.6	2.3	10.8	3.9	5.7	6.0	6.2	6.3	..	..	..	..	..	..	..
Nigeria	8.9	4.9	4.3	5.4	6.3	5.5	5.8	6.2	6.1	7.9	5.8	7.0	3.5	9.7	4.2
Rwanda	7.9	7.5	7.3	4.6	6.0	6.5	7.0	7.1	..	..	..	..	..	..	..
Senegal	4.1	2.1	3.5	4.0	4.5	4.8	4.7	4.7	..	..	..	..	..	..	..
Sierra Leone	8.9	6.0	15.2	20.1	4.0	-2.0	2.5	2.7	..	..	..	..	..	..	..
South Africa	3.5	3.6	2.5	1.9	1.4	2.2	2.5	2.7	1.4	3.7	1.2	5.1	-1.6	0.5	1.4
Sudan	6.3	-3.3	-10.1	-6.0	2.6	2.5	2.8	3.0	..	..	..	..	..	..	..
Swaziland	2.3	-0.7	1.9	2.8	2.0	2.2	2.6	2.8	..	..	..	..	..	..	..
Tanzania	7.0	6.4	6.9	7.0	7.0	7.2	6.8	7.0	..	..	..	..	..	..	..
Togo	2.2	4.9	5.9	5.1	5.2	5.0	4.9	4.7	..	..	..	..	..	..	..
Uganda	7.5	5.0	4.6	5.9	6.3	6.6	6.9	7.0	..	..	..	..	..	..	..
Zambia	5.6	6.8	7.3	6.4	6.4	6.3	6.5	6.7	..	..	..	..	..	..	..
Zimbabwe	-4.7	11.9	10.6	4.5	3.1	3.2	3.7	3.4	..	..	..	..	..	..	..

Source: World Bank, WDI, Haver Analytics, WEO
Note: Aggregates include countries with full national accounts and balance of payment data only
a. Annual percentage change
b. Quarter-over-quarter growth, seasonally adjusted and annualized
c. Compound average of the period 2000-10
d. Annual GDP is on fiscal year basis, as per reporting practice in the country
e. Preliminary for long-term average. Data was recently rebased; missing data up to 2003 was spliced with the earlier series.